For
MERRYN, EDERYN,
and
GWYDION MADAWC

FOREWORD TO 2013 EDITION
by Michael Barratt Brown

I first met Raymond Williams at an adult education conference with my friend Henry Collins when they were both working in adult education at Oxford, and I remember much enjoying his novel about his native Wales, *Border County*, first published in 1960. When I went onto the board of *Universities and Left Review*, we published an essay of Raymond's on the history of culture, some of which reappeared, in 1958, in *Culture and Society*. I don't think that I read the book until the 1963 edition, when we were both involved in *New Left Review*. I recall this history of Raymond's writing because it had a very considerable influence on my thinking and, indeed, on the thinking in left-wing circles on questions of the culture by which we were surrounded in Britain in the 1960s.

I do not intend to summarise Raymond's views. You can find that in the Introduction and most particularly in the Conclusion to this book, but I do wish to emphasise certain essential elements that I took into my own writing and teaching for adult students. The core of the book, between the Introduction and the Conclusion, consists of an extraordinarily rich scholarly review of the writers dealing with questions of culture and society, first in what he calls 'the Nineteenth Century Tradition', ranging from Burke and Cobbett via the industrial novels to Ruskin and William Morris. After an 'Inter-regnum' on Shaw and the critics of the state, Williams ends with a section on 'Twentieth Century Opinions', which in turn ranges from DH Lawrence to George Orwell. It was a magisterial performance.

Anyone teaching on English literature in adult classes would find all this invaluable material for class discussion, as I did; but in the Introduction and the Conclusion Raymond Williams draws certain conclusions from his studies of these works that I found quite compelling, and I absorbed them into my own work, not just my teaching, but much more widely, in work in schools, colleges, trade unions and international relations. Culture, I realised, was not just some decoration for the lives of an élite. The word has it origin in something that every gardener knows—the tending of natural growth. This applies to everyone, however well or badly we are tended. There is a common culture in every society. This is what can be built on in societies, in the 'rich associative life' (he takes the phrase from GDH Cole), which we all enjoy, apart from a few severely repressed or depressed. We all have mutual responsibilities, which make up the texture of our lives and engender acts of co-operation, as well as competition.

At the end of his book Williams writes already of the 'long revolution', the title of his next book, which will be needed to adjust our thinking to cope with the social, economic, industrial and environmental changes that are taking place all around us. He was one of the first to be concerned with environmental changes. The emphasis in the book is on the absolute necessity of building from below upwards and not from the top downward. Raymond had always been a very hesitant and critical member of the Communist Party, which operated top downward. He worked very happily with Edward Thompson in our attempt to make a real break in socialist thinking in the *New Left Review* and the New Left Clubs, and in the conference held in Raymond's rooms in Cambridge, which led, in 1967, to the publication of The New Left May Day Manifesto, edited by Stuart Hall, Edward Thomson and Raymond Williams.

Toward the end of his Conclusion, Raymond states quite unequivocally his philosophical position on the key question of inequality in a common culture. Our culture today is the inheritance of earlier ruling class cultures, but Raymond pins his faith on a working class culture emerging in time from the transitional period through which we are living, and insists that it will put its emphasis on community and solidarity as opposed to the individualism of 'bourgeois' society. Since Raymond was writing, it is this last which has, after Mrs. Thatcher, advanced most obviously. Raymond here issues a timely warning:

> 'A common culture is not, at any level, an equal culture. Yet equality of being is always necessary to it, or common experience will not be valued. A common culture can place no absolute restrictions on entry to any of its activities; this is the reality of the claim to equality of opportunity.'

And Raymond ends the book with a remarkable suggestion,

> 'The human crisis is always a crisis of understanding. What we genuinely understand we can do.'

You can apply that equally to socio-economic and environmental problems. There are great ingots of such wisdom in this book that give it its longevity.

FOREWORD

THE organizing principle of this book is the discovery that the idea of culture, and the word itself in its general modern uses, came into English thinking in the period which we commonly describe as that of the Industrial Revolution. The book is an attempt to show how and why this happened, and to follow the idea through to our own day. It thus becomes an account and an interpretation of our responses in thought and feeling to the changes in English society since the late eighteenth century. Only in such a context can our use of the word 'culture', and the issues to which the word refers, be adequately understood.

The book continues the enquiry which began with the founding of the review *Politics and Letters*, which I edited, with Mr Clifford Collins and Mr Wolf Mankowitz, between 1946 and 1948. Our object then was to enquire into and where possible reinterpret this tradition which the word 'culture' describes in terms of the experience of our own generation. I am permanently indebted to my former co-editors for what I learned with them in that first attempt. During the actual writing of the book, since 1950, I have again been particularly indebted to Mr Collins, and also to my colleague Mr Anthony McLean. I gained much benefit from discussing the work in progress with Humphry House and Francis Klingender, whose valuable work survives their early deaths. Others, among many who have helped me, whom I ought particularly to mention are Mr F. W. Bateson, Mr E. F. Bellchambers, Mr Henry Collins, Mr S. J. Colman and Mr H. P. Smith. My wife has argued the manuscript with me, line by line, to an extent which, in certain chapters, makes her virtually the joint author. But I cannot finally involve anyone but myself, either in my judgements or in my errors.

Because of the form of the book, I have not been able to include any detailed accounts of the changes in words and meanings to which I refer. I shall publish this supporting evidence, later, in a specialist paper on *Changes in English during the Industrial Revolution*. The brief accounts given in my text are subject to the usual dangers of summary, and the reader primarily interested in the words themselves must be referred to the paper mentioned, which adds some new evidence to the existing authorities.

While this book has been in the press I have been considering the directions in which further work in its field might profitably move, and it may be useful to note these. It seems to me, first, that we are arriving, from various directions, at a point where a new general theory of culture might in fact be achieved. In this book I have sought to clarify the tradition, but it may be possible to go on from this to a full restatement of principles, taking the theory of culture as a theory of relations between elements in a whole way of life. We need also, in these terms, to examine the idea of an expanding culture, and its detailed processes. For we live in an expanding culture, yet we spend much of our energy regretting the fact, rather than seeking to understand its nature and conditions. I think a good deal of factual revision of our received cultural history is necessary and urgent, in such matters as literacy, educational levels, and the press. We also need detailed studies of the social and economic problems of current cultural expansion, as means towards an adequate common policy. Finally, in the special field of criticism, we may be able to extend our methods of analysis, in relation to the re-definitions of creative activity and communication which various kinds of investigation are making possible. All this work will be difficult, but it may be helped by an understanding of the context of our present vocabulary in these matters, to which this book is offered as a contribution.

Parts of the book have previously appeared, in other forms, in *Essays in Criticism* and *Universities and Left Review.*

R. W.

CONTENTS

CONTENTS

Part III

TWENTIETH-CENTURY OPINIONS

AN OUTLINE OF DATES

The dates given are those in which the writers
discussed were aged 25

Edmund Burke	1754
Jeremy Bentham	1773
William Blake	1782
William Cobbett	1787
William Wordsworth	1795
Robert Owen	1796
S. T. Coleridge	1797
Robert Southey	1799
Lord Byron	1813
P. B. Shelley	1817
Thomas Arnold	⎧ 1820
John Keats	⎨ 1820
Thomas Carlyle	⎩ 1820
J. H. Newman	1826
Benjamin Disraeli	1829
F. D. Maurice	1830
John Stuart Mill	1831
Elizabeth Gaskell	1835
A. W. Pugin	⎧ 1837
Charles Dickens	⎩ 1837
John Ruskin	⎧ 1844
George Eliot	⎨ 1844
Charles Kingsley	⎩ 1844
Matthew Arnold	1847
William Morris	⎧ 1859
J. A. McN. Whistler	⎩ 1859
Walter Pater	1864
W. H. Mallock	1874
Bernard Shaw	⎧ 1881
Oscar Wilde	⎩ 1881

AN OUTLINE OF DATES

INTRODUCTION TO THE
1982 EDITION

IT IS now more than a quarter of a century since I wrote *Culture and Society*. I sometimes find, when I re-read it or parts of it, that it is like reading a book written by someone else. Yet it was in this book that I first found a position which expressed my sense of what had happened and was still happening in industrial civilisation, and in its art and thought. I have since developed and sometimes changed particular points and judgments, but I have not changed my view that one of the central ways of understanding the two extraordinary centuries which have so greatly changed the world and which underlie its now major crisis is through the detailed and complex thinking about culture which has been active and vibrant at every stage.

As the original Introduction explains, the book was formed around my discovery that the concept of culture, in its modern senses, came through at the time of the Industrial Revolution. The book was organised around the new kinds of problem and question which were articulated not only in the new sense of *culture* but in a whole group of closely associated words.* Thus the very language of serious inquiry and argument was in part changed and changing, and my purpose then was to follow this change through in the writing of the very diverse men and women who had contributed to this newly central kind of argument.

One of the questions I am now most often asked about the book is how I selected the writers I would discuss. Behind this question there is usually a sense that some kind of list or catalogue of such writers already existed, and that I included or excluded this one or that. But I have to say that when I was reading for the book no such list was known to me or has since been discovered. I do not mean that most of the writers were not already well known, but I do mean that, to the best of my knowledge, they had not been seen as connected in this way, around certain central themes. My actual preparation for the book was in fact a continually extending reading, without prepared lists or any real signposts. Indeed I remember several moments of something like panic when I discovered bodies of writing that I had not previously connected with the inquiry, but which were obviously relevant. The book, as a result, kept being shaped and reshaped. In the years since it was written, I have discovered more of these cases and could make other inclusions. But it may be possible to claim, as indeed many readers have said, that I got far enough to establish a sense of a tradition of writing about culture and society, which as a tradition was too little or not at all known, in its real complexity. There could then be subsequent inclusions, or indeed exclusions, but the sense that such a tradition existed was what the book had, in general, achieved. It is then, in a way, an ironic tribute to the success of the book that so many of its subsequent readers could take this tradition for granted, and then ask, often with good local reasons, why I had not included this or that contributor to so well-known a tradition.

Another regular question is why I centered the book on English writers, when there were so many obviously relevant writers in other languages and cultures. It is a fair question, and I certainly believe that both the book itself, and the many writers it discusses, need to be read alongside those other traditions, which bear, sometimes in common ways, sometimes with quite different approaches, on the same themes. Yet I am still sure that the book could only be formed, in its particular method, around this particular experience and tradition. The industrial revolution, which eventually swept or impinged on most of the world, began in England. The fundamentally new social and cultural relationships and issues which were part of that historically decisive transition were therefore first felt, in their intense and unprecedented immediacy, within this culture. At the beginning, and indeed for two or three generations, it was literally a problem of finding a language to express them. Thus though it is true that comparable changes happened in other societies, and new forms of thought and art were created to respond to them, often in equally or more penetrating and interesting ways than in these English writers, it is nevertheless of some permanent general importance to see what happened where it happened first. The warm responses to my book, in Italian or Japanese or German translation, or as so notably among North American readers, seem to confirm this belief.

There is then an important contemporary point. It was widely said, when *Culture and Society* was published in 1958, that it was one of the founding texts of the British New Left. It is still regularly said that this book, with the later *The Long Revolution*, combined with Richard Hoggart's *The Uses of Literacy* and E. P. Thompson's *William Morris* and *The Making of the English Working Class* to initiate a new intellectual and political tradition. That is for others to decide. The history is in fact quite complex. But I remember that in 1968 something different was being said. These books, or some of them, were still respected, but were often assigned to a kind of cultural radicalism which had since been outdistanced by a clearer, harder and indeed more traditional kind of socialism. I know that in any case I developed some of the arguments in that direction, for reasons I still support. But the way it looked in 1968 is different from the way it looked later, in 1978 or 1982. What had been confidently analysed, and in some cases dismissed, as the merely romantic critique of industrialism or industrial capitalism returned, in these later years, to make startling connections with the new ecological and radical-ecological movements. It was not that all or even most of the nineteenth-century forerunners had combined their sense of radical disturbance with the solutions that were being offered or sought in these new movements. Some of them simply looked backward, as indeed some in the new movements still do. Others looked forward, but only rarely in that temporarily confident way in which the basic modes of industrial civilisation were seen as the unproblematic ground for a new radical social order. As the crisis of our own years has continued, the openness, the diversity, the human commitments of these earlier writers came through, in a majority of cases, as the voices of fellow-strugglers rather than of historically outdated or periodised thinkers. The depth and extent of the crisis, that is to say, was something we could readily share from our own world with even the earliest of these contributors, and we were still, with them, looking for answers, having returned, by the sheer weight of events, to many of the same questions. I now often find it ironic that some of the newest and most important thinking of our own time, seeing the crises of the social order and of the natural order as inseparably linked, can be found in embryo or indeed in significant development in these earlier writers. But then it is finally encouraging rather than ironic, for new knowledge, new experience, new forms of hope, new groups and institutions, are taking the whole inquiry into dimensions which are much more than repetitive, and instead of being drawn back are pushed forward by these remarkable predecessors.

It is for this central reason that I can allow myself to hope that *Culture and Society* is still relevant to new contemporary readers. It is in any case widely used as a history of the thought and writing of this English tradition, and perhaps that is still enough. But I did not write it only as a history, as the Conclusion sufficiently shows. I began it in the post-1945 crisis of belief and affiliation. I used all the work for it as a way of finding a position from which I could hope to understand and act in contemporary society, necessarily through its history, which had delivered this strange, unsettling and exciting, world to us. It may not work in that way for others, but that is why it was written and how, by many more readers than I had hoped for, it has often been read.

Raymond Williams

Cambridge, 1982.

---

*NOTE: The paper on *Changes in English during the Industrial Revolution*, originally intended as an appendix to *Culture and Society*, developed much later into my book *Keywords* (1976), which contains my most recent research on the decisive new words and meanings.

INTRODUCTION

In the last decades of the eighteenth century, and in the first half of the nineteenth century, a number of words, which are now of capital importance, came for the first time into common English use, or, where they had already been generally used in the language, acquired new and important meanings. There is in fact a general pattern of change in these words, and this can be used as a special kind of map by which it is possible to look again at those wider changes in life and thought to which the changes in language evidently refer.

Five words are the key points from which this map can be drawn. They are *industry, democracy, class, art* and *culture*. The importance of these words, in our modern structure of meanings, is obvious. The changes in their use, at this critical period, bear witness to a general change in our characteristic ways of thinking about our common life: about our social, political and economic institutions; about the purposes which these institutions are designed to embody; and about the relations to these institutions and purposes of our activities in learning, education and the arts.

The first important word is *industry*, and the period in which its use changes is the period which we now call the Industrial Revolution. *Industry*, before this period, was a name for a particular human attribute, which could be paraphrased as 'skill, assiduity, perseverance, diligence'. This use of *industry* of course survives. But, in the last decades of the eighteenth century, *industry* came also to mean something else; it became a collective word for our manufacturing and productive institutions, and for their general activities. Adam Smith, in *The Wealth of Nations* (1776), is one of the first writers to use the word in this way, and from his time the development of this use is assured. *Industry*, with a capital letter, is thought of as a thing in itself—an institution, a body of activities—rather than simply a human attribute. *Industrious*, which described persons, is joined, in the nineteenth century, by *industrial*, which describes the institutions. The rapid growth in importance of these institutions is seen as creating a new system, which in the 1830s is first called *Industrialism*. In part, this is the acknowledgement of a series of very important technical changes, and of their transforming effect on methods of production. It is also, however, an acknowledgement of the effect of these changes on society as a whole, which is similarly transformed. The phrase *Industrial Revolution* amply confirms this, for the phrase, first used by French writers in the 1820s, and gradually adopted, in the course of the century, by English writers, is modelled explicitly on an analogy with the French Revolution of 1789. As that had transformed France, so this has transformed England; the means of change are different, but the change is comparable in kind: it has produced, by a pattern of change, a new society.

The second important word is *democracy*, which had been known, from the Greek, as a term for 'government by the people', but which only came into common English use at the time of the American and French Revolutions. Weekley, in *Words Ancient and Modern*, writes:

> It was not until the French Revolution that *democracy* ceased to be a mere literary word, and became part of the political vocabulary.[1]

In this he is substantially right. Certainly, it is in reference to America and France that the examples begin to multiply, at the end of the eighteenth century, and it is worth noting that the great majority of these examples show the word being used unfavourably: in close relation with the hated *Jacobinism*, or with the familiar *mob-rule*. England may have been (the word has so many modern definitions) a democracy since Magna Carta, or since the Commonwealth, or since 1688, but it certainly did not call itself one. *Democrats*, at the end of the eighteenth and the beginning of the nineteenth centuries, were seen, commonly, as dangerous and subversive mob agitators. Just as *industry* and its derived words record what we now call the Industrial Revolution, so *democracy* and *democrat*, in their entry into ordinary speech, record the effects, in England, of the American and French Revolutions, and a crucial phase of the struggle, at home, for what we would now call democratic representation.

Industry, to indicate an institution, begins in about 1776; *democracy*, as a practical word, can be dated from about the same time. The third word, *class*, can be dated, in its most important modern sense, from about 1772. Before this, the ordinary use of *class*, in English, was to refer to a division or group in schools and colleges: 'the usual Classes in Logick and Philosophy'. It is only at the end of the eighteenth century that the modern structure of *class*, in its social sense, begins to be built up. First comes *lower classes*, to join *lower orders*, which appears earlier in the eighteenth century. Then, in the 1790s, we get *higher classes*; *middle classes* and *middling classes* follow at once; *working classes* in about 1815; *upper classes* in the 1820s. *Class prejudice, class legislation, class consciousness, class conflict* and *class war* follow in the course of the nineteenth century. The *upper middle classes* are first heard of in the 1890s; the *lower middle class* in our own century.

It is obvious, of course, that this spectacular history of the new use of *class* does not indicate the *beginning* of social divisions in England. But it indicates, quite clearly, a change in the character of these divisions, and it records, equally clearly, a change in attitudes towards them. *Class* is a more indefinite word than *rank*, and this was probably one of the reasons for its introduction. The structure then built on it is in nineteenth-century terms: in terms, that is to say, of the changed social structure, and the changed social feelings, of an England which was passing through the Industrial Revolution, and which was at a crucial phase in the development of political democracy.

The fourth word, *art*, is remarkably similar, in its pattern of change, to *industry*. From its original sense of a human attribute, a 'skill', it had come, by the period with which we are concerned, to be a kind of institution, a set body of activities of a certain kind. An *art* had formerly been any human skill; but *Art*, now, signified a particular group of skills, the 'imaginative' or 'creative' arts. *Artist* had meant a skilled person, as had *artisan*; but *artist* now referred to these selected skills alone. Further, and most significantly, *Art* came to stand for a special kind of truth, 'imaginative truth', and *artist* for a special kind of person, as the words *artistic* and *artistical*, to describe human beings, new in the 1840s, show. A new name, *aesthetics*, was found to describe the judgement of art, and this, in its turn, produced a name for a special kind of person—*aesthete*. *The arts*—literature, music, painting, sculpture, theatre—were grouped together, in this new phrase, as having something essentially in common which distinguished them from other human skills. The same separation as had grown up between *artist* and *artisan* grew up between *artist* and *craftsman*. *Genius*, from meaning 'a characteristic disposition', came to mean 'exalted ability', and a distinction was made between it and *talent*. As *art* had produced *artist* in the new sense, and *aesthetics aesthete*, so this produced *a genius*, to indicate a special kind of person. These changes, which belong in time to the period of the other changes discussed, form a record of a remarkable change in ideas of the nature and purpose of art, and of its relations to other human activities and to society as a whole.

The fifth word, *culture*, similarly changes, in the same critical period. Before this period, it had meant, primarily, the 'tending of natural growth', and then, by analogy, a process of human training. But this latter use, which had usually been a culture *of* something, was changed, in the nineteenth century, to *culture* as such, a thing in itself. It came to mean, first, 'a general state or habit of the mind', having close relations with the idea of human perfection. Second, it came to mean 'the general state of intellectual development, in a society as a whole'. Third, it came to mean 'the general body of the arts'. Fourth, later in the century, it came to mean 'a whole way of life, material, intellectual and spiritual'. It came also, as we know, to be a word which often provoked either hostility or embarrassment.

The development of *culture* is perhaps the most striking among all the words named. It might be said, indeed, that the questions now concentrated in the meanings of the word *culture* are questions directly raised by the great historical changes which the changes in *industry*, *democracy* and *class*, in their own way, represent, and to which the changes in *art* are a closely related response. The development of the word *culture* is a record of a number of important and continuing reactions to these changes in our social, economic and political life, and may be seen, in itself, as a special kind of map by means of which the nature of the changes can be explored.

I have stated, briefly, the fact of the changes in these important words. As a background to them I must also draw attention to a number of other words which are either new, or acquired new meanings, in this decisive period. Among the new words, for example, there are *ideology, intellectual, rationalism, scientist, humanitarian, utilitarian, romanticism, atomistic; bureaucracy, capitalism, collectivism, commercialism, communism, doctrinaire, equalitarian, liberalism, masses, mediaeval* and *mediaevalism, operative* (noun), *primitivism, proletariat* (a new word for 'mob'), *socialism, unemployment; cranks, highbrow, isms* and *pretentious*. Among words which then acquired their now normal modern meanings are *business* (=trade), *common* (=vulgar), *earnest* (derisive), *Education* and *educational, getting-on, handmade, idealist* (=visionary), *Progress, rank-and-file* (other than military), *reformer* and *reformism, revolutionary* and *revolutionize, salary* (as opposed to 'wages'), *Science* (=natural and physical sciences), *speculator* (financial), *solidarity, strike* and *suburban* (as a description of attitudes). The field which these changes cover is again a field of general change, introducing many elements which we now point to as distinctively modern in situation and feeling. It is the relations within this general pattern of change which it will be my particular task to describe.

The word which more than any other comprises these relations is *culture*, with all its complexity of idea and reference. My overall purpose in the book is to describe and analyse this complex, and to give an account of its historical formation. Because of its very range of reference, it is necessary, however, to set the enquiry from the beginning on a wide basis. I had originally intended to keep very closely to *culture* itself, but, the more closely I examined it, the more widely my terms of reference had to be set. For what I see in the history of this word, in its structure of meanings, is a wide and general movement in thought and feeling. I shall hope to show this movement in detail. In summary, I wish to show the emergence of *culture* as an abstraction and an absolute: an emergence which, in a very complex way, merges two general responses—first, the recognition of the practical separation of certain moral and intellectual activities from the driven impetus of a new kind of society; second, the emphasis of these activities, as a court of human appeal, to be set over the processes of practical social judgement and yet to offer itself as a mitigating and rallying alternative. But, in both these senses, culture was not a response to the new methods of production, the new *Industry*, alone. It was concerned, beyond these, with the new kinds of personal and social relationship: again, both as a recognition of practical separation and as an emphasis of alternatives. The idea of *culture* would be simpler if it had been a response to industrialism alone, but it was also, quite evidently, a response to the new political and social developments, to *Democracy*. Again, in relation to this, it is a complex and radical response to the new problems of social class. Further, while these responses define bearings, in a given external area that was surveyed, there is also, in the formation of the meanings of *culture*, an evident reference back to an area of personal and apparently private experience, which was notably to affect the meaning and practice of art. These are the first stages of the formulation of the idea of culture, but its historical development is at least as important. For the recognition of a separate body of moral and intellectual activities, and the offering of a court of human appeal, which comprise the early meanings of the word, are joined, and in themselves changed, by the growing assertion of a whole way of life, not only as a scale of integrity, but as a mode of interpreting all our common experience, and, in this new interpretation, changing it. Where *culture* meant a state or habit of the mind, or the body of intellectual and moral activities, it means now, also, a whole way of life. This development, like each of the original meanings and the relations between them, is not accidental, but general and deeply significant.

My terms of reference then are not only to distinguish the meanings, but to relate them to their sources and effects.

INTRODUCTION

I shall try to do this by examining, not a series of abstracted problems, but a series of statements by individuals. It is not only that, by temperament and training, I find more meaning in this kind of personally verified statement than in a system of significant abstractions. It is also that, in a theme of this kind, I feel myself committed to the study of actual language: that is to say, to the words and sequences of words which particular men and women have used in trying to give meaning to their experience. It is true that I shall be particularly interested in the general developments of meaning in language, and these, always, are more than personal. But, as a method of enquiry, I have not chosen to list certain topics, and to assemble summaries of particular statements on them. I have, rather, with only occasional exceptions, concentrated on particular thinkers and their actual statements, and tried to understand and value them. The framework of the enquiry is general, but the method, in detail, is the study of actual individual statements and contributions.

In my First Part, I consider a number of nineteenth-century thinkers, of whom many if not all will be familiar to the informed reader, but whose relations, and even whose individual meanings, may be seen from this standpoint in a somewhat different light. I consider next, and more briefly, certain writers at the turn of the nineteenth into the twentieth century, who form, as I see them, a particular kind of inter-regnum. Then, in my Third Part, I consider some writers and thinkers of our own century, in an attempt to make the structure of meanings, and the common language in these matters, fully contemporary. Finally, in my Conclusion, I offer my own statement on an aspect of this common experience: not indeed as a verdict on the tradition, but as an attempt to extend it in the direction of certain meanings and values.

The area of experience to which the book refers has produced its own difficulties in terms of method. These, however, will be better appreciated, and judged, in the actual course of the enquiry. I ought perhaps to say that I expect the book to be controversial: not that I have written it for the sake of controversy as such, but because any such enquiry involves the discussion and the proposition of values, which are quite properly the subject of difference, and which affect even what we are in the habit of calling the known facts. I shall, at any rate, be glad to be answered, in whatever terms, for I am enquiring into our common language, on matters of common interest, and when we consider how matters now stand, our continuing interest and language could hardly be too lively.

PART I
A NINETEENTH-CENTURY TRADITION

CHAPTER I

CONTRASTS

THE mood of England in the Industrial Revolution is a mood of contrasts. The title, *Contrasts*, which Pugin was to make famous, epitomizes the habit of thinking of the early industrial generations. We can properly begin our own study by an essay in contrasts between lastingly influential men and ideas. My first contrast is between Edmund Burke and William Cobbett; my second between Robert Southey and Robert Owen.

1. Edmund Burke and William Cobbett

Edmund Burke has been called 'the first modern Conservative'; William Cobbett 'the first great tribune of the industrial proletariat'. Yet Cobbett began his political career in England under the patronage of William Windham, an intimate friend of Burke, and one who made Burke's principles his standard in politics. It was Windham, consciously the political heir of Burke, who welcomed back from the United States, in 1800, the famous young anti-Jacobin pamphleteer, William Cobbett. It was with money raised by Windham that Cobbett started publication of his famous *Political Register*, which became, and till Cobbett's death in 1835 continued, the most influential Radical publication in the land. The fierce young anti-Jacobin died a great Radical, who had been hunted to courtroom and prison, on charges of sedition, by others of the political heirs of Burke. But the association of Burke and Cobbett, through Windham, serves as an introduction to the more important association, which we should now make. In the convulsion of England by the struggle for political democracy and by the progress of the Industrial Revolution, many voices were raised in condemnation of the new developments, in the terms and accents of an older England. Of all these, two have survived as the most important: Burke and Cobbett. In spite of their great differences, this fact prevails. They attacked the new England from their experience of the old England, and, from their work, traditions of criticism of the new democracy and the new industrialism were powerfully begun: traditions which in the middle of the twentieth century are still active and important.

Burke's attack was upon democracy, as we now commonly understand it. The event which drew his fire was the Revolution in France, but his concern was not only with France; it was, perhaps primarily, with the running of a similar tide in England. He did not believe that this could be kept back, but his stand was none the less firm:

> You see, my dear Lord, that I do not go upon any difference concerning the best method of preventing the growth of a system which I believe we dislike in common. I cannot differ with you because I do not think *any* method can prevent it. The evil has happened; the thing is done in principle and in example; and we must wait the good pleasure of an Higher Hand than ours for the time of its perfect accomplishment in practice in this country and elsewhere. All I have done for some time past, and all I shall do hereafter, will only be to clear myself from having any hand, actively or passively, in this great change.[1]

Now that the change has happened, or is supposed to have happened, a man in such a position is evidently isolated. The confutation of Burke on the French Revolution is now a one-finger exercise in politics and history. We check the boiling by pouring in cold water. His writings on France are annotated as I have seen the story of the Creation in a Bible in a railway waiting-room: 'historically untrue'. This sort of thing is indeed so easy that we may be in danger of missing a more general point, which has to do less with his condemnations than with his attachments, and less with his position than with his manner of thinking. The quality of Burke is the quality indicated by Matthew Arnold, in his comment on him in *The Function of Criticism at the Present Time*:

> Almost alone in England, he brings thought to bear upon politics, he saturates politics with thought.[2]

Arnold himself is one of the political heirs of Burke, but

4

again this is less important than the kind of thinking which Arnold indicates by the verb 'saturates'. It is not 'thought' in the common opposition to 'feeling'; it is, rather, a special immediacy of experience, which works itself out, in depth, to a particular embodiment of ideas that become, in themselves, the whole man. The correctness of these ideas is not at first in question; and their truth is not, at first, to be assessed by their usefulness in historical understanding or in political insight. Burke's writing is an articulated experience, and as such it has a validity which can survive even the demolition of its general conclusions. It is not that the eloquence survives where the cause has failed; the eloquence, if it were merely the veneer of a cause, would now be worthless. What survives is an experience, a particular kind of learning; the writing is important only to the extent that it communicates this. It is, finally, a personal experience become a landmark.

My point can be illustrated in one very simple way. In politics Burke is, above all, the great recommender of prudence as the primary virtue of civil government. We know this; we receive it as an idea. Burke's formal opponents, knowing it, think they can destroy him when they can set against the principle such a sentence as this, from the tribute of a great admirer:

> His abilities were supernatural, and a deficiency of prudence and political wisdom alone could have kept him within the rank of mortals.[3]

As we look, now, at Burke's political career, we confirm the estimate of deficiency. Common prudence was lacking at one crisis after another, and his political wisdom, in the practical sense, was halting or negligible. Yet this does not affect his estimate of political virtue. Burke is one of that company of men who learn virtue from the margin of their errors, learn folly from their own persons. It is at least arguable that this is the most important kind of learning. Burke says of the leaders of the National Assembly:

> Their purpose everywhere seems to have been to evade and slip aside from *difficulty*. This it has been the glory of the great masters in all the arts to confront and to overcome; and when they had

overcome the first difficulty, to turn it into an instrument for new conquests over new difficulties; thus to enable them to extend the empire of their science; and even to push forward, beyond the reach of their original thoughts, the landmarks of the human understanding itself. Difficulty is a severe instructor, set over us by the supreme ordinance of a parental guardian and legislator, who knows us better than we know ourselves, as he loves us better too. . . . He that wrestles with us strengthens our nerves, and sharpens our skill. Our antagonist is our helper. This amicable conflict with difficulty obliges us to an intimate acquaintance with our object, and compels us to consider it in all its relations. It will not suffer us to be superficial. It is the want of nerves of understanding for such a task, it is the degenerate fondness for tricking short-cuts, and little fallacious facilities, that has in so many parts of the world created governments with arbitrary powers.[4]

The truth of this can be generally attested, and the wrestling is not less important, nor less fruitful, when under the shadow of general difficulty a man's antagonist is in certain aspects himself. Moreover, the connexion between the quality of this process in individuals and the quality of civil society is major and indisputable. We do not need to share Burke's support of the Bourbons against the Assembly to realize the authority of this:

If circumspection and caution are a part of wisdom, when we work only upon inanimate matter, surely they become a part of duty too, when the subject of our demolition and construction is not brick and timber, but sentient beings, by the sudden alteration of whose state, condition, and habits, multitudes may be rendered miserable. . . . The true lawgiver ought to have a heart full of sensibility. He ought to love and respect his kind, and to fear himself. It may be allowed to his temperament to catch his ultimate object with an intuitive glance; but his movements towards it ought to be deliberate. Political arrangement, as it is a work for social ends, is to be only wrought by social means. There mind must conspire with mind. . . . If I might venture to appeal to what is so much out of fashion in Paris, I mean to experience, I should tell you that in my course I have known and, according to my measure, have co-operated with great men; and I have never yet seen any plan which has not been mended by the observations of those who were much inferior in understanding to the person who took the lead in the business. By a slow but well-sustained progress, the effect of each step is watched; the good or ill success of the first gives light to us in the second; and so, from light to light, we are conducted with safety through the whole series. We see that the parts of the system do not clash. The evils latent in the most promising contrivances are provided for as they arise. One advantage is as little as possible sacrificed to another. We compensate, we reconcile, we balance.[5]

Nothing is more foolish than to suppose, as reformers of many kinds have done, that this is merely a recommendation of conservatism. It is equally foolish for conservatives to suppose that such conclusions are any kind of argument against the most radical social reform. Burke is describing a process, based on a recognition of the necessary complexity and difficulty of human affairs, and formulating itself, in consequence, as an essentially social and cooperative effort in control and reform. No particular policy can dispense with such recognitions; no description of policy, by a 'tricking short-cut', can arrogate them to itself.

Yet when this has been said, the direction of effort, the decision of what is necessary, remain to be discussed. Here, Burke belongs most certainly to what Arnold called an 'epoch of concentration'. It is not true to say that he resisted all reform, but his heaviest fire is reserved for all schemes of wholesale innovation or radical reconstruction:

> Reform is not a change in the substance or in the primary modification of the object, but a direct application of a remedy to the grievance complained of.[6]

Politics is a business of practical expediency, not of theoretical ideas. His comment on the unfortunate Dr Price can stand as a general comment on the whole philosophical and literary tradition which was promoting social change:

> Wholly unacquainted with the world in which they are so fond of meddling, and inexperienced in all its affairs, on which they pronounce with so much confidence, they have nothing of politics but the passions they excite.[7]

The point has been echoed by thousands of lesser men, and

7

is now a commonplace of diatribe, yet the criticism contained in the last clause keeps its force, and might even be applied to Burke himself. Even where the value of a tradition of thought in politics is most certainly to be acclaimed, this observation is not to be forgotten as an important limiting clause.

Burke served the causes of his day, and in particular the cause of opposition to democracy. He argued that the tendency of democracy was to tyranny, and he observed, further, that

> those who are subjected to wrong under multitudes are deprived of all external consolation. They seem deserted by mankind, overpowered by a conspiracy of their whole species.[8]

This again is an observation from experience. It did not need complete democracy for its realization; it was, in the bad times, Burke's own feeling about himself, under the sway of a majority opinion that was against him. This is not to deny that the observation about democracy may be reasonable. Yet, as the argument has gone since Burke's day, his position has come to seem paradoxical. It is commonly argued, in this kind of criticism of democracy, that the individual is oppressed by the mass, and that, generally speaking, virtues are individual in origin and are threatened by mass society. Burke had no experience of anything that could be called a mass society, but he could not in any case have accepted such an argument. His position, quite unequivocally, is that man as an individual left to himself is wicked; all human virtue is the creation of society, and is in this sense not 'natural' but 'artificial': 'art is man's nature'. The embodiment and guarantee of the proper humanity of man is the historical community. The rights of man include the right to be restrained:

> Government is a contrivance of human wisdom to provide for human *wants*. . . . Among these wants is to be reckoned the want, out of civil society, of a sufficient restraint upon their passions. Society requires not only that the passions of individuals should be subjected, but that even in the mass and body, as well as in the individuals, the inclinations of men should frequently be thwarted, their will controlled, and their passions brought into subjection.

This can only be done *by a power out of themselves*; and not, in the exercise of its function, subject to that will and to those passions which it is its office to bridle and subdue. In this sense the restraints on men, as well as their liberties, are to be reckoned among their rights.[9]

In so far as democracy is a system which enables individuals to decide how they should govern themselves (this is not its only definition, but it was a common one, in association with doctrines of economic individualism, when Burke was writing), this is a substantial criticism. As Burke says, in opposition to a main tenor of eighteenth-century thinking:

We are afraid to put men to live and trade each on his own private stock of reason; because we suspect that the stock in each man is small, and that the individuals would do better to avail themselves of the general bank and capital of nations and of ages.[10]

Seventy years later, this was to be the basis of Matthew Arnold's recommendation of Culture.

In opposition to the ideas of individualist democracy, Burke set the idea of a People:

In a state of *rude* nature there is no such thing as a people. A number of men in themselves have no collective capacity. The idea of a people is the idea of a corporation. It is wholly artificial; and made, like all other legal fictions, by common agreement. What the particular nature of that agreement was, is collected from the form into which the particular society has been cast.[11]

The whole progress of man is thus dependent, not only on the historical community in an abstract sense, but on the nature of the particular community into which he has been born. No man can abstract himself from this; nor is it his alone to change:

Society is indeed a contract. Subordinate contracts for objects of mere occasional interest may be dissolved at pleasure—but the state ought not to be considered nothing better than a partnership agreement in a trade of pepper and coffee, calico or tobacco, or some other such low concern, to be taken up for a little temporary interest, and to be dissolved by the fancy of the parties. It is to be looked on with other reverence; because it is not a partnership in things subservient only to the gross animal existence of a temporary and perishable

9

nature. It is a partnership in all science; a partnership in all art; a partnership in every virtue, and in all perfection. As the ends of such a partnership cannot be obtained in many generations, it becomes a partnership not only between those who are living, but between those who are living, those who are dead, and those who are to be born.[12]

It can now be observed that Burke shifts, in this argument, from *society* to *state*, and that the essential reverence for society is not to be confused, as Burke seems to confuse it, with that particular form of society which is the State at any given time. The observation is important, but Burke would not have been impressed by it. In his view, there was nothing in any way accidental about any particular form; the idea of society was only available to men in the form in which they had inherited it. Moreover, the progress of human society was 'the known march of the ordinary providence of God'; the inherited form was divine in origin and guidance, the instrument of God's will that man should become perfect:

Without . . . civil society man could not by any possibility arrive at the perfection of which his nature is capable, nor even make a remote and faint approach to it. . . . He who gave our nature to be perfected by our virtue, willed also the necessary means of its perfection—He willed therefore the state—He willed its connexion with the source and original archetype of all perfection.[13]

The difficulty about this position, of course, comes when the State form changes, as it had done in France, and yet is considered, in its new form, as a destroyer of civil society. If the creation of State forms is 'the known march of the ordinary providence of God', then even the great changes which Burke was resisting might be beyond human control. He recognized this himself, late in his life, although the recognition did not modify his resistance:

They who persist in opposing this mighty current in human affairs will appear rather to resist the decrees of Providence itself, than the mere designs of men.[14]

The difficulty serves to illustrate once again Burke's period. His doctrines rest on an experience of stability, containing imperfections, but not essentially threatened. As the current of change swelled, the affirmation became a desperate defence. And even while Burke was writing, the great tide of economic change was flowing strongly, carrying with it many of the political changes against which he was concerned to argue. He speaks from the relative stability of the eighteenth century against the first signs of the flux and confusion of the nineteenth century, but he speaks also against those rising doctrines which the eighteenth century had produced, and which were to become the characteristic philosophy of the change itself. In doing so, he prepared a position in the English mind from which the march of industrialism and liberalism was to be continually attacked. He established the idea of the State as the necessary agent of human perfection, and in terms of this idea the aggressive individualism of the nineteenth century was bound to be condemned. He established, further, the idea of what has been called an 'organic society', where the emphasis is on the interrelation and continuity of human activities, rather than on separation into spheres of interest, each governed by its own laws.

> A nation is not an idea only of local extent, and individual momentary aggregation; but it is an idea of continuity, which extends in time as well as in numbers and in space. And this is a choice not of one day, or one set of people, not a tumultuary and giddy choice; it is a deliberate election of the ages and of generations; it is a constitution made by what is ten thousand times better than choice, it is made by the peculiar circumstances, occasions, tempers, dispositions, and moral, civil, and social habitudes of the people, which disclose themselves only in a long space of time.[15]

Immediately after Burke, this complex which he describes was to be called the 'spirit of the nation'; by the end of the nineteenth century, it was to be called a national 'culture'.

Examination of the influence and development of these ideas belongs to my later chapters. It is sufficient to note here Burke's own definitions. It is in these terms that Burke has lasted, but the survival involves a separation of these ideas from the rest of Burke's statement. We see him, now, when we see him as a whole, crippled by many kinds of misunderstanding. We set his polemics against the subsequent 'known march'. He seems to us blind to many of the changes which, even as he wrote, were transforming England. How else, we ask, could he have written, in the middle of a sixty-year period which saw 3,209 Acts of Enclosure of traditional common land, such a sentence as this?:

> The tenant-right of a cabbage-garden, a year's interest in a hovel, the goodwill of an alehouse or a baker's shop, the very shadow of a constructive property, are more ceremoniously treated in our parliament, than with you the oldest and most valuable landed possessions.[16]

Of all English thinkers, Burke should have recognized most clearly the common ownership, through custom and pre-scription, of these four million acres that Parliament diverted into private hands. The point is not one of polemic against Burke; it is, rather, an indication of the flux of history and judgement. The 'organic society', with which Burke's name was to be associated, was being broken up under his eyes by new economic forces, while he protested elsewhere. The epitaph on all his polemic is this, in his own brilliant judgement:

> Wise men will apply their remedies to vices, not to names; to the causes of evil which are permanent, not to the occasional organs by which they act, and the transitory modes in which they appear. Otherwise you will be wise historically, a fool in practice. Seldom have two ages the same fashion in their pretexts and the same modes of mischief. Wickedness is a little more inventive. . . . It walks abroad, it continues its ravages, whilst you are gibbeting the carcase, or demolishing the tomb. You are terrifying yourselves with ghosts and apparitions, whilst your house is the haunt of robbers.[17]

The vigour of the insight serves only to underline the irony, when applied to Burke himself.

It is here, I think, that Cobbett is so relevant. Cobbett was sufficiently younger than Burke to live through the Napoleonic Wars and their aftermath, and to see the first effects in country and town of the whole complex of changes which we call the Industrial Revolution. He had nothing of Burke's depth of mind, but he had what in so confused a time was at least as important, an extraordinary sureness of instinct. There is more in common between Cobbett the anti-Jacobin and Cobbett the Radical than is usually supposed; there is the same arrogance, the same crudeness, the same appetite for a class of men that he could hate. Divested of his sureness of instinct, Cobbett is, in large measure, the type of the very worst kind of popular journalist. There have indeed been, since his day, a thousand petty Cobbetts, imitating the vices of the position and lacking the virtues. The fact serves to show, not only the continuity, but Cobbett's quality; for the sureness of instinct was no accident—it was, rather, vital and impregnable, a genuine embodiment of value.

'Wise men will apply their remedies to vices, not to names'; this, essentially, is the motto for Cobbett, and he was even helped in his wisdom, at this particularly confusing time, by his relative indifference to ideas. He could thunder, with Burke, against

> a Multitude of Horrid Barbarity, such as the eye never witnessed, the tongue never expressed, or the imagination conceived, until the commencement of the French Revolution.[18]

He could congratulate himself, on leaving the United States in 1800, on returning to his

> native land, where neither the moth of *Democracy* nor the rust of Federalism doth corrupt.[19]

But when he saw the condition of England, and in this instance the hiring out of pauper labour, he did not refer his reaction to any fixed categories, or fear the calling of names:

> Aye! you may wince; you may cry Jacobin and Leveller as long as you please. I wish to see the poor men of England what the poor men of England were when I was born; and from endeavouring to accomplish this wish, nothing but the want of the means shall make me desist.[20]

He saw, and understood, the changes in the countryside:

> The taxing and funding . . . system has . . . drawn the real property of the nation into fewer hands; it has made land and agriculture

c   13

objects of speculation; it has, in every part of the kingdom, moulded many farms into one; it has almost entirely extinguished the race of small farmers; from one end of England to the other, the houses which formerly contained little farmers and their happy families, are now seen sinking into ruins, all the windows except one or two stopped up, leaving just light enough for some labourer, whose father was, perhaps, the small farmer, to look back upon his half-naked and half-famished children, while, from his door, he surveys all around him the land teeming with the means of luxury to his opulent and overgrown master. . . . We are daily advancing to the state in which there are but two classes of men, *masters*, and *abject dependants*.[21]

This was always his major theme:

A labouring man, in England, with a wife and only three children, though he never lose a day's work, though he and his family be economical, frugal and industrious in the most extensive sense of these words, is not now able to procure himself by his labour a single meal of meat from one end of the year unto the other. Is this a state in which the labouring man ought to be?[22]

He contrasted apparent prosperity with actual poverty:

Here are resources! Here is wealth! Here are all the means of national power, and of individual plenty and happiness! And yet, at the end of these ten beautiful miles, covered with all the means of affording luxury in diet and in dress, we entered that city of Coventry, which, out of *twenty thousand inhabitants*, contained at that very moment upwards of *eight thousand miserable paupers*.[23]

So the indictment mounted, and was generalized:

England has long groaned under a *commercial system*, which is the most oppressive of all possible systems; and it is, too, a quiet, silent, smothering oppression that it produces, which is more hateful than all others.[24]

The terms of Cobbett's social criticism so much resemble later and more organized critiques that it is easy to forget the basis of experience from which he worked, and the values by which he judged. He called the new class system, most significantly, 'unnatural'. In controversy, he accused an opponent of trying to cut off the

14

chain of connection between the rich and the poor. You are for demolishing all small tradesmen. You are for reducing the community to two classes: *Masters* and *Slaves*. . . . When *master* and *man* were the terms, every one was in his place, and all were free. Now, in fact, it is an affair of *masters* and *slaves*. . . .[25]

The old social relations, in productive labour, were being replaced by men, reduced to 'hands', in the service of the

Seigneurs of the Twist, sovereigns of the Spinning Jenny, great Yeomen of the Yarn.[26]

The new industrial system was unnatural, and Cobbett could see 'much mischief' arising from such things as the new railways:

They are unnatural effects, arising out of the resources of the country having been drawn unnaturally together into great heaps. [2]

Unnatural is the constant emphasis, and the word is the keystone of a continuing tradition of criticism of the new industrial civilization.

Cobbett's reaction, however, is of two main kinds. There is the reaction of the countryman, which has become a major English tradition. Faced with the new industrial economy, and its kind of products and way of satisfying needs, he issued a manual of the England he remembered:

Cottage economy: containing information relative to the brewing of Beer, making of Bread, keeping of Cows, Pigs, Bees, Ewes, Goats, Poultry, and Rabbits, and relative to other matters deemed useful in the conducting of the affairs of a Labourer's Family.

It was a sign of the times, of course, that so much of this information should have to be conveyed in print, but the book epitomizes this part of Cobbett's positive reaction. He would salvage what he could of domestic industry and the traditional daily skills.

There is also, however, Cobbett's other reaction, which was, and still is, very much more controversial. In the misery that had fallen on the English poor, Cobbett stood fast against any kind of 'consolation'. He would have nothing to do with charity schemes, the dissemination of religious

15

tracts, or even with the kind of popular education then being recommended:

> The 'comforting' system necessarily implies *interference* on one side, and *dependence* on the other.[28]

He did not want violence, but he expected resistance. He expected, and watched with sympathy, all the efforts of the labouring poor to improve their conditions by their own action:

> I knew that all the palaver in the world, all the wheedling, coaxing, praying; I knew that all the blustering and threatening; I knew that all the teachings of all the Tract Societies; that all the imprisoning, whipping, and harnessing to carts and wagons; I knew that all these would fail to persuade the honest, sensible and industrious English labourer, that he had not an *indefeasible right to live*. . . . There is no man, not of a fiend-like nature, who can view the destruction of property that is now going on in the Southern counties without the greatest pain; but I stand to it, that it is the strict natural course of things, where the labourer, the producer, *will not starve*.[29]

In consequence, and at great personal risk, he opposed every kind of repression by State authority.

> To speak of them [the rioters], as *The Times* has done, as an organized rabble, easily beaten by the soldiers; and to say, that it may be desirable that the spirit should break out in all places at once, so that the trouble of subduing it may be the sooner over; to talk in this light and swaggering manner is calculated to swell discontent into rage and despair.[30]

He rejected the orthodox explanation of disorder as due to 'plots' and 'agitators':

> This is the circumstance that will most puzzle the ministry. They can find no *agitators*. It is a movement of the *people's own*.[31]

He condemned the institution of the Combination Acts, as a weapon against trade unionism:

> When it was found that men could not keep their families decently upon the wages that the rich masters chose to give them, and that the men would *not work*, and contrived to combine, so as to be able to live, for a while, without work; then it was, for the purposes in

view, found necessary to call this combining by the name of conspiracy; it was found necessary so to *torture the laws* as to punish men for demanding what they deemed the worth of their labour.[32]

He saw labour as the only property of the poor, and he demanded the same rights for this as for other property:

> The principle upon which all property exists is this: that a man has a right to do with it that which he pleases. That he has a right to sell it, or to keep it. That he has a right to refuse to part with it at all; or, if he choose to sell it, to insist upon any price that he chooses to demand: if this be not the case, a man has no property.[33]

The principle comes straight from the individualist thinking of the eighteenth century, but in being extended to a new kind of property and hence to a whole new class, it threatened the economic basis of a society conceived on just this principle. The new employer claimed his right to do as he willed with his own; Cobbett, on the same principle, claimed the same right for the workers.

Just as Cobbett had seen the emerging class-structure of the new society, so he saw its consequences in class-conflict:

> They [the workers] combine to effect a rise in wages. The masters combine against them. One side complains of the other; but, neither knows the *cause* of the turmoil, and the turmoil goes on. The different trades combine, and call their combination a GENERAL UNION. So that here is one class of society united to oppose another class.[34]

Cobbett saw this as inevitable, on the principle which he had put forward, and which the workers had themselves asserted. He did not think the problem was to be solved by the employers developing a better attitude to their workers; this was part of the 'comforting system', and was practised even by slave-owners towards their slaves. The workers would have no more status than slaves unless the traditional rights of property were extended to their only property, their labour. He wanted the working class to realize their position, in these terms. As he said in 1830, of the events in France:

> I am pleased at the Revolution, particularly on this account, that it makes the working classes see their real importance, and those who despise them see it too.[35]

17

Cobbett had discovered, in fact, the essential weakness, the inherent contradiction, in the theories of economic individualism. It might be more true to say that he had stumbled on it, in the coming together of his inheritance from the eighteenth century and of his attachment by instinct and experience to the labouring poor. He thus saw and approved, in its infancy, the course of the labour movement, and he knew that it would not be beaten by laws:

> Better call for a law to prevent those inconvenient things called spring-tides.[36]

That his assessment of this position was realistic, more realistic by far than that of the majority of his contemporaries, is now obvious.

As focal points of the criticism of the new industrial system, we have then Cobbett the countryman, with his attachments to a different way of life, and Cobbett the tribune, encouraging the rising labour movement. In the latter rôle he has been numerously succeeded, and, in the change of circumstance, replaced. In the former rôle he remains irreplaceable: the *Rural Rides*, and the values embodied in them, are still a landmark. It remains to note briefly two other aspects of his work: one expected, the other rather surprising. The first is his position on popular education, which is very much that of Dickens in *Hard Times*. He believed, for political reasons, that the working people must be in charge of their own educational movements; any other arrangement would be part of the 'comforting system', the incessant persuasion to 'be quiet'. Dickens was not interested in such a point, but he believed, with Cobbett, that knowledge abstracted from a whole way of life, and then used as a mould into which all young lives were to be cast, was inhuman and dangerous. Cobbett insisted that learning could not be separated from doing; and that good education arose from a whole way of life, and was a preparation for participation in it, rather than an isolated, 'book-learning', abstraction. The position is right, although it has been abused; Cobbett himself is often simply a Philistine. For the very economic and social changes which Cobbett was attacking were forcing a separation between learning and other human activity. Criticism of the separation was valuable; but it had to be made, more carefully perhaps than Cobbett could manage to make it, in positive terms of the unity of human activity, rather than in the negative terms of a prejudice against 'book-learning'. We shall see the later stages of this argument in other writers.

The other aspect of Cobbett's work is his surprising share of responsibility for that idealization of the Middle Ages which is so characteristic of nineteenth-century social criticism. As a literary movement, mediaevalism had been growing since the middle of the eighteenth century. Its most important aspect, for Cobbett, was its use of the monasteries as a standard for social institutions: the image of the working of a communal society as a welcome alternative to the claims of individualism. Burke made the point, in the *Reflections*; later, Pugin, Carlyle, Ruskin and Morris were all to make it, explicitly and influentially. It is a little surprising to find Cobbett in this company; his standard, normally, was 'the England into which I was born'. Yet not only did he make the point, he was responsible for a large measure of its popularization. He read Lingard's *History of England*, the work of a Catholic scholar, and used it, with characteristic licence, as the basis of his *History of the Protestant Reformation*. This book had, by contemporary standards, a huge circulation, and there must for some time have been many thousands of readers who came to these ideas through Cobbett rather than through contact with any of the more reliable sources. For Cobbett, as for many others, the attachment was one of instinct; the originating emotion was simply recoil from the very different social ideals of the rising industrialism.

Burke and Cobbett, when their thinking has been followed through, are very distinct, almost antagonistic figures. Burke did not live to give an opinion of Cobbett the Radical, but it is likely that he would have shared Coleridge's feelings in 1817:

> I entertain toward . . . Cobbetts . . . and all these creatures—and to the Foxites, who have fostered the vipers—a feeling more like hatred than I ever bore to other Flesh and Blood.[37]

Cobbett, as dogmatically, has left record of a characteristically limited view of Burke:

> How amusing it is to hear the world disputing and wrangling about the motives, and principles, and opinions of *Burke*! He had no notions, no principles, no opinions of his own, when he wrote his famous work. . . . He was a poor, needy dependant of a Boroughmonger, to serve whom, and please whom, he wrote; and for no other purpose whatever. . . . And yet, how many people read this man's writings as if they had flowed from his *own mind*. . . .[38]

Yet to put together the names of Burke and Cobbett is important, not only as contrast, but because we can only understand this tradition of criticism of the new industrial society if we recognize that it is compounded of very different and at times even directly contradictory elements. The growth of the new society was so confusing, even to the best minds, that positions were drawn up in terms of inherited categories, which then revealed unsuspected and even opposing implications. There was much overlapping, even in the opposite positions of a Cobbett and a Burke, and the continuing attack on Utilitarianism, and on the driving philosophy of the new industrialism, was to make many more strange affiliations: Marx, for instance, was to attack capitalism, in his early writings, in very much the language of Coleridge, of Burke, and—of Cobbett. Utilitarianism itself was to have unsuspected implications, and Liberalism was to divide into a confusion of meanings. It is no more than one would expect in the early stages of so great a change. The effort which men had to make, to comprehend and to affirm, was indeed enormous; and it is the effort, the learning, in experience which it is important for us to know. We can still be grateful that men of the quality of Burke and Cobbett, for all their differences, were there to try to learn and record, and so magnificently to affirm, to the last limits of their strength.

ii. Robert Southey and Robert Owen

If you propose to render civilization complete by extending it to those classes who are brutalized by the institutions of society, half the persons whom you address will ask how this is to begin? and the other half, where it is to end? Undoubtedly both are grave questions. Owen of Lanark indeed would answer both.[1]

This is Southey, in his character of Montesinos, in the *Colloquies* (*Sir Thomas More: or, Colloquies on the Progress and Prospects of Society;* 1829). The comment sketches for us the famous Mr Owen of Lanark, who, unlike the majority of his contemporaries who had realized the inadequacies of the new society, offered answers where they raised questions; offered confidence where they perceived difficulty; offered schemes, backed by practical success, which showed clearly where the process of completing civilization must begin and would end. Southey adds:

> But, because he promises too much, no trial is made of the good which his schemes might probably perform.[2]

There are, perhaps, other reasons than this.

Southey goes on to praise and to criticize Owen. He describes him as 'one of the three men who have in this generation given an impulse to the moral world', and continues:

> Clarkson and Dr Bell are the other two. They have seen the first fruits of their harvest. So I think would Owen ere this, if he had not alarmed the better part of the nation by proclaiming, upon the most momentous of all subjects, opinions which are alike fatal to individual happiness and to the general good. Yet I admire the man. . . . A craniologist, I dare say, would pronounce that the organ of theopathy is wanting in Owen's head, that of benevolence being so large as to have left no room for it.[3]

Southey is right in asserting, as Owen well knew, that Owen's attacks on religion, begun in 1817, led to a radical recasting of Owen's prospects and prevented the kind of harvest—an active benevolent system, of a paternal kind— which he had previously been preparing. But the man who is now seen as one of the founders of English socialism, and of the cooperative movement, requires an analysis more searching than that of a craniologist; there were other organs, not only in Owen, but in the society that determined his actual course.

Southey and Owen, in retrospect, stand as removed as Burke and Cobbett, in apparent principle. And Southey, to us, is the fainter figure: a life's work diluted to a few anthology poems, and marked in perpetuity by Byron's *Vision of Judgment:*

> He said—(I only give the heads)—he said,
> He meant no harm in scribbling; 'twas his way
> Upon all topics; 'twas, besides, his bread,
> Of which he butter'd both sides; 'twould delay
> Too long the assembly (he was pleased to dread)
> And take up rather more time than a day,
> To name his works—he would but cite a few—
> 'Wat Tyler'—'Rhymes on Blenheim'—'Waterloo'.[4]

In this, as in a hundred lesser passages, Southey was the stock butt as a turncoat and a reactionary, but a caricature is not a life, and there is more to Southey than this, just as there is more to Byron and Shelley than that they were (in Southey's phrase) members of 'the Satanic school'. In his social thinking at least, Southey remains an influential if unacknowledged figure; and his approval of Owen reminds us of the complexity of this difficult period. Where Cobbett sneered at Owen's 'parallelograms of paupers', Southey, with very many of the new generation of English industrial workers, approved. In a movement like Christian Socialism, the influence of both Southey and Owen can be clearly discerned. Yet Owen, in his main bearings, led to socialism and the cooperatives; Southey, with Burke and Coleridge, to the new conservatism. Southey's part in the latter movement, moreover, was no minor one; Smythe, for example, instanced the *Colloquies* as a main source of the ideas of Young England, and called Southey 'the real founder of the movement'.[5] What Southey said in 1816 could have been said by many throughout this generation, including many of those who attacked him:

> The great evil is the state of the poor, which . . . constantly exposes us to the horrors of a *bellum servile,* and sooner or later, if not remedied, will end in one.[6]

The *Colloquies* remains Southey's most important work in this field, but as early as 1807, in the *Letters from England by Don Manuel Alvarez Espriella,* he advanced the kind of criticism of the new manufacturing system which later became axiomatic in a number of different schools, and which is almost identical with the later observations of Owen. In this essential respect he did not change his opinions, and the *Colloquies* is only a fuller statement of a position which many thousands have inherited.

Sir Thomas More, in the *Colloquies,* is made to ask: 'Can a nation be too rich?' Southey, in the character of Montesinos, replies:

> I cannot answer that question without distinguishing between a people and a state. A state cannot have more wealth at its command than may be employed for the general good, a liberal expenditure in national works being one of the surest means for promoting national prosperity, and the benefit being still more evident of an expenditure directed to the purposes of national improvement. But a people may be too rich; because it is the tendency of the commercial, and more especially of the manufacturing system, to collect wealth rather than to diffuse it . . . great capitalists become like pikes in a fish-pond, who devour the weaker fish; and it is but too certain that the poverty of one part of the people seems to increase in the same ratio as the riches of another.[7]

Whereas the natural operations of commerce are wholly beneficial, and bind nation to nation and man to man, the effect of the manufacturing system is directly opposite in tendency:

> The immediate and home effect of the manufacturing system, carried on as it now is upon the great scale, is to produce physical and moral evil, in proportion to the wealth which it creates.[8]

Men are being reduced to machines, and

> he who, at the beginning of his career, uses his fellow-creatures as bodily machines for producing wealth, ends not infrequently in becoming an intellectual one himself, employed in continually increasing what it is impossible for him to enjoy.[9]

Meanwhile,

> the new cottages of the manufacturers (*i.e. workmen*) are . . . upon the manufacturing pattern . . . naked, and in a row. How is it, said I, that every thing which is connected with manufactures presents

such features of unqualified deformity? . . . Time cannot mellow them; Nature will neither clothe nor conceal them; and they remain always as offensive to the eye as to the mind.[10]

The items of this comprehensive indictment, and certain of its actual phrases, will be recognized as familiar by many who know Southey only as a 'renegade'. It is among the very earliest general judgements of this kind.

Southey's affirmation is as characteristic as his indictment, and is again a very early example of a position which has become general. The contrast with mediaeval society is one of its elements, although not greatly stressed. The very form of the *Colloquies*—the bringing of More to question the new society—indicates a conscious continuity with the first phase of the humanist challenge, in which many of the ideas now concentrated in the meaning of 'culture' were in fact laid down. Southey handles the historical contrast in this comment by More:

> Throughout the trading part of the community every one endeavours to purchase at the lowest price, and sell at the highest, regardless of equity in either case. Bad as the feudal times were, they were less injurious than these commercial ones to the kindly and generous feelings of human nature.[11]

The comment indicates also a central feature in Southey's attitude, and one which ranges him firmly with Owen. Criticizing orthodox political economy, on the grounds of its exclusion of moral considerations, Montesinos adds:

> [It discerns] the cause of all our difficulties . . ., not in the constitution of society, but of human nature.[12]

Complementary with this, Southey insists on the positive functions of government:

> There can be no health, no soundness in the state, till Government shall regard the moral improvement of the people as its first great duty. The same remedy is required for the rich and for the poor. . . . Some voluntary cast-aways there will always be, whom no fostering kindness and no parental care can preserve from self-destruction, but if any are lost for want of care and culture, there is a sin of omission in the society to which they belong.[13]

The word, *culture*, indicates here the line which was to be so extensively pursued: the setting-up, in opposition to the *laissez-faire* society of the political economists, of an idea of active and responsible government, whose first duty was the promotion of the general health of society. The idea, as was to become habitual, was linked with a respect for 'feeling'— More's comment, like Burke's, on the rise of the new society, is:

In came calculation, and out went feeling.[14]

Southey also puts forward a view of the humanizing effects of literature, which the author of *Utopia* would have recognized. In reply to More's grand indictment of the sinfulness of the nation, Montesinos replies:

There is hope to be derived from the humanizing effects of literature, which has now first begun to act upon all ranks.[15]

All these points are made by Southey very early in what was to become a major nineteenth-century tradition.

Southey's detailed proposals for reform are less interesting than his general affirmation: they include planned colonization, an improved parochial order, a more efficient police, a national system of education, universal religious instruction, savings-banks, and, finally,

perhaps by the establishment of Owenite communities among themselves, the labouring classes will have their comforts enlarged, and their well-being secured, if they are not wanting to themselves in prudence and good conduct.[16]

It is the familiar paternalist programme, but Owen, as must now be stressed, is rightly placed in such a context. Southey ends with an exchange of questions between Montesinos and More:

Montesinos: You would make me apprehend, then, that we have advanced in our chemical and mechanical discoveries faster than is consistent with the real welfare of society.

More: You cannot advance in them too fast, provided that the moral culture of the species keep pace with the increase of its material powers. Has it been so?[17]

You cannot advance in them too fast: this certainly would make sense to Owen. The real originality that gives value to Owen's work is that he begins from an acceptance of the vastly increased power which the Industrial Revolution had brought, and sees in just this increase of power the opportunity for the new moral world. He is the successful manufacturer, and not the scholar or poet; in temperament and personality he is at one with the new industrialists who were transforming England, but his vision of transformation is human as well as material. As the new generation of manufacturers would organize their places of work for production, or for profit, so he would organize England for happiness. He is as firmly paternalist, and as essentially authoritarian, as a Tory reformer like Southey, but he accepts, without equivocation, the increase of wealth as the means of culture.

Owen's *Observations on the Effect of the Manufacturing System* (1815) offers the now familiar general judgement:

> The general diffusion of manufactures throughout a country generates a new character in its inhabitants; and as this character is formed upon a principle quite unfavourable to individual or general happiness, it will produce the most lamentable and permanent evils, unless its tendency be counteracted by legislative interference and direction. The manufacturing system has already so far extended its influence over the British empire, as to effect an essential change in the general character of the mass of the people. This alteration is still in rapid progress, and, ere long, the comparatively happy simplicity of the agricultural peasant will be wholly lost amongst us. It is even now scarcely anywhere to be found, without a mixture of those habits which are the offspring of trade, manufactures, and commerce.[18]

Owen is thus with Southey, and against the political economists, in discerning the 'cause of all our difficulties', not in human nature, but in the 'constitution of society'. Further, he is stating, with hitherto unequalled clarity, the two propositions which have since been so widely affirmed:

(i) that a change in the conditions of production effects an essential change in the human producers;

(ii) that the Industrial Revolution was such a major change, and produced what was virtually a new kind of human being.

He attacks the change, as a matter of course:

> All ties between employers and employed are frittered down to the
> consideration of what immediate gain each can derive from the
> other. The employer regards the employed as mere instruments of
> gain, while these acquire a gross ferocity of character, which, if
> legislative measures shall not be judiciously devised to prevent its
> increase, and ameliorate the condition of this class, will sooner or
> later plunge the country into a formidable and perhaps inextricable
> state of danger.[19]

The choice, as Owen sees it, is between the new moral world
and anarchy.

The problem, as it presented itself to Owen, was one of
social engineering: the phrase gives exactly the right stress.
His basic principle he expresses in this way:

> Any general character, from the best to the worst, from the most
> ignorant to the most enlightened, may be given to any community,
> even to the world at large, by the application of proper means;
> which means are to a great extent at the command and under the
> control of those who have influence in the affairs of men.[20]

At times, and particularly in his very early writings, he is
not above expressing this principle in terms of the low
rationalism which one still encounters in discussion of
industrial relations:

> If, then, due care as to the state of your inanimate machines can
> produce such beneficial results, what may not be expected if you
> devote equal attention to your vital machines, which are far more
> wonderfully constructed? When you shall acquire a right knowledge
> of these, of their curious mechanism, of their self-adjusting powers,
> when the proper main-spring shall be applied to their varied move-
> ments—you will become conscious of their real value. . . . The more
> delicate, complex, living mechanism would be equally improved by
> being trained to strength and activity; . . . it would also prove true
> economy to keep it neat and clean; to treat it with kindness, that
> its mental movements might not experience too much irritating
> friction. . . . From experience which cannot deceive me, I venture
> to assure you, that your time and money so applied, if directed by
> a true knowledge of the subject, would return you, not five, ten,

or fifteen per cent for your capital so expended, but often fifty, and in many cases a hundred per cent.[21]

Against this element in Owen, the coarse scepticism of Cobbett reveals itself as a far superior human refinement.

Yet the spirit of Owen, in the main, is not fairly represented by his surrender to such a device of argument. The infant schools of New Lanark were original enough in their educational techniques, but they were far more innovating in their humanity and kindness. When Owen talked of creating human happiness, he was not serving an abstraction but an active and deeply impressive experience. His institution of these schools, so fascinatingly described on pages 186 to 196 of his autobiography, ranks as one of the major personal achievements of the century:

> The children were trained and educated without punishment or any fear of it, and were while in school by far the happiest human beings I have ever seen. . . . Human nature, its capacities and powers, is yet to be learned by the world.[22]

The whole enterprise at New Lanark, indeed, is so great a positive human achievement as to be virtually incredible, in such a field, in the years between the Luddites and Peterloo.

Always, it is Owen's experience that is impressive—the lived quality of his new view of society:

> I was completely tired of partners who were merely trained to buy cheap and sell dear. This occupation deteriorates, and often destroys, the finest and best faculties of our nature. From an experience of a long life, in which I passed through all the gradations of trade, manufactures and commerce, I am thoroughly convinced that there can be no superior character formed under this thoroughly selfish system. Truth, honesty, virtue, will be mere names, as they are now, and as they have ever been. Under this system there can be no true civilization; for by it all are trained civilly to oppose and often to destroy one another by their created opposition of interests. It is a low, vulgar, ignorant and inferior mode of conducting the affairs of society; and no permanent, general and substantial improvement can arise until it shall be superseded by a superior mode of forming character and creating wealth.[23]

Hazlitt first said, and others with and without acknowledgement have repeated, that Owen was 'a man of one idea'. Owen's comment on this is just:

> Had he said that I was a man of one fundamental principle and its practical consequences—he would have been nearer the truth. For instead of the knowledge that 'the character of man is formed *for* and not *by* him' being 'one idea'—it will be found to be, like the little grain of mustard seed, competent to fill the mind with new and true ideas, and to overwhelm in its consequences all other ideas opposed to it.[24]

Owen's tone, frequently, is messianic, and it becomes shrill, in the later years, with practical disappointment. Yet the 'one idea', with its essential hope, has certainly proved competent to fill the mind of England. On the one hand, Owen's idea of a new moral world, to be created by active government and a national system of education, merged significantly with the idea of positive culture which gained strength and wide adherence with the progress of the century. On the other hand, setting aside the principle of paternalism, the succeeding generations of the English industrial working people took upon themselves the realization of Owen's 'fundamental principle and its practical consequences'. We need only add, as a significant footnote, a question and answer from Owen's *Catechism of the New View of Society* (1817):

> *Q:* Is it not to be feared that such arrangements as you contemplate would produce a dull uniformity of character, repress genius, and leave the world without hope of future improvements?

> *A:* It appears to me that quite the reverse of all this will follow. . . . It is not easy to imagine, with our present ideas, what may be accomplished by human beings so trained and so circumstanced. . . . It is only when the obscurities by which society is now enveloped are in some degree removed, that the benefit . . . can be even in part appreciated.[25]

The answer, however locally convincing, is in terms of the idea which makes Owen significant in this tradition: that human nature itself is the product of a 'whole way of life', of a 'culture'.

CHAPTER II

THE ROMANTIC ARTIST

THAN the poets from Blake and Wordsworth to Shelley and Keats there have been few generations of creative writers more deeply interested and more involved in study and criticism of the society of their day. Yet a fact so evident, and so easily capable of confirmation, accords uneasily in our own time with that popular and general conception of the 'romantic artist' which, paradoxically, has been primarily derived from study of these same poets. In this conception, the Poet, the Artist, is by nature indifferent to the crude worldliness and materialism of politics and social affairs; he is devoted, rather, to the more substantial spheres of natural beauty and personal feeling. The elements of this paradox can be seen in the work of the Romantic poets themselves, but the supposed opposition between attention to natural beauty and attention to government, or between personal feeling and the nature of man in society, is on the whole a later development. What were seen at the end of the nineteenth century as disparate interests, between which a man must choose and in the act of choice declare himself poet or sociologist, were, normally, at the beginning of the century, seen as interlocking interests: a conclusion about personal feeling became a conclusion about society, and an observation of natural beauty carried a necessary moral reference to the whole and unified life of man. The subsequent dissociation of interests certainly prevents us from seeing the full significance of this remarkable period, but we must add also that the dissociation is itself in part a product of the nature of the Romantic attempt. Meanwhile, as some sort of security against the vestiges of the dissociation, we may usefully remind ourselves that Wordsworth wrote political pamphlets, that Blake was a friend of Tom Paine and was tried for sedition, that Coleridge wrote political journalism and social philosophy, that Shelley, in addition to this, distributed pamphlets in the streets, that Southey was a constant political commentator, that Byron spoke on the frame-riots and died as a volunteer in a political war; and, further, as must surely be obvious from the poetry of all the men named, that these activities were neither marginal nor incidental, but were essentially related to a large part of the experience from which the poetry itself was made. It is, moreover, only when we are blinded by the prejudice of the dissociation that we find such a complex of activities in any way surprising. For these two generations of poets lived through the crucial period in which the rise both of democracy and of industry was effecting qualitative changes in society: changes which by their nature were felt in a personal as well as in a general way. In the year of the French Revolution, Blake was 32, Wordsworth 19, Coleridge 17 and Southey 15. In the year of Peterloo, Byron was 31, Shelley 27, Keats 24. The dates are sufficient reminder of a period of political turmoil and controversy fierce enough to make it very difficult for even the least sensitive to be indifferent. Of the slower, wider, less observable changes that we call the Industrial Revolution, the landmarks are less obvious; but the lifetime of Blake, 1757 to 1827, is, in general, the decisive period. The changes that we receive as record were experienced, in these years, on the senses: hunger, suffering, conflict, dislocation; hope, energy, vision, dedication. The pattern of change was not background, as we may now be inclined to study it; it was, rather, the mould in which general experience was cast.

It is possible to abstract a political commentary from the writings of these poets, but this is not particularly important. The development of Wordsworth, Coleridge and Southey from differing degrees of revolutionary ardour in their youth to differing degrees of Burkean conservatism in their maturity is interesting. A distinction between the revolutionary principles of Shelley and the fine libertarian opportunism of Byron is useful. A reminder that Blake and Keats cannot be weakened to some ideal vagueness, but were, as men and poets, passionately committed to the tragedy of their period, is timely. In every case, however, the political criticism is now less interesting than the wider social criticism: those first apprehensions of the essential significance of the Industrial Revolution, which all felt and none revoked. Beyond this, again, is a different kind of response, which is a main root of the idea of culture. At this very time of political, social and economic change there is a radical change also in ideas of art, of the artist, and of their place in society. It is this significant change that I wish to adduce.

There are five main points: first, that a major change was taking place in the nature of the relationship between a writer and his readers; second, that a different habitual attitude towards the 'public' was establishing itself; third, that the production of art was coming to be regarded as one of a number of specialized kinds of production, subject to much the same conditions as general production; fourth, that a theory of the 'superior reality' of art, as the seat of imaginative truth, was receiving increasing emphasis; fifth, that the idea of the independent creative writer, the autonomous genius, was becoming a kind of rule. In naming these points, it is of course necessary to add at once that they are clearly very closely interrelated, and that some might be named as causes, and some as effects, were not the historical process so complex as to render a clear division impossible.

The first characteristic is clearly a very important one. From the third and fourth decades of the eighteenth century there had been growing up a large new middle-class reading public, the rise in which corresponds very closely with the rise to influence and power of the same class. As a result, the system of patronage had passed into subscription-publishing, and thence into general commercial publishing of the modern kind. These developments affected writers in several ways. There was an advance, for the fortunate ones, in independence and social status—the writer became a fully-fledged 'professional man'. But the change also meant the institution of 'the market' as the type of a writer's actual relations with society. Under patronage, the writer had at least a direct relationship with an immediate circle of readers, from whom, whether prudentially or willingly, as mark or as matter of respect, he was accustomed to accept and at times to act on criticism. It is possible to argue that this system gave the writer a more relevant freedom than that to which he succeeded. In any event, against the dependence, the occasional servility and the subjection to patronal caprice had to be set the direct relation of the act of writing with at least some part of society, personally known, and the sense, when relations were fortunate, that the writer 'belonged'. On the other hand, against the independence and the raised social status which success on the market commanded had to be set similar liabilities to caprice and similar obligations to please, but now, not liabilities to individuals personally known, but to the workings of an institution which seemed largely impersonal. The growth of the 'literary market' as the type of a writer's relations with his readers has been responsible for many fundamental changes of attitude. But one must add, of course, that such a growth is always uneven, both in its operations and in its effects. It is not perhaps until our own century that it is so nearly universal as to be almost dominant. By the beginning of the nineteenth century the institution was established, but it was nevertheless modified by many kinds of survival of earlier conditions. The important reactions to it were, however, laid down at this time.

One such reaction, evidently, is that named as the second point: the growth of a different habitual attitude towards the 'public'. Writers had, of course, often expressed, before this time, a feeling of dissatisfaction with the 'public', but in the early nineteenth century this feeling became acute and general. One finds it in Keats: 'I have not the slightest feel of humility towards the Public'; in Shelley: 'Accept no counsel from the simple-minded. Time reverses the judgement of the foolish crowd. Contemporary criticism is no more than the sum of the folly with which genius has to wrestle.' One finds it, most notably and most extensively, in Wordsworth:

Still more lamentable is his error who can believe that there is anything of divine infallibility in the clamour of that small though loud portion of the community, ever governed by factitious influence, which, under the name of the PUBLIC, passes itself upon the unthinking, for the PEOPLE. Towards the Public, the Writer hopes that he feels as much deference as it is entitled to; but to the People, philosophically characterized, and to the embodied spirit of their knowledge . . . his devout respect, his reverence, is due.[1]

33

It is, of course, easier to be respectful and reverent to 'the People, philosophically characterized', than to a Public, which noisily identifies itself. Wordsworth, in his conception of the People, is drawing heavily on the social theory of Burke, and for not dissimilar reasons. However the immediate argument went, whatever the reactions of actual readers, there was thus available a final appeal to 'the embodied spirit . . . of the People': that is to say, to an Idea, an Ideal Reader, a standard that might be set above the clamour of the writer's actual relations with society. The 'embodied spirit', naturally enough, was a very welcome alternative to the market. Obviously, such an attitude then affects the writer's own attitude to his work. He will not accept the market quotation of popularity:

> Away then with the senseless iteration of the word *popular* applied to new works in poetry, as if there were no test of excellence in this first of the fine arts but that all men should run after its productions, as if urged by an appetite, or constrained by a spell.[2]

He will continue to insist, in fact, on an Idea, a standard of excellence, the 'embodied spirit' of a People's knowledge, as something superior to the actual course of events, the actual run of the market. This insistence, it is worth emphasizing, is one of the primary sources of the idea of Culture. Culture, the 'embodied spirit of a People', the true standard of excellence, became available, in the progress of the century, as the court of appeal in which real values were determined, usually in opposition to the 'factitious' values thrown up by the market and similar operations of society.

The subjection of art to the laws of the market, and its consideration as a specialized form of production subject to much the same conditions as other forms of production, had been prefigured in much late-eighteenth-century thinking. Adam Smith had written:

> In opulent and commercial societies to think or to reason comes to be, like every other employment, a particular business, which is carried on by a very few people, who furnish the public with all the thought and reason possessed by the vast multitudes that labour.[3]

This is significant as a description of that special class of

34

persons who from the 1820s were to be called 'intellectuals'. It describes, also, the new conditions of specialization of the artist, whose work, as Adam Smith had said of knowledge, was now in fact

> purchased, in the same manner as shoes or stockings, from those whose business it is to make up and prepare for the market that particular species of goods.[4]

Such a position, and such a specialization of function, followed inevitably from the institution of commercial publishing. The novel, in particular, had quickly become a commodity; its main history as a literary form follows, as is well known, precisely the growth of these new conditions. But the effects were also obvious in poetry, on which the impact of a market relationship was inevitably severe. Alongside the rejection of the Public and of Popularity as standards of worth, increasing complaint was made that literature had become a trade. The two things, in fact, were normally treated together. Sir Egerton Brydges wrote in the 1820s:

> It is a vile evil that literature is become so much a trade all over Europe. Nothing has gone so far to nurture a corrupt taste, and to give the unintellectual power over the intellectual. Merit is now universally esteemed by the multitude of readers that an author can attract. . . . Will the uncultivated mind admire what delights the cultivated?[5]

Similarly in 1834 Tom Moore spoke of the

> lowering of standard that must necessarily arise from the extending of the circle of judges; from letting the mob in to vote, particularly at a period when the market is such an object to authors.[6]

He went on to distinguish between the 'mob' and the 'cultivated few'. It is obvious, here, how the adjective 'cultivated' contributed to the newly necessary abstractions, 'cultivation' and 'culture'. In this kind of argument, 'culture' became the normal antithesis to the market.

I have emphasized this new type of an author's relationship to his readers because I believe that such matters are always central in any kind of literary activity. I turn now to what is clearly a related matter, but one which raises the most difficult issues of interpretation. It is a fact that in this same period in which the market and the idea of specialist production received increasing emphasis there grew up, also, a system of thinking about the arts of which the most important elements are, first, an emphasis on the special nature of art-activity as a means to 'imaginative truth', and, second, an emphasis on the artist as a special kind of person. It is tempting to see these theories as a direct response to the actual change in relations between artist and society. Certainly, in the documents, there are some obvious elements of compensation: at a time when the artist is being described as just one more producer of a commodity for the market, he is describing himself as a specially endowed person, the guiding light of the common life. Yet, undoubtedly, this is to simplify the matter, for the response is not merely a professional one. It is also (and this has been of the greatest subsequent importance) an emphasis on the embodiment in art of certain human values, capacities, energies, which the development of society towards an industrial civilization was felt to be threatening or even destroying. The element of professional protest is undoubtedly there, but the larger issue is the opposition on general human grounds to the kind of civilization that was being inaugurated.

Romanticism is a general European movement, and it is possible to relate the new ideas, as they arise, solely to a larger system of ideas in European thinking as a whole. The influence of Rousseau, of Goethe, of Schiller and of Chateaubriand can certainly be traced. Indeed, if we consider the ideas in abstraction, we can take the idea of the artist as a special kind of person, and of the 'wild' genius, as far back as the Socratic definition of a poet in Plato's *Ion*. The 'superior reality' of art has a multitude of classical texts, and, within our period, is in obvious relation with the German idealist school of philosophy and its English dilution through Coleridge and Carlyle. These relations are important, yet an idea can perhaps only be weighed, only understood, in a particular mind and a particular situation. In England, these ideas that we call Romantic have to be understood in terms of the problems in experience with which they were advanced to deal.

A good example is a definition in one of the early documents of English Romanticism, Young's *Conjectures on Original Composition* (1759):

> An Original may be said to be of a *vegetable* nature; it rises spontaneously from the vital root of genius; it *grows*, it is not *made*; Imitations are often a sort of *manufacture*, wrought up by those *mechanics*, *art* and *labour*, out of pre-existent materials not their own.[7]

This is a piece of very familiar Romantic literary theory: contrasting the spontaneous work of genius with the formal imitative work bound by a set of rules. As Young also writes:

> Modern writers have a *choice* to make . . . they may soar in the regions of *liberty*, or move in the soft fetters of easy *imitation*.[8]

But what Young is saying when he defines an 'original' is, if we look at his terms, very closely linked with a whole general movement of society. It is certainly literary theory, but as certainly it is not being formulated in isolation. When he says of an original that 'it grows, it is not made', he is using the exact terms on which Burke based his whole philosophical criticism of the new politics. The contrast between 'grows' and 'made' was to become the contrast between 'organic' and 'mechanical' which lies at the very centre of a tradition which has continued to our own day. Again, when he defines an 'imitation', Young condemns it in terms of the very industrial processes which were about to transform English society: 'a sort of *manufacture, wrought up* by those *mechanics . . . out of pre-existent materials not their own*'. The point may or may not hold in literary theory; but these are certainly the terms and the implied values by which the coming industrial civilization was to be condemned.

Burke condemned the new society in terms of his experience (or his idealization) of the earlier society. But increasingly as the huge changes manifested themselves the condemnation became specialized, and, in a sense, abstract. One part of the specialization was the growth of the standard of Cultivation or Culture; another part, closely related to this and later in fact to combine with it, was the growth of

37

the new idea of Art. This new idea of a superior reality, and even of a superior power, is strikingly expressed by Blake:

> 'Now Art has lost its mental charms
> France shall subdue the World in Arms.'
> So spoke an Angel at my birth,
> Then said, 'Descend thou upon Earth.
> Renew the Arts on Britain's Shore,
> And France shall fall down and adore.
> With works of Art their armies meet,
> And War shall sink beneath thy feet.
> But if thy Nation Arts refuse,
> And if they scorn the immortal Muse,
> France shall the arts of Peace restore,
> And save thee from the Ungrateful shore.'
> Spirit, who lov'st Britannia's Isle,
> Round which the Fiends of Commerce smile. . . .[9]

In Blake, the professional pressures can be easily discerned, for he suffered badly in 'the desolate market where none come to buy'. He reminds us of Young, when he attacks

> the interest of the Monopolizing Trader who Manufactures Art by the Hands of Ignorant Journeymen till . . . he is Counted the Greatest Genius who can sell a Good-for-Nothing Commodity for a Great Price.[10]

But, equally, Blake's criticism goes far beyond the professional complaint: the Imagination which, for him, Art embodies is no commodity, but

> a Representation of what Eternally Exists, Really and Unchangeably.[11]

It is in such a light that the inadequacies of existing society and of the quality of life which it promotes are to be seen and condemned.

It is important to measure the strength of this claim, for we shall misunderstand it if we look only at some of the later divagations of the idea of Genius. The ambiguous word in Young's definition is 'Imitation', which in nearly all Romantic theory acquired a heavily derogatory sense. This is because 'imitation' was understood to mean 'imitation of works already done', that is to say conformity to a given set of rules. The eloquence deployed against the set of rules is both remarkable and, in the end, tedious. What was happening, technically, was no more than a change of convention, which when it is of any magnitude normally carries such eloquence as a by-product. To the degree that the change is more than a change in convention—and changes in convention only occur when there are radical changes in the general structure of feeling—the word 'Imitation' is particularly confusing. For indeed, in the best 'classicist' theory, Imitation is the term normally used to describe what Blake has just described, and what all the Romantic writers emphasized: 'a Representation of what Eternally Exists, Really and Unchangeably'. Imitation, at its best, was not understood as adherence to somebody else's rules; it was, rather, 'imitation of the universal reality'. An artist's precepts were not so much previous works of art as the 'universals' (in Aristotle's term) or permanent realities. This argument, really, had been completed in the writings of the Renaissance.

The tendency of Romanticism is towards a vehement rejection of dogmas of method in art, but it is also, very clearly, towards a claim which all good classical theory would have recognized: the claim that the artist's business is to 'read the open secret of the universe'. A 'romantic' critic like Ruskin, for example, bases his whole theory of art on just this 'classicist' doctrine. The artist perceives and represents Essential Reality, and he does so by virtue of his master faculty Imagination. In fact, the doctrines of 'the genius' (the autonomous creative artist) and of the 'superior reality of art' (penetration to a sphere of universal truth) were in Romantic thinking two sides of the same claim. Both Romanticism and Classicism are in this sense idealist theories of art; they are really opposed not so much by each other as by naturalism.

What was important at this time was the stress given to a mode of human experience and activity which the progress of society seemed increasingly to deny. Wordsworth might hold with particular conviction the idea of the persecuted genius, but there is a more general significance in his attitudes to poetry, and indeed to art as a whole:

> High is our calling, Friend!—Creative Art . . .
> Demands the service of a mind and heart
> Though sensitive, yet in their weakest part
> Heroically fashioned—to infuse
> Faith in the whispers of the lonely Muse
> While the whole world seems adverse to desert.[12]

These are the lines to the painter Haydon, in December 1815. They are significant for the additional reason that they mark the fusing into the common 'sphere of imaginative truth' of the two separate *arts*, or skills, of poetry and painting. While in one sense the market was specializing the artist, artists themselves were seeking to generalize their skills into the common property of imaginative truth. Always, this kind of emphasis is to be seen as a mode of defence: the defensive tone in Wordsworth's lines is very obvious, and in this they are entirely characteristic. At one level the defence is evidently compensatory: the height of the artists' claim is also the height of their despair. They defined, emphatically, their high calling, but they came to define and to emphasize because they were convinced that the principles on which the new society was being organized were actively hostile to the necessary principles of art. Yet, while to see the matter in this way is to explain the new emphasis, it is not to explain it away. What was laid down as a defensive reaction became in the course of the century a most important positive principle, which in its full implications was deeply and generally humane.

There are many texts from which this principle can be illustrated, but the most characteristic, as it is also among the best known, is Wordsworth's Preface of 1800 to the *Lyrical Ballads*. Here it is not only the truth but the general humanity of poetry which Wordsworth emphasizes: first, by attacking those

> who talk of Poetry as of a matter of amusement and idle pleasure; who will converse with us as gravely about a *taste* for poetry, as they express it, as if it were a thing as indifferent as a taste for rope-dancing, or Frontiniac or Sherry.[13]

The concept of *taste*—which implies one kind of relationship between writer and reader—is inadequate because

> it is a metaphor, taken from a *passive* sense of the human body, and transferred to things which are in their essence *not* passive—to intellectual *acts* and *operations*. . . . But the profound and the exquisite in feeling, the lofty and universal in thought and imagination . . . are neither of them, accurately speaking, objects of a faculty which could ever without a sinking in the spirit of Nations have been designated by the metaphor *Taste*. And why? Because without the exertion of a cooperating *power* in the mind of the Reader, there can be no adequate sympathy with either of these emotions: without this auxiliary impulse, elevated or profound passion cannot exist.[14]

This states in another way an important criticism of the new kind of social relationships of art: when art is a commodity, taste is adequate, but when it is something more, a more active relationship is essential. The 'something more' is commonly defined:

> Aristotle, I have been told, has said, that Poetry is the most philosophic of all writing: it is so: its object is truth, not individual and local, but general and operative; not standing upon external testimony, but carried alive into the heart by passion; truth which is its own testimony, which gives competence and confidence to the tribunal to which it appeals, and receives them from the same tribunal. . . . The Poet writes under one restriction only, namely, the necessity of giving immediate pleasure to a human Being possessed of that information which may be expected from him, not as a lawyer, a physician, a mariner, an astronomer, or a natural philosopher, but as a Man. . . . To this knowledge which all men carry about with them, and to these sympathies in which, without any other discipline than that of our daily life, we are fitted to take delight, the Poet principally directs his attention. . . . He is the rock of defence for human nature; an upholder and preserver, carrying everywhere with him relationship and love. In spite of difference of soil and climate, of language and manners, of laws and customs: in spite of things silently gone out of mind, and things violently destroyed; the Poet binds together by passion and knowledge the vast empire of human society, as it is spread over the whole earth, and over all time.[15]

This is the case which, in its essentials, was to be eloquently restated by Shelley in his *Defence of Poetry*. It is the case which extends through Ruskin and Morris into our own century, when Poetry, as Wordsworth would have approved, has been widened to Art in general. The whole tradition can be summed up in one striking phrase used by Wordsworth, where the poet, the artist in general, is seen as

> an upholder and preserver, carrying everywhere with him relationship and love.[16]

Artists, in this mood, came to see themselves as agents of the 'revolution for life', in their capacity as bearers of the creative imagination. Here, again, is one of the principal sources of the idea of Culture; it was on this basis that the association of the idea of the general perfection of humanity with the practice and study of the arts was to be made. For here, in the work of artists—'the first and last of all knowledge . . . as immortal as the heart of man'—was a practicable mode of access to that ideal of human perfection which was to be the centre of defence against the disintegrating tendencies of the age.

The emphasis on a general common humanity was evidently necessary in a period in which a new kind of society was coming to think of man as merely a specialized instrument of production. The emphasis on love and relationship was necessary not only within the immediate suffering but against the aggressive individualism and the primarily economic relationships which the new society embodied. Emphasis on the creative imagination, similarly, may be seen as an alternative construction of human motive and energy, in contrast with the assumptions of the prevailing political economy. This point is indeed the most interesting part of Shelley's *Defence*:

> Whilst the mechanist abridges, and the political economist combines, labour, let them beware that their speculations, for want of correspondence with those first principles which belong to the imagination, do not tend, as they have in modern England, to exasperate at once the extremes of luxury and want. . . . The rich have become richer, and the poor have become poorer; and the

vessel of the state is driven between the Scylla and Charybdis of anarchy and despotism. Such are the effects which must ever flow from an unmitigated exercise of the calculating faculty.[17]

This is the general indictment which we can see already forming as a tradition, and the remedy is in the same terms:

There is no want of knowledge respecting what is wisest and best in morals, government, and political economy, or at least, what is wiser and better than what men now practise or endure. But . . . we want the creative faculty to imagine that which we know; we want the generous impulse to act that which we imagine; we want the poetry of life: our calculations have outrun conception; we have eaten more than we can digest. . . . Poetry, and the Principle of Self, of which Money is the visible incarnation, are the God and Mammon of the world.[18]

The most obvious criticism of such a position as Shelley's is that, while it is wholly valuable to present a wider and more substantial account of human motive and energy than was contained in the philosophy of industrialism, there are corresponding dangers in specializing this more substantial energy to the act of poetry, or of art in general. It is this specialization which, later, made much of this criticism ineffectual. The point will become clearer in the later stages of our enquiry, where it will be a question of distinguishing between the idea of culture as art and the idea of culture as a whole way of life. The positive consequence of the idea of art as a superior reality was that it offered an immediate basis for an important criticism of industrialism. The negative consequence was that it tended, as both the situation and the opposition hardened, to isolate art, to specialize the imaginative faculty to this one kind of activity, and thus to weaken the dynamic function which Shelley proposed for it. We have already examined certain of the factors which tended towards this specialization; it remains now to examine the growth of the idea of the artist as a 'special kind of person'.

The word *Art*, which had commonly meant 'skill', became specialized during the course of the eighteenth century, first to 'painting', and then to the imaginative arts generally.

43

Artist, similarly, from the general sense of a skilled person, in either the 'liberal' or the 'useful' arts, had become specialized in the same direction, and had distinguished itself from *artisan* (formerly equivalent with *artist*, but later becoming what we still call, in the opposite specialized sense, a 'skilled worker'), and of course from *craftsman*. The emphasis on skill, in the word, was gradually replaced by an emphasis on sensibility; and this replacement was supported by the parallel changes in such words as *creative* (a word which could not have been applied to art until the idea of the 'superior reality' was forming), *original* (with its important implications of spontaneity and vitalism; a word, we remember, that Young virtually contrasted with *art* in the sense of skill), and *genius* (which, because of its root association with the idea of *inspiration*, had changed from 'characteristic disposition' to 'exalted special ability', and took its tone in this from the other affective words). From *artist* in the new sense there were formed *artistic* and *artistical*, and these, by the end of the nineteenth century, had certainly more reference to 'temperament' than to skill or practice. *Aesthetics*, itself a new word, and a product of the specialization, similarly stood parent to *aesthete*, which again indicated a 'special kind of person'.

The claim that the artist revealed a higher kind of truth is, as we have seen, not new in the Romantic period, although it received significant additional emphasis. The important corollary of the idea was, however, the conception of the artist's autonomy in this kind of revelation; his substantive element, for example, was now not faith but genius. In its opposition to the 'set of rules', the autonomous claim is of course attractive. Keats puts it finely:

> The Genius of Poetry must work out its own salvation in a man: It cannot be matured by law and precept, but by sensation and watchfulness in itself. That which is creative must create itself.[19]

Our sympathy with this rests on the emphasis on a personal discipline, which is very far removed from talk of the 'wild' or 'lawless' genius. The difference is there, in Keats, in the emphasis on 'the Genius of Poetry', which is impersonal as compared with the personal 'genius'. Coleridge put the same emphasis on law, with the same corresponding emphasis on autonomy:

> No work of true genius dares want its appropriate form, neither indeed is there any danger of this. As it must not, so genius cannot, be lawless; for it is even this that constitutes it genius—the power of acting creatively under laws of its own origination.[20]

This is at once more rational and more useful for the making of art than the emphasis, at least as common in Romantic pamphleteering, on an 'artless spontaneity'. Of the Art (sensibility) which claims that it can dispense with art (skill) the subsequent years hold more than enough examples.

As literary theory, the emphases of Keats and Coleridge are valuable. The difficulty is that this kind of statement became entangled with other kinds of reaction to the problem of the artist's relations with society. The instance of Keats is most significant, in that the entanglement is less and the concentration more. If we complete the sentence earlier quoted from him we find:

> I have not the slightest feel of humility towards the public, or to anything in existence,—but the eternal Being, the Principle of Beauty, and the Memory of Great Men.[21]

This is characteristic, as is the famous affirmation:

> I am certain of nothing but of the holiness of the Heart's affections, and the truth of Imagination. What the Imagination seizes as Beauty must be truth—whether it existed before or not—for I have the same idea of all our passions as of Love; they are all, in their sublime, creative of essential Beauty. . . . The Imagination may be compared to Adam's dream—he awoke and found it truth.[22]

But the account of the artist's personality which Keats then gives is, in his famous phrase, that of 'Negative Capability . . . when a man is capable of being in uncertainties, mysteries, doubts, without any irritable reaching after fact and reason'.[23] Or again:

> Men of Genius are great as certain ethereal Chemicals operating on the Mass of neutral intellect—but they have not any individuality, any determined Character—I would call the top and head of those who have a proper self, Men of Power.[24]

It is certainly possible to see this emphasis on passivity as a compensatory reaction, but this is less important than the fact that Keats's emphasis is on the poetic *process* rather than on the poetic *personality*. The theory of Negative Capability could degenerate into the wider and more popular theory of the poet as 'dreamer', but Keats himself worked finely, in experience, to distinguish between 'dreamer' and 'poet', and if in the second *Hyperion* his formal conclusion is uncertain, it is at least clear that what he means by 'dream' is something as hard and positive as his own skill. It is not from the fine discipline of a Keats that the loose conception of the romantic artist can be drawn.

Wordsworth, in the *Preface to Lyrical Ballads*, shows us most clearly how consideration of the poetic process became entangled with more general questions of the artist and society. In discussing his own theory of poetic language, he is in fact discussing communication. He asserts, reasonably and moderately, the familiar attitude to the Public:

> Such faulty expressions, were I convinced they were faulty at present, and that they must necessarily continue to be so, I would willingly take all reasonable pains to correct. But it is dangerous to make these alterations on the simple authority of a few individuals, or even of certain classes of men; for where the understanding of an Author is not convinced, or his feelings altered, this cannot be done without great injury to himself: for his own feelings are his stay and support.[25]

This has to be said on the one side, while at the same time Wordsworth is saying:

> The Poet thinks and feels in the spirit of human passions. How, then, can his language differ in any material degree from that of all other men who feel vividly and see clearly?[26]

And so:

> Among the qualities . . . enumerated as principally conducing to form a Poet, is implied nothing differing in kind from other men, but only in degree. . . . The Poet is chiefly distinguished from other men by a greater promptness to think and feel without immediate external excitement, and a greater power in expressing such thoughts and feelings as are produced in him in that manner. But

these passions and thoughts and feelings are the general passions and thoughts and feelings of men.[27]

Of these chief distinctions, while the first is a description of a psychological type, the second is a description of a skill. While the two are held in combination, the argument is plausible. But in fact, under the tensions of the general situation, it became possible to dissociate them, and so to isolate the 'artistic sensibility'.

The matter is exceptionally complex, and what happened, under the stress of events, was a series of simplifications. The obstruction of a certain kind of experience was simplified to the obstruction of poetry, which was then identified with it and even made to stand for it as a whole. Under pressure, art became a symbolic abstraction for a whole range of general human experience: a valuable abstraction, because indeed great art has this ultimate power; yet an abstraction nevertheless, because a general social activity was forced into the status of a department or province, and actual works of art were in part converted into a self-pleading ideology. This description is not offered for purposes of censure; it is a fact, rather, with which we have to learn to come to terms. There is high courage, and actual utility, if also simplification, in Romantic claims for the imagination. There is courage, also, in the very weakness which, ultimately, we find in the special pleading of personality. In practice there were deep insights, and great works of art; but, in the continuous pressure of living, the free play of genius found it increasingly difficult to consort with the free play of the market, and the difficulty was not solved, but cushioned, by an idealization. The last pages of Shelley's *Defence of Poetry* are painful to read. The bearers of a high imaginative skill become suddenly the 'legislators', at the very moment when they were being forced into practical exile; their description as 'unacknowledged', which, on the theory, ought only to be a fact to be accepted, carries with it also the felt helplessness of a generation. Then Shelley at the same time claims that the Poet

ought personally to be the happiest, the best, the wisest, and the most illustrious of men;[28]

47

where the emphasis, inescapably, falls painfully on the *ought*. The pressures, here personal as well as general, create, as a defensive reaction, the separation of poets from other men, and their classification into an idealized general person, 'Poet' or 'Artist', which was to be so widely and so damagingly received. The appeal, as it had to be, is beyond the living community, to the

mediator and . . . redeemer, Time.[29]

Over the England of 1821 there had, after all, to be some higher Court of Appeal. We are not likely, when we remember the lives of any of these men, to be betrayed into the irritability of prosecution, but it is well, also, if we can avoid the irritability of defence. The whole action has passed into our common experience, to lie there, formulated and unformulated, to move and to be examined. 'For it is less their spirit, than the spirit of the age.'[30]

CHAPTER III

MILL ON BENTHAM AND COLERIDGE

THE essays of John Stuart Mill on Jeremy Bentham and Samuel Taylor Coleridge are among the most remarkable documents of the intellectual history of the nineteenth century. Their recent reprinting, with an interesting introduction by Dr F. R. Leavis, was valuable and timely. The essays bring together what Mill called 'the two great seminal minds of England in their age', but the result, quite evident in a reading of the essays, is a bringing together not of two minds but of three. For to watch Mill being influenced by, and correcting, Bentham and Coleridge is absorbing and illuminating. We see not only the working of an individual and most able mind, but a process which has a general representative importance. Mill's attempt to absorb, and by discrimination and discarding to unify, the truths alike of the utilitarian and the idealist positions is, after all, a prologue to a very large part of the subsequent history of English thinking: in particular, to the greater part of English thinking about society and culture.

If we look at the matter in this way, we shall avoid the readiest mistake with regard to these essays: the mistake, that is, of supposing that we are reading an *impartial* judgement of the ideas of Bentham and Coleridge, an authoritative summing-up by a great neutral. Mill's tone is always so reasonable, and his professional skill in summary and distinction so evident, that such a conclusion seems positively invited. Yet the essays are not a judicial verdict; they are the effort of a particular mind—and a very distinguished one—to reconcile two deeply opposed positions. Mill believed that by the exercise of reason and patience all such differences could be resolved. Seeing the contrasted positions, as was his habit, in an almost solely rational light, he believed that reconciliation was possible, if only interest and prejudice could be (as he thought not impossible) set aside. But the essays are also an event, a particular stage, in Mill's own intellectual development. Written in 1838 and 1840, they belong to a period when Mill's reaction against Utilitarianism was at its most critical stage. The particular balance or appearance of balance which he here achieved was not afterwards fully maintained. The point is underlined when we remember that his Utilitarian friends did not see the essays as moving from the thesis of Bentham through the antithesis of Coleridge to a new synthesis; they saw them simply as apostasy, a surrender to 'German mysticism'. They may well, narrow dogmatists, have been wrong; but at least Mill did not impress them as a neutral. Further, almost immediately after the essay on Coleridge, Mill began moving away from the Coleridgian influence. In his *Political Economy*, and especially in his *Examination of Sir William Hamilton's Philosophy*, much of the assent here granted to Coleridge is deliberately withdrawn.

We may suitably begin our more detailed examination of the essays with a passage from the essay on Coleridge:

> All students of man and society who possess that first requisite for so difficult a study, a due sense of its difficulties, are aware that the besetting danger is not so much of embracing falsehood for truth, as of mistaking part of the truth for the whole. It might be plausibly maintained that in almost every one of the leading controversies, past or present, in social philosophy, both sides were in the right in what they affirmed, though wrong in what they denied; and that if either could have been made to take the other's views in addition to its own, little more would have been needed to make its doctrine correct.[1]

It is worth noting how completely intellectualist is Mill's method. For in life it is not whether the abstracted opinions of opposed thinkers might profitably complement each other, to make what is called a 'correct' doctrine. We have to ask, indeed, whether such a procedure would, even in itself, be useful, considering its tendency to isolate the 'doctrines' from those attachments, those particular valuations, those living situations, in which alone the 'doctrines' can be said to be active. The point is crucial, yet still the piety of Mill's hope is genuine. It is worth watching his account of the basic opposition:

Take for instance the question how far mankind have gained by civilization. One observer is forcibly struck by the multiplication of physical comforts; the advancement and diffusion of knowledge; the decay of superstition; the facilities of mutual intercourse; the softening of manners; the decline of war and personal conflict; the progressive limitation of the tyranny of the strong over the weak; the great works accomplished throughout the globe by the co-operation of multitudes: and he becomes that very common character, the worshipper of 'our enlightened age'.[2]

Here, fairly enough, is the abstract of Liberalism, and Mill continues:

Another fixes his attention, not upon the value of these advantages, but upon the high price which is paid for them; the relaxation of individual energy and courage; the loss of proud and self-relying independence; the slavery of so large a portion of mankind to artificial wants; their effeminate shrinking from even the shadow of pain; the dull unexciting monotony of their lives, and the passionless insipidity, and absence of any marked individuality, in their characters; the contrast between the narrow mechanical understanding, produced by a life spent in executing by fixed rules a fixed task, and the varied powers of the man of the woods, whose subsistence and safety depend at each instant upon his capacity of extemporarily adapting means to ends; the demoralizing effect of great inequalities in wealth and social rank; and the sufferings of the great mass of the people of civilized countries, whose wants are scarcely better provided for than those of the savage, while they are bound by a thousand fetters in lieu of the freedom and excitement which are his compensations.[3]

This is an aggregation of a number of kinds of criticism of what Mill calls 'Civilization', but which, from the detail of certain of its points, might better be called Industrialism. Mill remarks:

No two thinkers can be more entirely at variance than the two we have supposed—the worshippers of Civilization and of Independence, of the present and the remote past. Yet all that is positive in the opinions of either of them is true; and we see how easy it would be to choose one's path, if either half of the truth were the whole of it, and how great may be the difficulty of framing, as it is necessary to do, a set of practical maxims which combine both.[4]

This sounds reasonable, but the opposed positions as described by Mill contradict each other not only in valuation but, at certain points, in fact. The contrast is further confused by the inclusion of arguments which refer to different periods of history. Part of the criticism inherent in the latter position is criticism of the transition to industrialism; part again the contrast, not of the village labourer and the industrial worker, but of civilized man and Rousseau's Noble Savage—Mill's 'man of the woods'. It is then difficult to say which of the many points is 'positively true', and the idea of 'a set of practical maxims which combine both' seems absurd. Mill is, in fact, gathering opinions, and arbitrarily grouping them, rather than paying attention to the opposition of values engendered by different orders of experience, which arise from different ways of life. He is, at this point, nowhere near any kind of lived reality. A Cobbett from one position, a Coleridge from another, had their own views, in experience, of the 'high price paid for civilization'; but because their experience was actual, they were specific about the 'civilization'. Cobbett did not see 'the multiplication of physical comforts' and 'the sufferings of the great mass of the people' as opposing arguments; he saw them as aspects of one and the same civilization, and therefore, in their very contrast, a fact about the *kind* of civilization being experienced. Coleridge, in criticizing a 'narrow mechanical understanding', had something better to refer to as a positive than the 'man of the woods', about whom, after all, neither Rousseau nor Mill nor anyone likely to take part in the argument knew anything worth writing down; and whom we should have to define rather more precisely (savage? white trapper?) before we could say, even for the sake of argument, whether he is a just symbol of 'Independence'. I press these points because they show the degree to which Mill is apt to divorce opinions and valuations both from experience and from social reality.

He is on surer ground, and his normal grasp of his material returns, when he describes another opposition:

So again, one person sees in a very strong light the need which the great mass of mankind have of being ruled over by a degree of intelligence and virtue superior to their own. He is deeply im pressed with the mischief done to the uneducated and uncultivated by weaning them of all habits of reverence, appealing to them as a competent tribunal to decide the most intricate questions, and making them think themselves capable, not only of being a light to themselves, but of giving the law to their superiors in culture. He sees, further, that cultivation, to be carried beyond a certain point, requires leisure; that leisure is the natural attribute of a hereditary aristocracy; that such a body has all the means of acquiring intellectual and moral superiority; and he needs be at no loss to endow them with abundant motives to it.[5]

This summary is admirable. So too is Mill's exposition of the objections to it:

But there is a thinker of a very different description, in whose premises there is an equal portion of truth. This is he who says, that an average man, even an average member of an aristocracy, if he can postpone the interests of other people to his own calculations or instincts of self-interest, will do so; that all governments in all ages have done so, as far as they were permitted, and generally to a ruinous extent; and that the only possible remedy is a pure demo cracy, in which the people are their own governors, and can have no selfish interest in oppressing themselves.[6]

This is not the only line of objection to the former position, but it is the one which we should expect Mill to follow, the objection which would naturally occur to him, as one trained in the Utilitarian kind of thinking. He goes on to see the progress of this conflict of position in terms of the swing of the pendulum:

Every excess in either direction determines a corresponding re action; improvement consisting only in this, that the oscillation, each time, departs rather less widely from the centre, and an ever-increasing tendency is manifested to settle finally in it.[7]

It hardly needs emphasis that this view of the matter was to become a commonplace: when in doubt, the English imagine a pendulum. But still it is inadequate, since it is confined to the development of opinion and neglects the changing rela tions of those actual forces in society which seek to move in one or other direction. Yet Mill's statement of the opposing *political* doctrines is much more adequate than his exposition of what might be called the 'cultural' objections to modern industrial civilization. The methods and habits of Utilitarian thinking remained with him, even when he was questioning certain Utilitarian positions, or acknowledging the merits of positions reached in a different way. Consider, for instance, his famous distinction between his subjects:

> By Bentham, beyond all others, men have been led to ask themselves, in regard to any ancient or received opinion, Is it true? and by Coleridge, What is the meaning of it?[8]

This is just and illuminating, although we must not convict Coleridge of any disregard for truth. Yet, taking the distinction as it stands, there can be no doubt of the side on which Mill himself stands. His critique of Bentham is founded on the question, Is it true?:

> But *is* this fundamental doctrine of Bentham's political philosophy an universal truth?[9]

This, at all important points, is the tone of the enquiry. Similarly, with Coleridge, he is sifting for what he considers true, and setting aside what is false. There is a point, of course, at which one doubts whether there is any significant difference between the questions *Is it true?* and *What is the meaning of it?* But Mill's emphasis serves to underline very clearly his own habit of approach.

Mill is nearer to Bentham than to Coleridge in fundamentals. He is, by the same token, nearer to our own normal habits of thinking. One result of the essays, certainly, is a very damaging criticism of Bentham:

> Knowing so little of human feelings, he knew still less of the influences by which those feelings are formed: all the more subtle workings, both of the mind upon itself, and of external things upon the mind, escaped him; and no one, probably, who, in a highly instructed age, ever attempted to give a rule to all human conduct, set out with a more limited conception either of the agencies by which human conduct is, or of those by which it should be, influenced.[10]

The comment is a personal one, on Bentham; but it has

normally been seized on, by those who are opposed to Utilitarianism, as a general criticism of the system as a whole. It has become, now, an element in that familiar criticism of 'systematic' social thinking—a criticism which grounds itself on the principle that the systematizers have an inadequate knowledge of actual human nature. Mill is careful not to make this extension himself, and indeed how could he have done so? His own comment on himself lies too ready to hand:

> I never was a boy; never played at cricket; it is better to let Nature have her way.[11]

Or again:

> Even in the narrowest of my then associates, they being older men, their ratiocinative and nicely concatenated dreams were at some point or other, and in some degree or other, corrected and limited by their experience of actual realities, while I, a schoolboy fresh from the logic school, had never conversed with a reality, never seen one, knew not what manner of thing it was, had only spun, first other people's and then my own deductions from assumed premises.[12]

The notorious education which James Mill imposed on his son has been often abused, and with the support of texts like these. When I read such comments, I want always to enter the marginal note: 'yet the system, after all, produced John Stuart Mill'. For good or ill—and surely, in the main, it is for good—the severe training produced a fine example of a very fine kind of intelligence; that it is not the only kind is agreed. Systematic enquiry into the working of human institutions; systematic attempts to reform them, and to devise techniques for their further reformation: these are great positive human activities, and the objection to them, on the title of 'human nature', is not, under its most common auspices, very impressive. Mill, in emphasizing the personal deficiencies of Bentham, is not thereby rejecting the characteristic methods of Utilitarian thought. He is, rather, applying himself to the problems of a new situation, and a different one in certain radical respects from that which Bentham had been concerned to meet. The earlier Utilitarianism had been a wholly adequate doctrine for the rising middle class, seeking confirmation of its growing power through reforms directed against the privileges of the aristocracy. The doctrine had been coloured, throughout, by values appropriate to the new methods of production; it is true to say that this first period of Utilitarianism, in England, served to create the political and social institutions correspondent to the first stages of the Industrial Revolution. The climax of this effort was the Reform Bill of 1832. Mill, writing in the years immediately following the Bill, is concerned with the problems of the next phase. Bentham had claimed that good government depended upon the responsibility of the governors to

> persons whose interest, whose obvious and recognizable interest, accords with the end in view.[13]

The Reform Bill had gone a long way toward securing this, for that class which was directing the Industrial Revolution. But now Mill saw the inevitable extension of the principle, and that the 'numerical majority', whose 'obvious and recognizable interest' was to be served, had to be differently defined. The new item on the agenda was complete political democracy, and Mill, seeing the logical justice of this, from Bentham's premises as he understood them, saw also what he took to be the dangers of extension: in particular, a tyranny of opinion and prejudice—the 'will of the majority' overriding and perhaps suppressing minority opinion. When Cobbett had written his *Last Hundred Days of English Liberty*, his concern had been with the efforts of an authoritarian government to suppress the most dangerous advocates of reform. When Mill came to write his essay *On Liberty*, the emphasis had shifted and Mill had moved with his times. The central concern, now, was with the preservation of the rights of individuals and minorities against Public Opinion and the democratic State. And it was here that he found Coleridge so useful to him, particularly Coleridge's idea of the 'clerisy'—a nationally endowed class,

> for the cultivation of learning, and for diffusing its results among the community. . . . We consider the definitive establishment of this

fundamental principle to be one of the permanent benefits which
political science owes to the Conservative philosophers.[14]

Mill grounded his defence of individual liberty on other
main arguments, but he saw the usefulness, against the
tyranny of 'interest', of so apparently disinterested a class.

Even more than the danger of majority tyranny, Mill saw
when he was writing these essays the danger consequent on
the success of the first period of the Industrial Revolution,
of the national life being dominated by *laissez-faire*
commercialism:

> Bentham's idea of the world is that of a collection of persons
> pursuing each his separate interest and pleasure.[15]

This was freedom, or individual liberty, not as Mill the
intellectual had defined it, in terms of the freedom of
thought, but as the rising industrial class had defined it, with
the shadow of Bentham to support them, in terms of the
freedom 'to do as they willed with their own'. Faced with
this, Mill had to reconsider the bases of Utilitarian thought,
and he arrived, in consequence, at what is perhaps his
central judgement on Bentham:

> A philosophy like Bentham's . . . can teach the means of organizing
> and regulating the merely *business* part of the social arrange-
> ments. . . . It will do nothing (except sometimes as an instrument
> in the hands of a higher doctrine) for the spiritual interests of
> society; nor does it suffice of itself even for the material interests. . . .
> All he can do is but to indicate means by which, in any given state
> of the national mind, the material interests of society can be
> protected; saving the question, of which others must judge, whether
> the use of those means would have, on the national character, any
> injurious influence.[16]

Obviously, here, Coleridge's criticisms were relevant. There
were his famous questions, in the *Constitution of Church and
State:*

> Has the national welfare, have the weal and happiness of the people,
> advanced with the increase of the circumstantial prosperity? Is the
> increasing number of wealthy individuals that which ought to be
> understood by the wealth of the nation?[17]

Or again:

> It is not uncommon for 100,000 *operatives* (mark this word, for words *in this sense* are things) to be out of employment at once in the cotton districts, and, thrown upon parochial relief, to be dependent upon hard-hearted taskmasters for food. The Malthusian doctrine would indeed afford a certain means of relief, if this were not a twofold question. If, when you say to a man—'You have no claim upon me; you have your allotted part to perform in the world, so have I. In a state of nature, indeed, had I food, I should offer you a share from sympathy, from humanity; but in this advanced and artificial state of society, I cannot afford you relief; you must starve. You came into the world when it could not sustain you.' What would be this man's answer? He would say—'You disclaim all connection with me; I have no claims upon you? I can then have no duties towards you, and this pistol shall put me in possession of your wealth. You may leave a law behind you which shall hang me, but what man who saw assured starvation before him, ever feared hanging?' It is this accursed practice of ever considering *only* what seems *expedient* for the occasion, disjoined from all principle or enlarged systems of action, of never listening to the true and unerring impulses of our better nature, which has led the colder-hearted men to the study of political economy, which has turned our Parliament into a real committee of public safety. In it is all power vested; and in a few years we shall either be governed by an aristocracy, or, what is still more likely, by a contemptible demo-cratical oligarchy of glib economists, compared to which the worst form of aristocracy would be a blessing.[18]

It is a useful reminder of the complexity of reactions in this period to note that this comment of Coleridge's might almost have been written by Cobbett; certainly the starting point of the argument is one that Cobbett repeatedly used, and the expected answer of the poor man is one that he again and again emphasized.

What Mill seized on in Coleridge is fairly indicated by the phrase 'disjoined from all principle or enlarged systems of action'. For Mill was far too intelligent to suppose that the deficiencies of a particular system—here Benthamism—were any sort of argument against system as such. There is always a system of some kind: one system may be established and therefore confused with permanent 'human nature'; another system may challenge it and may be called, because it is still in the stage of doctrine, dogmatic and abstract. The argument against system as such is either fretful or ignorant. What appealed to Mill, in his reconsideration of Benthamism, was the emphasis implied in Coleridge's key word *enlarged*. He wanted *principle, or enlarged systems of action* as an improvement on a system competent only in 'the merely *business* part of the social arrangements', and insufficiently competent even in that. What might this new principle, or enlarged system, be?

> The peculiarity of the Germano-Coleridgian school is, that they saw beyond the immediate controversy, to the fundamental principles involved in all such controversies. They were the first (except a solitary thinker here and there) who inquired with any comprehensiveness or depth, into the inductive laws of the existence and growth of human society. . . . They thus produced, not a piece of party advocacy, but a philosophy of society, in the only form in which it is yet possible, that of a philosophy of history; not a defence of particular ethical or religious doctrines, but a contribution, the largest made by any class of thinkers, towards the philosophy of human culture.[19]

The last word of this extract must be given the emphasis, for indeed it is from the time of Coleridge on, as here so ably recognized by Mill, that the idea of Culture enters decisively into English social thinking. Mill continues:

> The same causes [*sc.* as those which had led to the new emphasis on historical studies] have naturally led the same class of thinkers to do what their predecessors never could have done, for the philosophy of human culture. For the tendency of their speculations compelled them to see in the character of the national education existing in any political society, at once the principal cause of its permanence as a society, and the chief source of its progressiveness: the former by the extent to which that education operated as a system of restraining discipline; the latter by the degree in which it called forth and invigorated the active faculties. Besides, not to have looked upon the culture of the inward man as the problem of problems, would have been incompatible with the belief which many of these

philosophers entertained in Christianity, and the recognition by all of them of its historical value, and the prime part which it has acted in the progress of mankind. But here too, let us not fail to observe, they rose to principles, and did not stick in the particular case. The culture of the human being had been carried to no ordinary height, and human nature had exhibited many of its noblest manifestations, not in Christian countries only, but in the ancient world, in Athens, Sparta, Rome; nay, even barbarians, as the Germans, or still more unmitigated savages, the wild Indians, and again the Chinese, the Egyptians, the Arabs, all had their own education, their own culture; a culture which, whatever might be its tendency upon the whole, had been successful in some respect or other. Every form of polity, every condition of society, whatever else it had done, had formed its type of national character. What that type was, and how it had been made what it was, were questions which the meta-physician might overlook, the historical philosopher could not. Accordingly, the views respecting the various elements of human culture and the causes influencing the formation of national character, which pervade the writings of the Germano-Coleridgian school, throw into the shade everything which had been effected before, or which has been attempted simultaneously by any other school. Such views are, more than anything else, the characteristic feature of the Goethian period of German literature; and are richly diffused through the historical and critical writings of the new French school, as well as of Coleridge and his followers.[20]

The emphasis on Culture, Mill decided, was the way to enlarge the Utilitarian tradition. He looked back to the state of affairs before the reforming movement into which he had been born, and concluded:

This was not a state of things which could recommend itself to any earnest mind. It was sure in no great length of time to call forth two sorts of men—the one demanding the extinction of the institutions and creeds which had hitherto existed; the other, that they be made a reality: the one pressing the new doctrines to their utmost consequences; the other reasserting the best meaning and purposes of the old. The first type attained its greatest height in Bentham; the last in Coleridge. We hold that these two sorts of men, who seem to be, and believe themselves to be, enemies, are in reality allies. The powers they wield are opposite poles of one great force of progression. What was really hateful and contemptible was the state which preceded them, and which each, in its way, has been striving now for many years to improve.[21]

Mill is simplifying, of course, when he speaks of alliance between these 'two sorts of men'. He is simplifying, in the way that is habitual to him, by abstracting the opinions and the speculative intentions from the particular interests and forces through which the opinions became active. Yet, having recognized the value of Benthamite reform, he had now found a way of expressing his conviction that the newly reformed industrial civilization was narrow and·inadequate. Coleridge had worked out this idea of Culture, the court of appeal to which all social arrangements must submit. We must now look at this idea more closely, in certain passages in the *Constitution of Church and State* which Mill does not quote. First, in Coleridge's fifth chapter:

> The permanency of the nation . . . and its progressiveness and personal freedom . . . depend on a continuing and progressive civilization. But civilization is itself but a mixed good, if not far more a corrupting influence, the hectic of disease, not the bloom of health, and a nation so distinguished more fitly to be called a varnished than a polished people, where this civilization is not grounded in cultivation, in the harmonious development of those qualities and faculties that characterize our humanity.[22]

Here, clearly, Coleridge is trying to set up a standard of 'health', to which a more certain appeal may be made than to the 'mixed good' of 'civilization'. He defines this standard in the word *cultivation*—the first time, in fact, that this word had been used to denote a general condition, a 'state or habit' of the mind. The word depends, of course, on the force of the important eighteenth-century adjective *cultivated*. What Coleridge here calls *cultivation* was elsewhere, as in Mill, to be called *culture*.

Coleridge makes the same general point again at the end of his discussion of the function of the National Church:

> And of especial importance is it to the objects here contemplated, that only by the vital warmth diffused by these truths throughout the many, and by the guiding light from the philosophy, which is

the basis of divinity, possessed by the few, can either the community or its rulers fully comprehend, or rightly appreciate, *the permanent distinction and the occasional contrast between cultivation and civilization*; or be made to understand this most valuable of the lessons taught by history, and exemplified alike in her oldest and her most recent records—that a nation can never be a too cultivated, but may easily become an over-civilized, race.[23]

'The permanent distinction, and the occasional contrast'; and Coleridge had already spoken of Cultivation as 'the ground, the necessary antecedent condition, of both . . . permanency and progressiveness'.

This idea of Cultivation, or Culture, was affirmed, by Coleridge, as a *social* idea, which should be capable of embodying true ideas of value. Mill had written:

Man is never recognized by Bentham as a being capable of pursuing spiritual perfection as an end.[24]

That man was so capable, that the pursuit of perfection was indeed his overriding business in life, was of course widely affirmed elsewhere, especially by Christian writers. But for Mill it was Coleridge who first attempted to define, in terms of his changing society, the *social* conditions of man's perfection. Coleridge's emphasis in his social writings is on *institutions*. The promptings to perfection came indeed from 'the cultivated heart'—that is to say, from man's inward consciousness—but, as Burke before him, Coleridge insisted on man's need for institutions which should confirm and constitute his personal efforts. Cultivation, in fact, though an inward was never a merely individual process. What in the eighteenth century had been an ideal of personality—a personal qualification for participation in polite society—had now, in the face of radical change, to be redefined, as a condition on which society as a whole depended. In these circumstances, cultivation, or culture, became an explicit factor in society, and its recognition controlled the enquiry into institutions.

We can now see that as a result of the changes in society at the time of the Industrial Revolution, cultivation could not be taken for granted as a process, but had to be stated as an absolute, an agreed centre for defence. Against mechanism, the amassing of fortunes and the proposition of utility as the source of value, it offered a different and a superior social idea. It became, indeed, the court of appeal, by which a society construing its relationships in terms of the cash-nexus might be condemned. Grounding itself on an idea of

> the harmonious development of those qualities and faculties that characterize our humanity,

this general condition, Cultivation, could be taken as the highest observable state of men in society, and the 'permanent distinction and occasional contrast' between it and *civilization* (the ordinary progress of society) drawn and emphasized. It was in this spirit that Coleridge examined the constitution of the State, and proposed the endowment within it of a class dedicated to the preservation and extension of cultivation. In his general approach he follows Burke; but where Burke had found the condition satisfied, within the traditional organization of society, Coleridge found the condition threatened, under the impact of change. In the face of the disintegrating processes of industrialism, cultivation had now more than ever to be socially assured. The social idea of Culture, now introduced into English thinking, meant that an idea had been formulated which expressed value in terms independent of 'civilization', and hence, in a period of radical change, in terms independent of the progress of society. The standard of perfection, of 'the harmonious development of those qualities and faculties that characterize our humanity', was now available, not merely to influence society, but to judge it.

The terms of Coleridge's proposals for an endowed class whose business should be 'general cultivation' are worth noting. He calls this class the Clerisy, or National Church, which

> in its primary acceptation, and original intention, comprehended the learned of all denominations; the sages and professors of . . . all the so-called liberal arts and sciences.[25]

He saw this class as the third estate of the realm.

> Now as in the first estate (*landowners*) the permanency of the nation was provided for; and in the second estate (*merchants and*

manufacturers) its progressiveness and personal freedom, while in the king the cohesion by interdependence, and the unity of the country, were established; there remains for the third estate only that interest which is the ground, the necessary antecedent condition, of both the former.[26]

The maintenance of this Clerisy, whose care was thus the 'necessary antecedent condition' for both 'permanency' and 'progressiveness', was to be assured by a specifically reserved portion of the national wealth, which Coleridge calls the 'Nationalty'. This would be its establishment, as a National Church; but the Church was not to be understood as only the 'Church of Christ', for this would 'reduce the Church to a religion', and thence to a mere sect. Theology, certainly, would give the 'circulating sap and life', but the object of the class as a whole was general cultivation:

> A certain smaller number were to remain at the fountainhead of the humanities, in cultivating and enlarging the knowledge already possessed, and in watching over the interests of physical and moral science; being likewise the instructors of such as constituted, or were to constitute, the remaining more numerous classes of the order. The members of this latter and far more numerous body were to be distributed throughout the country, so as not to leave even the smallest integral part or division without a resident guide, guardian, and instructor; the objects and final intention of the whole order being these—to preserve the stores and to guard the treasures of past civilization, and thus to bind the present with the past; to perfect and add to the same, and thus to connect the present with the future; but especially to diffuse through the whole community, and to every native entitled to its laws and rights, that quantity and quality of knowledge which was indispensable both for the understanding of those rights, and for the performance of the duties correspondent.[27]

The national property, which is to maintain this work,

> cannot rightfully, and . . . without foul wrong to the nation never has been, alienated from its original purposes.[28]

Where there has been such alienation, the State may rightly act to restore such property, and rededicate it to its original uses. This will be done through the 'National Church', but not necessarily through existing church organizations:

> I do not assert that the proceeds from the Nationalty cannot be rightfully vested, except in what we now mean by clergymen and the established clergy. I have everywhere implied the contrary.[29]

The idea, in all its aspects, bears the peculiar stamp of Coleridge's mind. In immediate terms, Mill's comment is probably just:

> By setting in a clear light what a national church establishment ought to be . . . he has pronounced the severest satire upon what in fact it is.[30]

Yet for Mill, and for us, the importance lies in the principle.

Mill found, then, in Coleridge, the *enlarged system of action* which he felt to be necessary. It is probably true to say that much of his later work is importantly affected by this enlargement of principle, although the directions which it took lie at some distance from the directions of those writers who consciously continued Coleridge's kind of enquiry. Mill's later work is dominated by two factors: his extension of the methods and claims of Utilitarian reform to the interests of the rising working-class; and his effort to reconcile democratic control with individual liberty. Such a programme was, indeed, to initiate the subsequent main line of English social thinking; its influence, not only on the Fabian kind of socialism, but on a wide area of characteristic modern legislation, is evident. No doubt Mill thought, as it is common to think, that the idea of culture, which had impressed him in Coleridge, was adequately provided for, in terms of a social institution, by the extending system of national education. In the latter half of the nineteenth century, Mill is so sensible, on particular issues, where a Carlyle or even a Ruskin is so patently absurd, that it is easy for us to conclude that Mill's enlarged, 'humanized' Utilitarianism was in fact the best outcome that could have been wished. Whether this is in fact so, whether this kind of development is indeed valuable to us, must be discussed at a later point in this enquiry, on the basis of our subsequent experience. What must be emphasized at this stage is the way in which what Mill took from Coleridge differs from what Coleridge himself offered: an emphasis which is certainly necessary if we are to understand the subsequent development of the idea of Culture. Mill uses the word *culture* in another important context, when he is describing, in his *Autobiography*, the effect on him, at a time of emotional crisis, of Wordsworth's poems. These poems, he writes,

> seemed to be the very culture of the feelings, which I was in quest of. In them I seemed to draw from a source of inward joy, of sympathetic and imaginative pleasure, which could be shared in by all human beings; which had no connexion with struggle or imperfection, but would be made richer by every improvement in the physical or social condition of mankind. From them I seemed to learn what would be the perennial sources of happiness, when all the greater evils of life shall have been removed.[31]

Such a conclusion is obviously relevant to his earlier account of the crisis itself:

> In this frame of mind it occurred to me to put the question directly to myself: 'Suppose that all your objects in life were realized; that all the changes in institutions and opinions which you are looking forward to, could be completely effected at this very instant: would this be a great joy and happiness to you?' And an irrepressible self-consciousness distinctly answered, 'No!' At this my heart sank within me; the whole foundation on which my life was constructed fell down.[32]

Mill puts the situation so clearly that we all understand him, and the movement of mind which he describes has, I suppose, become characteristic. These paragraphs are now the classical point of reference for those who decide that the desire for social reform is ultimately inadequate, and that art, the 'source of inward joy', is fortunately always there as an alternative. But this very common position, whether in Mill or others, is rather doubtful. Mill is recoiling from a solely rational organization of effort; this is only a recoil from the desire for social reform when such a desire has its roots in that kind of intellectual attachment. Many men have, like the early Mill, based their social thinking on that kind of attachment alone, and recoil under the inevitable extension of experience is then natural enough. The fact that, with sensitive men, the recoil takes the form of Mill's kind of attachment to poetry is also understandable. Poetry, as he describes it, is 'the very culture of the feelings', but it is not only this; it has 'no connexion with struggle or imperfection' —that is to say, it is a separate, ideal sphere. Democratic sentiments are retained: the pleasure will 'be made richer by every improvement in the physical or social condition of mankind'. Meanwhile, however, it is not only a promise but a refuge, a source of contact with 'the perennial sources of happiness'. And this has become a very common way of regarding poetry, and art in general, with the obvious implied judgement of the rest of man's social activity.

The basic objection to this way of regarding poetry is that it makes poetry a *substitute* for feeling. It does this because the normal method of intellectual organization, in minds of this kind, is a method which tends to deny the substance of feelings, to dismiss them as 'subjective' and therefore likely to obscure or hinder the ordinary march of thought. If the mind is a 'machine for thinking', then feeling, in the ordinary sense, is irrelevant to its operations. Yet the 'machine for thinking' inhabits a whole personality, which is subject, as in Mill's case, to complex stresses, and even to breakdown. Observing this situation, a mind organized in such a way conceives the need for an additional 'department', a special reserve area in which feeling can be tended and organized. It supposes, immediately, that such a 'department' exists in poetry and art, and it considers that recourse to this reserve area is in fact an 'enlargement' of the mind. Such a disposition has become characteristic, and both the practice and the appreciation of art have suffered from art being thus treated as a saving clause in a bad treaty.

There were elements in the Romantic idea of poetry which tended to indulge this kind of false attachment. The specialization of poetry to the function of 'a culture of the feelings' can be seen as part of the same movement of mind which produced the characteristic rational narrowness of Utilitarian thought. Feeling and thought, poetry and rational enquiry, appeared to be antitheses, to be 'chosen' between, or to be played off one against the other. But in fact they were antitheses within a disruption: the confusion of men haunted by this ghost of a 'mind'.

Coleridge, if Mill had attended to him, could have made this issue clear; made it clear, at least, as an issue, even if his own method of organization could not have been transferred. It was obviously impossible that Mill should realize Coleridge's kind of attachment to experience. A whole position like that of Coleridge cannot be offered for conviction; it is not, and could not be, a suasive element. The most that a man like Coleridge can offer is an instance, but, to the degree that one realizes Coleridge's position, one realizes also that an instance is indeed the most valuable thing that can be offered. The kind of thinking which we observe in Coleridge centres our attention, not on Mill's rationale of a society, but, almost wholly, on the *relations* between personal instance and social institution.

It is possible here only briefly to indicate Coleridge's fundamental approach. It is, perhaps, best described in a characteristically complicated sentence from a letter to Wordsworth:

> In short, the necessity of a general revolution in the modes of developing and disciplining the human mind by the substitution of life and intelligence . . . for the philosophy of mechanism, which, in everything that is most worthy of the human intellect, strikes *Death*, and cheats itself by mistaking clear images for distinct conceptions, and which idly demands conceptions where intuitions alone are possible or adequate to the majesty of the Truth. In short, facts elevated into theory—theory into laws—and laws into living and intelligent powers.[33]

Or again:

> The groundwork, therefore, of all true philosophy is the full apprehension of the difference between the contemplation of reason, namely, that intuition of things which arises when we possess ourselves, as one with the whole, which is substantial knowledge, and that which presents itself when transferring reality to the negations of reality, to the ever-varying framework of the uniform life, we think of ourselves as separated beings, and place nature in antithesis

to the mind, as object to subject, thing to thought, death to life. This is abstract knowledge, or the science of the mere understanding . . . which leads to a science of delusion then only when it would exist for itself instead of being the instrument of the former (that intuition of things which arises when we possess ourselves as one with the whole)—instead of being, as it were, a translation of the living word into a dead language, for the purposes of memory, arrangement, and general communication.[34]

The important distinction is between 'substantial knowledge' and 'abstract knowledge', but the function of the latter is not denied, a function of 'memory, arrangement, and general communication'. The contrast is not between 'thinking' and 'feeling', but between modes of both; the unity of the substantial modes of either is insisted upon:

My opinion is this: that deep thinking is attainable only by a man of deep feeling, and that all truth is a species of revelation. . . . It is *insolent* to *differ* from the public *opinion* in *opinion*, if it be only *opinion*.[35]

By deep feeling we make our *ideas dim*, and this is what we mean by our life, ourselves.[36]

This elevation of the spirit above the semblances of custom and the senses to a world of spirit, this life in the idea, even in the supreme and Godlike, which alone merits the name of life, and without which our organic life is but a state of somnambulism; this it is which affords the sole anchorage in the storm, and at the same time the substantiating principle of all true wisdom, the satisfactory solution of all the contradictions of human nature, of the whole riddle of the world. This alone belongs to and speaks intelligibly to all alike, the learned and the ignorant, if but the heart listens. For alike present in all, it may be awakened but it cannot be given. But let it not be supposed, that it is a sort of knowledge. No! it is a form of being, or indeed it is the only knowledge that truly *is*, and all other science is real only as far as it is symbolical of this.[37]

Of course, when Coleridge passes from instance to formulation he passes also into a more shadowy, and more debatable, activity. It is even possible to see how Mill made what he did of Coleridge's attempts at systematization. There is always in Coleridge a mixture of substantial and abstract knowledge, by his own definitions, and at times, easily enough, he mistook the one for the other. Yet in his major emphases he offers something so radically different from Bentham, and so different also from Mill's attempted 'enlargement', that his influence is not to be construed as that of a 'humanizing' check, but rather, for all its incompleteness of formulation, as an *alternative* conception of man and society. Still, such a conception 'may be awakened, but it cannot be given'.

It is from Coleridge, and later from Ruskin, that the construction of 'Culture' in terms of the arts may be seen to originate. Yet this, also, is only a partial conclusion, for the arts, essentially, are only a symbol for the kind of 'substantial knowledge' which Coleridge sought to describe. The same criterion is at least as necessary in other aspects of our whole activity. Coleridge was indeed, as Mill described him, a 'seminal mind'; but the seed, like that of the parable, has fallen on different kinds of ground. In Mill himself, it produced what I have called 'humanized Utilitarianism'. In Ruskin and Carlyle (in part working from the same sources as Coleridge) it nourished a particular set of social principles, very different from those of Mill, yet also not without their influence on the subsequent development of society. Later again, it joined with the influence of T. H. Green, and with the whole idealist school which approached the question of the functions of the State in ways which Coleridge would have recognized and valued. Yet a seminal mind, when it is that of a Coleridge, is not to be adequately judged by its solely intellectual harvest. Independently of this, and independently even of some of his own 'abstract knowledge', Coleridge has remained as an instance, in experience, of the very greatest value:

> I never before saw such an abstract of *thinking* as a pure act and energy—of thinking as distinguished from thought.[38]

CHAPTER IV

THOMAS CARLYLE

IN 1829, in the *Edinburgh Review*, Carlyle published his important essay, *Signs of the Times*. The essay was his first main contribution to the social thought of his time, yet it is perhaps also his most comprehensive contribution. It is a short essay, of little more than twenty pages, yet it states a general position which was to be the basis of all Carlyle's subsequent work, and which, moreover, was to establish itself in the general thinking of many other writers, and as a major element in the tradition of English social criticism.

It is not easy to distinguish the elements of influence which coalesced in this decisive statement. The influence of German thought in the preceding forty years is clear: the immediately relevant names are Goethe, Schiller, Jean Paul and Novalis. Carlyle had already read and written widely in this field, and the essay on Novalis, for example, written in the same year as *Signs of the Times*, shows evident relations to it. The contrast of *mechanical* and *dynamic* thinking is there, for instance, in a quotation from the *Fragments* in the second volume of the *Novalis Schriften* which he was reviewing. Many of the other ideas, and phrases, may be similarly traced. There are, again, signs of the influence of Coleridge, who himself had gone to many of the same sources, but had also individually developed them. Carlyle had already met Coleridge at this time, and the relation between the two men, if not always clear, is substantial. Carlyle is more systematic, as he is also more limited, than Coleridge: a hint from Coleridge becomes a position in Carlyle. These and other influences must be acknowledged, yet the originality of Carlyle's essay is still not essentially affected. The history of ideas is a dead study if it proceeds solely in terms of the abstraction of influences. What is important in a thinker like Carlyle is the quality of his direct response: the terms, the formulations, the morphology of ideas, are properly a secondary matter, and as properly, also,

the subject of influence. Carlyle is in this essay stating a
direct response to the England of his times: to Industrialism,
which he was the first to name: to the feel, the quality, of
men's general reactions—that structure of contemporary
feeling which is only ever apprehended directly; as well as
to the character and conflict of formal systems and points of
view. *Signs of the Times*, as a phrase, carries the right
emphasis.

The essay, although known to students, is not as generally
known as it deserves to be. More than anything else of
Carlyle's, it requires quotation. We can begin with the
general description:

> Were we required to characterize this age of ours by any single
> epithet, we should be tempted to call it, not an Heroical, Devotional,
> Philosophical, or Moral Age, but, above all others, the Mechanical
> Age. It is the Age of Machinery, in every outward and inward
> sense of that word. . . . Nothing is now done directly, or by hand;
> all is by rule and calculated contrivance.[1]

This proposition is illustrated, first by reference to the
changes in methods of production:

> On every hand, the living artisan is driven from his workshop, to
> make room for a speedier, inanimate one. The shuttle drops from
> the fingers of the weaver, and falls into iron fingers that ply it
> faster.[2]

Then, there are the consequent social changes:

> What changes, too, this addition of power is introducing into the
> Social System; how wealth has more and more increased, and at the
> same time gathered itself more and more into masses, strangely
> altering the old relations, and increasing the distance between the
> rich and the poor, will be a question for Political Economists, and a
> much more complex and important one than any they have yet
> engaged with.[3]

These are clear statements of a kind of analysis that has
continued and become familiar; it is easy, reading them, to
understand Marx's subsequent tribute to this aspect of
Carlyle's work. But Carlyle continues his analysis, in another

direction, which Matthew Arnold, writing *Culture and Anarchy*, could have acknowledged:

> Not the external and physical alone is now managed by machinery, but the internal and spiritual also. . . . The same habit regulates not our modes of action alone, but our modes of thought and feeling. Men are grown mechanical in head and in heart, as well as in hand. They have lost faith in individual endeavour, and in natural force, of any kind. Not for internal perfection, but for external combinations and arrangements, for institutions, constitutions—for Mechanism of one sort or other, do they hope and struggle. Their whole efforts, attachments, opinions, turn on mechanism, and are of a mechanical character.[4]

As examples of this, Carlyle adduces the following:

> An inward persuasion . . . that, except the external, there are no true sciences; that to the inward world (if there be any) our only conceivable road is through the outward; that, in short, what cannot be investigated and understood mechanically, cannot be investigated and understood at all.[5]

> The mighty interest taken in *mere political arrangements*. . . . Were the laws, the government, in good order, all were well with us; the rest would care for itself! . . . So devoted are we to this principle, and at the same time so curiously mechanical, that a new trade, specially grounded on it, has arisen among us, under the name of 'Codification', or code-making in the abstract; whereby any people, for a reasonable consideration, may be accommodated with a patent code;—more easily than curious individuals with patent breeches, for the people does *not* need to be measured first.[6]

> Mechanism has now struck its roots down into man's most intimate, primary sources of conviction; and is thence sending up, over his whole life and activity, innumerable stems—fruit-bearing and poison-bearing. . . . Intellect, the power man has of knowing and believing, is now nearly synonymous with Logic, or the mere power of arranging and communicating. Its implement is not Meditation, but Argument. . . . Our first question with regard to any object is not, What is it? but, How is it? . . . For every Why we must have a Wherefore. We have our little *theory* on all human and divine things.[7]

Religion is now . . . for the most part, a wise prudential feeling grounded on mere calculation . . . whereby some smaller quantum of earthly enjoyment may be exchanged for a far larger quantum of celestial enjoyment. Thus Religion too is Profit, a working for wages.[8]

This veneration for the physically Strongest has spread itself through Literature. . . . We praise a work, not as 'true', but as 'strong'; our highest praise is that it has 'affected' us. . . .[9]

Our . . . 'superior morality' is properly rather an 'inferior criminality', produced not by greater love of Virtue, but by greater perfection of Police; and of that far subtler and stronger Police, called Public Opinion.[10]

In all senses, we worship and follow after Power. . . . No man now loves Truth, as Truth must be loved, with an infinite love; but only with a finite love, and as it were *par amours*. Nay, properly speaking, he does not *believe* and know it, but only '*thinks*it', and that 'there is every probability'! He preaches it aloud, and rushes courageously forth with it—if there is a multitude huzzaing at his back; yet ever keeps looking over his shoulder, and the instant the huzzaing languishes, he too stops short.[11]

These are the faults of the *external* attachment, when viewed in the light of the inward claims. But:

To define the limits of these two departments of man's activity, which work into one another, and by means of one another, so intricately and inseparably, were by its nature an impossible attempt. Their relative importance . . . will vary in different times, according to the special wants and dispositions of those times. Meanwhile, it seems clear enough that only in the right co-ordination of the two, and the vigorous forwarding of *both*, does our true line of action lie. Undue cultivation of the inward or Dynamical province leads to idle, visionary, impracticable courses. . . . Undue cultivation of the outward, again, though less immediately prejudicial, and even for the time productive of many palpable benefits, must in the long-run, by destroying Moral Force, which is the parent of all other Force, prove not less certainly, and perhaps still more hopelessly, pernicious. This, we take it, is the grand characteristic of our age.[12]

THOMAS CARLYLE

Carlyle wants to see a restoration of balance, in the terms he has set. He is writing, not a rejection of his time, but a criticism of it:

> These dark features, we are aware, belong more or less to other ages, as well as to ours. This faith in Mechanism, in the all-importance of physical things, is in every age the common refuge of Weakness and blind Discontent. . . . We are aware also, that, as applied to ourselves in all their aggravation, they form but half a picture. . . . Neither, with all these evils more or less clearly before us, have we at any time despaired of the fortunes of society. Despair, or even despondency, in that respect, appears to us, in all cases, a groundless feeling. We have a faith in the imperishable dignity of man; in the high vocation to which, throughout this his earthly history, he has been appointed. . . . This age also is advancing. Its very unrest, its ceaseless activity, its discontent contains matter of promise. Knowledge, education are opening the eyes of the humblest; are increasing the number of thinking minds without limit. This is as it should be, for not in turning back, not in resisting, but only in resolutely struggling forward, does our life consist. . . . There is a deep-lying struggle in the whole fabric of society; a boundless grinding collision of the New with the Old. The French Revolution, as is now visible enough, was not the parent of this mighty movement, but its offspring. . . . The final issue was not unfolded in that country: nay it is not yet anywhere unfolded. Political freedom is hitherto the object of these efforts; but they will not and cannot stop there. It is towards a higher freedom than mere freedom from oppression by his fellow-mortal, that man dimly aims. Of this higher, heavenly freedom, which is 'man's reasonable service', all his noble institutions, his faithful endeavours and loftiest attainments, are but the body, and more and more approximated emblem.[13]

The criticism of the characteristics of the age is fundamental, but the dominant tone, especially of these last paragraphs, is surely very surprising to a twentieth-century reader. For us, now, such phrases as 'the imperishable dignity of man . . . the high vocation . . . resolutely struggling forward' are on one side of the argument; criticism of the 'faith in mechanism' on the other. The former argument now commonly neglects the criticism, while the latter, as commonly, has purged itself of strength and hope. The idea of balance is not usually one which suggests itself when we are thinking of Carlyle; but there is genuine balance in this essay, as well as a fine, and now rare, unity of insight and determination. A man who began in this way might well seem qualified to become the most important social thinker of his century.

There was a time, of course, when it was quite widely believed that this was in fact what Carlyle became. I suppose that no one believes this now, and certainly I do not wish to argue that it is so. The insight lasted in all his work; at his most savage he can still, on occasion, uncomfortably penetrate our normal assumptions. The limitation, as his life's work continued, is to be seen, primarily, in a false construction of basic issues of relationship. In this he is a victim of the situation which, in *Signs of the Times*, he had described. 'This veneration for the physically strongest has spread itself through Literature. . . . In all senses, we worship and follow after Power': these are the marks of the sickness which Carlyle observed, and to which he himself succumbed. The leading principle of all his later social writing is the principle of the strong Leader, the Hero, and the subjects who revere him. Carlyle, writing himself, becomes the caricature of such a hero. He sees, with a terrible clarity, the spiritual emptiness of the characteristic social relationships of his day, 'with Cash Payment as the sole nexus' between man and man '. . . and there are so many things which cash will not pay'.[14] The perception disqualifies him, wholly, from acquiescence in this construction of relationships; and he is therefore, without argument, a radical and a reformer. In this, however, he is isolated, feels himself isolated: the existing framework of relationships, the existing society, is against him, necessarily, because he is against it. He feels himself, in this situation, cut off from all fruitful social relationships; he has, in Burke's words, but by a force of circumstance which Burke overlooked, 'nothing of politics but the passions they excite'.[15] What he lacks, or feels himself to lack, is power; and yet he is conscious of power; conscious, too, of the superiority of his insight (which is not to be reduced to a merely personal conceit) into the

real problems of the day. Under this tension—the conclusion is not necessary, but it has been reached again and
again—he construes the generally desirable as what he
personally desires; he creates the image of the hero, 'the
strong man who stands alone', the leader, the leader
possessed by vision, who shall be listened to, revered,
obeyed. It is usual to explain this conclusion in terms of
Carlyle's personal psychology: impotence projecting itself
as power. But this, while relevant in so far as it can be
ascertained, does less than justice to the representative
quality of Carlyle's conclusion. The phenomenon is indeed
general, and has perhaps been especially marked in the last
six or seven generations. The explanation is mechanical
unless we discriminate, very carefully, about the purposes
for which the power is wanted. In Carlyle's case, essentially,
the purposes are positive and ennobling; the opposing
normality, of the society which he wished to reform, is
morally inferior to them in every way. This indeed is the
tragedy of the situation: that a genuine insight, a genuine
vision, should be dragged down by the very situation, the
very structure of relationships, to which it was opposed,
until a civilizing insight became in its operation barbarous,
and a heroic purpose, a 'high vocation', found its final
expression in a conception of human relationships which is
only an idealized version of industrial class-society. The
judgement, 'in all senses we worship and follow after Power',
returns indeed as a mocking echo.

The larger part of Carlyle's writing is the imaginative re-
creation of men of noble power. Lacking live men, we enter
a social contract with a biography. The writings on Crom-
well, on Frederick the Great, and on others, embody this
most curious of experiences: a man entering into personal
relations with history, setting up house with the illustrious
dead. The more relevant writings, now, are the essay on
Chartism, the lectures on *Heroes and Hero-Worship*, the
Latter-Day Pamphlets, *Past and Present*, and *Shooting
Niagara*. Yet the unity of Carlyle's work is such that almost
everything he wrote has a bearing on his main questions;
his most complete analysis of Mechanism, for example, is to
be found in *Sartor Resartus*, and it is there, also, in a brilliant

passage, that he named Industrialism for us, and gave it its first definition.

The essay on *Chartism*, published in 1839, is a fine example of his developed method and convictions. Written on the eve of the crisis of the Hungry Forties, it begins with characteristic insight:

> We are aware that, according to the newspapers, Chartism is extinct; that a Reform Ministry has 'put down the chimera of Chartism' in the most felicitous effectual manner. So say the newspapers;—and yet, alas, most readers of newspapers know withal that it is indeed the 'chimera' of Chartism, not the reality, which has been put down. . . . The living essence of Chartism has not been put down. Chartism means the bitter discontent grown fierce and mad, the wrong condition therefore or the wrong disposition, of the Working Classes of England. It is a new name for a thing which has had many names, which will yet have many. The matter of Chartism is weighty, deep-rooted, far-extending; did not begin yesterday; will by no means end this day or tomorrow.[16]

After this recognition, and the parallel recognition that it is no answer to call the discontent 'mad, incendiary, nefarious', Carlyle proposes the famous 'Condition-of-England' question:

> Is the condition of the English working people wrong; so wrong that rational working men cannot, will not, and even should not rest quiet under it?[17]

It is Cobbett's question, and in Cobbett's manner; and we have only to set such a question in the context of what passed in this period for political discussion to realize that the firmness of it, the essential and central strength of it— now so easily taken for granted—came by no kind of accident, but from a man with the qualities so often praised by Carlyle in others—a man strong and reverent.

When Dickens came to write *Hard Times*—a book in which there is a great deal of Carlyle—one of the things against which he turned his mocking invective was the procedure of systematic enquiry into just this 'Condition-of-England question'—Mr Gradgrind's Observatory, with its 'deadly statistical clock'. It is a measure of the difference between Carlyle and Dickens—an essential difference of human seriousness—that Carlyle makes no such trivial error. He criticizes imperfect statistics, but his demand, rightly, is for the evidence, for rational enquiry, so that the Legislature will not go on 'legislating in the dark'. The failure to seek such evidence he sees, again rightly, as a symptom of the spirit of *laissez-faire*. The essay becomes a full-scale assault on the *laissez-faire* idea:

> That self-cancelling Donothingism and *Laissez-faire* should have got so ingrained into our Practice, is the source of all these miseries.[18]

This eighteenth-century doctrine, as Carlyle calls it, struggled

> still to prolong itself into the Nineteenth—which, however, is no longer the time for it! . . . It was a lucky century that could get it so practised; a century which had inherited richly from its predecessors; and also which did, not unnaturally, bequeath to its successors a French Revolution, general overturn, and reign of terror;—intimating, in most audible thunder, conflagration, guillotinement, cannonading and universal war and earthquake, that such century with its practices had *ended*.[19]

The movement of which the French Revolution was a part is, however, not yet ended:

> These Chartisms, Radicalisms, Reform Bill, Tithe Bill, and infinite other discrepancy, and acrid argument and jargon that there is yet to be, are *our* French Revolution: God grant that we, with our better methods, may be able to transact it by argument alone.[20]

Carlyle recognizes part of this movement as the struggle for democracy. But to him, here as later, democracy is merely a negative solution:

> All men may see, whose sight is good for much, that in democracy can lie no finality; that with the completest winning of democracy there is nothing yet won—except emptiness, and the free chance to win.[21]

Carlyle sees democracy, in fact, as in one sense an expression of the same *laissez-faire* spirit: a cancelling of order and government, under which men can be left free to follow their own interests. Any such criticism of democracy, read now, is only too likely to meet immediate prejudice; we have all learned to shout 'fascist' at it. Yet the criticism has a certain justice, and is, indeed, a most relevant criticism of that kind of democracy which, for example, reached its climax in the Reform Bill of 1832. Whenever democracy is considered as solely a political arrangement, it is open to Carlyle's charge. A large part of the spirit of democracy in our kind of society is in fact the spirit of *laissez-faire*, extended to new interests and creating in consequence new kinds of problem.

Carlyle's call is for government; for more government, not less; more order, not less. This, he represents, is the demand of the English working people; and in essence he is again right, and has continued right—the characteristic movements of the English working class, while certainly democratic in the wide sense, have been in the direction of more government, more order, more social control. Carlyle, however, interprets this demand in his own way:

> What is the meaning of the 'five points', if we will understand them? What are all popular commotions and maddest bellowings, from Peterloo to the Place-de-Grève itself? Bellowings, *in*articulate cries as of a dumb creature in rage and pain; to the ear of wisdom they are inarticulate prayers: 'Guide me, govern me! I am mad and miserable, and cannot guide myself!' Surely of all 'rights of man', this right of the ignorant man to be guided by the wiser, to be, gently or forcibly, held in the true course by him, is the indisputablest. Nature herself ordains it from the first; Society struggles towards perfection by enforcing and accomplishing it more and more. If Freedom have any meaning, it means enjoyment of this right, wherein all other rights are enjoyed.[22]

In these last sentences, Carlyle is repeating a point that will be remembered from Burke, and, characteristically, it is again seen as the condition of 'Society struggling towards perfection'. Where Burke, however, saw an adequate ruling class ready made, Carlyle saw only the dereliction of duty by the governing classes in society. As his thinking develops, and particularly in his later writings, his call is to the classes with power to equip themselves for the right exercise of power: to make themselves an active and responsible governing class, and purge themselves of 'donothingism'. The call was addressed by Carlyle to the aristocracy, but it was most heeded in the middle class, where it became the basis of the appeal of reformers like Kingsley. The call to the aristocracy was meanwhile noted by Disraeli; the relations between Carlyle's *Chartism* and Disraeli's *Sybil* are very close.

Carlyle himself, more certainly in *Chartism* than elsewhere, had his own specific proposals. He was opposed, not only to the general spirit of *laissez-faire*, but to what he called Paralytic Radicalism, which, knowing the misery of industrial England, can refer it only to 'time and general laws'. He observes in his best manner:

> They are an unreasonable class who cry 'Peace, peace', when there *is* no peace. But what kind of class are they who cry, 'Peace, peace, have I not *told you* that there is no peace!'[23]

Carlyle's proposals, against these 'practical men', are two: first, popular education; second, planned emigration. The latter, which had indeed been a specific since the first impact of Malthus, and which Cobbett, for good reasons, had fiercely opposed, was to become a major element in reformist feeling. It was, of course, the surplus working people who were to emigrate, under the leadership (literally) of unemployed intellectuals and half-pay officers. The only thing in this proposal that reflects credit on Carlyle is his contingent contempt for the advice to 'stop breeding', again addressed only to the working poor. He is as eloquent against Malthus as Cobbett had been:

> Smart Sally in our alley proves all-too fascinating to brisk Tom in yours: can Tom be called on to make pause, and calculate the demand for labour in the British Empire first? . . . O wonderful Malthusian prophets! Millenniums are undoubtedly coming, must come one way or the other; but will it be, think you, by twenty millions of working people simultaneously striking work in that department?[24]

The other proposal, for Popular Education, was equally, and more fortunately, influential. Carlyle is for practical beginnings: 'the Alphabet first'—'the indispensable beginning of everything': 'handicraft . . . and the habit of the merest logic'. These things must be done, even while recognizing their inadequacy:

> An irreverent knowledge is no knowledge; may be a development of the logical or other handicraft faculty inward or outward; but is no culture of the soul of a man.[25]

The reservation is important; it is the reservation which the word *culture* was to embody, in criticism of many kinds of education. But Carlyle insisted, nevertheless, that fundamental, State-promoted education must be begun:

> To impart the gift of thinking to those who cannot think, and yet who could in that case think: this, one would imagine, was the first function a government had to set about discharging.[26]

Education is thus the central theme of the general demand for 'more government'.

The *Chartism* essay contains the greater part of what is best in Carlyle's social thinking. In practical effect—as in the proposals for popular education and planned emigration —it is not really very different from Utilitarianism; and in its call for more government it is a move in the same direction as that which the second phase of radical Utilitarianism was to take. The decisive emphasis is on the need to transform the social and human relationships hitherto dictated by the 'laws' of political economy. This emphasis, humane and general, was in fact to be more influential than Carlyle's alternative construction of heroic leadership and reverent obedience.

After *Chartism*, the balance, or comparative balance, of Carlyle's first positions is lost. *Past and Present* is eloquent, and the portrait of Abbot Samson and his mediaeval community is perhaps the most substantial, as it is also the most literal, of all the visions of mediaeval order which the critics of nineteenth-century society characteristically attempted. But, while it was possible to expose the deficiencies of Industrialism by contrast with selected aspects of a feudal civilization, the exercise was of no help to Carlyle, or to his readers, in the matter of perceiving the contemporary sources of community. The heroically drawn Samson, like

the figures celebrated in *Heroes and Hero-Worship*, under-
lines the steady withdrawal from genuinely social thinking
into the preoccupations with personal power. In the *Latter-
Day Pamphlets* the decisive shift has taken place; it is to the
existing holders of power—the Aristocracy, the 'Captains of
Industry'[27]—that Carlyle looks for leadership in the reorganization of society; the call is only for them to fit themselves for such leadership, and to assume it. By the time of
Shooting Niagara this call has become a contemptuous
absolutism, and the elements which made the former
criticism humane have virtually disappeared. The recognition of the dignity of common men has passed into the kind
of contempt for the 'masses'—Swarmery, 'Sons of the Devil,
in overwhelming majority',[28] 'blockheadism, gullibility,
bribeability, amenability to beer and balderdash'[29]—which
has remained a constant element in English thought.

The idea of culture as the whole way of living of a people
receives in Carlyle a marked new emphasis. It is the ground
of his attack on Industrialism: that a society, properly so
called, is composed of very much more than economic
relationships, with 'cash payment the sole nexus':

> 'Supply and demand' we will honour also; and yet how many
> 'demands' are there, entirely indispensable, which have to go else-
> where than to the shops, and produce quite other than cash, before
> they can get their supply.[30]

The emphasis which Carlyle commonly gave to these other
kinds of demand is closely related to his characteristic conception of the 'genius', the 'hero as man of letters'. He saw
the neglect of such a man, and of the values which he represented, as a main symptom of the disorganization of
society by the forces which elsewhere he attacked:

> Complaint is often made, in these times, of what we call the dis-
> organized condition of society: how ill many arranged forces of
> society fulfil their work; how many powerful forces are seen
> working in a wasteful, chaotic, altogether unarranged manner. It
> is too just a complaint, as we all know. But perhaps, if we look at
> this of Books and the Writers of Books, we shall find here, as it
> were, the summary of all other disorganization;—a sort of *heart*,

from which, and to which, all other confusion circulates in the
world. . . . That a wise great Johnson, a Burns, a Rousseau, should
be taken for some idle nondescript, extant in the world to amuse
idleness, and have a few coins and applause thrown in, that he
might live thereby; *this* perhaps, as before hinted, will one day seem
a still absurder phasis of things. Meanwhile, since it is the spiritual
always that determines the material, this same Man-of-Letters
Hero must be regarded as our most important modern person. He,
such as he may be, is the soul of all. What he teaches, the whole
world will do and make. The world's manner of dealing with him
is the most significant feature of the world's general position.[31]

The relation of this to the Romantic idea of the artist is
clear. Carlyle was a contemporary of the younger generation
of Romantic poets, and his views on this subject are very
similar to those of, say, Shelley. This can be readily seen
when Carlyle writes of his 'Man-of-Letters Hero':

Whence he came, whither he is bound, by what ways he arrived,
by what he might be furthered on his course, no one asks. He is an
accident in society. He wanders like a wild Ishmaelite, in a world
of which he is as the spiritual light, either the guidance or the
misguidance.[32]

Carlyle's share in the formation of the characteristic modern
idea of the artist (to use our own generic term) must, then, be
acknowledged. The specific development of this idea as one
of the main lines of criticism of the new kind of industrial
society must again be noted. It is here that the idea of culture
as the body of arts and learning, and the idea of culture as a
body of values superior to the ordinary progress of society,
meet and combine. Carlyle, even when he appealed to the
leadership of the aristocracy and captains of industry, never
failed to emphasize this other conception of a 'spiritual
aristocracy', a highly cultivated and responsible minority,
concerned to define and emphasize the highest values at
which society must aim. In the general anger of *Shooting
Niagara* he warns this class to set aside Poetry and Fiction,
in order to 'write the History of England as a kind of Bible',
and to concentrate on rethinking of our basic social assumptions. But this, although significant of Carlyle—it is his own

kind of work, as poetry was Shelley's—does not change the
central emphasis, on the need for a *class* of such men—
'Writing and Teaching Heroes'—whose concern is with the
quality of the national life. This had been Coleridge's idea of
the National Church, the Clerisy. Carlyle, in different terms,
makes the same proposal, for an 'organic Literary Class'. He
is not sure of the best arrangements for such a class, but

> If you ask, Which is the worst? I answer: This which we now
> have, that Chaos should sit umpire in it; this is the worst.[33]

It is not a question of 'money-furtherances' to individual
writers:

> The result to individual Men of Letters is not the momentous one;
> they are but individuals, an infinitesimal fraction of the great body;
> they can struggle on, and live or else die, as they have been wont.
> But it deeply concerns the whole society, whether it will set its
> *light* on high places, to walk thereby. . . . I call this anomaly of a
> disorganic Literary Class the heart of all other anomalies, at once
> product and parent.[34]

The idea of such an *élite*, for the common good of society,
has not been lost sight of, down to our own day. All that
now needs emphasis, with Carlyle as with Coleridge, and
as with Matthew Arnold after them, is that the then existing
organization of society, as they understood it, offered no
actual basis for the maintenance of such a class. The
separation of the activities grouped as 'culture' from the
main purposes of the new kind of society was the ground of
complaint:

> Never, till about a hundred years ago, was there seen any figure of a
> Great Soul living apart in that anomalous manner; endeavouring
> to speak forth the inspiration that was in him by Printed Books,
> and find place and subsistence by what the world would please to
> give him for doing that. Much had been sold and bought, and left
> to make its own bargain in the market place; but the inspired
> wisdom of a Heroic Soul never till then, in that naked manner.[35]

This was the immediate criterion by which the faulty
organization, the narrow purposes, of the new society might
be perceived. It is in these terms, reinforced by more general

conclusions, that Culture came to be defined as a separate entity and a critical idea.

Of Carlyle himself, much more might be said. He was in every way so remarkable a man that the contrast between the ideas which he deposited and the total experience within which they had immediate meaning holds more than the common irony. His influence was deep and wide, and we shall catch many echoes of him as we proceed, down to our own century. The faults, alike of the man and of his influence, remain obvious. But there is one common word of his which continues to express his essential quality: the word *reverence*, not for him, but in him: the governing seriousness of a living effort, against which every cynicism, every kind of half-belief, every satisfaction in indifference, may be seen and placed, in an ultimate human contrast.

CHAPTER V

THE INDUSTRIAL NOVELS

OUR understanding of the response to industrialism would be incomplete without reference to an interesting group of novels, written at the middle of the century, which not only provide some of the most vivid descriptions of life in an unsettled industrial society, but also illustrate certain common assumptions within which the direct response was undertaken. There are the facts of the new society, and there is this structure of feeling, which I will try to illustrate from *Mary Barton*, *North and South*, *Hard Times*, *Sybil*, *Alton Locke*, and *Felix Holt*.

Mary Barton (1848)

Mary Barton, particularly in its early chapters, is the most moving response in literature to the industrial suffering of the 1840s. The really impressive thing about the book is the intensity of the effort to record, in its own terms, the feel of everyday life in the working-class homes. The method, in part, is that of documentary record, as may be seen in such details as the carefully annotated reproduction of dialect, the carefully included details of food prices in the account of the tea-party, the itemized description of the furniture of the Bartons' living-room, and the writing-out of the ballad (again annotated) of *The Oldham Weaver*. The interest of this record is considerable, but the method has, nevertheless, a slightly distancing effect. Mrs Gaskell could hardly help coming to this life as an observer, a reporter, and we are always to some extent conscious of this. But there is genuine imaginative re-creation in her accounts of the walk in Green Heys Fields, and of tea at the Bartons' house, and again, notably, in the chapter *Poverty and Death* where John Barton and his friend find the starving family in the cellar. For so convincing a creation of the characteristic feelings and responses of families of this kind (matters more determining than the material details on which the reporter is apt to concentrate) the English novel had to wait, indeed, for the early writing of D. H. Lawrence. If Mrs Gaskell never quite manages the sense of full participation which would finally authenticate this, she yet brings to these scenes an intuitive recognition of feelings which has its own sufficient conviction. The chapter *Old Alice's History* brilliantly dramatizes the situation of that early generation brought from the villages and the countryside to the streets and cellars of the industrial towns. The account of Job Legh, the weaver and naturalist, vividly embodies that other kind of response to an urban industrial environment: the devoted, lifelong study of living creatures—a piece of amateur scientific work, and at the same time an instinct for living creatures which hardens, by its very contrast with its environment, into a kind of crankiness. In the factory workers walking out in spring into Green Heys Fields; in Alice Wilson, remembering in her cellar the ling-gathering for besoms in the native village that she will never again see; in Job Legh, intent on his impaled insects—these early chapters embody the characteristic response of a generation to the new and crushing experience of industrialism. The other early chapters movingly embody the continuity and development of the sympathy and cooperative instinct which were already establishing a main working-class tradition.

The structure of feeling from which *Mary Barton* begins is, then, a combination of sympathetic observation and of a largely successful attempt at imaginative identification. If it had continued in this way, it might have been a great novel of its kind. But the emphasis of the method changes, and there are several reasons for this. One reason can be studied in a curious aspect of the history of the writing of the book. It was originally to be called *John Barton*. As Mrs Gaskell wrote later:

> Round the character of John Barton all the others formed themselves; he was my hero, *the* person with whom all my sympathies went.[1]

And she added:

> The character, and some of the speeches, are exactly a poor man I know.[1]

The change of emphasis which the book subsequently

underwent, and the consequent change of title to *Mary Barton*, seem to have been made at the instance of her publishers, Chapman and Hall. The details of this matter are still obscure, but we must evidently allow something for this external influence on the shape of the novel. Certainly the John Barton of the later parts of the book is a very shadowy figure. In committing the murder, he seems to put himself not only beyond the range of Mrs Gaskell's sympathy (which is understandable), but, more essentially, beyond the range of her powers. The agony of conscience is there, as a thing told and sketched, but, as the crisis of 'my hero; *the* person with whom all my sympathies went', it is weak and almost incidental. This is because the novel as published is centred on the daughter—her indecision between Jem Wilson and 'her gay lover, Harry Carson'; her agony in Wilson's trial; her pursuit and last-minute rescue of the vital witness; the realization of her love for Wilson: all this, the familiar and orthodox plot of the Victorian novel of sentiment, but of little lasting interest. And it now seems incredible that the novel should ever have been planned in any other way. If Mrs Gaskell had written 'round the character of Mary Barton all the others formed themselves', she would have confirmed our actual impression of the finished book.

Something must be allowed for the influence of her publishers, but John Barton must always have been cast as the murderer, with the intention perhaps of showing an essentially good man driven to an appalling crime by loss, suffering and despair. One can still see the elements of this in the novel as we have it, but there was evidently a point, in its writing, at which the flow of sympathy with which she began was arrested, and then, by the change of emphasis which the change of title records, diverted to the less compromising figure of the daughter. The point would be less important if it were not characteristic of the structure of feeling within which she was working. It is not only that she recoils from the violence of the murder, to the extent of being unable even to enter it as the experience of the man conceived as her hero. It is also that, as compared with the carefully representative character of the early chapters, the murder itself is exceptional. It is true that in 1831 a Thomas Ashton, of Pole Bank, Werneth, was murdered under somewhat similar circumstances, and that the Ashton family appear to have taken the murder of Carson as referring to this. Mrs Gaskell, disclaiming the reference in a letter to them, turned up some similar incidents in Glasgow at about the same time. But in fact, taking the period as a whole, the response of political assassination is so uncharacteristic as to be an obvious distortion. The few recorded cases only emphasize this. Even when one adds the cases of intimidation, and the occasional vitriol-throwing during the deliberate breaking of strikes, it remains true, and was at the time a subject of surprised comment by foreign observers, that the characteristic response of the English working people, even in times of grave suffering, was not one of personal violence. Mrs Gaskell was under no obligation to write a representative novel; she might legitimately have taken a special case. But the tone elsewhere is deliberately representative, and she is even, as she says, modelling John Barton on 'a poor man I know'. The real explanation, surely, is that John Barton, a political murderer appointed by a trade union, is a dramatization of the *fear of violence* which was widespread among the upper and middle classes at the time, and which penetrated, as an arresting and controlling factor, even into the deep imaginative sympathy of a Mrs Gaskell. This fear that the working people might take matters into their own hands was widespread and characteristic, and the murder of Harry Carson is an imaginative working-out of this fear, and of reactions to it, rather than any kind of observed and considered experience.

The point is made clearer when it is remembered that Mrs Gaskell planned the murder herself, and chose, for the murderer, 'my hero, *the* person with whom all my sympathies went'. In this respect the act of violence, a sudden aggression against a man contemptuous of the sufferings of the poor, looks very much like a projection, with which, in the end, she was unable to come to terms. The imaginative choice of the act of murder and then the imaginative recoil from it have the effect of ruining the necessary integration of feeling in the whole theme. The diversion to Mary Barton, even allowing for the publishers' influence, must in fact have been welcome.

Few persons felt more deeply than Elizabeth Gaskell the sufferings of the industrial poor. As a minister's wife in Manchester, she actually saw this, and did not, like many other novelists, merely know it by report or occasional visit. Her response to the suffering is deep and genuine, but pity cannot stand alone in such a structure of feeling. It is joined, in *Mary Barton*, by the confusing violence and fear of violence, and is supported, finally, by a kind of writing-off, when the misery of the actual situation can no longer be endured. John Barton dies penitent, and the elder Carson repents of his vengeance and turns, as the sympathetic observer wanted the employers to turn, to efforts at improvement and mutual understanding. This was the characteristic humanitarian conclusion, and it must certainly be respected. But it was not enough, we notice, for the persons with whom Mrs Gaskell's sympathies were engaged. Mary Barton, Jem Wilson, Mrs Wilson, Margaret, Will, Job Legh—all the objects of her real sympathy—end the book far removed from the situation which she had set out to examine. All are going to Canada; there could be no more devastating conclusion. A solution within the actual situation might be hoped for, but the solution with which the heart went was a cancelling of the actual difficulties and the removal of the persons pitied to the uncompromised New World.

North and South (1855)

Mrs Gaskell's second industrial novel, *North and South*, is less interesting, because the tension is less. She takes up here her actual position, as a sympathetic observer. Margaret Hale, with the feelings and upbringing of the daughter of a Southern clergyman, moves with her father to industrial Lancashire, and we follow her reactions, her observations and her attempts to do what good she can. Because this is largely Mrs Gaskell's own situation, the integration of the book is markedly superior. Margaret's arguments with the mill-owner Thornton are interesting and honest, within the political and economic conceptions of the period. But the emphasis of the novel, as the lengthy inclusion of such arguments suggests, is almost entirely now on attitudes *to* the working people, rather than on the attempt to reach, imaginatively, their feelings about their lives. It is interesting, again, to note the manner of the working-out. The relationship of Margaret and Thornton and their eventual marriage serve as a unification of the practical energy of the Northern manufacturer with the developed sensibility of the Southern girl: this is stated almost explicitly, and is seen as a solution. Thornton goes back to the North

> to have the opportunity of cultivating some intercourse with the hands beyond the mere 'cash nexus'.[2]

Humanized by Margaret, he will work at what we now call 'the improvement of human relations in industry'. The conclusion deserves respect, but it is worth noticing that it is not only under Margaret's influence that Thornton will attempt this, but under her patronage. The other manufacturers, as Thornton says, 'will shake their heads and look grave' at it. This may be characteristic, but Thornton, though bankrupt, can be the exception, by availing himself of Margaret's unexpected legacy. Money from elsewhere, in fact—by that device of the legacy which solved so many otherwise insoluble problems in the world of the Victorian novel—will enable Thornton, already affected by the superior gentleness and humanity of the South, to make his humanitarian experiment. Once again Mrs Gaskell works out her reaction to the insupportable situation by going—in part adventitiously—outside it.

Hard Times (1854)

> Ordinarily Dickens's criticisms of the world he lives in are casual and incidental—a matter of including among the ingredients of a book some indignant treatment of a particular abuse. But in *Hard Times* he is for once possessed by a comprehensive vision, one in which the inhumanities of Victorian civilization are seen as fostered and sanctioned by a hard philosophy, the aggressive formulation of an inhumane spirit.[3]

This comment by F. R. Leavis on *Hard Times* serves to distinguish Dickens's intention from that of Mrs Gaskell in *Mary Barton*. *Hard Times* is less imaginative observation than an imaginative judgement. It is a judgement of social attitudes, but again it is something more than *North and South*. It is a thorough-going and creative examination of the dominant philosophy of industrialism—of the hardness that Mrs Gaskell saw as little more than a misunderstanding, which might be patiently broken down. That Dickens could achieve this more comprehensive understanding is greatly to the advantage of the novel. But against this we must set the fact that in terms of human understanding of the industrial working people Dickens is obviously less successful than Mrs Gaskell: his Stephen Blackpool, in relation to the people of Mary Barton, is little more than a diagrammatic figure. The gain in comprehension, that is to say, has been achieved by the rigours of generalization and abstraction; *Hard Times* is an analysis of Industrialism, rather than experience of it.

The most important point, in this context, that has to be made about *Hard Times* is a point about Thomas Gradgrind. Josiah Bounderby, the other villain of the piece, is a simple enough case. He is, with rough justice, the embodiment of the aggressive money-making and power-seeking ideal which was a driving force of the Industrial Revolution. That he is also a braggart, a liar and in general personally repellent is of course a comment on Dickens's method. The conjunction of these personal defects with the aggressive ideal is not (how much easier things would be if it were) a necessary conjunction. A large part of the Victorian reader's feelings against Bounderby (and perhaps a not inconsiderable part of the twentieth-century intellectual's) rests on the older and rather different feeling that trade, as such, is gross. The very name (and Dickens uses his names with conscious and obvious effect), incorporating *bounder*, incorporates this typical feeling. The social criticism represented by *bounder* is, after all, a rather different matter from the question of aggressive economic individualism. Dickens, with rough justice, fuses the separate reactions, and it is easy not to notice how one set of feelings is made to affect the other.

The difficulty about Thomas Gradgrind is different in character. It is that the case against him is so good, and his refutation by experience so masterly, that it is easy for the modern reader to forget exactly *what* Gradgrind is. It is surprising how common is the mistake of using the remembered name, Gradgrind, as a class-name for the hard Victorian employer. The valuation which Dickens actually asks us to make is more difficult. Gradgrind is a Utilitarian: seen by Dickens as one of the *feeloosofers* against whom Cobbett thundered, or as one of the *steam-engine intellects* described by Carlyle. This line is easy enough, but one could as easily draw another: say, Thomas Gradgrind, Edwin Chadwick, John Stuart Mill. Chadwick, we are told, was 'the most hated man in England', and he worked by methods, and was blamed for 'meddling', in terms that are hardly any distance from Dickens's Gradgrind. Mill is a more difficult instance (although the education of which he felt himself a victim will be related, by the modern reader, to the Gradgrind system). But it seems certain that Dickens has Mill's *Political Economy* (1849) very much in mind in his general indictment of the ideas which built and maintained Coketown. (Mill's reaction, it may be noted, was the expressive 'that creature Dickens'.⁴) It is easy now to realize that Mill was something more than a Gradgrind. But we are missing Dickens's point if we fail to see that in condemning Thomas Gradgrind, the representative figure, we are invited also to condemn the kind of thinking and the methods of enquiry and legislation which in fact promoted a large measure of social and industrial reform. One wonders, for example, what a typical Fabian feels when he is invited to condemn Gradgrind, not as an individual but as a type. This may, indeed, have something to do with the common error of memory about Gradgrind to which I have referred. Public commissions, Blue Books, Parliamentary legislation—all these, in the world of *Hard Times*—are Gradgrindery.

For Dickens is not setting Reform against Exploitation. He sees what we normally understand by both as two sides of the same coin, Industrialism. His positives do not lie in social improvement, but rather in what he sees as the elements of human nature—personal kindness, sympathy, and forbearance. It is not the model factory against the satanic mill, nor is it the humanitarian experiment against selfish exploitation. It is, rather, individual persons against the System. In so far as it is social at all, it is the Circus against Coketown. The schoolroom contrast of Sissy Jupe and Bitzer is a contrast between the education, practical but often inarticulate, which is gained by living and doing, and the education, highly articulated, which is gained by systemization and abstraction. It is a contrast of which Cobbett would have warmly approved; but in so far as we have all (and to some extent inevitably) been committed to a large measure of the latter, it is worth noting again what a large revaluation Dickens is asking us to make. The instinctive, unintellectual, unorganized life is the ground, here, of genuine feeling, and of all good relationships. The Circus is one of the very few ways in which Dickens could have dramatized this, but it is less the circus that matters than the experience described by Sleary:

> that there ith a love in the world, not all Thelf-interetht after all, but thomething very different . . . it hath a way of ith own of calculating or not calculating, which thomehow or another ith at leatht ath hard to give a name to, ath the wayth of the dogth ith.[5]

It is a characteristic conclusion, in a vitally important tradition which based its values on such grounds. It is the major criticism of Industrialism as a whole way of life, and its grounds in experience have been firm. What is essential is to recognize that Dickens saw no social expression of it, or at least nothing that could be 'given a name to'. The experience is that of individual persons. Almost the whole organization of society, as Dickens judges, is against it. The Circus can express it because it is not part of the industrial organization. The Circus is an end in itself, a pleasurable end, which is instinctive and (in certain respects) anarchic. It is significant that Dickens has thus to go outside the industrial situation to find any expression of his values. This going outside is similar to the Canada in which *Mary Barton* ends, or the legacy of Margaret Hale. But it is also more than these, in so far as it is not only an escape but a positive assertion of a certain kind of experience, the denial of which was the real basis (as Dickens saw it) of the hard times.

It was inevitable, given the kind of criticism that Dickens was making, that his treatment of the industrial working people should have been so unsatisfactory. He recognizes them as objects of pity, and he recognizes the personal devotion in suffering of which they are capable. But the only conclusion he can expect them to draw is Stephen Blackpool's:

Aw a muddle![6]

This is reasonable, but the hopelessness and passive suffering are set against the attempts of the working people to better their conditions. The trade unions are dismissed by a stock Victorian reaction, with the agitator Slackbridge. Stephen Blackpool, like Job Legh, is shown to advantage because he will not join them. The point can be gauged by a comparison with Cobbett, whose criticism of the System is in many ways very similar to that of Dickens, and rests on so many similar valuations, yet who was not similarly deceived, even when the trade unions came as a novelty to him. The point indicates a wider comment on Dickens's whole position.

The scathing analysis of Coketown and all its works, and of the supporting political economy and aggressive utilitarianism, is based on Carlyle. So are the hostile reactions to Parliament and to ordinary ideas of reform. Dickens takes up the hostility, and it serves as a comprehensive vision, to which he gives all his marvellous energy. But his identification with Carlyle is really negative. There are no social alternatives to Bounderby and Gradgrind: not the time-serving aristocrat Harthouse; not the decayed gentlewoman Mrs Sparsit; nowhere, in fact, any active Hero. Many of Dickens's social attitudes cancel each other out, for he will use almost any reaction in order to undermine any normal representative position. *Hard Times*, in tone and structure, is the work of a man who has 'seen through' society, who has found them all out. The only reservation is for the passive and the suffering, for the meek who shall inherit the earth but not Coketown, not industrial society. This primitive feeling, when joined by the aggressive conviction of having found everyone else out, is the retained position of an adolescent. The innocence shames the adult world, but also essentially rejects it. As a whole response, *Hard Times* is more a symptom of the confusion of industrial society than an understanding of it, but it is a symptom that is significant and continuing.

Sybil, or The Two Nations (1845)

Sybil can be read now as the production of a future Conservative Prime Minister, and hence in the narrow sense as a political novel. The elements of political pleading are indeed evident in any reading of it. Their curiosity, their partisanship and their opportunism are matched only by their brilliance of address. The novel would be fascinating if it were only political. The stucco elegance of Disraeli's writing has a consonance with one kind of political argument. What is intolerable in his descriptions of persons and feelings becomes in his political flights a rather likeable panache. The descriptions of industrial squalor are very like those of Dickens on Coketown: brilliant romantic generalizations—the view from the train, from the hustings, from the printed page—yet often moving, like all far-seeing rhetoric. There are similar accounts of the conditions of the agricultural poor which need to be kept in mind against the misleading contrasts of *North and South*. Again, in a quite different manner, there is in *Sybil* the most spirited description of the iniquities of the tommy-shop, and of the practical consequences of the system of truck, to be found anywhere. Disraeli's anger—the generalized anger of an outsider making his way—carries him often beyond his formal text. The hostile descriptions of London political and social life are again generalization, but they have, doubtless, the same rhetorical significance as those of the forays among the poor. Anyone who is prepared to give credit to Disraeli's unsupported authority on any matter of social fact has of course mistaken his man, as he would similarly mistake Dickens. But Disraeli, like Dickens, is a very fine generalizing analyst of cant, and almost as fine a generalizing rhetorician of human suffering. Both functions, it must be emphasized, are reputable.

In terms of ideas, *Sybil* is almost a collector's piece. There is this, for instance, from Coleridge:

But if it have not furnished us with abler administration or a more illustrious senate, the Reform Act may have exercised on the country at large a beneficial influence? Has it? Has it elevated the tone of the public mind? Has it cultured the popular sensibilities to noble and ennobling ends? Has it proposed to the people of England a higher test of national respect and confidence than the debasing qualification universally prevalent in this country since the fatal introduction of the system of Dutch finance? Who will pretend it? If a spirit of rapacious covetousness, desecrating all the humanities of life, has been the besetting sin of England for the last century and a half, since the passing of the Reform Act the altar of Mammon has blazed with triple worship. To acquire, to accumulate, to plunder each other by virtue of philosophic phrases, to propose a Utopia to consist only of WEALTH and TOIL, this has been the breathless business of enfranchised England for the last twelve years, until we are startled from our voracious strife by the wail of intolerable serfage.[7]

It is true that this is political, a part of the grand assault on Whiggery. But the terms of the assault are familiar, as part of a much wider criticism. Or again this, which was to re-appear in our own century with an air of original discovery:

'. . . There is no community in England; there is aggregation, but aggregation under circumstances which make it rather a dis-sociating than a uniting principle. . . . It is a community of purpose that constitutes society . . . without that, men may be drawn into contiguity, but they still continue virtually isolated.'

'And is that their condition in cities?'

'It is their condition everywhere; but in cities that condition is aggravated. A density of population implies a severer struggle for existence, and a consequent repulsion of elements brought into too close contact. In great cities men are brought together by the desire of gain. They are not in a state of cooperation, but of isolation, as to the making of fortunes; and for all the rest they are careless of neighbours. Christianity teaches us to love our neighbour as ourself; modern society acknowledges no neighbour.'[8]

These views of the Chartist Stephen Morley were the common element in a number of varying political positions. They have remained the terms of a basic criticism of Industrialism.

The two nations, of rich and poor, have of course become

famous. The basis of the attempt to make one nation of them is the restoration to leadership of an enlightened aristocracy. For,

'There is a change in them, as in all other things,' . . . said Egremont.

'If there be a change,' said Sybil, 'it is because in some degree the people have learnt their strength.'

'Ah! dismiss from your mind those fallacious fancies,' said Egremont. 'The people are not strong; the people never can be strong. Their attempts at self-vindication will end only in their suffering and confusion.'[9]

It is, of course, the familiar injunction, in Cobbett's words, to 'be quiet', and the familiar assumption of the business of regeneration by others—in this case 'the enlightened aristocracy'. Disraeli shared the common prejudices about the popular movement: his account of the initiation of Dandy Mick into a Trade Union—

'. . . you will execute with zeal and alacrity . . . every task and injunction that the majority of your brethren . . . shall impose upon you, in furtherance of our common welfare, of which they are the sole judges: such as the chastisement of Nobs, the assassination of oppressive and tyrannical masters, or the demolition of all mills, works and shops that shall be deemed by us incorrigible.'[10]

—is characteristically cloak-and-dagger. This must be acknowledged alongside the shrewder assessment:

The people she found was not that pure embodiment of unity of feeling, of interest, and of purpose which she had pictured in her abstractions. The people had enemies among the people: their own passions; which made them often sympathize, often combine, with the privileged.[11]

This shrewdness might well have been also applied to some of Disraeli's other abstractions, but perhaps that was left for later, in the progress of his political career.

The passages quoted are near the climax of that uniting of Egremont, 'the enlightened aristocrat', and Sybil, 'the daughter of the People', which, in the novel, is the symbolic creation of the One Nation. This, again, is the way the heart goes, and it is the novel's most interesting illustration. For

Sybil, of course, is only theoretically 'the daughter of the People'. The actual process of the book is the discovery that she is a dispossessed aristocrat, and the marriage bells ring, not over the achievement of One Nation, but over the uniting of the properties of Marney and Mowbray, one agricultural, the other industrial: a marriage symbolical, indeed, of the political development which was the actual issue. The restored heiress stands, in the general picture, with Margaret Thornton's legacy, with Canada, and with the Horse-Riding. But it is significant of Disraeli's shrewdness that, through the device, he embodied what was to become an actual political event.

Alton Locke, Tailor and Poet (1850)

In part, *Alton Locke* is in the orthodox sense an 'exposure': an informed, angry and sustained account of sweated labour in the 'Cheap and Nasty' clothing trade. Much of it can still be read in these terms, with attention and sympathy. It is fair to note, however, that in respect of this theme the Preface is more effective than the novel, and for the unexpected reason that it is more specific.

The wider intention of the book is rather different. It is really a story of conversion: of the making of a Chartist in the usual sense, and of his remaking in Kingsley's sense. This is the basic movement in a book which is extremely discursive in mood. The earlier chapters are perhaps the most effective: the caricature of the Baptist home; the indignant realism of the apprenticeship in the sweating-rooms; the generalized description of the longing from the 'prison-house of brick and iron' for the beauty apprehended as knowledge and poetry. The beginnings of Alton Locke in political activity are also, in general outline, convincing. With them, however, begins also the major emphasis on argument, on prolonged *discussion* of events, which is evidently Kingsley's motive and energy. Often this discussion is interesting, particularly as we recognize the familiar popularization of Carlyle and of the ideas which Carlyle concentrated. This merges, from the time of the conversion (the curious chapter *Dreamland*), into the Christian Socialist arguments with which Kingsley's name is commonly identified. It is doubtful whether much attention of a different kind, attention, that is, other than to the genealogy of ideas, can be given to all these parts of the book. A very large part of it is like reading old newspapers, or at least old pamphlets. The issues are there, but the terms are arbitrary and the connexions mechanical. The book is not an 'autobiography' but a tract.

We need note here only the conclusion, alike of the story and of the argument. Once again, the motive to Chartism, to a working-class political movement, has been sympathetically set down (it was on this score that Kingsley and others were thought of as 'advanced' or 'dangerous' thinkers). But again the effort is seen finally as a delusion: in effect—'we understand and sympathize with your sufferings which drove you to this, but what you are doing is terribly mistaken':

> 'Ay,' she went on, her figure dilating, and her eyes flashing, like an inspired prophetess, 'that is in the Bible! What would you more than that? That is your charter; the only ground of all charters. You, like all mankind, have had dim inspirations, confused yearnings after your future destiny, and, like all the world from the beginning, you have tried to realise, by self-willed methods of your own, what you can only do by God's inspiration, God's method. . . . Oh! look back, look back, at the history of English Radicalism for the last half-century, and judge by your own deeds, your own words; were you fit for those privileges which you so frantically demanded? Do not answer me, that those who had them were equally unfit; but thank God, if the case be indeed so, that your incapacity was not added to theirs, to make confusion worse confounded. Learn a new lesson. Believe at last that you are in Christ, and become new creatures. With those miserable, awful farce tragedies of April and June, let old things pass away, and all things become new. Believe that your kingdom is not of this world, but of One whose servants must not fight.'[12]

It is not surprising after this that the destiny of the hero is—once again—emigration. Alton Locke dies as he reaches America, but his fellow-Chartist, Crossthwaite, will come back after seven years.

The regeneration of society, according to Kingsley's

Cambridge preface to the book, will meanwhile proceed under the leadership of a truly enlightened aristocracy. It will be a movement towards democracy, but not to that 'tyranny of numbers' of which the dangers have been seen in the United States. For:

> As long, I believe, as the Throne, the House of Lords, and the Press, are what, thank God, they are, so long will each enlargement of the suffrage be a fresh source not of danger, but of safety; for it will bind the masses to the established order of things by that loyalty which springs from content; from the sense of being appreciated, trusted, dealt with not as children, but as men.[13]

Felix Holt (1866)

Felix Holt was not published till 1866, but we can set beside it a passage from a letter of George Eliot's, written to J. Sibree in 1848, just after the French Revolution of that year:

> You and Carlyle . . . are the only two people who feel just as I would have them—who can glory in what is actually great and beautiful without putting forth any cold reservations and incredulities to save their credit for wisdom. I am all the more delighted with your enthusiasm because I didn't expect it. I feared that you lacked revolutionary ardour. But no—you are just as *sans-culottish* and rash as I would have you. . . . I thought we had fallen on such evil days that we were to see no really great movement—that ours was what St Simon calls a purely critical epoch, not at all an organic one; but I begin to be glad of my date. I would consent, however, to have a year clipt off my life for the sake of witnessing such a scene as that of the men of the barricades bowing to the image of Christ, 'who first taught fraternity to men'. One trembles to look into every fresh newspaper lest there should be something to mar the picture. . . . I should have no hope of good from any imitative movement at home. Our working classes are eminently inferior to the mass of the French people. In France the *mind* of the people is highly electrified; they are full of ideas on social subjects; they really desire social *reform*—not merely an acting out of Sancho Panza's favourite proverb, 'Yesterday for you, today for me'. The revolutionary animus extended over the whole nation, and embraced the rural population—not merely, as with us, the artisans of the

towns. Here there is so much larger a proportion of selfish radicalism and unsatisfied brute sensuality (in the agricultural and mining districts especially) than of perception or desire of justice, that a revolutionary movement would be simply destructive, not constructive. Besides, it would be put down. . . . And there is nothing in our Constitution to obstruct the slow progress of *political* reform. This is all we are fit for at present. The social reform which may prepare us for great changes is more and more the object of effort both in Parliament and out of it. But we English are slow crawlers.[14]

The distinctions in this are doubtful, but the tone indicates an intelligence of a different order from the other novelists discussed. We are interested in Mrs Gaskell or Kingsley or Disraeli because of what they testified; with George Eliot there is another interest, because of the quality of the witness.

This quality is evident in *Felix Holt*, which as a novel has a quite different status from those previously discussed. It has also, however, much in common with them. The formal plot turns on the familiar complications of inheritance in property, and Esther, with her inherited breeding showing itself in poor circumstances, has something in common with Sybil. As with Sybil, her title to a great estate is proved, but there the comparison with Disraeli ends. Harold Transome is, like Egremont, a second son; like him, he turns to the reforming side in politics. But George Eliot was incapable of resting on the image of an Egremont, the figurehead of the enlightened gentleman. Harold Transome is a coarser reality, and it is impossible that Esther should marry him. She renounces her claim and marries Felix Holt. It is as if Sybil had renounced the Mowbray estates and married Stephen Morley. I do not make any claim for the superior reality of George Eliot's proceedings. The thing is as contrived, in the service of a particular image of the desirable, as Disraeli's very different dénouement. George Eliot works with a rather finer net, but it is not in such elements of the novel that her real superiority is apparent.

Nor again is there much superiority in her creation of Felix Holt himself. He is shown as a working-man radical, determined to stick to his own class, and to appeal solely to the energies of 'moral force'. He believes in sobriety and education, argues for social rather than merely political reform, and wants to be

> a demagogue of a new sort; an honest one, if possible, who will tell the people they are blind and foolish, and neither flatter them nor fatten on them.[15]

It is not easy, at any time, to say whether a character 'convinces'. We are all apt, in such questions, to impose our own conceptions both of the probable and the desirable. But one can usually see, critically, when a character comes to existence in a number of aspects, forming something like the image of a life; and, alternatively, when a character is fixed at a different and simpler stage: in the case of Felix Holt, at a physical appearance and a set of opinions. Mrs Gaskell could conceive the early John Barton in much these terms, but, because other substance was lacking, she had virtually to dismiss him as a person when the course of action found necessary on other grounds went beyond the limits of her sympathy. Felix Holt, like Alton Locke, is conceived as a more probable hero: that is to say, as one whose general attitude is wholly sympathetic to the author, and who is detached from him only by a relative immaturity. Like Alton Locke, Felix Holt becomes involved in a riot; like him, he is mistaken for a ringleader; like him, he is sentenced to imprisonment. This recurring pattern is not copying, in the vulgar sense. It is rather the common working of an identical fear, which was present also in Mrs Gaskell's revision of John Barton. It is at root the fear of a sympathetic, reformist-minded member of the middle classes at being drawn into any kind of mob violence. John Barton is involved in earnest, and his creator's sympathies are at once withdrawn, to the obvious detriment of the work as a whole. Sympathy is transferred to Jem Wilson, mistakenly accused, and to Margaret's efforts on his behalf, which have a parallel in Esther's impulse to speak at the trial of Felix Holt. But the basic pattern is a dramatization of the fear of being involved in violence: a dramatization made possible by the saving clause of innocence and mistaken motive, and so capable of redemption. What is really interesting is that the conclusion of this kind of dramatization is then taken as proof of the rightness of the author's original reservations. The people are indeed dangerous, in their constant tendency to blind disorder. Anyone sympathizing with them is likely to become involved. Therefore (a most ratifying word) it can be sincerely held that the popular movements actually under way are foolish and inadequate, and that the only wise course is dissociation from them.

Of course, that there is inadequacy in any such movement is obvious, but the discriminations one would expect from a great novelist are certainly not drawn in *Felix Holt*. Once again Cobbett is a touchstone, and his conduct at his own trial after the labourers' revolts of 1830 is a finer demonstration of real maturity than the fictional compromises here examined. Cobbett, like nearly all men who have worked with their hands, hated any kind of violent destruction of useful things. But he had the experience and the strength to enquire further into violence. He believed, moreover, what George Eliot so obviously could not believe, that the common people were something other than a mob, and had instincts and habits something above drunkenness, gullibility and ignorance. He would not have thought Felix Holt an 'honest demagogue' for telling the people that they were 'blind and foolish'. He would have thought him rather a very convenient ally of the opponents of reform. George Eliot's view of the common people is uncomfortably close to that of Carlyle in *Shooting Niagara*: 'blockheadism, gullibility, bribeability, amenability to beer and balderdash'. This was the common first assumption, and was the basis for the distinction (alike in her 1848 comment and in *Felix Holt*) between 'political' and 'social' reform. The former is only 'machinery'; the latter is seen as substance. The distinction is useful, but consider this very typical speech by Felix Holt:

> The way to get rid of folly is to get rid of vain expectations, and of thoughts that don't agree with the nature of things. The men who have had true thoughts about water, and what it will do when it is turned into steam and under all sorts of circumstances, have made themselves a great power in the world: they are turning the wheels of engines that will help to change most things. But no engines

would have done, if there had been false notions about the way water would act. Now, all the schemes about voting, and districts, and annual Parliaments, and the rest, are engines, and the water or steam—the force that is to work them—must come out of human nature—out of men's passions, feelings, and desires. Whether the engines will do good work or bad depends on these feelings.[16]

But the 'engines' mentioned are, after all, particular engines, proposed to do different work from the engines previously employed. It is really mechanical to class all the engines together and to diminish their importance, when in fact their purposes differ. The new proposals are an embodiment of 'passions, feelings, and desires': alternative proposals, supported by alternative feelings, so that a choice can properly be made. The real criticism, one suspects, is of 'thoughts that don't agree with the nature of things', and this 'nature of things' can either be a supposedly permanent 'human nature', or else, as probably, the supposedly immutable 'laws of society'. Among these 'laws', as Felix Holt's argument continues, is the supposition that among every hundred men there will be thirty with 'some soberness, some sense to choose', and seventy, either drunk or 'ignorant or mean or stupid'. With such an assumption it is easy enough to 'prove' that a voting reform would be useless. George Eliot's advice, essentially, is that the working men should first make themselves 'sober and educated', under the leadership of men like Felix Holt, and then reform will do some good. But the distinction between 'political' and 'social' reform is seen at this point at its most arbitrary. The abuses of an unreformed Parliament are even dragged in as an argument against parliamentary reform—it will only be more of the same sort of thing. The winning through political reform of the means of education, of the leisure necessary to take such opportunity, of the conditions of work and accommodation which will diminish poverty and drunkenness: all these and similar aims, which were the purposes for which the 'engines' were proposed, are left out of the argument. Without them, the sober responsible educated working man must, presumably, spring fully armed from his own ('drunken, ignorant, mean and stupid') head.

It has passed too long for a kind of maturity and depth in experience to argue that politics and political attachments are only possible to superficial minds; that any appreciation of the complexity of human nature necessarily involves a wise depreciation of these noisy instruments. The tone—'cold reservations and incredulities to save their credit for wisdom'—is often heard in *Felix Holt*:

Crying abuses—'bloated paupers', 'bloated pluralists', and other corruptions hindering men from being wise and happy—had to be fought against and slain. Such a time is a time of hope. Afterwards, when the corpses of those monsters have been held up to the public wonder and abhorrence, and yet wisdom and happiness do not follow, but rather a more abundant breeding of the foolish and unhappy, comes a time of doubt and despondency. . . . Some dwelt on the abolition of all abuses, and on millennial blessedness generally; others, whose imaginations were less suffused with exhalations of the dawn, insisted chiefly on the ballot-box.[17]

The wise shake of the head draws a complacent answering smile. But what I myself find in such a passage as this, in the style ('suffused with exhalations of the dawn'; 'millennial blessedness generally') as in the feeling ('a more abundant breeding of the foolish and unhappy'), is not the deep and extensive working of a generous mind, but rather the petty cynicism of a mind that has lost, albeit only temporarily, its capacity for human respect.

Felix Holt's opinions are George Eliot's opinions purged of just this element, which is a kind of intellectual fatigue. It is the mood of the 'sixties—of *Shooting Niagara* and *Culture and Anarchy*—holding an incompetent post-mortem on the earlier phases of Radicalism. Felix Holt himself is not so much a character as an impersonation: a rôle in which he again appears in the *Address to Working Men, by Felix Holt*, which George Eliot was persuaded to write by her publisher. Here the dangers of active democracy are more clearly put:

The too absolute predominance of a class whose wants have been of a common sort, who are chiefly struggling to get better and more food, clothing, shelter, and bodily recreation, may lead to hasty measures for the sake of having things more fairly shared which, even if they did not fail . . . would at last debase the life of the nation.[18]

Reform must proceed

> not by any attempt to do away directly with the actually existing
> class distinctions and advantages . . . but by the turning of Class
> Interests into Class Functions. . . . If the claims of the unendowed
> multitude of working men hold within them principles which must
> shape the future, it is not less true that the endowed classes, in their
> inheritance from the past, hold the precious material without which
> no worthy, noble future can be moulded.[19]

George Eliot, in this kind of thinking, is very far from her
best. Her position, behind the façade of Felix Holt, is that
of a Carlyle without the energy, of an Arnold without the
quick practical sense, of an anxiously balancing Mill without
the intellectual persistence. Yet it is clear that, inadequate
as her attempt at a position may be, it proceeds, though not
fruitfully, from that sense of society as a complicated inheritance which is at the root of her finest work. In *Felix Holt*,
this sense is magnificently realized at the level of one set of
personal relationships—that of Mrs Transome, the lawyer
Jermyn and their son Harold Transome. In *Middlemarch*,
with almost equal intensity, this realization is extended to a
whole representative section of provincial society. Always,
at her best, she is unrivalled in English fiction in her creation
and working of the complication and consequence inherent
in all relationships. From such a position in experience she
naturally sees society at a deeper level than its political
abstractions indicate, and she sees her own society, in her
own choice of word, as 'vicious'. Her favourite metaphor for
society is a network: a 'tangled skein'; a 'tangled web'; 'the
long-growing evils of a great nation are a tangled business'.
This, again, is just; it is the ground of her finest achievements. But the metaphor, while having a positive usefulness
in its indication of complexity, has also a negative effect. For
it tends to represent social—and indeed directly personal—
relationships as passive: acted upon rather than acting. 'One
fears', she remarked, 'to pull the wrong thread, in the
tangled scheme of things.' The caution is reasonable, but
the total effect of the image false. For in fact every element
in the complicated system is active: the relationships are
changing, constantly, and any action—even abstention;

certainly the impersonation of Felix Holt—affects, even if only slightly, the tensions, the pressures, the very nature of the complication. It is a mark, not of her deep perception, but of the point at which this fails, that her attitude to society is finally so negative: a negativeness of detail which the width of a phrase like 'deep social reform' cannot disguise. The most important thing about George Eliot is her superb control of particular complexities, but this must not be stated in terms of an interest in 'personal' relationships as opposed to 'social' relationships. She did not believe, as others have tried to do, that these categories are really separate: 'there is no private life which has not been determined by a wider public life', as she remarks near the beginning of *Felix Holt*. Yet it is a fact that when she touches, as she chooses to touch, the lives and the problems of working people, her personal observation and conclusion surrender, virtually without a fight, to the general structure of feeling about these matters which was the common property of her generation, and which she was at once too hesitant to transcend, and too intelligent to raise into any lively embodiment. She fails in the extension which she knows to be necessary, because indeed there seems 'no right thread to pull'. Almost any kind of social action is ruled out, and the most that can be hoped for, with a hero like Felix Holt, is that he will in the widest sense keep his hands reasonably clean. It is indeed the mark of a deadlock in society when so fine an intelligence and so quick a sympathy can conceive no more than this. For patience and caution, without detailed intention, are very easily converted into acquiescence, and there is no right to acquiesce if society is known to be 'vicious'.

These novels, when read together, seem to illustrate clearly enough not only the common criticism of industrialism, which the tradition was establishing, but also the general structure of feeling which was equally determining. Recognition of evil was balanced by fear of becoming involved. Sympathy was transformed, not into action, but into withdrawal. We can all observe the extent to which this structure of feeling has persisted, into both the literature and the social thinking of our own time.

CHAPTER VI

J. H. NEWMAN AND MATTHEW ARNOLD

I N his *Discourse VII, On the Scope and Nature of University Education* (1852), Newman wrote:

It were well if the English, like the Greek language, possessed some definite word to express, simply and generally, intellectual proficiency or perfection, such as 'health', as used with reference to the animal frame, and 'virtue' with reference to our moral nature. I am not able to find such a term;—talent, ability, genius, belong distinctly to the raw material, which is the subject-matter, not to that excellence which is the result, of exercise and training. When we turn, indeed, to the particular kinds of intellectual perfection, words are forthcoming for our purpose, as, for instance, judgement, taste, and skill; yet even these belong, for the most part, to powers or habits bearing upon practice or upon art, and not to any perfect condition of the intellect, considered in itself. Wisdom, again, which is a more comprehensive word than any other, certainly has a direct relation to conduct and to human life. Knowledge, indeed, and Science express purely intellectual ideas, but still not a state or habit of the intellect; for knowledge, in its ordinary sense, is but one of its circumstances, denoting a possession or influence; and science has been appropriated to the subject-matter of the intellect, instead of belonging at present, as it ought to do, to the intellect itself. The consequence is that, on an occasion like this, many words are necessary, in order, first, to bring out and convey what is surely no difficult idea in itself—that of the cultivation of the intellect as an end; next, in order to recommend what surely is no unreasonable object; and lastly, to describe and realize to the mind the particular perfection in which that object consists.[1]

The most surprising fact about this paragraph is that Newman does not meet the want of 'some definite word' with the word 'culture'. The staple of his argument is clearly connected with the ideas of 'cultivated' and 'cultivation' as defined by Coleridge. He is moreover, in his concluding phrases, virtually announcing the task which Arnold was about to

undertake in *Culture and Anarchy*. Elsewhere, he in fact
made the essential connexion with 'culture':

> And so, as regards intellectual culture, I am far from denying
> utility in this large sense as the end of education, when I lay it down,
> that the culture of the intellect is a good in itself and its own end. . . .
> As the body may be sacrificed to some manual or other toil . . . so
> may the intellect be devoted to some specific profession; and I do
> not call *this* the culture of the intellect. Again, as some member or
> organ of the body may be inordinately used and developed, so may
> memory or imagination or the reasoning faculty; and *this* again is
> not intellectual culture. On the other hand, as the body may be
> tended, cherished, and exercised with a simple view to its general
> health, so may the intellect also be generally exercised in order to
> its perfect state; and this *is* its cultivation.[2]

The proposition is in terms of the 'general health' of the
mind, as in Coleridge's distinction between the 'hectic of
disease' of one kind of civilization, and the 'bloom of health'
of a civilization 'grounded in cultivation'. Health is Newman's standard for the body; his standard for the mind is
perfection:

> There is a physical beauty and a moral: there is a beauty of person,
> there is a beauty of our moral being, which is natural virtue; and
> in like manner there is a beauty, there is a perfection, of the intellect.
> There is an ideal perfection in these various subject-matters, towards
> which individual instances are seen to rise, and which are the
> standards for all instances whatever.[3]

This, again, is within the tradition, from Burke to Arnold.
The work of perfection, which Arnold was to name as
Culture, received increasing emphasis in opposition to the
powerful Utilitarian tendency which conceived education as
the training of men to carry out particular tasks in a particular kind of civilization. Coleridge, Newman and others set
a different ideal:

> the harmonious development of those qualities and faculties that
> characterize our humanity.[4]

This part of the preparation for Matthew Arnold's work
is now clear. But, by the time he came to write, there was

also another consideration: the general reaction to the social effects of full industrialism, and in particular to the agitation of the industrial working class. One stock reaction to this agitation is well known in Macaulay's phrase 'we must educate our masters'. Macaulay, characteristically, argued that the 'ignorance' of the 'common people' was a danger to property, and that therefore their education was necessary. Carlyle, on the other hand, had rejected any argument for education based on grounds of social expediency: 'as if . . . the first function (of) a government were not . . . to impart the gift of thinking'.[5] Kingsley, in his Cambridge Preface to *Alton Locke*, recommended the new Working Men's Colleges:

> Without insulting them by patronage, without interfering with their religious opinions, without tampering with their independence in any wise, but simply on the ground of a common humanity, they (*i.e. members of the University of Cambridge*) have been helping to educate these men, belonging for the most part, I presume, to the very class which this book sets forth as most unhappy and most dangerous—the men conscious of unsatisfied and unemployed intellect. And they have their reward in a practical and patent form. Out of these men a volunteer corps is organized, officered partly by themselves, partly by gentlemen of the University: a nucleus of discipline, loyalty, and civilisation for the whole population of Cambridge.[6]

Kingsley's last sentence, his 'practical and patent reward', is something of a revision of his earlier reason: 'simply on the ground of a common humanity'. But however phrased, and however now interpreted, the response itself is evident. We can see it very clearly in an extract from a speech by F. D. Maurice to the Manchester, Ancoats and Salford Working Men's College, in 1859:

> Now while we were thinking about these things, and thinking earnestly about them, there came that awful year 1848, which I shall always look upon as one of the great epochs of history. . . . I do say that when I think how it has affected the mind and the heart of the people of England; yes, of all classes of Englishmen. . . . I hear one intelligent man and another confessing; 'Ten years ago

we thought differently. But all of us have acquired since that time, a new sense of our relation to the working-class.' . . . It did cause us to fear, I own; but it was not fear for our property and position; it was the fear that we were not discharging the responsibilities, greater than those which rank or property imposes, that our education laid upon us. . . . We believed and felt that unless the classes in this country which had received any degree of knowledge more than their fellows were willing to share it with their fellows, to regard it as precious because it bound them to their fellows, England would fall first under an anarchy, and then under a despotism. . . .[7]

This was the reaction, and Maurice added a note on method:

What we wanted, if possible, was to make our teaching a bond of intercourse with the men whom we taught. How that could be, we might never have found out. But the working men themselves had found it out. We heard in 1853 that the people of Sheffield had founded a People's College. The news seemed to us to mark a new era in education. We had belonged to Colleges. They had not merely given us a certain amount of indoctrination in certain subjects; they had not merely prepared us for our particular professions; they had borne witness of a culture which is the highest of all culture. . . .[8]

This aspect of the preparation of Arnold's ground could hardly be more evident: 'culture', quite explicitly, is offered as the alternative to 'anarchy'. The need for popular education might be met in a number of ways; the Utilitarians, in particular, had been early in the field. But Maurice's emphasis is that of Coleridge and Newman. The general opposition to Utilitarianism, and the alarmed reaction to increasing working-class power, here came together in a most significant way.

One other aspect of Arnold's inheritance needs to be briefly examined: the important attitudes which he had learned from his father. Thomas Arnold's liberalism, in the difficult 1830s, was best expressed in his *Englishman's Register* (1831), and in the letters to the *Sheffield Courant* at the beginning and to the *Hertford Reformer* at the end of the decade. These are all worth reading, but only two or three points need be noted here. There is, for instance, this characteristic emphasis:

> When I call the great evil of England the unhappy situation in which the poor and the rich stand towards each other, I wish to show that the evil is in our feelings quite as much or more than in our outward condition.[9]

The period is one of revolution:

> We have been living, as it were, the life of three hundred years in thirty. All things have made a prodigious start together—or rather all that could have done so, and those that could not have, therefore, been left at a long distance behind.[10]

One proper response is Education:

> Education, in the common sense of the word, is required by a people before poverty has made havoc among them; at that critical moment when civilization makes its first burst, and is accompanied by an immense commercial activity.[11]

The other, deeper response is to end the habit of *laissez-faire*:

> . . . one of the falsest maxims which ever pandered to human selfishness under the name of political wisdom. . . . We stand by and let this most unequal race take its own course, forgetting that the very name of society implies that it shall not be a mere race, but that its object is to provide for the common good of all.[12]

This is the new humane liberalism, which can join itself with attitudes drawn from quite other ways of thinking, as here:

> The unwieldy and utterly unorganized mass of our population requires to be thoroughly organized. Where is the part of our body into which minute blood-vessels and nerves of the most acute sensibility are not insinuated, so that every part there is truly alive?[13]

This is the 'organic' stress, as in Coleridge, and it is not surprising that such a liberal as a father had such a liberal as a son.

We can now turn to Matthew Arnold's important definition of Culture, which at last gives the tradition a single watchword and a name. His purpose in *Culture and Anarchy*, he writes, is to recommend culture as the great help out of our present difficulties; culture being a pursuit of our total perfection by means of getting to know, on all the matters which most concern us, the best which has been thought and said in the world; and, through this knowledge, turning a stream of fresh and free thought upon our stock notions and habits, which we now follow staunchly but mechanically, vainly imagining that there is a virtue in following them staunchly which makes up for the mischief of following them mechanically.[14]

The quotation often stops halfway, as if perfection were to be striven for merely by 'getting to know'. As is clear, Arnold intends this only as a first stage, to be followed by the re-examination of 'stock notions and habits'. And further:

Culture, which is the study of perfection, leads us . . . to conceive of true human perfection as a *harmonious* perfection, developing all sides of our humanity; and as a *general* perfection, developing all parts of our society.[15]

Culture, then, is both study and pursuit. It is not merely the development of 'literary culture', but of 'all sides of our humanity'. Nor is it an activity concerning individuals alone, or some part or section of society; it is, and must be, essentially *general*.

Culture and Anarchy is, first, a description of this attitude; second, a re-examination of certain dominant nineteenth-century 'notions and habits'; and third, a consideration of the bearings of this position on the progress of society. In all three elements, Arnold draws heavily on the thinkers who had immediately preceded him: in particular on Coleridge, Burke, Newman and Carlyle. Yet the work is original in tone and in certain of its examples and emphases. It was written, moreover, in a rather different social situation. Its impact was immediate, and it has remained more influential than any other single work in this tradition.

Arnold begins with a point familiar to us from Carlyle and Coleridge:

In our modern world . . . the whole civilization is, to a much greater degree than the civilization of Greece and Rome, mechanical and external, and tends constantly to become more so.[16]

This is the social fact, and the corresponding social attitudes are described, in the usual phrase, as an over-valuation of 'machinery': means valued as ends. The first piece of 'machinery', or stock notion, is Wealth:

> Nine Englishmen out of ten at the present day believe that our greatness and welfare are proved by our being so very rich.[17]

The people who believe this are the 'Philistines'. And:

> Culture says: 'Consider these people then, their way of life, their habits, their manners, the very tones of their voice; look at them attentively; observe the literature they read, the things which give them pleasure, the words which come forth out of their mouths, the thoughts which make the furniture of their minds; would any amount of wealth be worth having with the condition that one was to become just like these people by having it?'[18]

This is a paragraph which one kind of reader will appreciatively underline. He will enjoy the spectacle of 'these people', with their *British Banner* and their tea-meetings, as he enjoyed Josiah Bounderby of Coketown. I am sorry to dissent, but there is something in the tone which reminds us that Arnold not only popularized the tradition, but brought down on it the continuing charges of priggishness and spiritual pride. The damage done by the stock notion of Wealth is its narrowing of human ideals to a single end, which is really only a means. The question, certainly, is what quality of life the wealth is used to sustain. Arnold asked this question, but included in his answer a stock reaction to 'the vulgar' which is surely vulgar in itself. The description of spiritual perfection, in Newman, comes through with a remarkable purity that commands respect even where assent is difficult. In Arnold, on the other hand, the spiritual ideal is too often flanked by a kind of witty and malicious observation better suited to minor fiction. The most bitter opponent of Newman could never have called him a prig, and Burke, at the height of his prejudices, retains an always admirable strength. Arnold has neither this inviolability nor this power.

This may be seen again in his attack on the 'stock notion' of Progress, in *Friendship's Garland*:

J. H. NEWMAN AND MATTHEW ARNOLD

Your middle-class man thinks it is the highest pitch of development and civilization when his letters are carried twelve times a day from Islington to Camberwell, and from Camberwell to Islington, and if railway trains run to-and-fro between them every quarter of an hour. He thinks it is nothing that the trains only carry him from an illiberal, dismal life at Camberwell to an illiberal, dismal life at Islington; and the letters only tell him that such is the life there.[19]

The bearing of the question is again fruitful, but Arnold's demonstration of the point depends, first, on prior assent to the judgement 'illiberal' and 'dismal', and, second, on the inclusion of 'Islington' and 'Camberwell', which are really false particulars, very similar in function to Mr Eliot's 'Camden Town and Golders Green'. One might say that the light penetrates, but that it is hardly accompanied by sweetness. The literary method, rather, is that of a soured romanticism, of which we have had sufficient examples in the stock notions about 'Subtopia' in our own day.

The fact is that in the developed social structure of a fully industrialized society few reactions of any kind could escape an admixture of largely self-regarding feelings of class. The worst harm done by the 'stock notion' of class, a notion receiving constant assent from the material structure of society, was that it offered category feelings about human behaviour, based on a massing and simplifying of actual individuals, as an easy substitute for the difficulties of personal and immediate judgement. Arnold had many useful things to say about class, but it is one of the 'stock notions and habits' whose influence he did not wholly escape.

What Arnold had to say about Industry and Production, as 'stock notions', seems to me admirable. It is of a piece with the ideas of Carlyle, Ruskin, and, in our own day, Tawney. But his best treatment of a stock notion is his discussion of Freedom. It is very much what Burke had said in the early part of the *Reflections*, but it is admirably enriched and extended by Arnold's contact with the high period of Liberalism.

Freedom . . . is a very good horse to ride, but to ride somewhere. You . . . think that you have only to get on the back of your horse

Freedom . . . and to ride away as hard as you can, to be sure of coming to the right destination. If your newspapers can say what they like, you think you are sure of being well-informed.[20]

The text is still apt, and unanswerable. Arnold was an excellent analyst of the deficiencies of the gospel of 'doing as one likes': partly because of his reliance on the traditional idea of man's business as the 'pursuit of perfection'; and partly, in social terms, because he lived through a period in which the freedom of one group of people to do as they liked was being challenged by that much larger group who were being 'done by as others liked'. He saw the consequences, in both spheres: the danger of spiritual anarchy when individual assertion was the only standard; the danger of social anarchy as the rising class exerted its power.

Yet the most influential part of Arnold's work is not his treatment of the 'stock notions', but his effort to give his revaluation a practical bearing in society. It is often said (and his tone, at times, lends unfortunate support) that Arnold recommends a merely selfish personal cultivation: that although he professes concern about the state of society, the improvement of this state must wait on the process of his internal perfection:

> The culture we recommend is, above all, an inward operation. . . .
> Culture . . . places human perfection in an *internal* condition.[21]

But this, if Arnold has been read, can be only a deliberate misunderstanding. For example:

> Perfection, as culture conceives it, is not possible while the individual remains isolated. The individual is required, under pain of being stunted and enfeebled in his own development if he disobeys, to carry others along with him in his march towards perfection, to be continually doing all he can to enlarge and increase the volume of the human stream sweeping thitherward [22]

Or again:

> 'The fewer there are who follow the way to perfection, the harder that way is to find.' So all our fellowmen, in the East of London and elsewhere, we must take along with us in the progress towards perfection, if we ourselves really, as we profess, want to be perfect;

and we must not let the worship of any fetish, any machinery, such as manufactures or population—which are not, like perfection, absolute goods in themselves, though we think them so—create for us such a multitude of miserable, sunken and ignorant human beings, that to carry them all along with us is impossible, and perforce they must for the most part be left by us in their degradation and wretchedness.[23]

The position is quite clear, and it is evidently in line with the basic criticism of Industrialism, and with the traditional reaction to the accumulating evidence of poverty and suffering. Others had argued for a new national education, but none with the authority or effect of Arnold. Those who accuse him of a policy of 'cultivated inaction' forget not only his arguments but his life. As an Inspector of schools, and independently, his effort to establish a system of general and humane education was intense and sustained. There is nothing of the dandy in Arnold's fight against the vicious mechanism of the Revised Code. On a number of similar educational matters of great importance he showed a fine capacity for detailed application of principles that in his theoretical writings are often open to a charge of vagueness. *Culture and Anarchy*, in fact, needs to be read alongside the reports, minutes, evidence to commissions and specifically educational essays which made up so large a part of Arnold's working life.

When we have said this, we may have rescued Arnold from a common and insupportable charge, but we have not finally construed either his significance or his effect. The most interesting point to consider is his recommendation of the State as the agent of general perfection. Here, in part, he is following the ideas, and the language, of Burke. He speaks, characteristically, of

ways which are naturally alluring to the feet of democracy, though in this country they are novel and untried ways. I may call them the ways of Jacobinism. Violent indignation with the past, abstract systems of renovation applied wholesale, a new doctrine drawn up in black and white for elaborating down to the very smallest details a rational society for the future—these are the ways of Jacobinism.[24]

'I may call them the ways of Jacobinism' (they had been called this for three-quarters of a century). In any event, we are now well used to this kind of criticism as typical of the opposition to 'State' power. In Arnold, as in Burke, this is not the conjunction; the argument against 'State' power depends, nearly always, on who is the 'State'. Arnold's position is that of Burke:

> He who gave our nature to be perfected by our virtue willed also the necessary means of its perfection: He willed therefore the State.[25]

Arnold, similarly, imagined the State as the 'centre of light and authority', the organ of the 'best self'. But how, in practical terms, was this centre to be composed? Burke had accepted the existing ruling class as, though imperfect, the natural 'centre of light and authority'. Arnold, though he looked at each class in turn, could find none which seemed to him at all qualified for so high a duty. The aristocracy (Barbarians) were, as a class, useless, because their characteristic virtues were those created by the business of defending the *status quo*. Their very vigour in this defence made them inaccessible to the free play of new ideas, on which 'light and authority' must depend. The middle classes (Philistines) were also useless, because of their attachment to an *external* civilization. Their faith in 'machinery' (Wealth, Industry, Production, Progress) and in individual success denied, respectively, the 'harmonious' and the 'general' pursuit of perfection. As for the working classes (Populace), they either shared with the middle classes the attachment to external civilization, wishing only to become Philistine as quickly as possible; or else they were merely degraded and brutal, the repository of darkness rather than of light.

Others might see all this, and consequently fear the idea of State power, which could only be the embodiment of the interest of one or other of these classes. And if this were indeed true, could the State, in practical terms, be considered as a likely 'centre of light and authority' at all?

> But how to organize this authority, or to what hands to entrust the wielding of it? How to get your *State*, summing up the right reason

of the community, and giving effect to it, as circumstances may require, with vigour? And here I think I see my enemies waiting for me with a hungry joy in their eyes. But I shall elude them.[26]

He saw his enemies waiting indeed; and we too, who are not his enemies, still wait, and are still, in a sense, hungry. One is glad to see Arnold eluding the nineteenth-century pack; or to see him enjoying the thought of doing so, even if the glint has a certain ridiculous effect. The problem, however, remained a most difficult one. The existing social classes, the ordinary candidates for power, were in Arnold's view inadequate for its proper exercise. The political conflict was merely a deadlock of their imperfections. For these reasons a State was needed, as an adequate and transcending organ. The classes were the embodiment of our ordinary selves; to embody our best self we must create a State. But by what means, and through what persons? Arnold's answer depends on what he called the 'remnant'. In each class, he argued, there existed, alongside the characteristic majority, a minority, a number of 'aliens', who were not disabled by the ordinary notions and habits of their class:

> persons who are mainly led, not by their class spirit, but by a general *humane* spirit, by the love of human perfection.[27]

In such persons the 'best self' is active, and they can try, in a number of ways, to awaken the 'best self' that is latent in all men but is obscured by the inadequacies of class ideology and habit. The means of awakening will include education, poetry and criticism. Education will base itself on 'the best that has been thought and written in the world'. By extending and communicating this record of the 'best self' of humanity it will create an adequate general knowledge and a standard of effective thinking. Poetry, as a distinct organ of the 'best self' of men, will set a standard of 'beauty, and of a human nature perfect on all sides'. In this sense, adding to itself a 'religious and devout energy', it can 'work on a broader scale for perfection, and with greater masses of men', and can therefore 'save us', by providing a lasting and actual standard of the 'best self'. Finally, criticism, as in his general writings Arnold exemplified it, is a further part of the same process: a creation, by the free play of intelligence, of 'the authority of the best self'. These ways might be dismissed as impractical, but

> it may truly be averred . . . that at the present juncture the centre of movement is not in the House of Commons. It is in the fermenting mind of the nation; and his is for the next twenty years the real influence who can address himself to this.[28]

Whatever we may think of this as an answer, we can easily recognize in its mood and attitude a position which since Arnold's day has been widely and sincerely held. It is attacked as a slow and timid programme, but those who hold to it are entitled to ask whether any quick and ready alternative for the achievement of Arnold's ends has in fact, in the ninety years since he wrote, manifested itself.

Nevertheless, there is a real ambiguity in the position, and this must be examined. For it is not merely the influence of the best individuals that Arnold is recommending; it is the embodiment of this influence in the creation of a State. On this point, Arnold quotes Wilhelm von Humboldt:

> Humboldt's object in this book (*The Sphere and Duties of Government*) is to show that the operation of government ought to be severely limited to what directly and immediately relates to the security of person and property. Wilhelm von Humboldt, one of the most beautiful souls that have ever existed, used to say that one's business in life was first to perfect oneself by all the means in one's power, and secondly to try and create in the world around one an aristocracy, the most numerous that one possibly could, of talents and characters. He saw, of course, that in the end, everything comes to this—that the individual must act for himself, and must be perfect in himself; and he lived in a country, Germany, where people were disposed to act too little for themselves, and to rely too much on the Government. But even thus, such was his flexibility, so little was he in bondage to a mere abstract maxim, that he saw very well that for his purpose itself, of enabling the individual to stand perfect on his own foundations and to do without the State, the action of the State would for long, long years be necessary. And soon after he wrote his book on *The Sphere and Duties of Government*, Wilhelm von Humboldt became Minister of Education in Prussia; and from

his ministry all the great reforms which give the control of Prussian education to the State . . . take their origin.[29]

The relevance of this to Arnold's immediate purposes in State education is clear and important. He backs it up with a quotation from Renan:

A Liberal believes in liberty, and liberty signifies the non-intervention of the State. *But such an ideal is still a long way off from us, and the very means to remove it to an indefinite distance would be precisely the State's withdrawing its action too soon.*[30]

The point helps in a local argument, but the position in which it leaves the general argument is this: that the State itself must be the principal agent through which the State as a 'centre of authority and light' is to be created. Yet the existing State, loaded with such an agency, is in fact, on Arnold's showing, subject to the deadlock of the existing and inadequate social classes. The aristocracy uses the power and dignity of the State as an instrument of protection of its own privileges. The middle class, reacting against this, seeks only to diminish State power, and to leave perfection to those 'simple natural laws' which somehow arise out of un-regulated individual activity. It scarcely seems likely, if Arnold is right about these classes, that any actual State, expressing the power of one or other of them, or a dead-locked compromise, could undertake the all-important function which he proposes. The State which for Burke was an actuality has become for Arnold an idea.

The position is further complicated by the nature of Arnold's reaction to his third great class, the Populace. The working class was organizing itself. It was, as Arnold put it, 'our playful giant', which was

beginning to assert and put in practice an Englishman's right to do what he likes; his right to march where he likes, meet where he likes, enter where he likes, hoot as he likes, threaten as he likes, smash as he likes. All this, I say, tends to anarchy.[31]

This reaction, as we know, is a typical one, and Arnold's fears run deep:

He comes in immense numbers, and is rather raw and rough. . . .
And thus that profound sense of settled order and security, without

which a society like ours cannot live and grow at all, some-times seems to be beginning to threaten us with taking its departure.[32]

So great indeed is the threat that, for resisting it, even the lovers of culture may prize and employ fire and strength.[33]

With this sort of thing in his mind, Arnold's idea of the State as a 'centre of authority' takes on a new colouring.

For us, who believe in right reason, in the duty and possibility of extricating and elevating our best self, in the progress of humanity towards perfection—for us, the framework of society, that theatre on which this august drama has to unroll itself, is sacred; *and who-ever administers it,* and however we may seek to remove them from their tenure of administration, yet, while they administer, we steadily and with undivided heart support them in repressing anarchy and disorder; because without order there can be no society, and without society there can be no human perfection.[34]

It is here, at so vital a point, that we see Arnold surrendering to a 'stock notion or habit' of his class. The organizing, and at times demonstrating, working class was not, on any showing, seeking to destroy society as such. It was seeking by such methods as were available to it, to change the particular ordering of society which then prevailed. Often, indeed, it sought only the remedy of some particular grievance. For Arnold to confuse the particular, temporary ordering of interests, which was indeed being threatened, with human society as such, is the confusion which else-where he so clearly analysed: the confusion between 'machinery' and 'purpose'. The existing 'framework of society' is always 'machinery'. Arnold, who found it in so many ways so inadequate, should have known that this was so; and restrained his 'right reason' from the talk of 'fire and strength'. He is, indeed, ready for change. He looks forward 'cheerfully and hopefully' to a 'revolution by due course of law'. But can it honestly be said that the working people asked for anything other than this, in the terms of their own experience? Arnold might defend himself from a charge of simple authoritarianism by arguing that he is concerned only to ensure that necessary 'minimum of order' which would allow the civilizing and humanizing process to be sustained. But again, can it now honestly be said that this was threatened, when Arnold was writing? Further, we must remember that Arnold was asking, not for the Liberal 'minimum of order', but, essentially, for the maximum of order: the State to become a real 'centre of authority'. When the emphasis on State power is so great, any confusion between that ideal State which is the agent of perfection, and this actual State which embodies particular powers and interests, becomes dangerous and really disabling.

The case is one which Arnold, detached from his particular position, would readily understand. A prejudice overcomes 'right reason', and a deep emotional fear darkens the light. It is there in his words: *hoot, bawl, threaten, rough, smash*. This is not the language of 'a stream of fresh thought', nor is the process it represents any kind of 'delicacy and flexibility of thinking'. Calm, Arnold rightly argued, was necessary. But now the Hyde Park railings were down, and it was not Arnold's best self which rose at the sight of them. Certainly he feared a general breakdown, into violence and anarchy, but the most remarkable facts about the British working-class movement, since its origin in the Industrial Revolution, are its conscious and deliberate abstention from general violence, and its firm faith in other methods of advance. These characteristics of the British working class have not always been welcome to its more romantic advocates, but they are a real human strength, and a precious inheritance. For it has been, always, a positive attitude: the product not of cowardice and not of apathy, but of moral conviction. I think it had more to offer to the 'pursuit of perfection' than Matthew Arnold, seeing only his magnified image of the Rough, was able to realize.

One final point must be made about Arnold's use of the idea of Culture. Culture is right knowing and right doing; a process and not an absolute. This, indeed, is Arnold's doctrine. But his emphasis in detail is so much on the importance of knowing, and so little on the importance of doing, that Culture at times seems very like the Dissenters' Salvation: a thing to secure first, to which all else will then be added. There is surely a danger of allowing Culture also to become a fetish: 'freedom is a very good horse to ride, but to ride somewhere'. Perfection is a 'becoming', culture is a process, but a part of the effect of Arnold's argument is to create around them a suggestion that they are known absolutes. One of the elements in this effect is his style. In a sentence like this, for example—

> Culture looks beyond machinery, culture hates hatred, culture has one great passion, the passion for sweetness and light.[35]

—it is difficult not to feel the pressure of Saint Paul's description of Charity, and it seems not improbable that there has been a (perhaps unconscious, but in any case invalid) transference of emotion from the old concept to the new. Culture as a substitute for religion is a very doubtful quantity, especially when it is taken, as so often, in its narrowest sense. I agree, from a different standpoint, with Newman's comment on the result:

> Accordingly, virtue being only one kind of beauty, the principle which determines what is virtuous is, not conscience, but *taste*.[36]

The implied relaxation has been lived through, and at its worst it has not been very edifying, at its best not very convincing, to watch.

Moreover, this kind of intonation of 'culture' seems to be largely responsible for the common English hostility to the word, which has in some respects been damaging. I have found no hostile or derisive reference before 1860, but in this immediate context such references are common. J. C. Shairp comments in 1870 on the 'artificiality' of the word.[37] Frederic Harrison refers to 'this same . . . *sauerkraut* or *culture*',[38] in the course of arguing that Arnold makes 'culture' mean whatever suits himself. Now, the challenge of the valuations concentrated in the idea of culture was bound to provoke hostility from defenders of the existing system. With such hostility, one wants no kind of truce. Yet this essential conflict has been blurred by adventitious effects. Almost all the words standing for learning, seriousness and reverence have in fact been compromised, and the struggle against this ought not to be hindered by our own faults of tone and feeling. The attachment to culture which disparages science; the attachment which writes off politics as a narrow and squalid misdirection of energy; the attachment which appears to criticize manners by the priggish intonation of a word: all these, of which Arnold and his successors have at times been guilty, serve to nourish and extend an opposition which is already formidable enough. The idea of culture is too important to be surrendered to this kind of failing.

The difficulty of tone indicates, however, a more general difficulty. Arnold learned from Burke, from Coleridge and from Newman, but he was differently constituted from each of them. Burke rested on an existing society, and on a faith. Coleridge drew nourishment, in a period of transition, from the values known from the old kind of society, and again from a faith. Newman, more certainly than either, based his thinking on a convinced experience of the divine order. Arnold learned from them, but he had learned, also, from the reformers who rejected the old kind of society and from the thinkers who had asserted, against the claims of the divine order, the supremacy of human reason. For Coleridge the idea of Cultivation had at least a vestigial relation to an actual society: the relation is there in the word, with its dependence on the social idea of the cultivated man. For Newman, culture had a reality in experience, as an element of the divine perfection. Arnold grasped at these holds, but he had also commitments elsewhere. And it may of course be argued that, being thus committed, he was nearer the actual truth. Culture was a process, but he could not find the material of that process, either, with any confidence, in the society of his own day, or, fully, in a recognition of an order that transcended human society. The result seems to be that, more and more, and against his formal intention, the process becomes an abstraction. Moreover, while appearing to resemble an absolute, it has in fact no absolute ground. The difficulty can be seen in such a paragraph as this:

> Perfection will never be reached; but to recognize a period of transformation when it comes, and to adapt themselves honestly and rationally to its laws, is perhaps the nearest approach to perfection

of which men and nations are capable. No habits or attachments should prevent their trying to do this; nor indeed, in the long run, can they. Human thought, which made all institutions, inevitably saps them, resting only in that which is absolute and eternal.[39]

The general tone of this is convincing and admirable, but the final reservation—the desperate grasp in the last phrase at a traditional hold—is disabling, once he has conceded so much. Human thought 'makes' and 'saps' *all* institutions, yet must rest, finally, in something 'absolute and eternal': that is to say, by his own argument, in something above and beyond 'institutions'. In Newman, this position might make sense; he could at least have said clearly what the 'absolute and eternal' was. Arnold, however, was caught between two worlds. He had admitted reason as the critic and destroyer of institutions, and so could not rest on the traditliona society which nourished Burke. He had admitted reason— 'human thought'—as the maker of institutions, and thus could not see the progress of civil society as the working of a divine intention. His way of thinking about institutions was in fact relativist, as indeed a reliance on 'the best that has been thought and written in the world' (and on that alone) must always be. Yet at the last moment he not only holds to this, but snatches also towards an absolute: and *both are Culture*. Culture became the final critic of institutions, and the process of replacement and betterment, yet it was also, at root, beyond institutions. This confusion of attachment was to be masked by the emphasis of a word.

Arnold is a great and important figure in nineteenth-century thought. His recognition of 'a period of transformation when it comes' was deep and active, as the strength of his essay on *Equality* clearly shows. Even the final breakdown in his thinking (as I judge it to be) is extremely important, as the mark of a continuing and genuine confusion. We shall, if we are wise, continue to listen to him, and, when the time comes to reply, we can hardly speak better than in his own best spirit. For if we centre our attention on a tradition of thinking rather than on an isolated man, we shall not be disposed to underrate what he did and what he represented, nor to neglect what he urged us, following him, to do. As he himself wrote:

> Culture directs our attention to the natural current there is in human affairs, and its continual working, and will not let us rivet our faith upon any one man and his doings. It makes us see, not only his good side, but also how much in him was of necessity limited and transient. . . .[40]

CHAPTER VII

ART AND SOCIETY

A. W. Pugin, John Ruskin, William Morris

AN essential hypothesis in the development of the idea of culture is that the art of a period is closely and necessarily related to the generally prevalent 'way of life', and further that, in consequence, aesthetic, moral and social judgements are closely interrelated. Such a hypothesis is now so generally accepted, as a matter of intellectual habit, that it is not always easy to remember that it is, essentially, a product of the intellectual history of the nineteenth century. One of the most important forms of the hypothesis is, of course, that of Marx, to which I shall return. But there is another line, of great importance in nineteenth-century England, in which the important names are Pugin, Ruskin and Morris. As an idea, the relation between periods of art and periods of society is to be found earlier, in Europe, in the work of, among others, Vico and Herder and Montesquieu. But the decisive emphasis in England begins in the 1830s, and it is an emphasis which was at once novel and welcome. Sir Kenneth Clark in *The Gothic Revival* is explicit about the novelty:

> Standard writers of art criticism—Aristotle, Longinus, and Horace —all described art as something imposed, so to speak, from without. The idea of style as something organically connected with society, something which springs inevitably from a way of life, does not occur, as far as I know, in the Eighteenth Century.[1]

And that the new emphasis was welcome, a development which other currents of thinking had prepared, may be judged from the extraordinary influence which first Pugin, and later Ruskin, almost immediately exerted. If we remember the direction of parts of the Romantic theory of art, and the examination, in Coleridge and Carlyle, of the relations between 'culture' and 'civilization', we shall see that, in fact, the ground had been very well prepared.

'The history of architecture is the history of the world,'

Pugin wrote, in his *Apology for the Present Revival of Christian Architecture in England* (1843). 'Different nations have given birth to so many various styles of Architecture, each suited to their climate, customs, and religion,' he had written earlier, in 1835, in *Contrasts: or a Parallel between the Noble Edifices of the Middle Ages, and Corresponding Buildings of the Present Day, shewing the Present Decay of Taste*. Pugin was writing, of course, with evident polemical and practical intent; his concern, as another title shows, was to define the *True Principles of Pointed or Christian Architecture* (1841), so that 'the present degraded state of ecclesiastical buildings' might be remedied. In his advocacy of the Gothic style he had, of course, been widely preceded. His father, A. C. Pugin, had edited two volumes of *Specimens of Gothic Architecture*, and Shaw, Savage and especially James Wyatt had, among other architects, tried to build in this way. The new element in the younger Pugin was his insistence that revival of the style must depend on revival of the feelings from which it originally sprang: the architectural revival must be part of a general religious, and truly Catholic, revival. This controlling principle is evident in his remark in the Preface to the second edition of *Contrasts*: '*revivals of ancient architecture*, although erected *in*, are not buildings *of*, the nineteenth century'. Such a judgement serves to distinguish Pugin from the Gothic Revivalists who had preceded him. He was not offering Gothic as one of a number of possible styles from which the competent architect might choose, but rather as the embodiment of 'true Christian feeling', which, understood in this way, might be helped to revive. It is very curious, of course, to find this principle of the necessary relation between art and its period being enunciated in the context of a revivalist tract. This paradox was to have its own effect on the subsequent history of 'Gothic' building. Yet the dominant mediaevalism, here as elsewhere in nineteenth-century thought, had by-products more important than its formal advocacy. The most important element in social thinking which developed from the work of Pugin was the use of the art of a period to judge the quality of the society that was producing it. To this, Pugin himself made a notable contribution.

In the text of the *Contrasts*, he writes, significantly:

> The erection of churches, like all that was produced by zeal or art in ancient days, has dwindled down into a mere trade. . . . They are erected by men who ponder between a mortgage, a railroad, or a chapel, as the best investment of their money, and who, when they have resolved on relying on the persuasive eloquence of a cushion-thumping, popular preacher, erect four walls, with apertures for windows, cram the same full of seats, which they readily let; and so greedy after pelf are these chapel-raisers, that they form dry and spacious vaults underneath, which are soon occupied, at a good rent, by some wine and brandy merchant.[2]

This kind of extension, from an architectural to a social judgement, is brilliantly continued in the actual contrasts, the paired engravings. A contrast of altars is immediately followed by the *Contrasted Residences for the Poor*: the one a Benthamite Panopticon, with its attendant Master, armed with whip and leg-irons, its diet-sheet of bread, gruel and potatoes, and its pauper dead being carried away for dissection; the other a monastery, in a natural relationship with its surrounding countryside, with its kindly master, its well-clothed poor, its religious burials, and its diet-sheet of beef, mutton, bacon, ale and cheese. The 'past and present' theme occurs again, in social terms, in the contrasted public conduits, of which the modern version, surmounted by a lamp-post, is set in front of the police-station: the pump is locked, and a child who wants to drink is being warned off by a constable carrying a truncheon. The widest contrast, however, is between a 'Catholic town in 1440' and 'The Same Town in 1840'. It is not only that several of the mediaeval churches have been spoiled, architecturally, and have been interspersed with bare dissenting chapels. It is also that the abbey is ruined, and is now bordered by an ironworks; that the churchyard of St Michael's on the Hill is now occupied by a 'New Parsonage House and Pleasure Grounds'; and that in addition to such new institutions as a 'Town Hall and Concert Room' and a 'Socialist Hall of Science' there are, dominating the foreground, the New Jail (again a panopticon), the Gas Works and the Lunatic Asylum. From criticizing a change of architecture, Pugin has arrived at criticizing a civilization; and he does so in terms that became familiar enough during the remaining part of the century. The relations with Carlyle, Ruskin and Morris, and with figures in our own century, are clear and unmistakable.

Both Ruskin and Morris were, in fact, unkind in their references to Pugin; but this is mainly due to their difference from him, and from each other, in matters of belief. Ruskin, for example, wanted to capture Gothic for Protestantism, and was therefore bound to oppose Pugin; whereas for Morris, Pugin's prejudice against anything to do with the working-class movement was sufficiently distasteful.

Ruskin, more than any other nineteenth-century figure, is now very difficult to approach. One has indeed to cut one's way back to him through a mass of irrelevant material and reactions. The successors of Lytton Strachey have applied to him, as to Carlyle, an almost wholly irresponsible biographical attention; while his own more interesting writings are comparatively little read. It is worth turning back to the comment of a contemporary reader, which will indicate the more general problem:

> I don't know whether you look out for Ruskin's books whenever they appear. His little book on the *Political Economy of Art* contains some magnificent passages, mixed up with stupendous specimens of arrogant absurdity on some economical points. But I venerate him as one of the great teachers of the day. The grand doctrines of truth and sincerity in art, and the nobleness and solemnity of our human life, which he teaches with the inspiration of a Hebrew prophet, must be stirring up young minds in a promising way.[3]

The writer is George Eliot, in a letter to Miss Sara Hennell. If one takes her comment point by point, and sets it beside the conventional modern reaction, the difficulty of a return to Ruskin becomes sufficiently apparent. We should, of course, be far less sure than she was of his 'arrogant absurdity on some economical points'. It is true that Ruskin has now no sort of authority as an economist, but his approach to social and economic problems is very much nearer our own than is the normal approach of his contemporaries. With George Eliot's reservation discounted, however, we should begin a different kind of amendment. 'The grand doctrines of truth and sincerity in art', if indeed such a formulation meant anything to us at all, would be merely a cue for our rejection of Ruskin's aesthetics. 'The nobleness and solemnity of our human life', when we had pondered the phrase, would seem a very general thing to begin teaching upon. 'The inspiration of a Hebrew prophet', and the 'magnificent passages', indicate only why Ruskin is now reputed so difficult to read. And the Ruskin Societies are dead, the books with their extraordinary titles neglected, while we occupy ourselves with a discussion of his sexual life more sterile than any nullity. Yet, without question, Ruskin must still be read if the tradition is to be understood. It does not seem to me (as it does to Dr Leavis) 'fairly easy to say what his place and significance are'. The reading has to be done, and in relation to the tradition—otherwise we shall fall into the other error, of Mr Graham Hough, in assuming that 'the new ideas about the arts and their relations to religion and the social order all (seem) to originate somewhere in the dense jungle of Ruskin's works'. Ruskin is best understood, and necessarily read, as a major contributor to the development of our complex ideas of Culture.

Ruskin was an art critic before he was a social critic, but his work must now be seen as a whole. The worst biographies have put into circulation a number of discreditable motives for his 'transfer of interest' from art to society. It has been suggested that his social criticism

> was a passing-on of the indictment of Effie, a suit for nullity proclaimed against England.[4]

Mr Wilenski, who can see the crudity of this, implies that the social criticism was the result of Ruskin's failure to capture something called the 'Art Dictatorship' in the fifties. But in fact the nature of Ruskin's thinking, and of the tradition as a whole, made the inclusive examination of both art and society a quite natural thing. There is, also, sufficient evidence of Ruskin's direct reaction to the evils of industrialism; and it is perhaps we, not Ruskin, who are on questionable ground when we suppose that social criticism requires some special (usually disreputable) explanation. It remains true, however, that Ruskin's social criticism would not have taken the same form if it had not arisen, as it did inevitably, from his kind of thinking about the purposes of art. The central nature of Ruskin's concern may be seen in one of his early definitions of Beauty:

> By the term Beauty . . . properly are signified two things. First, that external quality of bodies . . . which, whether it occur in a stone, flower, beast, or in man, is absolutely identical; which . . . may be shown to be in some sort typical of the Divine attributes, and which therefore I . . . call Typical Beauty: and secondarily, the appearance of felicitous fulfilment of function in living things, more especially of the joyful and right exertion of perfect life in man; and this kind of beauty I . . . call Vital Beauty.[5]

Here, indeed, is the basis of his whole work. In his criticism of art, his standard was always this 'Typical Beauty', the absolute evidence, in works of art, of the 'universal grand design'. In his social criticism, his concern was with the 'felicitous fulfilment of function in living things', and with the conditions of the 'joyful and right exertion of perfect life in man'. The absolute standard of perfection in works of art; the conditions of perfection in man: these are the common bases of the tradition. Both sides of Ruskin's work are comprised in an allegiance to the same single term, Beauty; and the idea of Beauty (which in his writings is virtually interchangeable with Truth) rests fundamentally on belief in a universal, divinely appointed order. The art criticism and the social criticism, that is to say, are inherently and essentially related, not because one follows from the other, but because both are *applications*, in particular directions, of a fundamental conviction.

The purpose of art, according to Ruskin, is to reveal aspects of the universal 'Beauty' or 'Truth'. The artist is one who, in Carlyle's words, 'reads the open secret of the universe'. Art is not 'imitation', in the sense of illusionist representation, or an adherence to the rules of models; but Art *is* 'imitation', in the older sense of an embodiment of aspects of the universal, 'ideal' truth. These essential doctrines were ready to Ruskin's hand, from Romantic theory, and there was the additional emphasis, seen in Pugin and the ideas of *The Ecclesiologist* and the Camden Society, on the necessary goodness (moral goodness) of the artist, charged with this high function of revelation. Any corruption of the artist's nature would blur or distort his capacity for realizing and communicating the ideal, essential beauty. But, Ruskin added (and here again he is influenced by the Pugin relation between the quality of a society and the quality of its art), it is impossible, finally, for the artist to be good if his society is corrupt. Ruskin's constant definition of this theme is now unfashionable, but is still significant.

> The art of any country *is the exponent of its social and political virtues*. The art, or general productive and formative energy, of any country, is an exact exponent of its ethical life. You can have noble art only from noble persons, associated under laws fitted to their time and circumstances.[6]

The question of the 'goodness' of the artist is, however, at times ambiguous. At times, he must be good in order to reveal essential Beauty; at other times he is good *because* he reveals essential Beauty—other criteria of goodness are irrelevant. The latter will be recognized as characteristic of what was later called 'aestheticism', a body of feeling from which Ruskin is not always distinct. Consider, for example:

> As the great painter is not allowed to be indignant or exclusive, it is not possible for him to nourish his (so-called) spiritual desires, as it is to an ordinarily virtuous person. Your ordinarily good man absolutely avoids, either for fear of getting harm, or because he has no pleasure in such places or people, all scenes that foster vice, and all companies that delight in it. . . . But you can't learn to paint of blackbirds, nor by singing hymns. You must be in the wildness of the midnight masque—in the misery of the dark street at dawn . . . —on the moor with the wanderer or the robber. . . . Does a man die at your feet, your business is not to help him, but to note the colour of his lips; does a woman embrace her destruction before you, your business is not to save her, but to watch how she bends her arms.[7]

So extreme a position, of a subsequently familiar kind, is not, however, Ruskin's normal conclusion. The aberration, here as in the more general movement, sprang from the implications of the claim of the artist as an instrument of revelation, in conflict with a corrupt society: one in which morality, normally, was little more than negative. Ruskin, characteristically, insisted on the need for positive spiritual goodness in artists, and it is only occasionally that he is betrayed into that substitution of art for life which is, perhaps, always latent in a conception of the artist as one who reveals a more than ordinary reality. Certainly, as a rule, he did not grant exemption to artists from common ethical considerations. He insisted, rather, on the contrary: on the artist's rôle as an agent of general perfection, and on the dependence of this on his positive personal goodness.

So moral an emphasis became unfashionable, but Ruskin, although he described the greatest art as that which was 'capable of arousing the greatest number of the greatest ideas', did not in fact separate the 'great ideas' from the actual business of painting:

> It is well when we have strong moral or poetical feeling manifested in painting, to mark this as the best part of the work; but it is not well to consider as a thing of small account the painter's language in which that feeling is conveyed; for if that language be not good and lovely, the man indeed may be a just moralist or a great poet, but he is not a *painter*, and it was wrong of him to paint. . . . If the man be a painter indeed, and have the gift of colours and lines, what is in him will come from his hand freely and faithfully; and the language itself is so difficult and so vast, that the mere possession of it argues that the man is great, and that his works are worth reading. . . . Neither have I ever seen a good expressional work without high artistical merit; and that this is ever denied is only owing to the narrow view which men are apt to take both of expression and of art; a narrowness consequent on their own especial practice and habits of thought.[8]

Thus a man is not a good artist merely because he has good ideas, but, rather, the artist's apprehension of good ideas is an intrinsic element of his artist's skill. The quality of seeing, the special quality of apprehension of essential form: these are the particular faculties through which the artist reveals the essential truth of things. His goodness, as artist, depends on these special qualities; but then, to communicate, he depends on the existence of these same qualities, in some degree, in others; he depends, that is to say, on their active presence in society. Here is a main line to Ruskin's radical criticisms of nineteenth-century society: for he finds such qualities generally lacking, prevented from emergence by an imposed mechanical habit of apprehension. In these circumstances, a great national art was impossible.

Once again, a particular kind of experience, here most powerfully identified with the arts, is being used as a standard of the health of a civilization. In a civilization in which such kinds of experience are being constantly overlaid by the attitudes of industrialism, Ruskin argues not only that a national art is impossible, but that the civilization itself is therefore bad. The key words of the opposition of kinds of experience are, once again, *mechanical* and *organic*. For what the artist perceives is 'organic', not 'external', form. The universal life which he reveals is that organic life, Ruskin's 'Typical Beauty', which is common throughout the universe, and is in fact the form of God. The artist sees this typical beauty as a whole process: art is not merely the product of an 'aesthetic' faculty, but an operation of the whole being. The artist's goodness is also his 'wholeness', and the goodness of a society lies in its creation of the conditions for 'wholeness of being'. The decisive stage in Ruskin's formulation of this position was in the work preparatory to his *Stones of Venice*. He was judging artists by their degree of 'wholeness', and, when he found variations of degree, he sought to explain them by corresponding variations in the 'wholeness' of man's life in society:

> so forcing me into the study of the history of Venice herself; and through that into what else I have traced or told of the laws of national strength and virtue.[9]

The transition to social criticism is then quite natural, within the forms of Ruskin's thinking. It is best understood, as I have indicated, in the context of a *general* transition between thinking about art and thinking about society: the transition which is marked, in all its complexity of reference, by the changes in the meanings of *culture*. The 'organic society', the 'whole way of life', and similar phrases, are certainly open to charges of obscurity, but they are not in any case likely to be understood except by reference to conceptions of experience, largely drawn from the practice and study of art, which are their basis and substance. We have seen how the idea of 'wholeness', as a distinguishing quality of the mind of the artist, led Ruskin into a criticism of society by the same criterion, which was in fact to be most influential. We must now see how his conception of Beauty directed his continuing social thinking. The artist's standard was 'Typical' Beauty, but, related to this, and extending beyond the sphere of art, was the other category, 'Vital Beauty':

> the felicitous fulfilment of function in living things, more especially of the joyful and right exertion of perfect life in man.[10]

This, throughout Ruskin's work, was to be the standard by which a society must be judged: whether in its essential order it created the conditions for such a fulfilment. The relation of such a standard to the ideas of Burke, Coleridge, Carlyle and Arnold is evident: the central word of all these ideas, in their reference to society, is the *perfection* of man. In Ruskin, it will be noted, it is the *exertion*, rather than the *discovery*, of 'perfect life in man'; and it is 'felicitous fulfilment of *function*'—the word *function* carrying an inescapable reference to the idea of design. It is here, as in all generally conservative criticism of *laissez-faire* society, that the greatest difficulty shows itself. If Ruskin's criticisms of the nineteenth-century economy are examined piecemeal, he may at times be seen as a socialist forerunner—as indeed he has been often described. It is perhaps true that the ideas of an 'organic' society are an essential preparation for socialist theory, and for the more general attention to a 'whole way of life', in opposition to theories which consistently reduce social to individual questions, and which support legislation of an individualist as opposed to a collectivist kind. But the theories can hardly be abstracted from actual social situations, and the 'organic' theory has in fact been used in support of very different, and even opposing, causes. The detail of much of Ruskin's criticism of a *laissez-faire* society was in fact perfectly acceptable to socialists; but the ideas of *design* and *function*, as he expressed them, supported not a socialist idea of society but rather an authoritarian idea, which included a very emphatic hierarchy of classes. One who learned much from him, J. A. Hobson, put this point precisely:

> This organic conception everywhere illuminates his theory and his practical constructive policy: it gives order to his conception of the different industrial classes and to the relations of individual members of each class: it releases him from the mechanical atomic notion of equality, and compels him to develop an orderly system of interdependence sustained by authority and obedience.[11]

In this respect Ruskin is very far from socialism, as, for similar reasons, was Carlyle. It is, however, perhaps one of the most important facts about English social thinking in the nineteenth century that there grew up, in opposition to a *laissez-faire* society, this organic conception, stressing interrelation and interdependence. This conception was at one point the basis of an attack on the conditions of men in 'industrial production', the 'cash-nexus' their only active relation, and on the claims of middle-class political democracy. Meanwhile, at another point it was the basis of an attack on industrial capitalism, and on the limitations of triumphant middle-class liberalism. One kind of conservative thinker, and one kind of socialist thinker, seemed thus to use the same terms, not only for criticizing a *laissez-faire* society, but also for expressing the idea of a superior society. This situation has persisted, in that 'organic' is now a central term both in this kind of conservative thinking and in Marxist thinking. The common enemy (or, if it is preferred, the common defender of the true faith) is Liberalism.

Burke was perhaps the last serious thinker who could find the 'organic' in an existing society. As the new industrial society established itself, critics like Carlyle and Ruskin could find the 'organic' image only in a backward look: this is the basis of their 'mediaevalism', and of that of others. It was not, in this tradition, until Morris that this image acquired a distinctly future reference—the image of socialism. Even in Morris, as we shall see, the backward reference is still important and active. Ruskin, like Carlyle, was one of the destroyers of Liberalism: this may now be seen as his merit. It is for his destructive social criticism that he is important.

The basic indictment is in the chapter *On the Nature of Gothic*:

The great cry that rises from all our manufacturing cities, louder than their furnace blast, is all in very deed for this—that we manufacture everything there except men; we blanch cotton, and strengthen steel, and refine sugar, and shape pottery; but to brighten, to strengthen, to refine or to form a single living spirit, never enters into our estimate of advantages. And all the evil to which that cry is urging our myriads can be met only in one way: not by teaching or preaching, for to teach them is but to show them their misery, and to preach to them, if we do nothing more than preach, is to mock at it. It can be met only by a right understanding on the part of all classes, of what kinds of labour are good for men, raising them, and making them happy.[12]

'A right understanding of what kinds of labour': this is the fundamental emphasis. Not labour for profit, or for production, or for the smooth functioning of the existing order; but the 'right kind of labour'—'the felicitous fulfilment of function in living things'. A society is to be governed by no other purposes than what is 'good for men, raising them, and making them happy'—'the joyful and right exertion of perfect life in man'. Immediately, as part of the same argument, Ruskin introduces his criterion of 'wholeness':

We have much studied and much perfected, of late, the great civilized invention of the division of labour; only we have given it a false name. It is not, truly speaking, the labour that is divided; but the men:—Divided into mere segments of men—broken into small fragments and crumbs of life. . . . You are put to stern choice in this matter. You must either make a tool of the creature, or a man of him. You cannot make both. . . . It is verily this degradation of the operative into a machine, which, more than any other evil of the times, is leading the mass of the nations everywhere into vain, incoherent, destructive struggling for a freedom of which they cannot explain the nature to themselves. Their universal outcry against wealth, and against nobility, is not forced from them either by the pressure of famine, or by the sting of mortified pride. These do much, and have done much, in all ages; but the foundations of society were never yet shaken as they are at this day. It is not that men are ill fed, but that they have no pleasure in the work by which they make their bread, and therefore look to wealth as the only means of pleasure. It is not that men are pained by the scorn of the upper classes, but they cannot endure their own; for they feel that the kind of labour to which they are condemned is verily a degrading one, and makes them less than men.[13]

This emphasis on the 'kind of labour' created by an industrial system was to be widely adopted. It is the basis of Ruskin's social values: the contrast between the 'kind of labour' which the system made necessary, and the 'right kind of labour'. The contrast is supported by his important analysis of Wealth. Wealth, he argues, is that which 'avails for life'. It is, as everyone agrees, the possession of 'goods', but 'goods' cannot be a neutral word; it involves, necessarily, a positive valuation. Wealth is not automatically equivalent with possessions and production, for of these some part are Wealth, and some part (in the useful word that Ruskin coined) Illth. Wealth is 'the possession of useful things, which we can use'. And 'usefulness' is determined by 'Intrinsic Value', that is to say the extent to which it 'avails for life'. Intrinsic value is

independent of opinion, and of quantity. Think what you will of it, gain how much you may of it, the value of the thing itself is neither greater nor less. For ever it avails, or avails not; no estimate can raise, no disdain repress, the power which it holds from the Maker of things and of men.[14]

Value is intrinsic because it is a part of the 'universal grand design'. It must not, in this sense, be confused with 'exchange value', which is only the price its possessor will take for some labour or commodity. Intrinsic value is not determined by this, which is a temporary and often defective estimate. Value rests properly only in the fitness of such labour or commodity as a means to 'the joyful and right exertion of perfect life in man'.

This position was necessarily a fundamental challenge to the nineteenth-century system of production, and to the 'laws of political economy' which supported it. Value, wealth, labour were taken out of the jurisdiction of the law of supply and demand, and related to a wholly different social judgement. In asserting this Ruskin was also, necessarily, asserting the idea of a social *order*. At the root of all his thinking is his idea of 'function'—the fulfilment of each man's part in the general design. Such a fulfilment was only possible if society was regulated in terms of the general design: a society must regulate itself by attention to 'intrinsic values' primarily, and anything which prevented this must be swept away. But a system of production geared only to the laws of supply and demand made regulation impossible, for it reduced men to available labour and thus made impossible any 'whole fulfilment' of their ultimate function as human beings. There could be only one right economy: that which led men to 'the joyful and right exertion of perfect life'. Political economy was

neither an art nor a science; but a system of conduct and legislature, founded on the sciences, directed by the arts, and impossible, except under certain conditions of moral culture.[15]

To these 'conditions of moral culture', and to an economic order morally determined, the principal obstacle was an economic system based on competition:

Government and Co-operation are . . . the Laws of Life. Anarchy and Competition the Laws of Death.[16]

Thus, the contrast between culture and anarchy was again made, but now in terms that directly challenged the basic principles of nineteenth-century industrial economy. Not only was the supply of real 'wealth' impossible under such conditions: production, at hazard, being both wealth and illth. But also the effects of competition extended to consumption. Wealth was 'the possession of useful articles *which we can use*'.[17] So that even if the existing system always produced useful articles, the kind of society which it also produced made just distribution and wise consumption difficult or impossible. And since 'intrinsic value' depended not only on the value of the thing in itself, but, by its relation to 'function' in the general design, on its right and valuable *use*, the question of the wealth of a society could not be settled by attention to production only, but necessarily involved the whole life of a society. A society had to be judged in terms of all its making and using, and in terms of all the human activities and relationships which the methods of manufacture and consumption brought into existence.

A good example of Ruskin's assertion of this principle is contained in a speech made at Bradford:

> You must remember always that your business, as manufacturers, is to form the market, as much as to supply it. If, in short-sighted and reckless eagerness for wealth, you catch at every humour of the populace as it shapes itself into momentary demand—if, in jealous rivalry with neighbouring States, or with other producers, you try to attract attention by singularities, novelties, and gaudinesses, to make every design an advertisement, and pilfer every idea of a successful neighbour's, that you may insidiously imitate it, or pompously eclipse—no good design will ever be possible to you, or perceived by you. You may, by accident, snatch the market; or, by energy, command it; you may obtain the confidence of the public, and cause the ruin of opponent houses; or you may, with equal justice of fortune, be ruined by them. But whatever happens to you, this, at least, is certain, that the whole of your life will have been spent in corrupting public taste and encouraging public extravagance. Every preference you have won by gaudiness must have been based on the purchaser's vanity; every demand you have created by novelty has fostered in the consumer a habit of discontent; and when you retire into inactive life, you may, as a subject of consolation for your declining years, reflect that precisely according to the extent of your past operations, your life has been successful in retarding the arts, tarnishing the virtues, and confusing the manners of your country.[18]

This is Ruskin at his best, and the passage, for all the calculation of its rhetoric, comes through to our own century and our own social situation with all the penetration of genius. What is interesting also is that Ruskin is here discussing *design*—'industrial design' as we should now call it. The argument is a practical example of his refusal to treat aesthetic questions in isolation: good design in industry, he argued, depended on the right organization of industry, and this in turn, through labour and consumption, on the right organization of society. He made the point in a negative way, in another speech at Bradford, where he had been invited to lecture in the Town Hall on the best style of building for a new Exchange:

> I do not care about this Exchange, because you don't. . . . You think you may as well have the right thing for your money. You know there are a great many odd styles of architecture about; you don't want to do anything ridiculous; you hear of me, among others, as a respectable architectural man-milliner; and you send for me, that I may tell you the leading fashion; and what is, in our shops, for the moment, the newest and sweetest thing in pinnacles.[19]

But architecture was the expression of a whole way of life, and the only appropriate style for their Exchange would be one

> built to your great Goddess of 'Getting-on'. . . . I can only at present suggest decorating its frieze with pendant purses; and making its pillars broad at the base, for the sticking of bills.[20]

The tone of this sufficiently indicates the nature of Ruskin's attack on nineteenth-century society. There is something of Pugin in it, and something of Arnold; but, more certainly than either of these, Ruskin pressed home his criticism to the actual economic system which seemed to him to be at the root of the matter. Arnold's is very much more the flexible intelligence, but he falls notably short of Ruskin in terms of penetration. The difference may be seen, perhaps, in the fact that when the essays composing *Unto this Last* were published in the *Cornhill*, the editor discontinued them because of violent protest and indignation; whereas *Culture and Anarchy*, when started through the same medium, was at least tolerated. Ruskin, in the opinion of his contemporaries, was not only 'stupendously and arrogantly absurd . . . on some economical points'; he was writing in a deliberate attempt to alter an economic system. Arnold on the other hand, where he was opposed, was blamed as a prig; the 'bookish and pedantic' dismissal was easily available, and the criticism did not hurt in the same way. Yet both Arnold and Ruskin are, in the end, victims of abstraction in their social criticism: Arnold, because he shirked extending his criticism of ideas to criticism of the social and economic system from which they proceeded; Ruskin, as becomes apparent in his proposals for reform, because he was committed to an idea of 'inherent design' as a model for society —a commitment which led him into a familiar type of general replanning of society on paper, without close attention to existing forces and institutions. His criticism is always close, because he saw industrialism and hated it. His proposals for reform, on the other hand, are abstract and dull.

The basic idea of 'organic form' produced, in Ruskin's thinking about an ideal society, the familiar notion of a paternal State. He wished to see a rigid class-structure corresponding to his ideas of 'function'. It was the business of government, he argued, to produce, accumulate, and distribute real wealth, and to regulate and control its consumption. Government was to be guided in this by the principles of intrinsic value which became apparent in any right reading of the universal design. Democracy must be rejected: for its conception of the equality of men was not only untrue; it was also a disabling denial of order and 'function'. The ruling class must be the existing aristocracy, properly trained in its function:

> The office of the upper classes . . . as a body, is to keep order among their inferiors, and raise them always to the nearest level with themselves of which those inferiors are capable.[21]

This of course is Carlyle again, but it is interesting to notice also that Ruskin's definition of the three functional orders of aristocracy corresponds exactly with that of Coleridge: first estate, landowners; second estate, merchants and manufacturers; third estate, 'scholars and artists' (Coleridge's 'clerisy'). These three groups, working together, would ensure order, initiate 'honest production and just distribution', and, by the training of taste, develop 'wise consumption'. All would be educated by the State, and receive salaries from it, for the proper performance of these functions. Below this ruling class, the basic form of society would be the 'guild', with a variety of grades for each kind of work. The guilds would take over the functions of the existing capitalist employer, and would regulate conditions of work and quality of product. Finally, at the base of this edifice would be a class whose business was the 'necessarily inferior labour'. This class would include criminals, men on probation, and a certain number of 'volunteers' from the aristocracy. The Commonwealth thus established would ensure 'felicitous fulfilment of function', and the 'joyful and right exertion of perfect life in man'! Moreover, it would rest

upon a foundation of eternal law, which nothing can alter nor overthrow.[22]

Ruskin's scheme has its relations with many earlier and later conceptions of society. But the problem, when it had been drawn up, was what to do about getting it implemented. There was no force to which Ruskin could appeal, and increasingly, as he got older, he narrowed his range to that of local, small-scale experiment. The Guild of Saint George was established, with himself as Master; Carlyle, who had always a shrewd sense of the practical, said at once that such a thing was nonsense. It was not, however, Ruskin's personal nonsense alone; this is where the biographical emphasis is most misleading. This kind of deadlock, followed by absurd attempts to break it, is really a general phenomenon. The image of a society organized in terms of value is recurring and inevitable. In Ruskin, as in so many others, the failure was one of realization. His society was an image without energy, because the necessary social commitment could not or would not be made. And because this is a general phenomenon, we have to look at the deadlock very carefully. It is not enough to rationalize it and blame Ruskin for, say, 'mediaevalism'. In fact, Ruskin knew quite well that mediaevalism was inadequate:

We don't want either the life or the decorations of the thirteenth century back again; and the circumstances with which you must surround your (*sc,* Bradford) workmen are those simply of happy modern English life . . . The designs you have now to ask for from your workmen are such as will make modern English life beautiful. All that gorgeousness of the Middle Ages, beautiful as it sounds in description, noble as in many respects it was in reality, had, nevertheless, for foundation and for end, nothing but the pride of life—the pride of the so-called superior classes; a pride which supported itself by violence and robbery, and led in the end to the destruction both of the arts themselves and the States in which they flourished.[23]

This was a just recognition that the real issues were always immediate and contemporary, and that the establishment of a new kind of society had to begin in conditions of the old anarchy which it sought to replace. Beyond this recognition, however, Ruskin cannot help us. His remarkable and admirable enquiry into the values of his society brought us to this point, but could not take us past it. And it is precisely here that our attention is drawn to the man most immediately and deeply influenced by Ruskin, William Morris. The significance of Morris in this tradition, is that he sought to attach its general values to an actual and growing social force: that of the organized working class. This was the most remarkable attempt that had so far been made to break the general deadlock.

Morris's own retrospective account of his development is clear and interesting:

> Before the uprising of *modern* Socialism almost all intelligent people either were, or professed themselves to be, quite contented with the civilization of this century. Again, almost all of these really were thus contented, and saw nothing to do but to perfect the said civilization by getting rid of a few ridiculous survivals of the barbarous ages.[24a]

(This, evidently, is Morris's judgement of the utilitarian liberals.)

> To be short, this was the *Whig* frame of mind, natural to the modern prosperous middle-class men, who, in fact, as far as mechanical progress is concerned, have nothing to ask for, if only Socialism would leave them alone to enjoy their plentiful style. But besides these contented ones there were others who were not really contented, but had a vague sentiment of repulsion to the triumph

of civilization, but were coerced into silence by the measureless power of Whiggery.[24b]

(*Civilization*, in this last sentence, is used in a Coleridgian sense, as a limited term. In the previous sentence, the limiting function of *mechanical* is also evident. These are the traditional terms.)

> Lastly, there were a few who were in open rebellion against the said Whiggery—a few, say two, Carlyle and Ruskin. The latter, before my days of practical socialism, was my master towards the ideal.[24c]

Thus Morris acknowledges both the tradition and his own extension of it. He now restates the grounds of the opposition to 'civilization':

> Apart from the desire to produce beautiful things, the leading passion of my life has been and is hatred of modern civilization. . . . What shall I say concerning its mastery of and its waste of mechanical power, its commonwealth so poor, its enemies of the commonwealth so rich, its stupendous organization—for the misery of life! Its contempt of simple pleasures, which everyone could enjoy but for its folly? Its eyeless vulgarity which has destroyed art, the one certain solace of labour? . . . The struggles of mankind for many ages had produced nothing but this sordid, aimless, ugly confusion; the immediate future seemed to me likely to intensify all the present evils by sweeping away the last survivals of the days before the dull squalor of civilization had settled down on the world. This was a bad look-out indeed, and, if I may mention myself as a personality and not as a mere type, especially so to a man of my disposition, careless of metaphysics and religion, as well as of scientific analysis, but with a deep love of the earth and the life on it, and a passion for the history of the past of mankind. Think of it! Was it all to end in a counting-house on the top of a cinder-heap, with Podsnap's drawing-room in the offing, and a Whig committee dealing out champagne to the rich and margarine to the poor in such convenient proportions as would make all men contented together, though the pleasure of the eyes was gone from the world, and the place of Homer was to be taken by Huxley.[24d]

This kind of opposition is by now very familiar, and we can see in it elements of Carlyle, Ruskin and Pugin, and of the

149

popularization of these ideas in Dickens. There is also, significantly, the anti-scientific element: the Romantic prejudice that a mechanical civilization had been created by a mechanical science, and that science was attempting to substitute for art. One would have expected Morris to remember, as he elsewhere insisted, that the offered substitute for art was bad art; and that it was not scientific enquiry (however indifferent to it Morris might personally be) but the organization of economic life, which had produced the misery and the vulgarity. Keeping this point aside, we pass to Morris's important new emphasis:

> So there I was in for a fine pessimistic end of life, if it had not somehow dawned on me that amidst all this filth of civilization the seeds of a great change, what we others call Social-Revolution, were beginning to germinate. . . . (This) prevented me, luckier than many others of artistic perceptions, from crystallizing into a mere railer against 'progress' on the one hand, and on the other from wasting time and energy in any of the numerous schemes by which the quasi-artistic of the middle classes hope to make art grow when it has no longer any root, and thus I became a practical Socialist. . . . Surely any one who professes to think that the question of art and cultivation must go before that of the knife and fork (and there are some who do propose that) does not understand what art means, or how that its roots must have a soil of a thriving and unanxious life. Yet it must be remembered that civilization has reduced the workman to such a skinny and pitiful existence, that he scarcely knows how to frame a desire for any life much better than that which he now endures perforce. *It is the province of art to set the true ideal of a full and reasonable life before him,* a life to which the perception and creation of beauty, the enjoyment of real pleasure that is, shall be felt to be as necessary to man as his daily bread, and that no man, and no set of men, can be deprived of this except by mere opposition, which should be resisted to the utmost.[25]

The social revolution, then, was to be the answer to the deadlock of the 'railers against progress'. The priority of 'cultivation' is set aside, in terms that remind one of Cobbett. Yet, unlike Cobbett, Morris uses the idea of culture, in particular in its embodiment in art, as a positive criterion: 'the true ideal of a full and reasonable life'. Like Cobbett,

Morris would have nothing set as a priority over the claims of working men to an improvement in their conditions; but unlike Cobbett, who set his objective in terms of a remembered society, Morris, like Blake or Ruskin, sets his social objective in terms of the fulness of life which art especially reveals.

Morris's principal opponent, in fact, was Arnold. The word 'culture', because it was associated in his mind with Arnold's conclusions, is usually roughly handled:

> In the thirty years during which I have known Oxford more damage has been done to art (and therefore to literature) by Oxford 'culture' than centuries of professors could repair—for, indeed, it is irreparable. These coarse brutalities of 'light and leading' make education stink in the nostrils of thoughtful persons, and . . . are more likely than is Socialism to drive some of us mad. . . . I say that to attempt to teach literature with one hand while it destroys history with the other is a bewildering proceeding on the part of 'culture'.[26]

The point of this was Morris's opposition to the 'modernization' of Oxford:

> I wish to ask if it is too late to appeal to the mercy of the 'Dons' to spare the few specimens of ancient town architecture which they have not yet had time to destroy. . . . Oxford thirty years ago, when I first knew it, was full of these treasures; but Oxford 'culture', cynically contemptuous of the knowledge which it does not know, and steeped to the lips in the commercialism of the day, has made a clean sweep of most of them.[27]

As so often, a particular argument is here entangled with a much more general judgement. This is very typical of Morris's method, which is often no more than a kind of generalized swearing. Yet the general argument is there, when he troubles to control it. Oxford was for him a test-case, on the issue whether culture could be saved from commercialism by isolating it:

> There are of the English middle class, today . . . men of the highest aspirations towards Art, and of the strongest will; men who are most deeply convinced of the necessity to civilization of surrounding

men's lives with beauty; and many lesser men, thousands for what I know, refined and cultivated, follow them and praise their opinions: but both the leaders and the led are incapable of saving so much as half a dozen commons from the grasp of inexorable Commerce: they are as helpless in spite of their culture and their genius as if they were just so many overworked shoemakers: less lucky than King Midas, our green fields and clear waters, nay the very air we breathe, are turned not to gold (which might please some of us for an hour maybe) but to dirt; and to speak plainly we know full well that under the present gospel of Capital not only there is no hope of bettering it, but that things grow worse year by year, day by day.[28]

For indeed, Morris argues, the commercial habits of the middle class can destroy even those things which many individual members of the middle-class value. It is this commercialism which has destroyed even such a centre of alternative values as Oxford:

What is it, for instance, that has destroyed the Rouen, the Oxford of my elegant poetic regret? Has it perished for the benefit of the people, either slowly yielding to the growth of intelligent change and new happiness? or has it been, as it were, thunderstricken by the tragedy which mostly accompanies some great new birth? Not so. Neither phalangstere nor dynamite has swept its beauty away, its destroyers have not been either the philanthropist or the Socialist, the cooperator or the anarchist. It has been sold, and at a cheap price indeed: muddled away by the greed and incompetence of fools who do not know what life and pleasure mean, who will neither take them themselves nor let others have them.[29]

To the constant question of this tradition—'can the middle classes regenerate themselves?'—Morris returned a decided No. The middle classes cannot or will not *change* the consequences of industrialism; they will only try to escape them, in one of two ways. Either:

Men get rich now in their struggles not to be poor, and because their riches shield them from suffering from the horrors which are a necessary accompaniment of the existence of rich men; e.g., the sight of slums, the squalor of a factory country, the yells and evil language of drunken and brutalized poor people.[30]

This way, an energetic entry into commercialism in order to escape its consequences, is a kind of Moral Sinking Fund, which continues to be heavily subscribed. The other way is the way of 'minority culture':

> Nothing made by man's hand can be indifferent: it must be either beautiful and elevating, or ugly and degrading; and those things that are without art are so aggressively; they wound it by their existence, and they are now so much in the majority that the works of art we are obliged to set ourselves to seek for, whereas the other things are the ordinary companions of our everyday life; so that if those who cultivate art intellectually were inclined never so much to wrap themselves in their special gifts and their high cultivation, and so live happily, apart from other men, and despising them, they could not do so: they are as it were living in an enemy's country; at every turn there is something lying in wait to offend and vex their nicer sense and educated eyes: they must share in the general discomfort—and I am glad of it.[31]

The cultivated were indeed 'aliens', as Arnold had called them, but they were helpless to prevent further damage, even to themselves. Forty years of publicized revival of the arts had shown, Morris argued, not an improvement in the quality of things seen, but even a deterioration:

> The world is everywhere growing uglier and more commonplace, in spite of the conscious and very strenuous efforts of a small group of people towards the revival of art, which are so obviously out of joint with the tendency of the age, that while the uncultivated have not even heard of them, the mass of the cultivated look upon them as a joke, and even that they are now beginning to get tired of.[32]

Art, Morris argued, in line with his tradition, depends on the quality of the society which produces it. There is no salvation in

> art for art's sake . . . of (which) a school . . . does, in a way, theoretically at least, exist at present. Its watchword (is) a piece of slang that does not mean the harmless thing it seems to mean . . . An art cultivated professedly by a few, and for a few, who would consider it necessary—a duty, if they could admit duties—to despise

the common herd, to hold themselves aloof from all that the world has been struggling for from the first, to guard carefully every approach to their palace of art . . . that art at last will seem too delicate a thing for even the hands of the initiated to touch; and the initiated must at last sit still and do nothing—to the grief of no one.[33]

The hope for art was not here, but in the belief that

the cause of Art is the cause of the people. . . . One day we shall win back Art, that is to say the pleasure of life; win back Art again to our daily labour.[34]

This, at the end of the century, is a rejection of the specialization of 'Art' which was common at its beginning. But the terms of the rejection are in part a result of the specialization. In particular, Morris profits from Ruskin's thinking about art and labour, as here:

Nothing should be made by man's labour which is not worth making; or which must be made by labour degrading to the makers. . . . Simple as that proposition is . . . it is a direct challenge to the death to the present system of labour in civilized countries. . . . The aim of art (is) to destroy the curse of labour by making work the pleasurable satisfaction of our impulse towards energy, and giving to that energy hope of producing something worth the exercise.[35]

Art had become a particular quality of labour. Delight in work had been widely destroyed by the machine-system of production, but, Morris argued, it was the system, rather than the machines as such, which must be blamed.

If the necessary reasonable work be of a mechanical kind, I must be helped to do it by a machine, not to cheapen my labour, but so that as little time as possible may be spent upon it. . . . I know that to some cultivated people, people of the artistic turn of mind, machinery is particularly distasteful . . . (but) it is the allowing machines to be our masters and not our servants that so injures the beauty of life nowadays. In other words, it is the token of the terrible crime we have fallen into of using our control of the powers of Nature for the purpose of enslaving people, we careless meantime of how much happiness we rob their lives of.[36]

That Morris could feel like this is of considerable importance. He was himself a hand-craftsman, and he had a respect born from experience for work of that kind. In his Utopian writings, the removal of machines from the process of work is often emphasized. Yet the reaction 'Morris—handicrafts—get rid of the machines' is as misleading as the reaction 'Ruskin—Gothic—mediaevalism'. The regressive elements are present in Morris, as they were in Ruskin. These elements seek to compensate for the difficulties in the way of practical realization of certain qualities of life; and because their function is compensatory, they are often sentimental. Yet, although their reference is to the past, their concern is with the present and the future. When we stress, in Morris, the attachment to handicrafts, we are, in part, rationalizing an uneasiness generated by the scale and nature of his social criticism. Morris wanted the end of the capitalist system, and the institution of socialism, so that men could decide for themselves how their work should be arranged, and where machinery was appropriate. It was obviously convenient to many of his readers, and to many of Ruskin's readers, to construe all this as a campaign to end machine-production. Such a campaign could never be more than an affectation, but it is less compromising than Morris's campaign to end capitalism, which lands one directly in the heat and bitterness of political struggle. It is most significant that Morris should have been diluted in this way. The dilution stresses what are really the weaker parts of his work, and neglects what is really strong and alive. For my own part, I would willingly lose *The Dream of John Ball* and the romantic socialist songs and even *News from Nowhere*—in all of which the weaknesses of Morris's general poetry are active and disabling, if to do so were the price of retaining and getting people to read such smaller things as *How we Live, and How we might Live, The Aims of Art, Useful Work versus Useless Toil,* and *A Factory as it might be.* The change of emphasis would involve a change in Morris's status as a writer, but such a change is critically inevitable. There is more life in the lectures, where one feels that the whole man is engaged in the writing, than in any of the prose and verse romances. These seem so clearly the product of a fragmentary consciousness—of that very state of mind which

Morris was always trying to analyse. Morris is a fine political writer, in the broadest sense, and it is on that, finally, that his reputation will rest. The other and larger part of his literary work bears witness only to the disorder which he felt so acutely. He was not a Hopkins to make art 'when the time seemed unpropitious'. The nearest figure to him, in his own century, is Cobbett: with the practice of visual instead of rural arts as the controlling sanity from which the political insights sprang. And as with Cobbett, we come to accept the impatience and the ritual swearing as the price of the vitality, which has its own greatness.

It remains to look briefly at Morris's socialism, since it grew out of the tradition which we have been examining. He is often mentioned by modern members of the Labour Party, but usually in terms that suggest a very limited acquaintance with his actual ideas. He is, for instance, something very different from an orthodox Fabian. Socialism, for him, is not merely

> substituting business-like administration in the interests of the public for the old Whig muddle of *laissez-faire* backed up by coercion.[37]

This was the socialism the utilitarians had come to, but Morris, always, applied to socialism the modes of judgement which had been developed in opposition to utilitarianism. This, for example: Socialism might

> gain higher wages and shorter working hours for the working men themselves: industries may be worked by municipalities for the benefit both of producers and consumers. Working-people's houses may be improved, and their management taken out of the hands of commercial speculators. In all this I freely admit a great gain, and am glad to see schemes tried which would lead to it. But great as the gain would be, the ultimate good of it . . . would, I think, depend on *how* such reforms were done; in what spirit; or rather what else was being done, while these were going on. . . .[38]

This is a familiar kind of argument, from the tradition, and Morris confirms it in its usual terms:

> The great mass of what most non-socialists at least consider at present to be socialism, seems to me nothing more than a *machinery*

of socialism, which I think it probable that socialism *must* use in its militant condition; and which I think it *may* use for some time after it is practically established; but does not seem to me to be of its essence.[39]

Yet the result of this point of view is not modification of the Socialist idea, but its emphasis. Morris wonders

whether, in short, the tremendous organization of civilized commercial society is not playing the cat and mouse game with us socialists. Whether the Society of Inequality might not accept the quasi-socialist machinery above mentioned, and work it for the purpose of upholding that society in a somewhat shorn condition, maybe, but a safe one. . . . The workers better treated, better organized, helping to govern themselves, but with no more pretence to equality with the rich, nor any more hope for it than they have now.[40]

This insight into what has been perhaps the actual course of events since his death is a measure of Morris's quality as a political thinker. Yet it is no more than an application, under new circumstances, of the kind of appraisal which the century's thinking about the meanings of culture had made available. The arts defined a quality of living which it was the whole purpose of political change to make possible:

I hope we know assuredly that the arts we have met together to further are necessary to the life of man, if the progress of civilization is not to be as causeless as the turning of a wheel that makes nothing.[41]

Socialist change was the means to a recovery of purpose. The limitation of such change to 'machinery' would only be possible

on the grounds that the working people have ceased to desire real socialism and are contented with some outside show of it joined to an increase in prosperity enough to satisfy the cravings of men who do not know what the pleasures of life might be if they treated their own capacities and the resources of nature reasonably with the intention and expectation of being happy.[42]

The business of a socialist party is not only to organize political and economic change. It is, more vitally, to foster and extend a real socialist consciousness, among working men, so that finally

> they understand themselves to be face to face with false society, themselves the only possible elements of true society.[43]

We realize the tradition behind Morris even as, in this remarkable way, he gives a radically new application to its ideas. For Morris is here announcing the extension of the tradition into our own century, and setting the stage for its continuing controversy.

PART II

INTERREGNUM

INTERREGNUM

THE pivotal figure of the tradition which has been examined, and which we shall see continued and extended to our own day, is William Morris. In the middle of the twentieth century Morris remains a contemporary thinker, for the directions which he indicated have become part of a general social movement. Yet he belongs, essentially, with the great Victorian rebels, sharing with them an energy, an expansion, a willingness to generalize which marks him, from our own period of critical specialism, as an historic figure. The life went out of that kind of general swearing and homily soon after Morris's death, and we look at it now post-mortem with mixed feelings of respect and suspicion.

It is almost true that there are no periods in thought; at least, within a given form of society. But if there are, the chances of reign and century deal hardly with them. The temper which the adjective Victorian is useful to describe is virtually finished in the 1880s; the new men who appear in that decade, and who have left their mark, are recognizably different in tone. To the young Englishman in the 1920s, this break was the emergence of the modern spirit, and so we have tended to go on thinking. But now, from the 1950s, the bearings look different. The break comes no longer in the generation of Butler, Shaw, Wilde, who are already period figures. For us, our contemporaries, our moods, appear in effect after the war of 1914-1918. D. H. Lawrence is a contemporary, in mood, in a way that Butler and Shaw are clearly not. As a result, we tend to look at the period 1880-1914 as a kind of interregnum. It is not the period of the masters, of Coleridge or of George Eliot. Nor yet is it the period of our contemporaries, of writers who address themselves, in our kind of language, to the common problems that we recognize. I shall then treat the writers of that period who have affected our thinking about culture, in a brief, separate section. If they were neglected altogether, certain important links would be missing. Yet we shall not find in them, except perhaps in Hulme, anything very new:

a working-out, rather, of unfinished lines; a tentative re-direction. Such work requires notice, but suggests brevity.

1. W. H. Mallock

Mallock's *The New Republic* is as good a starting point for this period as could be found: not so much as a foretaste of what is to come but as a valediction to the period we are leaving. The evident if fragile brilliance of *The New Republic* has commanded for Mallock less readers than one might reasonably expect. His later work, which gains in substance as it loses in brilliance, has been almost wholly neglected.

The plan of *The New Republic*, which was published in 1877 when Mallock was twenty-eight, is the bringing together in a weekend house-party of a number of the figures we have been discussing, together with the other masters of Mallock's twenties. Matthew Arnold is there as Mr Luke, Ruskin as Mr Herbert, Pater as Mr Rose, Jowett as Dr Jenkinson, together with figures representing Herbert Spencer, W. K. Clifford, Violet Fane, and others who were more important to Mallock than they can now be to us. Their discussion of an ideal republic is made the occasion for a number of very brilliant parodies; the book has about the weight, in terms of ideas, of Aldous Huxley's early novels. It is interesting to see the relative respect and disrespect with which Mallock treats his figures: Pater, for instance, is savaged in a way that Huxley has made familiar ('his two topics are self-indulgence and art'); Arnold is little more than a dandy and a bore; Ruskin, though shown as theatrical, is still evidently respected. These are the uses of the book as a document: the tradition seen at a certain point in time through the eyes of an intelligent critic.

The second chapter of the third book is particularly useful. For example:

'You mean then,' said Miss Merton, 'that a man of the highest culture is a sort of emotional *bon vivant*?'

'That surely is hardly a fair way—' began Laurence.

'Excuse me, my dear Laurence,' broke in Mr Luke in his most magnificent of manners, 'it is perfectly fair—it is admirably fair. Emotional *bon vivant*!' he exclaimed. 'I thank Miss Merton for teaching me that word! for it may remind us all,' Mr Luke continued, drawing out his words slowly, as if he liked the taste of them, 'how near our view of the matter is to that of a certain Galilean peasant—of whom Miss Merton has perhaps heard—who described the highest culture by just the same metaphor, as a hunger and a thirst after righteousness. Our notion of it differs only from his, from the *Zeitgeist* having made it somewhat wider.'[1]

The irony of 'just the same metaphor' retains its relevance even if we wish to rescue Arnold from Mr Luke. The subsequent direction of the argument about culture is towards Otho Laurence's (the host's) definition—

'It *is* with the life about us that all our concern lies; and culture's double end is simply this—to make us appreciate that life, and to make that life worth appreciating.'[2]

—and then its dilution into

'the aim of culture is to make us better company as men and women of the world.'[3]

It is on this weakened preoccupation that the wrath of Mr Herbert's theatrical sermon descends:

'Will art, will painting, will poetry be any comfort to you? You have said that these were magic mirrors which reflected back your life for you. Well—will they be any better than the glass mirrors in your drawing-rooms, if they have nothing but the same listless orgy to reflect? . . . What, then, shall you do to be saved? Rend your hearts, I say, and do not mend your garments. . . .'[4]

This is as far as the house-party gets, except for a discriminating renewal of invitations.

Mallock is not concerned, in *The New Republic*, to commit himself, but his later work shows him as perhaps the most able conservative thinker of the last eighty years. The mood of the later books is sceptical and critical, and Mallock is not to be recommended to socialists, or even democrats, who have merely received a doctrine and want to keep it. *The Limits of Pure Democracy* (1917) anticipates, and is better written than, those many books presenting a similar thesis which have appeared since 1945. The political and economic arguments must be referred elsewhere, but the result, in social thinking, is Mallock's dictum:

Only through oligarchy does civilized democracy know itself.[5]

In the second chapter of Book VII, Mallock works this idea out in terms of culture:

In each of the three lives—that of knowledge, that of aesthetic appreciation and that of religion—on which the quality of social intercourse in a civilized country depends, the activities of the few play a part of such supreme importance that were their activities absent the mass of the citizens, whatever their material wealth, would be unlettered, superstitious, and half-brutal barbarians, as many newly enriched men on the outskirts of civilization actually are today.[6]

It is the truth of democratic theory that

whatever the few may add to the possible things of civilization, the many must, according to their several talents, share them.[7]

But there will be nothing to share if the oligarchy (or minority) is not recognized and maintained:

the many can prosper only through the participation in benefits which, in the way alike of material comfort, opportunity, culture and social freedom, would be possible for no one unless the many submitted themselves to the influence or authority of the super-capable few.[8]

Two other points from *The Limits of Pure Democracy* may be briefly noted: Mallock's discussion of the idea of Equality of Opportunity, in terms of wages and of education. He says of the idea in general:

The demand for equality of opportunity may, indeed, wear on the surface of it certain revolutionary aspects; but it is in reality—it is in its very nature—a symptom of moderation, or rather of an un-intended conservatism, of which the masses of normal men cannot, if they would, divest themselves. The very meaning of the word 'opportunity'—a word saturated as it is with implications—is enough in itself to show this. For if the ideal demand of pure democracy were realized, and the social conditions of all men made equal by force of law, there would be no such thing as opportunity equal or unequal, for anybody. . . . The desire for equality of opportunity—the desire for the right to rise—in so far as it is really experienced by the morally typical man of all ages and nations, is a desire that everybody (he himself, as included in 'everybody', being a prominent figure in his thoughts) shall have an opportunity of achieving by his own talents, if he can, some position or condition which is not equal, but which is, on the contrary, superior to any position or condition which is achievable by the talents of all.[9]

He then argues that, as applied to wage negotiations, the advocates of equality of opportunity invariably in practice seek, not absolute equality, but relative equality: that is to say, wages graduated in proportion to effort, skill, length of training, etc., with an insistence on the 'maintenance of their proper graduation'. What is demanded (if Mallock's argument may be paraphrased) is an equal opportunity to become unequal. It is so, also, he argues, in the advocacy of popular education; what is emphasized is giving a chance to gifted but poor children, so that they may better themselves. The idea assumes

the existence of some average mass, whose capacities and whose wages represent those normal lots, by their upward distance from which those ampler lots are measured, which opportunity offers to talents above the average.[10]

A large part of democratic sentiment, therefore, is in Mallock's view merely a demand for the right to become a member of the oligarchy. But when this demand is, by the theory of pure democracy, granted to every member of society, there can only be disillusion. Democratic theory is a sentimental reassurance that the thing can be done; but the facts of society, and of production in all its aspects, will demand major inequalities, corresponding to differences of effort and ability, and these will be assessed on a basis of fact rather than on that self-estimate which democratic theory, in its encouragement of everyone, seems to support. The 'masses' can only, in following this path, be deluded or disillusioned. It is better, then, to recognize that the general welfare depends on exceptional ability and effort, which have to be stimulated and maintained, and to recognize, in consequence, that oligarchy is not the opposite of democracy, but its necessary complement. The confusion between government and social contribution, in this argument, is comparatively easy to spot. But the 'aristocracy of talent', which Carlyle had first defined, was a popular notion in this period, as may be seen in Shaw and Wells. We can see now its inevitable confusion with arbitrary inequalities, and we limit Mallock accordingly. Yet the democratic idea needed its sceptics, and Mallock, always, is shrewd enough to be attended to.

11. The 'New Aesthetics'

If the 'eighties and 'nineties in England had really produced a new aesthetics, it might have stood greatly to their credit. But what was called, from Pater in the late 'sixties, the new doctrine of 'art for art's sake', was really little more than a restatement of an attitude which properly belongs to the first generations of the Romantics. The most extreme form of this restatement is to be found in Whistler, but in Pater and Wilde, who have been associated with Whistler's position, the continuity from the earlier tradition is quite evident. We need trace only the point at which this kind of reaffirmation swung over, in certain extreme statements, to something approaching its negation.

What we sometimes suppose to be a change in ideas is perhaps properly identified as a change—a change for the worse—in prose. This is particularly evident in the case of Pater, whose ideas, when visible through the gauze, are the ideas of Wordsworth, of Shelley and of Arnold. The conclusion of the essay on Wordsworth is the obvious illustration of this. Pater writes:

That the end of life is not action but contemplation—*being* as distinct from *doing*—a certain disposition of the mind: is, in some shape or other, the principle of all the higher morality. In poetry, in art, if you enter into their true spirit at all, you touch this principle, in a measure: these, by their very sterility, are a type of beholding for the mere joy of beholding. To treat life in the spirit of art, is to make life a thing in which means and ends are identified: to encourage such treatment, the true moral significance of art and poetry. . . . Not to teach lessons, or enforce rules, or even to stimulate us to noble ends; but to withdraw the thoughts for a little while from the mere machinery of life, to fix them, with appropriate emotions, on the spectacle of those great facts in man's existence which no machinery affects. . . . To witness this spectacle with appropriate emotions is the aim of all culture.[1]

The elements of continuity in this statement are clear: the distinction between 'being' and 'doing', the criticism of 'mere machinery', the description of this 'true moral significance of art and poetry' as 'culture'—this to the very words is no more than a summing-up of the long preceding tradition. And it is doubtful whether Pater believed that he was saying anything different when he wrote the notorious sentence in the Conclusion (1868) to *The Renaissance*:

> Of this wisdom, the poetic passion, the desire of beauty, the love of art for art's sake, has most; for art comes to you professing frankly to give nothing but the highest quality to your moments as they pass, and simply for those moments' sake.[2]

For Pater is here saying no more than Mill said when he described poetry as 'a culture of the feelings'. If we disapprove the attitude in Pater, we must similarly disapprove it in Mill—I suggested, in my discussion of Mill, its inadequacy. Yet Mill is approvingly quoted, while Pater is commonly dismissed in a cloud of roses and stars. The composition of this curious cloud is indeed the whole point. It is not Pater's doctrine that is commonly rejected; indeed, an austere technician like I. A. Richards seems, in the question of doctrine, to be very close to Pater, yet the reaction is quite different. What we reject in Pater is his instances, and the substance of these instances is his style at its worst. It has been to us, we say, but as the sound of lyres and flutes; and when we repeat these words, we do not hear any particular instruments. To recommend the saving power of sensibility is, always, to invite attention to one's instances, even if these lie only in the language of the recommendation. Pater, as a teacher, is enrolled in the Grand Old Cause, and the rejection of his teaching implies, properly, a rejection of the whole Romantic position from Keats to Arnold. The first emphasis of culture was an emphasis of the function of

167

certain kinds of thought and feeling in the whole life of man: a function properly described as moral. Pater argues this function within the major tradition; in his general statements he is at one with his peers. Yet repeatedly, in his instances, he embodies the negative element which is always latent in this position: the reduction of a whole process, characterized by its movement and its interactions, to a fragmentary, isolated product—Pater's image of the contemplating being, who has struggled 'with those forms till its secret is won from each, and then lets each fall back into its place, in the supreme, artistic view of life'.[3] His apotheosis of La Gioconda is typical of this image, but his relation to art is such that he seems genuinely unable to distinguish between the condition of a work of art—a made thing, containing within itself an achieved stillness—and the condition of any life, which is not made but making, and which can only in phantasy be detached from a continuous process and a whole condition. Pater's kind of sensibility thus reduces a general and active proposition to what is, in effect, its negation. Art for art's sake is a reasonable maxim for the artist, when creating, and for the spectator when the work is being communicated; at such times, it is no more than a definition of attention. The negative element is the phantasy—usually explicable—that a man can himself become, can confuse himself with, a made work. The phantasy is common enough for Pater to be comprehended; it is indeed a general distortion of the emphasis on culture, which otherwise Pater clearly continues and conveys.

Whistler is Pater vulgarized, yet the vulgarity is in a way a gain. Unlike Pater, he rejects the received thesis, in particular the thesis of Ruskin. In opposition to the belief that in the past, and especially in the Middle Ages, there was a greater general regard for art and a fuller integration of it with the common life, Whistler asserted:

> Listen! There never was an artistic period. There never was an art-loving nation. . . . If Art be rare today, it was seldom heretofore. It is false, this teaching of decay. . . . False again, the fabled link between the grandeur of Art and the glories and virtues of the State, for Art feeds not upon nations, and peoples may be wiped from the face of the earth, but Art *is*.[4]

INTERREGNUM

This is only Pater's practical separation of art and life (a separation resting on their confusion, and on the consequent reduction of life to the condition of art) extended and jumped up into a kind of theory, which is then entirely opposed to the tradition which Pater in his general statements had continued. 'Listen!' says Whistler, and we have listened. We agree that 'this teaching of decay' is at any rate partly false; we agree also with his onslaught on 'Taste':

> 'Taste' has long been confounded with capacity, and accepted as sufficient qualification for the utterance of judgment. . . . Art is joyously received as a matter of opinion; and that it should be based upon laws as rigid and defined as those of the . . . sciences, is a supposition no longer to be tolerated by modern cultivation. . . . The millennium of Taste sets in.[5]

It is no more than Wordsworth was saying, eighty years earlier, but it is relevant, as is the observation

> Art is upon the Town! . . . to be coaxed into company, as a proof of culture and refinement.[6]

These are reasonable criticisms of a fashionable ethos, but Whistler is at once too shallow and too confused to make anything further of them. For example, a statement like the following is useful:

> Humanity takes the place of Art, and God's creations are excused by their usefulness. Beauty is confounded with virtue, and, before a work of art, it is asked: 'What good shall it do?'[7]

Newman had drawn attention to a similar confusion between 'beauty' and virtue, and to the deficiencies of 'Taste', but what we have now to notice in Whistler is an acceptance of the simple converse: art takes the place of humanity, and virtue is not merely distinguished from beauty, but made irrelevant. There are times, in reading Pater, when one sees how this position was prepared, and it is in Pater's accents that Whistler makes his only positive point:

> We have then but to wait—until with the mark of the gods upon him—there come among us again the chosen—who shall continue what has gone before. Satisfied that, even were he never to appear,

the story of the beautiful is already complete—hewn in the marbles of the Parthenon—and broidered, with the birds, upon the fan of Hokusai—at the foot of Fusi-Yama.[8]

The accents of this cannot disguise its servility: an essential servility which made possible Whistler's spurts of arrogance. This degree of abstraction of Art and 'the beautiful', this reduction of man to the status of a humble spectator, compose together a lifeless caricature—yet bearing a caricature's relations to its original—of the positive affirmations of Shelley or of Keats. In Whistler, the Romantic trap has been sprung.

Oscar Wilde, by comparison, is a traditional figure. His immediate reply to Whistler's account of the artist is the sober (if in vocabulary self-conscious)

> an artist is not an isolated fact, he is the resultant of a certain *milieu* and a certain entourage.[9]

In *The Soul of Man under Socialism*, he repeats a familiar point from Arnold and Pater:

> The true perfection of man lies, not in what man has, but in what man is.[10]

The right activity of man, he argues elsewhere, is

> not *doing*, but *being*, and not *being* merely, but *becoming*.[11]

The 'true ideal' of man is 'self-culture'; and culture is made possible by a 'transmission of racial experience', which 'the critical spirit alone . . . (makes) perfect'.[12]

The 'new aesthetics', as expounded by Wilde, had three principles: first, that 'art never expresses anything but itself'; second, that 'all bad art comes from returning to Life and Nature, and elevating them into ideals'; third, that 'Life imitates Art far more than Art imitates Life'.[13] In consequence, Wilde finds,

> all art is immoral . . . for emotion for the sake of emotion is the aim of art, and emotion for the sake of action is the aim of life, and of that practical organization of life that we call society. Society, which is the beginning and basis of morals, exists simply for the concentration of human energy . . . Society often forgives the criminal; it never forgives the dreamer. . . . While in the opinion

of society, Contemplation is the gravest sin of which any citizen can be guilty, in the opinion of the highest culture it is the proper occupation of man.[14]

Wilde stands in this with Pater and Arnold, but his attitudes to society are, though consistent with this, unexpected. For example:

> Civilization requires slaves.... Unless there are slaves to do the ugly, horrible, uninteresting work, culture and contemplation become almost impossible. Human slavery is wrong, insecure, and demoralizing. On mechanical slavery, on the slavery of the machine, the future of the world depends.... At present machinery competes against man. Under proper conditions machinery will serve man.... The machines will be the new slaves.[15]

This is a good example of the Wildean paradox, no longer merely verbal, but embodying a real adjustment and advance in feeling. The same may be said of his claims for socialism:

> The chief advantage that would result from the establishment of Socialism is, undoubtedly, the fact that Socialism would relieve us from that sordid necessity of living for others which, in the present condition of things, presses so hardly upon almost everybody.[16]

This might appear modish, but it is based on a real perception:

> Selfishness is not living as one wishes to live, it is asking others to live as one wishes to live.[17]

In its context, this is a valuable criticism of a dominative mood which is characteristic alike of Arnold's Philistines and of some of their socialist opponents. In turning the phrases of didactic respectability, Wilde often reached a feeling that is in fact more generally humane:

> The virtues of the poor may be readily admitted, and are much to be regretted.... The best amongst the poor are never grateful. They are ungrateful, discontented, disobedient, and rebellious. They are quite right to be so.[18]

Art is not an argument against social change, but its corollary:

> Socialism will . . . restore society to its proper condition of a thoroughly healthy organism, and ensure the material well-being

of each member of the community. It will, in fact, give Life its proper basis and its proper environment. But for the full development of Life to its highest mode of perfection, something more is needed. What is needed is Individualism.[19]

Art, as 'the most intense form of individualism that the world has known', is an epitome of the life that social change will make generally possible. But it is not merely to be contrasted with 'materialism':

> Men . . . rage against Materialism, as they call it, forgetting that there has been no material improvement that has not spiritualized the world.[20]

Thus, while the 'new aesthetics' rests essentially on a denial of society, and Wilde in the end is no exception, yet, in Wilde, the pursuit of an isolated aesthetic pleasure is accompanied by a general humanity which is a real ground for respect. If he remains the fastidious spectator of a common life, he is yet intelligent enough to realize that the basis of cultivated individual living will have to be redrawn on less degrading general terms. He, rather than Pater, is the first of the minor inheritors of Arnold, whose general position he repeats, without the Victorian ballast which is Arnold's moral stability, but with much the same irony—that of the desperate, chiding spectator—narrowed and hardened to a sharper and more conscious wit. In being the prodigal of a most respectable tradition, Wilde showed, perhaps, what the tradition had still to learn.

iii. George Gissing

If the difficulty of obtaining recent editions of his work is any guide, Gissing is now generally neglected, although he holds his place in the text-books. Yet if *The Way of all Flesh*, *Tono Bungay*, or *The Man of Property* can still be usefully read, so, without question, can Gissing's *New Grub Street* or *The Nether World*. The interest of Gissing in the present context lies in two aspects of his work: his analysis of literature as a trade, which makes *New Grub Street* a minor classic; and his social observations and attitudes, in such

novels as *The Nether World* and *Demos*, which provide
evidence of a significant and continuing process. The
interest of the first point is enhanced by its date: Gissing
wrote *New Grub Street* in 1891, at the crucial time for an
observation of the effects on literature of the new journalism
and the new kind of market. These effects are dramatized in
the novel in the contrast between the novelist Reardon, who
fails and dies, and Jasper Milvain, the 'new' kind of writer.
Milvain's exposition is characteristic:

> 'Just understand the difference between a man like Reardon and a
> man like me. He is the old type of unpractical artist; I am the
> literary man of 1882. He won't make concessions, or, rather, he
> can't make them; he can't supply the market. . . . Literature nowa-
> days is a trade. Putting aside men of genius, who may succeed by
> mere cosmic force, your successful man of letters is your skilful
> tradesman. He thinks first and foremost of the markets; when one
> kind of goods begins to go off slackly, he is ready with something
> new and appetizing. He knows perfectly all the possible sources of
> income. Whatever he has to sell he'll get payment for it from all
> sorts of various quarters. . . . Reardon can't do that kind of thing;
> he's behind his age; he sells a manuscript as if he lived in Sam
> Johnson's Grub Street. But our Grub Street of today is quite a
> different place: it is supplied with telegraphic communication, it
> knows what literary fare is in demand in every part of the world,
> its inhabitants are men of business, however seedy.'[1]

A now familiar case has hardly ever been better put. And
Gissing sees to it that these observations by Milvain, at the
outset of his career, are amply justified by the action. At the
end of the book, Milvain lies back 'in dreamy bliss', married
to Reardon's widow, editor of *The Current*, and having
written a respectful notice of 'The Novels of Edwin
Reardon'.

If Milvain is one portent, the entrepreneur Whelpdale is
another. Having played with the idea of 'Novel-writing
taught in ten lessons', he finds his true destiny in 'one of the
most notable projects of modern times':

> 'Let me explain my principle. I would have the paper address itself
> to the quarter-educated; that is to say, the great new generation

that is being turned out by the Board schools, the young men and women who can just read, but are incapable of sustained attention. People of this kind want something to occupy them in trains and on 'buses and trams. As a rule they care for no newspapers except the Sunday ones; what they want is the lightest and frothiest of chit-chatty information—bits of stories, bits of description, bits of scandal, bits of jokes, bits of statistics, bits of foolery. . . . No article in the paper is to measure more than two inches in length, and every inch must be broken into at least two paragraphs.'[2]

The project materializes; the periodical *Chat* is renamed *Chit-Chat*, and so transformed that

in a month's time all England was ringing with the fame of this noble new development of journalism.[3]

Gissing is writing, of course, after *Tit-Bits*, if only by a few years, but his estimate of attitudes, which are less easily recorded than methods, is at once interesting and convincing. The exploration of detail at the various levels of New Grub Street, which reaches as far as the Reading Room of the British Museum, carries a general conviction. The book is not likely to be read by any kind of writer, now, without a number of wry recognitions. And it is so representative and so thorough that it is extraordinary that it should not be more generally read.

The figure of Reardon, and in a lesser degree that of Harold Biffen, author of the realistic novel *Mr Bailey, Grocer*, are evidently, within the limits of such correspondences, related to Gissing himself. The achievement of a degree of irony towards Biffen, as part of the relatively mature general tone of the novel, marks indeed an important stage in Gissing's development. His novels after 1891 (he had remarried in 1890) are perhaps better, but in many ways less interesting, than his work in the 'eighties, as a very young man, when the pressure on him was at its most severe. *Demos* (1886) and *The Nether World* (1889) are not great or even very good novels; but they have considerable interest from the fact that they stand in the direct line of succession from the 'industrial novels' of the 1840s. It is interesting to see what has happened to the structure of feeling there indicated with the passing of forty years.

INTERREGNUM

One's first reaction is that the essential structure has not changed at all. If Gissing is less compassionately observant than Mrs Gaskell, less overtly polemical than Kingsley, still *The Nether World* and *Demos* would be sympathetically endorsed by either of them, or by their typical readers. Yet Gissing does introduce an important new element, and one that remains significant. He has often been called 'the spokesman of despair', and this is true in both meanings of the phrase. Like Kingsley and Mrs Gaskell, he writes to describe the true conditions of the poor, and to protest

> against those brute forces of society which fill with wreck the abysses of the nether world.[4]

Yet he is also the spokesman of another kind of despair: the despair born of social and political disillusion. In this he is a figure exactly like Orwell in our own day, and for much the same reasons. Whether one calls this honesty or not will depend on experience.

The Nether World, though marked by this latter element, is primarily a simple descriptive novel centred on two characters, Sidney Kirkwood and Jane Snowdon, who are part of the ideal mode of earlier novels of this type:

> In each life little for congratulation. He with the ambitions of his youth frustrated; neither an artist, nor a leader of men in the battle for justice. She, no saviour of society by the force of a superb example; no daughter of the people, holding wealth in trust for the people's needs. Yet to both was their work given. Unmarked, unencouraged save by their love of uprightness and mercy, they stood by the side of those more hapless, brought some comfort to hearts less courageous than their own. Where they abode it was not all dark.[5]

This is, of course, a Victorian solution: a dedication to charity, shrunk to an almost hidden scale, within an essential resignation.

In *Workers in the Dawn* (1880) Gissing had been an evident radical, but the sentimentality of the title indicates the precariousness of the attachment. He came to be disillusioned, but the process of this, as one follows it in the novels, is less a discovery of reality than a document of a particular category of feeling, which we can call 'negative identification'. Gissing himself puts the best description of this into the mouth of one of the predecessors of Reardon, in the novel *The Unclassed* (1884):

> 'I often amuse myself with taking to pieces my former self. I was not a conscious hypocrite in those days of violent radicalism, working-man's-club lecturing, and the like; the fault was that I understood myself as yet so imperfectly. That zeal on behalf of the suffering masses was nothing more nor less than disguised zeal on behalf of my own starved passions. I was poor and desperate, life had no pleasures, the future seemed hopeless, yet I was overflowing with vehement desires, every nerve in me was a hunger which cried to be appeased. . . . I identified myself with the poor and ignorant; I did not make their cause my own, but my own cause theirs.'[6]

This is the negative identification which has been responsible for a great deal of adolescent socialism and radicalism, in particular in the adolescent who is breaking away from (or, as in Gissing's personal history, has fallen foul of) the social standards of his own class. The rebel (or, as in Gissing, the outcast—he was sent down from his college at Manchester on an issue of personal conduct) finds available to him an apparent cause, on behalf of the outcast of society, in a mood of rebellion. He identifies himself with this, often passionately. But the identification will involve an actual relationship, and, at this stage, the rebel faces his new crisis. It is not only that he will normally be reluctant to accept the discipline of the cause; it is also, and more essentially, that the outcast class, whom he has thought of as noble (outcast= himself= noble) are in fact nothing of the kind, but are very mixed in character, containing very good and very bad, and in any case living in ways that differ from his own. I do not say that it is not then possible for him to go on; there have been some useful rebels who began in this way. But clearly in the ordinary case there will be disillusion. The cause will not be precisely his cause; the oppressed will have intentions and attachments and faults of their own. The rebel will react within his own terms: either violently—these people are a menace—'the brute domination of the quarter-educated mob'; or soberly—these people cannot be helped—reform is useless, we need a deep, underlying change. Or else (as has happened in our own generation, with a transfer of identification from the working masses, as in the 'thirties, to the oppressed colonial populations, as now) he will find a new cause. I do not seek to minimize the difficulties of such men, but I would insist that their accounts of their progress form documents, not of a discovered reality, but of their own emotional pressures and recoils. Gissing found the London poor repulsive, in the mass; his descriptions have all the generalizing squalor of a Dickens or an Orwell. There are two points here. First, it does not come as news to anyone born into a poor family that the poor are not beautiful, or that a number of them are lying, shiftless and their own worst enemies. Within an actual social experience, these things can be accepted and recognized; we are dealing after all with actual people under severe pressure. A man like Gorki can record the faults of the poor (in his *Autobiography* and elsewhere) with an unfailing and quite unsentimental alertness. But a Gorki would not suppose that this was an argument against change, or a reason for dissatisfaction with the popular cause. He was never subject to that kind of illusion because that was not the material of his attachment, which grew within a whole reality. Second, the faults of the poor, as they are seen from within a whole situation, are different—more individualized, and related to different standards—from those seen by the rebel whose identification is merely negative. Gissing sees real faults, but generalizes them—his use of an abstract figure like Demos makes this process clear. He sees also what to him are faults, but what, objectively, are no more than differences. A good local example of this occurs in *Demos*, where the shiftless 'Arry speaks, and receives Gissing's comment:

> 'A clerk's, of course.'
> He pronounced the word 'clerk' as it is spelt; it made him seem yet more ignoble.[7]

This example is to be recommended to Mr Russell Kirk, a modern American conservative who, describing Gissing as a 'proletarian novelist', finds in Gissing's discovery of the ignobility of the poor a Conservative witness.[8] What Gissing is here discovering, of course—and an American is well placed to appreciate it—is a trivial difference of speech habit which only his own ambiguous emotion permits him to interpret as 'ignoble'. There is a good deal of this in Gissing. There is some wonderful nonsense, also in *Demos*,[9] about the final distinction between a lady and an upstart being the way she closes her lips. Absurd local examples can be confirmed in Gissing's whole treatment. The general compassion is tempered by a different emotion: the desire of the outcast from another class, who in material circumstances is not to be distinguished from the amorphous ignoble poor, to emphasize all the differences that are possible, and to insist that they are real and important—the attitude to working-class speech (a thing in itself not at all uniform) is characteristic of this. Anyone now in Gissing's position, or in one resembling it, can gain from a critical reading of these social novels, in their exposure of a number of prejudices and false positions, towards which this situation by its own pressures urges them.

It is better that a man like Gissing should write *Demos* or *The Nether World* than that he should write *Workers in the Dawn*. Nothing is to be gained from a simple negative identification, as in the latter, whereas its breakdown can be instructive. And it is breakdown that we must stress. We do not learn from *Demos* that social reform is hopeless; we learn about Gissing's prejudices and difficulties. The case he sets himself to prove is instructive: that a socialist working man, Richard Mutimer, on inheriting a fortune by what amounts to an accident, will inevitably deteriorate personally, and will end by diluting his principles. This does not surprise me, but it is interesting that Gissing thought this an analogue of social reform—the book is sub-titled *A Story of English Socialism*. Mutimer's destiny is always predictable, down to the point where, poor again, and seeking only to serve the working people, he is, in part through his own carelessness, in part through real error, stoned to death by those whom he sought to help. We do not need to ask whose martyrdom this is, and in terms of the structure of feeling we return it to *Felix Holt*: if you get involved, you get into trouble.

There remains, finally, a more general line to be drawn. After *New Grub Street*, Gissing returns to his proper study, that of the condition of exile and loneliness; but both before and after the change there is a significant pattern: the disillusion with social reform is transmuted to an attachment to art. It is so in Waymark, who had described the negative identification in *The Unclassed*. It is so in *Demos*, where it is embodied in the figure of Stella, the wife of a 'literary socialist', Westlake, who has points of relation to William Morris ('the man who wrote "Daphne"!'[10]). The description in this latter instance will serve generally:

> there is a work in the cause of humanity other than that which goes on so clamorously in lecture-halls and at street-corners . . . the work of those whose soul is taken captive of loveliness, who pursue the spiritual ideal apart from the world's tumult.[11]

The relation of this to the 'new aesthetics' is clear enough, and Westlake if he had really been Morris would have had something relevant to say about it. But the attachment, except in its resting on a false, because partial, antithesis, is certainly to be respected. In its extension—for it is how 'the world's tumult' is mediated that is always crucial—Gissing reverts to an early strand in the development of the idea of culture: to rural values, the old order uncorrupted by commercialism, the distrust of industry and science (the latter 'the remorseless enemy of mankind'). Hubert Eldon, the squire, saves the beautiful Wanley valley from the coarse, industry-spreading Socialist, Richard Mutimer. Within this old order, guaranteed by the Englishman's love of 'Common Sense . . . that Uncommon Sense', and his distrust of abstractions, virtue can reside. It is a matter of opinion, I suppose, whether one finds this a convincing peroration, or, in the world's tumult, the desperate rationalization of a deeply sensitive, deeply lonely man.

IV. Shaw and Fabianism

> 'Do I at last see before me that old and tried friend of the working classes, George Bernard Shaw? How are you, George?'
> . . . I was not then old, and had no other feeling for the working classes than an intense desire to abolish them and replace them by sensible people.[1]

This is the right way, with Gissing still in mind, to approach the social thinking of Shaw. It is a point which he often makes:

> When the Socialist movement in London took its tone from lovers of art and literature ... it was apt to assume that all that was needed was to teach Socialism to the masses (vaguely imagined as a huge crowd of tramplike saints) and leave the rest to the natural effect of sowing the good seed in kindly virgin soil. But the proletarian soil was neither virgin nor exceptionally kindly. ... The blunt truth is that ill used people are worse than well used people: indeed this is at bottom the only good reason why we should not allow anyone to be ill used. ... We should refuse to tolerate poverty as a social institution not because the poor are the salt of the earth, but because 'the poor in a lump are bad'.[2]

Such negative criticism is useful (it is the point made in Turgeniev's *Virgin Soil*), but Shaw's conviction of the essential badness of the poor is very close to Gissing (compare *Pygmalion* with Gissing's 'Arry). It exists, however, within a still deeper feeling, which is fundamental to Shaw:

> We have to confess it: Capitalist mankind in the lump is detestable. ... Both rich and poor are really hateful in themselves. For my part I hate the poor and look forward eagerly to their extermination. I pity the rich a little, but am equally bent on their extermination. The working classes, the business classes, the professional classes, the propertied classes, the ruling classes, are each more odious than the other: they have no right to live: I should despair if I did not know that they will all die presently, and that there is no need on earth why they should be replaced by people like themselves. ... And yet I am not in the least a misanthrope. I am a person of normal affections.[3]

If we look at this sentiment, soberly, we shall probably recognize it as one of the perennial sources of politics. The description of available mankind as 'capitalist mankind' is so plausible a gambit, to be followed by adherence to a system, and prophecy of a new kind of man, that what in its direct terms might not be easily confessed is soon rationalized as a humanitarian concern. It is not that one doubts Shaw's kindliness, his 'normal affections', but that one sees these, quite clearly, as pre-social affections: attachments that can hardly be mediated in any adult world. The choice of the word 'extermination' is hardly an accident; it betrays the dissociated violence of the feeling, which is still compatible with private kindliness. 'Yahoo' is perhaps never shouted but by sensitive, kindly, lonely men.

As a basis for Shaw's politics, the feeling is rational. The hatefulness of men, his period had taught him to believe, is not final; it is merely the stamp of their incomplete evolution. The agency of this evolution is still, however, in question. The socialism which promises regeneration by the coming to power of the working class will obviously not be acceptable: the odious can hardly negotiate the noble. In one way or another, regeneration is something that will have to be done *for* mankind; but then by whom? Marxist revolution is merely an old-fashioned liberal romanticism. Owenite revolution, the belief that man will accept the new moral world as soon as he is clearly told about it, is also incredible. Yet, despite the facts of human continuity, the odious need not at all 'be replaced by people like themselves'. A revolutionary discontinuity has to be achieved in the context of a disbelief in revolutions. In the end, Shaw never got out of this dilemma, but for a time, and especially in the 'eighties and 'nineties, he went along with a particular English tradition, which culminated in Fabianism. If the existing classes were odious, there was always, in Arnold's term, the 'remnant': men moved by general feelings of humanity. If the appeals of Carlyle and Ruskin for the aristocracy to resume its functions had failed, there was always the other aristocracy, the aristocracy of intellect. Shaw, determined on socialism, chose these means of its attainment.

Shaw's association with Fabianism is of great importance, for it marks the confluence of two traditions which had been formerly separate and even opposed. Fabianism, in the orthodox person of Sidney Webb, is the direct inheritor of the spirit of John Stuart Mill; that is to say, of a utilitarianism refined by experience of a new situation in history. Shaw, on the other hand, is the direct successor of the spirit of Carlyle and of Ruskin, but he did not go the way of his elder successor, William Morris. In attaching himself to Fabianism, Shaw was, in effect, telling Carlyle and Ruskin to go to school with Bentham, telling Arnold to get together with Mill. One sees, even as early as *Fabian Essays* (1889), his doubts of this, when, having sketched a policy of gradual reform, he writes:

> Let me, in conclusion, disavow all admiration for this inevitable, but sordid, slow, reluctant, cowardly path to justice. I venture to claim your respect for those enthusiasts who still refuse to believe that millions of their fellow creatures must be left to sweat and suffer in hopeless toil and degradation, whilst parliaments and vestries grudgingly muddle and grope towards paltry instalments of betterment. The right is so clear, the wrong so intolerable, the gospel so convincing, that it seems to them that it *must* be possible to enlist the whole body of workers—soldiers, policemen, and all—under the banner of brotherhood and equality; and at one great stroke to set Justice on her rightful throne. Unfortunately, such an army of light is no more to be gathered from the human product of nineteenth-century civilization than grapes are to be gathered from thistles. But if we feel glad of that impossibility . . . if we feel anything less than acute disappointment and bitter humiliation at the discovery . . . then I submit to you that our institutions have corrupted us to the most dastardly degree of selfishness.[4]

This is Shaw at his best, but the feeling he describes is not a feeling that would have occurred to the normal Fabian. Certainly, Sidney Webb gives one no such impression. To Webb, socialism was the straightforward business of evolution:

> Historic fossils are more dangerous . . . but against the stream of tendencies they are ultimately powerless. . . . The main stream which has borne European society towards Socialism during the past 100 years is the irresistible progress of Democracy. . . . The economic side of the democratic ideal is, in fact, Socialism itself. . . . The landlord and the capitalist are both finding that the steam-engine is a Frankenstein which they had better not have raised; for with it comes inevitably urban Democracy, the study of Political Economy, and Socialism.[5]

On this, with its calm, admirable assumption of steady progress, William Morris's comment may be recalled: the Fabians, he said, very much underrate the strength of the tremendous organization under which we live. . . . Nothing but a tremendous force can deal with this force; it will not suffer itself to be dismembered, nor to lose anything which really is its essence without putting forth all its force in resistance; rather than lose anything which it considers of importance, it will pull the roof of the world down upon its head.[6]

(Webb, oddly, had also been thinking about Samson, but in different terms: 'the industrial revolution has left the laborer a landless stranger in his own country. The political evolution is rapidly making him its ruler. Samson is feeling for his grip on the pillars.'[7] There is some significance in the different application of the metaphor.)

Of Webb's evolutionary argument, with its formidable list of public administrative arrangements already in force, Morris added:

He is so anxious to prove the commonplace that our present industrial system embraces some of the machinery by means of which a Socialist system *might* be worked . . . that his paper tends to produce the impression of one who thinks that we are already in the first stages of socialistic life.[8]

Webb's mistake, for Morris, was to

overestimate the importance of the *mechanism* of a system of society apart from the *end* towards which it may be used.[9]

These are the precise terms in which, from Carlyle to Arnold, the utilitarians had always been criticized.

The argument between Morris and Webb, between communism and social democracy, still rages; neither has yet been proved finally right. But it is significant to take the argument thirty or forty years on from *Fabian Essays*, and to compare Webb's Introduction to the 1920 edition with Shaw's Preface to that of 1931. Webb, in 1920, is admirably himself: the intervening lines are traced and annotated; the questions formerly neglected are lucidly posed and discussed:

We evidently attached quite insufficient importance to Trade Unionism. . . . We were similarly unappreciative of the Co-operative Movement. . . . We went far astray in what was said about Unemployment. . . . And whilst we were strong on Liberty and Fraternity . . . we were apt to forget Equality.[10]

These defects, however, have been remedied: the reader is referred to the relevant works.

Shaw's Preface is wholly different in tone. He refers to Morris as 'the greatest Socialist of that day', and, on the central issue of the Fabian adherence to constitutional change, which Morris had opposed, adds:

> It is not so certain today as it seemed in the 'eighties that Morris was not right.[11]

Shaw had, of course, lived to see Fascism, which could not be blandly overlooked as a fossil. He had also, however, lived through the essential disillusion which haunts his statements of the 'eighties. Socialism might be for Mill or Webb the 'economic obverse' of democracy, but was the faith in democracy real?

> The naked truth is that democracy, or government by the people through votes for everybody, has never been a complete reality; and to the very limited extent to which it has been a reality it has not been a success. The extravagant hopes which have been attached to every extension of it have been disappointed. . . . If there were any disfranchised class left for our democrats to pin their repeatedly disappointed hopes on, no doubt they would still clamour for a fresh set of votes to jump the last ditch into their Utopia; and the vogue of democracy might last a while yet. Possibly there may be here and there lunatics looking forward to votes for children, or for animals, to complete the democratic structure. But the majority shows signs of having had enough of it.[12]

Capitalism, he argues, has produced such ignorance, particularly as a result of the division of labour, that

> we should die of idiocy through disuse of our mental faculties if we did not fill our heads with romantic nonsense out of illustrated newspapers and novels and plays and films. Such stuff keeps us alive; but it falsifies everything for us so absurdly that it leaves us more or less dangerous lunatics in the real world.[13]

In consequence,

> the more power the people are given the more urgent becomes the need for some rational and well-informed superpower to dominate

them and disable their inveterate admiration of international murder and national suicide.[14]

Here the wheel has come full circle, and Shaw is back with Carlyle. We have to set 'dominate . . . and disable' with 'exterminate' as significant marks of feeling, but Shaw remains to be listened to. In the mood that brought him to Fabianism, he goes on with proposals for a real elective aristocracy, which should inaugurate socialism and equality. In the mood of his earlier disillusion, he concludes:

> Since all moral triumphs, like mechanical triumphs, are reached by trial and error, we can despair of Democracy and despair of Capitalism without despairing of human nature: indeed if we did not despair of them as we know them we should prove ourselves so worthless that there would be nothing left for the world but to wait for the creation of a new race of beings capable of succeeding where we have failed.[15]

This is the ironic twist of the Fabian adherence to evolution as a social model: that it comes, in Shaw, to an evolution of humanity beyond man. The twist, perhaps, was always there, in the deeply humane man who hated what he called 'capitalist mankind'. The situation has, in modern social thinking, a representative significance, and Shaw is always so articulate and so penetrating that he remains a classical point to which we are bound, in wisdom, to refer.

v. Critics of the State

In terms of industrial action, the Labour movement has gone its own way: at times, indeed, to the point where a Fabian might conclude that it was feeling for its grip on the pillars. But the political actions of the Labour movement as a recognizable body have, in general, been under Fabian direction; we now live, in certain evident respects, in a Webb world. The identification of socialism with State action is the clear result of this, and the identification points a further argument, within the tradition which we are considering. Hilaire Belloc wrote *The Servile State*, and with Chesterton continued a mediaevalist sentiment that we have already traced to this point. The conclusions of this type of criticism have led down to a number of books in our own time, with Hayek's *The Road to Serfdom* as exemplar. Also, however, within the interregnum, there was an important body of socialist criticism of the State, in the Guild Socialist movement inaugurated by Penty, Orage and Hobson, and later continued by Cole. These currents of opinion are the direct inheritors of elements of the nineteenth-century tradition.

Belloc's argument is that capitalism as a system is breaking down, and that this is to be welcomed. A society in which a minority owns and controls the means of production, while the majority are reduced to proletarian status, is not only wrong but unstable. Belloc sees it breaking down in two ways—on the one hand into State action for welfare (which pure capitalism cannot embody); on the other hand into monopoly and the restraint of trade. There are only two alternatives to this system: socialism, which Belloc calls collectivism; and the redistribution of property on a significant scale, which Belloc calls distributivism. Our social difficulties will not be understood if they are regarded as the product of the Industrial Revolution: modern society was not formed by the growth of industry, but by the fact that

> capitalism was here in England before the Industrial System. . . . England, the seed-plot of the Industrial System, was *already* captured by a wealthy oligarchy *before* the series of great discoveries began.[1]

Modern society, with its propertied minority and its propertyless proletariat, was not created by the Industrial Revolution:

> No such material cause determined the degradation from which we suffer. It was the deliberate action of men, evil will in a few and apathy of will among the many. . . .[2]

The root of our present evils was in fact the Reformation, and the seizure of the monastic lands. This created a landed oligarchy and destroyed the civilization of the late Middle Ages, where the distributive system of property and the organization of the guilds had been slowly creating a society in which all men should be 'economically free through the possession of capital and land'.[3] The recovery of economic freedom through socialism is in fact impossible: collectivist measures will merely make capitalism endurable, within its essential terms. What is being brought into being is not a collectivist but a servile State, in which

> the mass of men shall be constrained *by law* to labour to the profit of a minority, but, as the price of such constraint, shall enjoy a security which the old Capitalism did not give them.[4]

Such a State will be a smoothly running 'machine', in which all 'human and organic complexity'[5] will be absent; this is why it appeals to the tidy-minded bureaucrat who is one main type of socialist reformer. The other type, the idealist, when he sees that property cannot simply be confiscated, and that 'buying-out' is not really a change in property-holding but may even be a new endowment of the capitalists, will concentrate on getting the owners to recognize their responsibilities, on the promise of complementary responsibilities undertaken by the wage-earners. Here again, but now increasingly bound by law, the reforming measures will be producing the servile State.

Belloc's is a very relevant criticism, which still invites attention. It was never clear, however, how distributivism was to be effected, except in a general way by recovery of the old faith. The redistribution of property, Belloc emphasized, had to be in significant amounts, and it was this that capitalism could not allow. He added:

> those to whom the argument for existing small property appeals— those whom our Capitalist press bemuses with the mere numbers of holders in Railway stock or the National Debt—were hardly of the kind who would follow a serious economic discussion.[6]

It is at the point where Belloc leaves off that the Guild Socialist emphasis begins. A. J. Penty, a direct inheritor of Ruskin and Morris, noted first 'the prejudice against Mediaeval society which has been created by lying historians in the past',[7] and continued:

> To Mediaeval social arrangements we shall return, not only because we shall never be able to regain complete control over the economic forces in society except through the agency of restored Guilds, but because it is imperative to return to a simpler state of society. . . .

When any society develops beyond a certain point, the human mind is unable to get a grip of all the details necessary to its proper ordering.[8]

The result of such development is a spirit of anarchy, which is 'rife today', and 'is a sign that modern society is beginning to break up'.[9] The growing disrespect for all kinds of authority is legitimate, but it may

develop into a revolt against authority and culture in general. . . . To those who realize the dependence of a healthy social system on living traditions of culture it is a matter of some concern. For whereas a false culture like the academic one of today tends to separate people by dividing them in classes and groups and finally isolating them as individuals, a true culture like the great cultures of the past unites them. . . . The recovery of such a culture is one of our most urgent needs.[10]

The Fabian road of collectivism is firmly rejected:

It never presumed to be an artistic ideal. It has ended in not even daring to be a human one. The Anti-Socialist who told us that Socialism left human nature out of account stands justified.[11]

The needs of human nature are identical with 'the needs of art in industry'.[12] The Fabian programme is 'far too intellectual and too little human ever to get at grips with the realities of life'.[13] The psychology of its supporters leads them to seek 'an external order' because they lack 'any personal organizing principle'.[14] Such efforts are plausible, but

the Leisure State and the Servile State are complementary—the one involves the other.[15]

The Guild programme, offered as an alternative, proposed:

the abolition of the wage-system, and the establishment of self-government in industry through a system of national guilds working in conjunction with other democratic functional organizations in the community.

The last phrase of this was an amendment from the original 'in conjunction with the State', and shows the high-water point of this kind of criticism. As a programme, the establishment of guilds became immensely difficult and controversial when it encountered problems of detail. G. D. H. Cole, alone among the Guildsmen, was competent to translate an emphasis into a practical proposition, but even he, in the full development of his work, transforms the programme into an emphasis within existing forms of social organization. Because of these practical difficulties, which lie not only in the discovery of a social force to realize such a programme, but also in the question of the compatibility of 'self-government in industry' with a high degree of economic concentration, it has been easy, too easy, to overlook the value both of the emphasis and of the criticism of other kinds of socialist programme. The underlying problem, as restated by Cole in 1941, is that of 'democracy face to face with hugeness'.[16] The dangers of powerful central authority, and of a general bureaucratic organization, to which the Guild Socialists drew attention, have become increasingly obvious since they were writing. Further, the dangers of socialism conceived merely as 'machinery' have become increasingly apparent, and have already produced a restlessness, particularly in matters of industrial organization, among the working class. The gradual dropping of the reliance on mediaeval ideas and patterns was of course inevitable, but the line of thinking which is summed up in the word 'community', rather than in the word 'state', remains an essential element of our tradition. Its reliance on nineteenth-century thinking about culture is clear and important.

From a number of directions, the emphasis on 'community' has received increasing support. Many now agree with Cole, in a point that goes back to the beginning of this tradition, in Burke, that the political

democrats set out to strip the individual naked in his relations to the State, regarding all the older social tissue as tainted with aristocratic corruption or privileged monopoly. Their representative democracy was atomistically conceived in terms of millions of voters, each casting his individual vote into a pool which was somehow mystically to boil up into a General Will. No such transmutation happened, or could happen. Torn away from his fellows, from the small groups which he and they had been painfully learning to manage, the individual was lost. He could not control the State: it was too big for him. Democracy in the State was a great aspiration; but in practice it was largely a sham.[17]

Cole points out, however, that all kinds of voluntary democratic associations, based on a real collective experience, have in fact grown up, and that it is to this 'vital associative life' that we must look for the reality of democracy. The Guild Socialists failed in their effort to extend this over society as a whole, but their emphasis was, and remains, creative and indispensable.

vi. T. E. Hulme

If the interregnum began with the minor scepticism of Mallock, it ends with a major scepticism, and its only novelty, in the work of T. E. Hulme. For Hulme challenged the tradition at its roots, in ways that have since taken on a wide and representative significance. He died at thirty-four, and his work embodies no complete system, but the emphases which he made in his preparatory work, to be seen in the volume *Speculations* which was collected after his death, challenge certain aspects of the inherited ways of thinking with power and effect.

Hulme's basic point is that the humanist tradition, which has dominated Europe since the Renaissance, is breaking up; and that this is to be welcomed, since the fundamental beliefs of humanism are in fact false. He sees romanticism as the extreme development of humanism, and is concerned to reject it, and to prepare for a radical transformation of society, according to different principles which he calls classical. His distinction between romanticism and the classical is made in this way:

Here is the root of all romanticism: that man, the individual, is an infinite reservoir of possibilities; and if you can so rearrange society by the destruction of oppressive order then these possibilities will have a chance and you will get Progress. One can define the classical quite clearly as the exact opposite to this. Man is an extraordinarily fixed and limited animal whose nature is absolutely constant. It is only by tradition and organization that anything decent can be got out of him.[1]

This is to be supplemented by another definition:

> All Romanticism springs from Rousseau, and the key to it can be found even in the first sentence of the Social Contract. . . . In other words, man is by nature something wonderful, of unlimited powers, and if hitherto he has not appeared so, it is because of external obstacles and fetters, which it should be the main business of social politics to remove. What is at the root of the contrasted system of ideas . . . the classical, pessimistic, or, as its opponents would have it, the reactionary ideology? This system springs from the exactly contrary conception of man; the conviction that man is by nature bad or limited, and can consequently only accomplish anything of value by disciplines, ethical, heroic, or political.[2]

Thus far, Hulme is doing little more than restate Burke, although Burke did not use this Romantic/Classical distinction. In his analysis of the driving force of the French Revolution, and in his rejection of its principles, Hulme echoes Burke quite evidently. From this kind of analysis and rejection there came, we must remember, an important part of the idea of culture, with its emphasis on order as against the dominant individualism. But from its beginning in Burke, and in a direct line down to Arnold, this emphasis on order was associated with the idea of perfectibility—the gradual perfection of man through cultivation. Hulme rejects this:

> The whole subject has been confused by the failure to recognize the *gap* between the regions of vital and human things, and that of the *absolute* values of ethics and religion. We introduce into human things the *Perfection* that properly belongs only to the divine, and thus confuse both human and divine things by not clearly separating them. . . . We place *Perfection* where it should not be—on this human plane. As we are painfully aware that nothing *actual* can be *perfect*, we imagine the perfection to be not where we are, but some distance along one of the roads. This is the essence of all Romanticism. . . . If we continue to look with satisfaction along these roads, we shall always be unable to understand the religious attitude. . . .

It is the closing of all the roads, this realization of the *tragic* significance of life, which makes it legitimate to call all other attitudes
shallow.[3]

Thus, even if the Romantic view that 'man is intrinsically
good, spoilt by circumstance' is rejected, its alternative, in
Hulme, is not 'that he is intrinsically limited, but disciplined
by order and tradition' towards perfection; it is, rather, 'that
he is intrinsically limited, but disciplined by order and tradition to something fairly decent'.[4] The idea of perfection is
wrongly imported from the quite separate religious sphere.
Romanticism is 'spilt religion',[5] and in the same way
culture, by the time of Arnold's definition of it, would also
be, for Hulme, 'spilt religion'.

This argument is Hulme's major contribution; it has
since been widely popularized, notably by T. S. Eliot. The
events of the twentieth century have contributed to its
acceptability. In so far as the Romantics have been rejected,
it is in these terms. But it is necessary to remember that our
thinking about culture has in itself outgrown Romanticism,
yet not in Hulme's way. While Hulme's alternatives are the
only alternatives, our experience of a violent century will
deny the Romantic complacencies, only to offer us a new
complacency. It may seem strange to describe Hulme's
classicism as complacent, yet so, I think, it has been in effect.
The pressure of the alternatives makes us suppose that we
have to choose between considering man as 'intrinsically
good' or 'intrinsically limited', and then, in a desperate
world, we are invited to look at the evidence. I can perhaps
best describe these alternatives, however, as pre-cultural.
Neither version of man takes its origin from a view of man
in society, man within a culture; both are based on speculation about his isolated, pre-social condition. Hulme points,
rightly, to the 'pseudo-categories' of Romanticism, and to
the more general 'pseudo-categories' of humanism. As a
negative critique, this is entirely useful, and it is merely
sentimental to blame it for its pessimism. The contrast of
pessimism and optimism, at these ultimate levels, is to be
seen, rather, as yet another pair of limiting alternatives,
which any adequate thinking about culture will find

irrelevant. My own view is that Hulme is himself confined by a 'pseudo-category', one of

> a number of abstract ideas, of which we are as a matter of fact unconscious. We do not see them, but see other things through them.[6]

This pseudo-category is the acceptance, as fact, of an ultimate, essential condition of man: a nature which underlies, and precedes, his actual manifestation in particular circumstances. It is not that we may not speculate on this, but that if we accept it we are accepting something which no man can ever experience as a fact. We are then erecting a pseudo-category which prevents us from thinking adequately about culture at all, for to think about culture can only be to think about common experience. I agree with Hulme that romanticism is 'spilt religion'. I think also that much of the early definition of culture was also 'spilt religion'. But I see what he calls romanticism and what he calls 'the classical' as alternative versions within a pseudo-category. There is in fact no reason why we should accept either. Experience moves within an actual situation, in directions which the forces within that situation will alone determine. A version of man as perfectible or limited, a spirit of humane optimism or of tragic pessimism, can be imported into this situation, but as little more than a posture. As interpretation any such attitude may be important, but as programme any is irrelevant. At its worst, such an attitude merely rationalizes the phantasy of being above the common situation, able to direct it by taking thought in this way or in that. Hulme wanted hard, bare, unsentimental thinking, but he hardly achieved it. His function was the replacement of one rationalization by another, but we cannot think about culture until we are rid of both. The acceptance of actual experience, commitment to a real situation from which by no effort of abstraction we can escape, is harder than Hulme supposed, and needs a pulling-down of further pseudo-categories which he, in common with his direct successors, failed to notice. The psychology that is revealed in *Cinders*, his notes for a *Weltanschauung*, indicates well enough the barriers against experience which he had to erect.

From his basic position, Hulme derived certain views on politics, and certain important views on art. In politics, he was concerned to reject the idea of Progress as the product of 'democratic romanticism', and to point out that it proceeded from a 'body of middle-class thought',[7] which had no necessary connexion with the working-class movement. His own view was that

> no theory that is not fully moved by the conception of justice asserting the equality of men, and which cannot offer something to all men, deserves or is likely to have any future.[8]

With this in mind, he approved Sorel's critique of democratic ideology, distinguishing it from other kinds of criticism:

> Some of these are merely dilettante, having little sense of reality, while others are really vicious, in that they play with the idea of inequality.[9]

All this is useful as far as it goes, but he never took the points further, and found little practical allegiance. The combination of 'revolutionary economics' with the 'classical' spirit in ethics seemed to him likely to be emancipating, but the combination has not yet occurred, in practice, except in the degrading caricature of Fascism, with which Hulme in certain moods can be associated, but from which he is essentially to be distinguished because of his adherence to equality, a saving clause which some of his successors either dropped or never possessed.

The views on art are more important, if only because they have become the commonplaces of English criticism. This is not only so in language—his advocacy of a 'dry hardness'[10]; his description of the Romantic attitude as 'poetry that isn't damp isn't poetry at all',[11] or of romanticism as 'always flying, flying over abysses, flying up into the eternal gases . . . the word infinite in every other line'.[12] It is so also in certain now characteristic doctrines: the rejection of naturalism, the theory of 'geometrical art',[13] the belief in 'lines which are clean, clear-cut, and mechanical',[14] the view of the coming relation between art and machinery: 'it has nothing whatever to do with the superficial notion that one must beautify machinery. It is not a question of dealing with machinery in the spirit and with the methods of existing art, but of the creation of a new art having an organization, and governed by principles, which are at present exemplified unintentionally, as it were, in machinery.'[15] In all this, Hulme is a genuine forerunner: the first important anti-Romantic critic.

He accepts wholly, of course, the nineteenth-century view of the relation between the principles of a society and the character of its art. He interprets the new movements in art as the first signs of a general change in principles, just as he has interpreted the art of past periods in terms of this kind of change. He is an extraordinarily stimulating critic, and his place at the head of the tradition which we associate with Eliot, or in another category with Read, requires recognition and emphasis. The questions which we are then left with are important: whether the new mood in art, the rejection of Romanticism, is in fact based on Hulme's 'classical' view of man, carrying it along, as it were inevitably, with it; or whether, in noticing and helping to form this mood, Hulme was responding correctly but interpreting wrongly, within his 'pseudo-category'. These are questions which we might wish Hulme had lived to help us answer; his death in action in 1917 was in every way a loss. But they are questions, also, which carry us beyond the interregnum, into our own immediate period.

PART III
TWENTIETH-CENTURY
OPINIONS

CHAPTER I

D. H. LAWRENCE

IT is easy to be aware of Lawrence's great effect on our thinking about social values, but it is difficult, for a number of reasons, to give any exact account of his actual contribution. It is not only that the public projection of him is very different from his actual work, and that this has led to important misunderstandings (that he believed that 'sex solves everything'; that he was 'a precursor of the Fascist emphasis on blood'). These, in the end, are matters of ignorance, and ignorance, though always formidable, can always be faced. The major difficulties are, I think, two in number. First, there is the fact that Lawrence's position, in the question of social values, is an amalgam of original and derived ideas. Yet, because of the intensity with which he took up and worked over what he had learned from others, this is, in practice, very difficult to sort out. Secondly, Lawrence's main original contribution is as a novelist, yet his general writing, in essays and letters, which for obvious reasons expresses most clearly his social ideas, cannot really be separated or judged apart from the novels. For example, his vital study of relationships, which is the basis of his original contribution to our social thinking, is naturally conducted in the novels and stories, and has constantly to be turned to for evidence, even though it is very difficult, for technical reasons, to use it just as evidence. Again, he has certain clear positives, which appear in a central position in his general arguments, yet which again depend on what he learned, and shows, in the writing of the novels. We can quote him, for example, on vitality, or on spontaneity, or on relationship, but to realize these, as the matters of substance which for him they were, we can only go, as readers, to this or that novel.

The thinker of whom one is most often reminded, as one goes through Lawrence's social writings, is Carlyle. There is more than a casual resemblance between the two men, in a number of ways, and anyone who has read

Carlyle will see the continuity of such writing as this, in Lawrence:

> The Pisgah-top of spiritual oneness looks down upon a hopeless squalor of industrialism, the huge cemetery of human hopes. This is our Promised Land. . . . The aeroplane descends and lays her eggshells of empty tin-cans on the top of Everest, in the Ultima Thule, and all over the North Pole; not to speak of tractors waddling across the inviolate Sahara and over the jags of Arabia Petraea, laying the same addled eggs of our civilization, tin cans, in every camp-nest. . . .[1]
>
> . . . It is the joy for ever, the agony for ever, and above all, the fight for ever. For all the universe is alive, and whirling in the same fight, the same joy and anguish. The vast demon of life has made himself habits which, except in the whitest heat of desire and rage, he will never break. And these habits are the laws of our scientific universe. But all the laws of physics, dynamics, kinetics, statics, all are but the settled habits of a vast living incomprehensibility, and they can all be broken, superseded, in a moment of great extremity.[2]

The bitter sweep of this critique of industrialism; this vibrant repetitive hymn to the 'vast incomprehensibility': these, across eighty years, belong uniquely to Lawrence and Carlyle, and the resemblance, which is not only imitation, is remarkable. Lawrence takes over the major criticism of industrialism from the nineteenth-century tradition, on point after point, but in tone he remains more like Carlyle than any other writer in the tradition, then or since. There is in each the same mixture of argument, satire, name-calling, and sudden wild bitterness. The case is reasoned and yet breaks again and again into a blind passion of rejection, of which the tenor is not merely negative but annihilating—a threshing after power, which is to be known, ultimately, only in that force of mystery at the edge of which the human articulation breaks down. The impact of each man on the generation which succeeded him is remarkably similar in quality: an impact not so much of doctrines as of an inclusive, compelling, general revelation.*

* I have read, since writing this paragraph, Dr Leavis's censure (in *D. H. Lawrence, Novelist*) on a comparison of Lawrence with Carlyle. He traces the comparison to Desmond MacCarthy, and predicts that it will 'recur.' Well, here it is, but not, so far as I am concerned, from that source. As my comparison stands, I see no reason for withdrawal.

D. H. LAWRENCE

The points which Lawrence took over from the nine-teenth-century tradition can be briefly illustrated. There is, first, the general condemnation of industrialism as an attitude of mind:

The industrial problem arises from the base forcing of all human energy into a competition of mere acquisition.[3]

Then, when narrowed to competitive acquisitiveness, human purpose is seen as debased to 'sheer mechanical materialism':

When pure mechanization or materialism sets in, the soul is auto-matically pivoted, and the most diverse of creatures fall into a common mechanical unison. This we see in America. It is not a homogeneous, spontaneous coherence so much as a disintegrated amorphousness which lends itself to perfect mechanical unison.[4]

Mechanical, disintegrated, amorphous: these are the continuing key words to describe the effect of the industrial priorities on individuals and on the whole society. It is this condition of mind, rather than industry as such, which is seen as having led to the ugliness of an industrial society, on which Lawrence is always emphatic:

The real tragedy of England, as I see it, is the tragedy of ugliness. The country is so lovely: the man-made England is so vile. . . . It was ugliness which betrayed the spirit of man, in the nineteenth century. The great crime which the moneyed classes and promoters of industry committed in the palmy Victorian days was the con-demning of the workers to ugliness, ugliness, ugliness: meanness and formless and ugly surroundings, ugly ideals, ugly religion, ugly hope, ugly love, ugly clothes, ugly furniture, ugly houses, ugly relation-ship between workers and employers. The human soul needs actual beauty even more than bread.[5]

Or again:

The blackened brick dwellings, the black slate roofs glistening their sharp edges, the mud black with coal-dust, the pavements wet and black. It was as if dismalness had soaked through and through every-thing. The utter negation of natural beauty, the utter negation of the gladness of life, the utter absence of the instinct for shapely beauty which every bird and beast has, the utter death of the human intuitive faculty was appalling. . . .[6]

Lawrence is here carrying on a known judgement, yet with his own quick perception and in his own distinctive accent. This kind of observation has to be made again and again, in every generation, not only because the atmosphere of industrialism tends to breed habituation, but also because (in ironic tribute to the strength of the tradition of protest) it is common to shift the ugliness and evil of industrialism out of the present, back into the 'bad old days'. The reminder that the thing is still here has repeatedly to be issued. Lawrence is little concerned, historically, with the origins of industrialism. For him, in this century, it is a received fact, and at the centre of it is the 'forcing of all human energy into a competition of mere acquisition'—the common element in all the diverse interpretations of which the tradition is composed.

Lawrence's starting point is, then, familiar ground. The inherited ideas were there to clarify his first sense of crisis. When we think of Lawrence, we concentrate, understandably, on the adult life, in all its restless dedication. That he was the son of a miner adds, commonly, a certain pathetic or sentimental interest; we relate the adult life back to it, in a personal way. But the real importance of Lawrence's origins is not and cannot be a matter of retrospect from the adult life. It is, rather, that his first social responses were those, not of a man observing the processes of industrialism, but of one caught in them, at an exposed point, and destined, in the normal course, to be enlisted in their regiments. That he escaped enlistment is now so well known to us that it is difficult to realize the thing as it happened, in its living sequence. It is only by hard fighting, and, further, by the fortune of fighting on a favourable front, that anyone born into the industrial working class escapes his function of replacement. Lawrence could not be certain, at the time when his fundamental social responses were forming, that he could so escape. That he was exceptionally gifted exacerbated the problem, although later it was to help towards solving it. Yet the problem of adjustment to the disciplines of industrialism, not merely in day-to-day matters, but in the required basic adjustments of feeling, is common and general. In remembering the occasional 'victories'—the

escapes from the required adjustment—we forget the in-
numerable and persistent defeats. Lawrence did not forget,
because he was not outside the process, meeting those who
had escaped, and forming his estimate of the problem from
this very limited evidence. For him, rather, the *whole* process
had been lived, and he was the more conscious of the general
failure, and thus of the general character of the system:

> In my generation, the boys I went to school with, colliers now,
> have all been beaten down, what with the din-din-dinning of Board
> Schools, books, cinemas, clergymen, the whole national and human
> consciousness hammering on the fact of material prosperity above all
> things.[7]

Lawrence could not have written this, with such a phrase as
'all been beaten down', if the pressures had not been so
intensely and personally felt. In the early stages of the imposition of the industrial system, an observer could see adult
men and women, grown to another way of life, being 'beaten
down' into the new functions and the new feelings. But once
industrialism was established, an *observer* could hardly see
this. Tension would be apparent to him only in those who
had escaped, or half-escaped. The rest, 'the masses', would
normally appear to him fully formed—the 'beating down'
had happened, and he had not seen it. It thus became
possible for men in such a position to believe, and with a
show of reason to argue, that the residual majority, the
'masses', had, essentially, got the way of life they wanted, or,
even, the way of life they deserved—the way 'best fitted' for
them. Only an occasional generous spirit could construct,
from his own experience, the vision of an alternative possibility; even this, because it had to be vision, was always in
danger of simplification or sentimentality. The outstanding
value of Lawrence's development is that he was in a position
to know the living process as a matter of common rather than
of special experience. He had, further, the personal power of
understanding and expressing this. While the thing was being lived, however, and while the pressures were not theoretic
but actual, the inherited criticism of the industrial system was
obviously of the greatest importance to him. It served to
clarify and to generalize what had otherwise been a confused

and personal issue. It is not too much to say that he built his whole intellectual life on the foundation of this tradition. A man can live only one life, and the greater part of Lawrence's strength was taken up by an effort which in terms of ideas achieved perhaps less than had already been reached by different paths. Lawrence was so involved with the business of getting free of the industrial system that he never came seriously to the problem of changing it, although he knew that since the problem was common an individual solution was only a cry in the wind. It would be absurd to blame him on these grounds. It is not so much that he was an artist, and thus supposedly condemned, by romantic theory, to individual solutions. In fact, as we know, Lawrence spent a good deal of time trying to generalize about the necessary common change; he was deeply committed, all his life, to the idea of re-forming society. But his main energy went, and had to go, to the business of personal liberation from the system. Because he understood the issue in its actual depth, he knew that this liberation was not merely a matter of escaping a routine industrial job, or of getting an education, or of moving into the middle class. These things, in Lawrence's terms, were more of an evasion than what he actually came to do. Mitigation of the physical discomforts, of the actual injustices, or of the sense of lost opportunity, was no kind of liberation from the 'base forcing of all human energy into a competition of mere acquisition'. His business was the recovery of other purposes, to which the human energy might be directed. What he lived was the break-out, not theoretically, nor in any Utopian construction, but as it was possible to him, in immediate terms, in opposition alike to the 'base forcing' and to his own weakness. What he achieved, in his life, was an antithesis to the powerful industrial thesis which had been proposed for him. But this, in certain of its aspects, was never more than a mere rejection, a habit of evasion: the industrial system was so strong, and he had been so fiercely exposed to it, that at times there was little that he or any man could do but run. This aspect, however, is comparatively superficial. The weakness of the exclusively biographical treatment of Lawrence, with its emphasis on the restless wanderings and the approach to any way of life but his own, lies in the fact that these things were only contingencies, whereas the dedication, and the value, were in the 'endless venture into consciousness', which was his work as man and writer.

Lawrence is often dramatized as the familiar romantic figure who 'rejects the claims of society'. In fact, he knew too much about society, and knew it too directly, to be deceived for long by anything so foolish. He saw this version of individualism as a veneer on the consequences of industrialism.

> We have frustrated that instinct of community which would make us unite in pride and dignity in the bigger gesture of the citizen, not the cottager.[8]

The 'instinct of community' was vital in his thinking: deeper and stronger, he argued, than even the sexual instinct. He attacked the industrial society of England, not because it offered community to the individual, but because it frustrated it. In this, again, he is wholly in line with the tradition. If in his own life he 'rejected the claims of society', it was not because he did not understand the importance of community, but because, in industrial England, he could find none. Almost certainly, he underestimated the degree of community that might have been available to him: the compulsion to get away was so fierce, and he was personally very weak and exposed. But he was rejecting, not the claims of society, but the claims of industrial society. He was not a vagrant, to live by dodging; but an exile, committed to a different social principle. The vagrant wants the system to stay as it is, so long as he can go on dodging it while still being maintained by it. The exile, on the contrary, wants to see the system changed, so that he can come home. This latter is, in the end, Lawrence's position.

Lawrence started, then, from the criticism of industrial society which made sense of his own social experience, and which gave title to his refusal to be 'basely forced'. But alongside this ratifying principle of denial he had the rich experience of childhood in a working-class family, in which most of his positives lay. What such a childhood gave was certainly not tranquillity or security; it did not even, in the ordinary sense, give happiness. But it gave what to Lawrence was more important than these things: the sense of close quick relationship, which came to matter more than anything else. This was the positive result of the life of the family in a small house, where there were no such devices of eparation of children and parents as the sending-away to school, or the handing-over to servants, or the relegation to nursery or playroom. Comment on this life (usually by those who have not experienced it) tends to emphasize the noisier factors: the fact that rows are always in the open; that there is no privacy in crisis; that want breaks through the small margin of material security and leads to mutual blame and anger. It is not that Lawrence, like any child, did not suffer from these things. It is rather that, in such a life, the suffering and the giving of comfort, the common want and the common remedy, the open row and the open making-up, are all part of a continuous life which, in good and bad, makes for a whole attachment. Lawrence learned from this experience that sense of the continuous flow and recoil of sympathy which was always, in his writing, the essential process of living. His idea of close spontaneous living rests on this foundation, and he had no temptation to idealize it into the pursuit of happiness: things were too close to him for anything so abstract. Further, there is an important sense in which the working-class family is an evident and mutual economic unit, within which both rights and responsibilities are immediately contained. The material processes of satisfying human needs are not separated from personal relationships; and Lawrence knew from this, not only that the processes must be accepted (he was firm on this through all his subsequent life, to the surprise of friends for whom these things had normally been the function of servants), but also that a common life has to be made on the basis of a correspondence between work relationships and personal relationships: something, again, which was only available, if at all, as an abstraction, to those whose first model of society, in the family, had been hierarchical, separative and inclusive of the element of paid substitute labour—Carlyle's 'cash-nexus'. The intellectual critiques of industrialism as a system were therefore reinforced and prepared for by all he knew of primary relationships. It is no accident that the early chapters of *Sons and Lovers* are at once a marvellous re-creation of this close, active, contained family life, and also in general terms an indictment of the pressures of industrialism. Almost all that he learned in this way was by contrasts, and this element of contrast was reinforced by the accident that he lived on a kind of frontier, within sight both of industrial and of agricultural England. In the family and out of it, in the Breach and at Haggs Farm, he learned on his own senses the crisis of industrial England. When the family was broken by the death of his mother, and when the small world of the family had to be replaced by the world of wages and hiring, it was like a personal death, and from then on he was an exile, in spirit and later in fact.

The bridge across which he escaped was, in the widest sense, intellectual. He could read his way out in spirit, and he could write his way out in fact. It has recently been most valuably emphasized, by F. R. Leavis, that the provincial culture which was available to him was very much more rich and exciting than the usual accounts infer. The chapel, the literary society attached to it, the group of adolescents with whom he could read and talk: these were not the 'drab, earnest institutions' of the observers' clichés, but active, serious, and, above all, wholehearted in energy. What they lacked in variety and in contact with different ways of living was to a large extent balanced by just that earnestness, which is so much larger and finer a thing than the fear of it which has converted the word into a gesture of derision. Lawrence's formal education, it must be remembered, was also by no means negligible.

This then, in summary, is the background of Lawrence's inherited ideas and social experience. It remains to examine his consequent thinking about community, at the centre of his discussion of social values. This depends on what was his major 'venture into consciousness': the attempt to realize that range of living, human energy which the existing system had narrowed and crippled. He put one of his basic beliefs in this way:

> You can have life two ways. Either everything is created from the mind, downwards; or else everything proceeds from the creative

quick, outwards into exfoliation and blossom. . . . The actual living quick itself is alone the creative reality.[9]

Lawrence's exploration was into this 'creative reality', not as an idea, but in its actual processes:

> The quick of self is *there*. You needn't try to get behind it. As leave try to get behind the sun.[10]

This 'quick of self', in any living being, is the basis of individuality:

> A man's self is a law unto itself, not unto *himself*, mind you. . . . The living self has one purpose only: to come into its own fulness of being. . . . But this coming into full, spontaneous being is the most difficult thing of all. . . . The only thing man has to trust to in coming to himself is his desire and his impulse. But both desire and impulse tend to fall into mechanical automatism: to fall from spontaneous reality into dead or material reality. . . . All education must tend against this fall; and all our efforts in all our life must be to preserve the soul free and spontaneous . . . the life-activity must never be degraded into a fixed activity. There can be no ideal goal for human life. . . . There is no pulling open the buds to see what the blossom will be. Leaves must unroll, buds swell and open, and *then* the blossom. And even after that, when the flower dies and the leaves fall, *still* we shall not know. . . . We know the flower of today, but the flower of tomorrow is all beyond us.[11]

Lawrence wrote nothing more important than this, although he wrote it differently, elsewhere, using different terms and methods. The danger is that we recognize this too quickly as 'Laurentian' (that 'gorgeous befeathered snail of an *ego* and a personality'[12] which Lawrence and his writing could be at their worst), and accept it or pass it by without real attention. For it is quite easy to grasp as an abstraction, but very difficult in any more substantial way. In all Lawrence's writing of this kind one is reminded of Coleridge, whose terms were essentially so different, and yet whose emphasis was so very much the same: an emphasis, felt towards in metaphor, on the preservation of the 'spontaneous life-activity' against those rigidities of category and abstraction, of which the industrial system was so powerful a particular embodiment. This sense of life is not obscurantism, as it is

sometimes represented to be. It is a particular wisdom, a
particular kind of reverence, which at once denies, not only
the 'base forcing of all human energy into a competition of
mere acquisition', but also the dominative redirection of this
energy into new fixed categories. I believe that it sets a
standard, in our attitudes to ourselves and to other human
beings, which can in experience be practically known and
recognized, and by which all social proposals must submit
themselves to be judged. It can be seen, as a positive, in
thinkers as diverse as Burke and Cobbett, as Morris and
Lawrence. It is unlikely to reach an agreed end in our
thinking, but it is difficult to know where else to begin. We
have only the melancholy evidence of powerful and clashing
movements that begin elsewhere. When this is so, every
renewed affirmation counts.

For Lawrence, the affirmation led on to an interesting
declaration of faith in democracy, but this was something
rather different from the democracy of, say, a Utilitarian:

> So, we know the first great purpose of Democracy: that each man
> shall be spontaneously himself—each man himself, each woman
> herself, without any question of equality or inequality entering in
> at all; and that no man shall try to determine the being of any other
> man, or of any other woman.[13]

At first sight, this looks like, not democracy, but a kind of
romantic anarchism. Yet it is more than this, essentially,
even though it remains very much a first term. Our question
to those who would reject it must rest on the phrase 'no man
shall try to determine the being of any other man'. We must
ask, and require the answer, of anyone with a social philosophy, whether this principle is accepted or denied. Some of
the most generous social movements have come to fail
because, at heart, they have denied this. And it is much the
same, in effect, whether such determination of human beings
is given title by the abstractions of production or service, of
the glory of the race or good citizenship. For 'to try to
determine the being of any other man' is indeed, as Lawrence
emphasized, an arrogant and base forcing.

To Lawrence, the weakness of modern social movements
was that they all seemed to depend on the assumption of a

'fixed activity' for man, the 'life activity' forced into fixed ideals. He found this

> horribly true of modern democracy—socialism, conservatism, bolshevism, liberalism, republicanism, communism: all alike. The one principle that governs all the *isms* is the same: the principle of the idealized unit, the possessor of property. Man has his highest fulfilment as a possessor of property: so they all say, really.[14]

And from this he concludes:

> All discussion and idealizing of the possession of property, whether individual or group or State possession, amounts now to no more than a fatal betrayal of the spontaneous self. . . . Property is only there to be used, not to be possessed . . . possession is a kind of illness of the spirit. . . . When men are no longer obsessed with the desire to possess property, or with the parallel desire to prevent another man's possessing it, then, and only then, shall we be glad to turn it over to the State. Our way of State-ownership is merely a farcical exchange of words, not of ways.[15]

In this, Lawrence is very close to the socialism of a man like Morris, and there can be little doubt that he and Morris would have felt alike about much that has subsequently passed for socialism.

Lawrence's attitude to the question of equality springs from the same sources in feeling. He writes:

> Society means people living together. People *must* live together. And to live together, they must have some Standard, some *Material* Standard. This is where the Average comes in. And this is where Socialism and Modern Democracy come in. For Democracy and Socialism rest upon the Equality of Man, which is the Average. And this is sound enough, so long as the Average represents the real basic material needs of mankind: basic material needs: we insist and insist again. For Society, or Democracy, or any Political State or Community exists not for the sake of the individual, nor should ever exist for the sake of the individual, but simply to establish the Average, in order to make living together possible: that is, to make proper facilities for every man's clothing, feeding, housing himself, working, sleeping, mating, playing, according to his necessity as a common unit, an average. Everything beyond that common necessity depends on himself alone.[16]

D. H. LAWRENCE

This idea of equality is 'sound enough'. Yet when it is not
a question of material needs but of whole human beings,

> we cannot say that all men are equal. We cannot say $A=B$. Nor
> can we say that men are unequal. We may not declare that
> $A=B+C$. . . . One man is neither equal nor unequal to another
> man. When I stand in the presence of another man, and I am my
> own pure self, am I aware of the presence of an equal, or of an
> inferior, or of a superior? I am not. When I stand with another
> man, who is himself, and when I am truly myself, then I am only
> aware of a Presence, and of the strange reality of Otherness. There
> is me, and there is *another being.* . . . There is no comparing or
> estimating. There is only this strange recognition of *present other-*
> *ness.* I may be glad, angry, or sad, because of the presence of the
> other. But still no comparison enters in. Comparison enters only
> when one of us departs from his own integral being, and enters the
> material mechanical world. Then equality and inequality starts at
> once.[17]

This seems to me to be the best thing that has been written
about equality in our period. It gives no title to any defence
of material inequality, which in fact is what is usually
defended. But it removes from the idea of equality that
element of mechanical abstraction which has often been felt
in it. The emphasis on relationship, on the recognition and
acceptance of 'present otherness', could perhaps only have
come from a man who had made Lawrence's particular
'venture into consciousness'. We should remember the
emphasis when Lawrence, under the tensions of his exile,
falls at times into an attitude like that of the later Carlyle,
with an emphasis on the recognition of 'superior' beings and
of the need to bow down and submit to them. This 'following
after power', in Carlyle's phrase, is always a failure of the
kind of relationship which Lawrence has here described: the
impatient frustrated relapse into the attempt to 'determine
another man's being'. Lawrence can show us, more clearly
than anyone, where in this he himself went wrong.

I have referred to the tensions of exile, and this aspect of
Lawrence's work should receive the final stress. In his basic
attitudes he is so much within the tradition we have been
following, has indeed so much in common with a socialist

like Morris, that it is at first difficult to understand why his influence should have appeared to lead in other directions. One reason, as has been mentioned, is that he has been vulgarized into a romantic rebel, a type of the 'free individual'. There is, of course, just enough in his life and work to make this vulgarization plausible. Yet it cannot really be sustained. We have only to remember this:

> Men are free when they are in a living homeland, not when they are straying and breaking away.[18]

And again:

> Men are free when they belong to a living, organic, believing community, active in fulfilling some unfulfilled, perhaps unrealized purpose.[19]

But this in practice was the cry of an exile: of a man who wanted to commit himself, yet who rejected the terms of the available commitments. Lawrence's rejection had to be so intense, if he was to get clear at all, that he was led into a weakness, which found its rationalization. He kept wanting to see a change in society, but he could conclude:

> Every attempt at preordaining a new material world only adds another last straw to the load that already has broken so many backs. If we are to keep our backs unbroken, we must deposit all property on the ground, and learn to walk without it. We must stand aside. And when many men stand aside, they stand in a new world; a new world of man has come to pass.[20]

This is the end of the rainbow: the sequel to that Rananim which had been one more in the series of attempts to evade the issues: an idealized substitute community, whether Pantisocracy, New Harmony, or the Guild of St George. Lawrence's point is that the change must come first in feeling, but almost everything to which he had borne witness might have shown how much 'in the head' this conclusion was. He knew all about the processes of 'beating down'. He knew, none better, how the consciousness and the environment were linked, and what it cost even an exceptional man to make his ragged breathless escape. There is something false, in the end, in the way he tries to separate the material

D. H. LAWRENCE

issues and the issues in feeling, for he had had the opportunity of knowing, and indeed had learned, how closely inter-
meshed these issues were. It is not a question of the old
debate on which conditions are primary. It is that in
actuality the pressures, and the responses creating new
pressures, form into a whole process, which

> is *there*. You needn't try to get behind it. As leave try to get behind
> the sun.

Lawrence came to rationalize and to generalize his own
necessary exile, and to give it the appearance of freedom.
His separation of the material issues from the issues in
consciousness was an analogy of his own temporary condition. There is something, in the strict sense, suburban about
this. The attempt to separate material needs, and the ways in
which they are to be met, from human purpose and the
development of being and relationship, is the suburban
separation of 'work' and 'life' which has been the most
common response of all to the difficulties of industrialism.
It is not that the issues in consciousness ought to be set
aside while the material ends are pursued. It is that because
the process is whole, so must change be whole: whole in
conception, common in effort. The 'living, organic, believing
community' will not be created by standing aside, although
the effort towards it in consciousness is at least as important
as the material effort. The tragedy of Lawrence, the working-
class boy, is that he did not live to come home. It is a
tragedy, moreover, common enough in its incidence to
exempt him from the impertinences of personal blame.

The venture into consciousness remains, as a sufficient
life's work. Towards the end, when he had revisited the
mining country where the pressures of industrialism were
most explicit and most evident, he shaped, as a creative
response, the sense of immediate relationship which informs
Lady Chatterley's Lover, and which he had earlier explored
in *The Rainbow*, *Women in Love* and *St Mawr*. This is only
the climax of his exploration into those elements of human
energy which were denied by the 'base forcing', and which
might yet overthrow it. It is profoundly important to realize
that Lawrence's exploration of sexual experience is made,

213

always, in this context. To isolate this exploration, as it was tempting for some of his readers to do, is not only to misunderstand Lawrence but to expose him to the scandal from which, in his lifetime, he scandalously suffered. 'This which we are must cease to be, that we may come to pass in another being'[21]: this, throughout, is the emphasis. And, just as the recovery of the human spirit from the base forcing of industrialism must lie in recovery of 'the creative reality, the actual living quick itself', so does this recovery depend on the ways in which this reality can be most immediately apprehended: 'the source of all life and knowledge is in man and woman, and the source of all living is in the interchange and meeting and mingling of these two'.[22] It is not that sexual experience is 'the answer' to industrialism, or to its ways of thinking and feeling. On the contrary, Lawrence argues, the poisons of the 'base forcing' have extended themselves into this. His clearest general exposition of this comes in the essay on Galsworthy, where he derides the proposition of 'Pa-assion', and its related promiscuity, as alternatives to the emphasis on money or property which follows from men being 'only materially and socially conscious'. The idea of sex as a reserve area of feeling, or as a means of Byronic revolt from the conventions of money and property (a Forsyte turning into an anti-Forsyte), is wholly repugnant to Lawrence. People who act in this way are 'like all the rest of the modern middle-class rebels, not in rebellion at all; they are merely social beings behaving in an anti-social manner'.[23] The real meaning of sex, Lawrence argues, is that it 'involves the whole of a human being'. The alternative to the 'base forcing' into the competition for money and property is not sexual adventure, nor the available sexual emphasis, but again a return to the 'quick of self', from which whole relationships, including whole sexual relationships, may grow. The final emphasis, which all Lawrence's convincing explorations into the 'quick of self' both illumine and realize, is his criticism of industrial civilization:

If only our civilization had taught us . . . how to keep the fire of sex clear and alive, flickering or glowing or blazing in all its varying degrees of strength and communication, we might, all of us, have lived all our lives in love, which means we should be kindled and full of zest in all kinds of ways and for all kinds of things.[24]

Or again, as an adequate summary of the whole 'venture into consciousness':

Our civilization . . . has almost destroyed the natural flow of common sympathy between men and men, and men and women. And it is this that I want to restore into life.[25]

CHAPTER II

R. H. TAWNEY

T HE author of *Religion and the Rise of Capitalism* is a professional historian, subject at once to disciplines and limitations which the prophets and critics of the nineteenth century did not observe. Yet it seems to be true that the work of a whole school of economic and social historians in our own century has been directed, essentially, to the detailed investigation of the general judgements which, from the nineteenth century, they inherited. The outline was received, and the professional researches were directed towards the details of its area, and at times to its revision.

Tawney, more clearly perhaps than any other historian in this century, begins not so much from the received general outline (for this is hardly a distinguishing characteristic) as from the inherited judgements and questions. The influence in particular of Ruskin and of Arnold is difficult not to discern; and behind this influence, as we have seen, is a whole nineteenth-century tradition. A work like *Religion and the Rise of Capitalism* illustrates most clearly the difference between professional historian and general critic. Yet, if we compare it with a work like Southey's *Colloquies*, which stands near the head of the tradition, we remark not only the gain—the achievement of detailed exposition over scattered assertion—but also in moral terms the continuity. This emphasis on the moral terms is the most important, and the ratifying, quality of Tawney's work. It is no accident that alongside his formal historical enquiries he should have published such works as *Equality* and *The Acquisitive Society*: works which are historically informed certainly, but which are informed also with those special qualities of personal experience and affirmed morality which bring them within the categories of the traditional great debate. Tawney's importance is that he is a social critic and a moralist who brings to his discharge of these functions the particular equipment of a professional historian.

Equality and *The Acquisitive Society* are important contributions to the tradition. *Equality* is the more important, but *The Acquisitive Society* is a fine restatement and revaluation of a traditional case. The emphasis of both books can be marked by a sentence from the second chapter of *The Acquisitive Society*:

> As long as men are men, a poor society cannot be too poor to find a right order of life, nor a rich society too rich to have need to seek it.[1]

The challenge of such an attitude is, as always, radical.

The two most important elements in *The Acquisitive Society* are the general discussion of changes in social theory, and the analysis of the idea of Industrialism. The former is summarized in this way:

> The difference between the England of Shakespeare, still visited by the ghosts of the Middle Ages, and the England which emerged in 1700 from the fierce polemics of the last two generations, was a difference of social and political theory even more than of constitutional and political arrangements. Not only the facts, but the minds which appraised them, were profoundly modified. . . . The natural consequence of the abdication of authorities which had stood, however imperfectly, for a common purpose in social organization, was the gradual disappearance from social thought of the idea of purpose itself. Its place in the eighteenth century was taken by the idea of mechanism. The conception of men as united to each other, and of all mankind as united to God, by mutual obligations arising from their relation to a common end, ceased to be impressed upon men's minds.[2]

Thus far, the essence of this argument would have been familiar to Southey, Coleridge or Arnold, as it is also the ground-swell of the eloquent protests of Burke. Tawney continues his argument, however, with an appreciation of the new Liberalism which would then have been impossible:

> In the modern revulsion against economic tyranny, there is a disposition to represent the writers who stand on the threshold of the age of capitalist industry as the prophets of a vulgar materialism, which would sacrifice every human aspiration to the pursuit of riches. No interpretation could be more misleading. . . . The grand enemy of the age was monopoly; the battlecry with which enlighten-

ment marched against it was the abolition of privilege; its ideal was a society where each man had free access to the economic opportunities which he could use and enjoy the wealth which by his efforts he had created. That school of thought represented all, or nearly all, that was humane and intelligent in the mind of the age. It was individualistic, not because it valued riches as the main end of man, but because it had a high sense of human dignity, and desired that men should be free to become themselves.[3]

The movements of liberalism and enlightenment were, Tawney argues, wholly necessary, but their doctrines, historically considered, were 'crystallized . . . while the new industrial order was still young and its effects unknown'. The nineteenth-century individualism which succeeded to this heritage is in a different state:

It seems to repeat the phrases of an age which expired in producing them, and to do so without knowing it. For since they were minted by the great masters, the deluge has changed the face of economic society and has made them phrases and little more.[4]

The old liberating ideas were carried forward without criticism into a new society, of which they became the dogmas:

Behind their political theory, behind the practical conduct, which, as always, continues to express theory long after it has been discredited in the world of thought, lay the acceptance of absolute rights to property and to economic freedom as the unquestioned centre of social organization.[5]

Tawney's whole subsequent argument is a criticism of these dogmas. He criticizes the 'absolute right to property' very much in the terms of a Tory Romantic: the right to property is seen as conditional on the obligation to service. He is, however, less sanguine that the urging of this principle on the existing owners of property will produce any sensible change. He is forced, rather, to the advocacy of socialism as the only discernible means of restoring the idea and the practice of social property. This principle is the basis of all his most interesting recommendations.

His criticism of the other dogma, of economic freedom, is also socialist in character. But he combines this with a criticism of 'Industrialism' which must be seen, at this date, as a radical criticism of much socialist policy. The criticism of 'industrialism' rests heavily on Ruskin and Arnold, and much of it is in their exact terms. He sees industrialism as a fetish: the exaggeration of one of the necessary means for the maintenance of society into a central and overriding end. He compares it with the Prussian fetish of militarism, and continues:

> Industrialism is no more the necessary characteristic of an economically developed society than militarism is a necessary characteristic of a nation which maintains military forces. . . . The essence of industrialism . . . is not any particular method of industry, but a particular estimate of the importance of industry, which results in it being thought the only thing that is important at all, so that it is elevated from the subordinate place which it should occupy among human interests and activities into being the standard by which all other interests and activities are judged.[6]

The Acquisitive Society was written in 1921, and it is a measure of its insight (as well as a symptom of that 'practical conduct which continues to express theory long after it has been discredited in the world of thought') that the examples which Tawney gives of this 'perversion' should be so startlingly relevant, a full generation later, to the practice of both our major political parties:

> When a Cabinet Minister declares that the greatness of this country depends upon the volume of its exports, so that France, which exports comparatively little, and Elizabethan England, which exported next to nothing, are presumably to be pitied as altogether inferior civilizations, that is Industrialism. It is the confusion of one minor department of life with the whole of life. . . . When the Press clamours that the one thing needed to make this island an Arcadia is productivity, and more productivity, and yet more productivity, that is Industrialism. It is the confusion of means with ends.[7]

Tawney's debt to Arnold, in this, will have been noted; as also, in another example, his debt to Ruskin:

> So to those who clamour, as many now do, 'Produce! Produce!' one simple question may be addressed:—'Produce what?' Food,

clothing, house-room, art, knowledge? By all means! But if the
nation is scantily furnished with these things had it not better stop
producing a good many others which fill shop windows in Regent
Street? . . . What can be more childish than to urge the necessity
that productive power should be increased, if part of the productive
power which exists already is misapplied?[8]

In part, this observation rests on the traditional appeal for
the rejection of 'illth' which Ruskin and Morris would
have approved. But Tawney takes the argument an important stage further. It is not only the lack of purpose in
society which distorts human effort; it is also the existence
and the approval of inequality. It was in 1929 that Tawney
addressed himself fully to this latter problem, in the lectures
that were published as *Equality*.

Here, once again, Tawney's starting point is Arnold, but
as before he expands a moral observation into a detailed and
practical argument. Tawney argues, basically, from the
existence of economic crisis, and concludes that efforts to
overcome this crisis in any lasting way are consistently
brought to nothing by the fact of social inequality. He draws
attention to the surprise of foreign observers at the emphasis
on class in England, and continues:

Here are these people, they (the observers) say, who, more than any
other nation, need a common culture, for, more than any other,
they depend on an economic system which at every turn involves
mutual understanding and continuous cooperation, and who, more
than any other, possess, as a result of their history, the materials by
which such a common culture might be inspired. And, so far from
desiring it, there is nothing, it seems, which they desire less.[9]

The foundations of a common culture, he insists, are
economic; their condition is a large measure of equality. But
to raise the question of equality in England is to encounter
at once 'doleful voices and rushings to and fro'. The
questioner will be told at once not only that the doctrine is
poisonous, wicked and impracticable, but that in any case it
is a 'scientific impossibility'. Tawney goes on:

It is obvious that the word 'Equality' possesses more than one
meaning, and that the controversies surrounding it arise partly, at

least, because the same term is employed with different connotations. . . . On the one hand, it may affirm that men are, on the whole, very similar in their natural endowments of character and intelligence. On the other hand, it may assert that, while they differ profoundly as individuals in capacity and character, they are equally entitled as human beings to consideration and respect. . . . If made in the first sense, the assertion of human equality is clearly untenable. . . . The acceptance of that conclusion, nevertheless, makes a somewhat smaller breach in equalitarian doctrines than is sometimes supposed, for such doctrines have rarely been based on a denial of it. . . . When observers from the dominions, or from foreign countries, are struck by inequality as one of the special and outstanding characteristics of English social life, they do not mean that in other countries differences of personal quality are less important than in England. They mean, on the contrary, that they are more important, and that in England they tend to be obscured or obliterated behind differences of property and income, and the whole elaborate façade of a society that, compared with their own, seems stratified and hierarchical.[10]

Yet still, in England, the debate on equality is normally continued as if the proposition were absolute equality of character and ability. In fact, however:

the equality which all these thinkers emphasize as desirable is not equality of capacity or attainment, but of circumstances, and institutions, and manner of life. The inequality which they deplore is not inequality of personal gifts, but of the social and economic environment. . . . Their view . . . is that, because men are men, social institutions—property rights, and the organization of industry, and the system of public health and education—should be planned, as far as is possible, to emphasize and strengthen, not the class differences which divide, but the common humanity which unites, them.[11]

Tawney adds two further arguments. First, that equality is not to be rejected on the grounds that human beings differ in their needs: 'equality of provision is not identity of provision'. Second (and in my view of the greatest importance), that

in order to justify inequalities of circumstance or opportunity by reference to differences of personal quality, it is necessary . . . to show that the differences in question are relevant to the in-equalities.[12]

It is not an argument against women's suffrage that women are physically weaker than men, nor an argument for slavery that men differ in intelligence. Further, it is not an argument for economic inequality that 'every mother knows her children are not equal': it has then to be asked 'whether it is the habit of mothers to lavish care on the strong and neglect the delicate'. Nor, finally, is it an argument for inequality that it is supported by 'economic laws'; these 'laws' are relative to circumstances and institutions, and these are determined by 'the values, preferences, interests and ideals which rule at any moment in a given society'.

Much of the remainder of *Equality* is devoted to advocacy of Tawney's specific remedies; in particular, an extension of the social services, and the conversion of industry to a social function with the status and standards of a profession. It is difficult to disagree with the humanity of his arguments, but it is difficult also not to feel, as of much of the writing in this tradition, that although it recognizes what Tawney calls 'the lion in the path' it yet hopes that the path can be followed to the end by converting both traveller and lion to a common humanity. For Tawney, one of the noblest men of his genera-tion, the attitude is evidently habitual. The inequality and the avoidable suffering of contemporary society are subject, 'while men are men', to a moral choice; when the choice has been made, it is then only a matter of deliberate organization and collective effort. 'When the false gods depart', as he says in another metaphor, 'there is some hope, at least, of the arrival of the true.' Tawney, above all, is a patient exorcizer; he meets the false gods with irony, and appeals, meanwhile, over their heads to the congregation, in the accents of a confident humanism. Yet the irony is, at times, disquieting, although it accounts for much of the charm of his writing:

A nation is not civilized because a handful of its members are successful in acquiring large sums of money and in persuading their fellows that a catastrophe will occur if they do not acquire it, any more than Dahomey was civilized because its king had a golden stool and an army of slaves, or Judea because Solomon possessed a thousand wives and imported apes and peacocks, and surrounded the worship of Moloch and Ashtaroth with an impressive ritual.[13]

This manner is very characteristic of his general works, and produces at times the sense of an uneasy combination between argument and filigree. The irony, one suspects, is defensive, as it was with Arnold, from whom in essentials it derives. It is not merely a literary device for good-humoured acceptance, which seems incumbent on some Englishmen when they feel they are going against the grain of their society. It is also, one cannot help feeling, a device for lowering the tension when, however, the tension is necessary. It is a particular kind of estimate of the opposition to be expected, and it is, of course, in essentials, an underestimate. No believer in any god will be affected by the smiling insinuation of a missionary that the god's real name is Mumbo-Jumbo; he is altogether more likely merely to return the compliment. Tawney's manner before the high priests is uneasy. He seems to feel, as Arnold felt, that they are his kind of men, and will understand his language: if they do not, he has only to say it again. The spectacle contrasts uneasily and unfavourably with Tawney's manner in direct address beyond them: the steady exposition of his argument that contemporary society will move merely from one economic crisis to another unless it changes both its values and the system which embodies them. The manner of exposition occupies, fortunately, the bulk of his work.

The discussion of 'Equality and Culture', which is obviously very important, is conducted in both moods, but we can, fairly, omit the apes and peacocks. His position is at the outset the traditional one:

> What matters to a society is less what it owns than what it is and how it uses its possessions. It is civilized in so far as its conduct is guided by a just appreciation of spiritual ends, in so far as it uses its material resources to promote the dignity and refinement of the individual human beings who compose it.[14]

Thus far, Tawney is saying what Coleridge or Ruskin would approve. He continues, however:

> Violent contrasts of wealth and power, and an undiscriminating

devotion to institutions by which such contrasts are maintained and heightened, do not promote the attainment of such ends, but thwart it.[15]

The new recognition is just, and of his period. Tawney is concerned less with the defence of culture against industrialism than with the making of a 'common culture'. The main objection to this is the representative objection of Clive Bell: that culture depends on standards, and standards on a cultivated minority; a cultivated minority is not compatible with the pursuit of equality, which would merely be a levelling-down to mediocrity.

Tawney's answer to this objection is interesting, although it is difficult to feel that he meets the point about 'levelling down' with more than a sidetracking device of argument. It is not really relevant to point out that England has already 'a dead-level of law and order' and that this is generally approved. He observes, justly:

> Not all the ghosts which clothe themselves in metaphors are equally substantial, and whether a level is regrettable or not depends, after all, upon what is levelled.[16]

The argument, however, is about the levelling of standards, and on this, essentially, Tawney has nothing to say.

The essence of his reply is more general. The maintenance of economic inequality, he argues, tends to 'pervert what Mr Bell calls the sense of values':

> to cause men, in the strong language of the Old Testament, 'to go a-whoring after strange gods', which means, in the circumstances of today, staring upwards, eyes goggling and mouths agape, at the antics of a third-rate Elysium, and tormenting their unhappy souls, or what, in such conditions, is left of them, with the hope of wriggling into it.[17]

This collateral argument, that economic inequality while possibly maintaining a genuinely cultivated minority maintains also and more prominently 'sham criteria of eminence', is valid. We can agree also with the point he repeats from Arnold: experience does not suggest that

> in modern England, at any rate, the plutocracy, with its devotion to the maxim, *Privatim opulentia, publice egestas*, is, in any special

sense, the guardian of such activities (*the labours of artist or student*), or that, to speak with moderation, it is noticeably more eager than the mass of the population to spend liberally on art, or education, or the things of the spirit.[18]

Yet, equally, it would be a forcible observation, as it was in Arnold, to reverse the proposition and ask whether the 'mass' is a probable guardian. We can say that the argument about culture is not in itself an argument for economic inequality, but the recommendation of a common culture requires something more than a *tu quoque*.

If we look, finally, at Tawney's central statement on culture, we shall observe the same kind of difficulty. He writes:

> It is true that excellence is impossible in the absence of severe and exacting standards of attainment and appreciation. . . . In order, however, to escape from one illusion, it ought not to be necessary to embrace another. If civilization is not the product of the kitchen garden, neither is it an exotic to be grown in a hot-house. . . . Culture may be fastidious but fastidiousness is not culture. . . . Culture is not an assortment of aesthetic sugar-plums for fastidious palates, but an energy of the soul. . . . When it feeds on itself, instead of drawing nourishment from the common life of mankind, it ceases to grow, and, when it ceases to grow, it ceases to live. In order that it may be, not merely an interesting museum specimen, but an active principle of intelligence and refinement, by which vulgarities are checked and crudities corrected, it is necessary, not only to preserve intact existing standards of excellence, and to diffuse their influence, but to broaden and enrich them by contact with an ever-widening range of emotional experiences and intellectual interests. The association of culture with a limited class, which is enabled by its wealth to carry the art of living to a high level of perfection, may achieve the first, but it cannot, by itself, achieve the second. It may refine, or appear to refine, some sections of a community, but it coarsens others, and smites, in the end, with a blight of sterility, even refinement itself. It may preserve culture, but it cannot extend it; and, in the long run, it is only by its extension that, in the conditions of today, it is likely to be preserved.[19]

As a reply to the case for minority culture this is reasonable. Not that its language is wholly admirable: the sugar-plums belong with the apes and peacocks, while 'hothouse', 'museum specimen', 'sterility', and so on, have become the nodes of a familiar kind of journalism. The uncertainty of the language marks, in fact, an important evasion of feeling. The case for extension (the entirely appropriate word) is strong; the dangers of limitation are real and present. But to think of the problem as one of 'opening the museums' or of putting the specimens in the market-place is to capitulate to a very meagre idea of culture. Tawney's position is both normal and humane. But there is an unresolved contradiction, which phrases about broadening and enriching merely blur, between the recognition that a culture must grow and the hope that 'existing standards of excellence' may be preserved intact. It is a contradiction which, among others, the defenders of inequality will be quick to exploit. The question that has to be faced, if we may put it for a moment in one of Tawney's analogies, is whether the known gold will be more widely spread, or whether, in fact, there will be a change of currency. If the social and economic changes which Tawney recommends are in fact effected, it is the latter, the change of currency, which can reasonably be expected. For those to whom this is a feared disaster, Tawney's reassurances are not likely to be convincing. For others, impressed by Tawney's consistent humanity and convinced of the need for radical social change, the analysis, while decent, is likely to seem lacking in depth. Tawney is the last important voice in that tradition which has sought to humanize the modern system of society on its own best terms. This is the mark both of his achievement and his limitations. We may properly end, however, by stressing the achievement, for Tawney is one of the very few thinkers in this century who, in the qualities of reverence, dedication and courage, ranks with his nineteenth-century predecessors.

CHAPTER III

T. S. ELIOT

W E can say of Eliot what Mill said of Coleridge, that an 'enlightened Radical or Liberal' ought 'to rejoice over such a Conservative'.[1] We can do this even if, in the wisdom of our generation, we feel 'enlightened' as a kind of insult. For it is not only that, as Mill said, 'even if a Conservative philosophy were an absurdity, it is well calculated to drive out a hundred absurdities worse than itself', or that such a thinker is 'the natural means of rescuing from oblivion truths which Tories have forgotten, and which the prevailing schools of Liberalism never knew'.[2] It is also that, if Eliot is read with attention, he is seen to have raised questions which those who differ from him politically must answer, or else retire from the field. In particular, in his discussion of culture, he has carried the argument to an important new stage, and one on which the rehearsal of old pieces will be merely tedious.

In writing *The Idea of a Christian Society*, Eliot adopts an emphasis of Coleridge:

> In using the term 'Idea' of a Christian Society I do not mean primarily a concept derived from the study of any societies which we may choose to call Christian: I mean something that can only be found in an understanding of the end to which a Christian Society, to deserve the name, must be directed. . . . My concern . . . will . . . be . . . with the question, what—if any—is the 'idea' of the society in which we live? to what end is it arranged?[3]

From this he goes on to criticize a formidable public platitude:

> The current terms in which we describe our society, the contrasts with other societies by which we—of the 'Western Democracies'—eulogize it, only operate to deceive and stupefy us. To speak of ourselves as a Christian society, in contrast to that of Germany (1939) or Russia, is an abuse of terms. We mean only that we have a society in which no one is penalized for the *formal profession* of

227

Christianity; but we conceal from ourselves the unpleasant knowledge of the real values by which we live.[4]

The effect of this observation resembles very closely the
effect of Coleridge's observations on the idea of a National
Church. Under such precision, the 'hundred absurdities'
may be seen for what they are.

The observation is characteristic of the tone of the whole
work. Eliot's enquiry springs from a crisis of feeling in
September 1938:

> It was not a disturbance of the understanding: the events them-
> selves were not surprising. Nor, as became increasingly evident, was
> our distress due merely to disagreement with the policy and
> behaviour of the moment. The feeling which was new and un-
> expected was a feeling of humiliation, which seemed to demand an
> act of personal contrition, of humility, repentance and amendment;
> what had happened was something in which one was deeply
> implicated and responsible. It was not, I repeat, a criticism of the
> government, but a doubt of the validity of a civilization. . . . Was
> our society, which had always been so assured of its superiority and
> rectitude, so confident of its unexamined premises, assembled
> round anything more permanent than a congeries of banks,
> insurance companies and industries, and had it any beliefs more
> essential than a belief in compound interest and the maintenance of
> dividends?[5]

The manner of this question belongs, quite evidently, to the
tradition. And the feelings of humiliation and implication
remind one of earlier feelings in a different crisis: the reaction to Chartism in the 1830s and 1840s.

A Christian community, Eliot argues, is one 'in which
there is a unified religious-social code of behaviour'.[6] A
Christian organization of society would be one 'in which the
natural end of man—virtue and well-being in community—
is acknowledged for all, and the supernatural end—
beatitude—for those who have the eyes to see it'.[7] As
things are, however,

> a great deal of the machinery of modern life is merely a sanction
> for un-Christian aims . . . it is not only hostile to the conscious
> pursuit of the Christian life in the world by the few, but to the
> maintenance of any Christian society *of* the world.[8]

A Christian society will not be realized merely by a change of this 'machinery', yet any contemplation of it must lead to

> such problems as the hypertrophy of the motive of Profit into a social ideal, the distinction between the *use* of natural resources and their exploitation, the use of labour and its exploitation, the advantages unfairly accruing to the trader in contrast to the primary producer, the misdirection of the financial machine, the iniquity of usury, and other features of a commercialized society which must be scrutinized on Christian principles. . . . We are being made aware that the organization of society on the principle of private profit, as well as public destruction, is leading both to the deformation of humanity by unregulated industrialism, and to the exhaustion of natural resources, and that a good deal of our material progress is a progress for which succeeding generations may have to pay dearly.[9]

Industrialism, when it is unregulated, tends to create not a society but a mob. The religious-social complex on which a Christian organization of society may be built is thus weakened or destroyed:

> In an industrialized society like that of England, I am surprised that the people retains as much Christianity as it does. . . . In its religious organization, we may say that Christendom has remained fixed at the stage of development suitable to a simple agricultural and piscatorial society, and that modern material organization—or if 'organization' sounds too complimentary, we will say 'complication'—has produced a world for which Christian social forms are imperfectly adapted.[10]

In such a state of disintegration, or unbalance, material or physical improvement can be no more than secondary:

> A mob will be no less a mob if it is well fed, well clothed, well housed, and well disciplined.[11]

From Liberalism we are likely to inherit only the fruits of its disorder, while Democracy, in terms of which we tend to define our social ends, means too many things to mean anything at which a society can direct its whole life. In this criticism of Liberalism and Democracy, Eliot is essentially repeating Carlyle: that both are movements *away* from something, and that they may either arrive at something very different from what was intended, or else, in social terms, arrive at nothing positive at all.

The Idea of a Christian Society, in its general effect, serves rather to distinguish a Christian idea of society from other ideas with which it has become entangled, or by which it is evidently denied, than to formulate anything in the nature of a programme. Eliot's business is to confess an attitude, and it is an essential part of this attitude that the formulation of programmes cannot have priority. He observes, for instance, in a passage which leads directly to the kind of enquiry undertaken in *Notes towards the Definition of Culture*:

> You cannot, in any scheme for the reformation of society, aim directly at a condition in which the arts will flourish: these activities are probably by-products for which we cannot deliberately arrange the conditions. On the other hand, their decay may always be taken as a symptom of some social ailment to be investigated.[12]

And he goes on to observe

> the steady influence which operates silently in any mass society organized for profit, for the depression of standards of art and culture. The increasing organization of advertisement and propaganda—or the influencing of masses of men by any means except through their intelligence—is all against them. The economic system is against them; the chaos of ideals and confusion of thought in our large scale mass education is against them; and against them also is the disappearance of any class of people who recognize public and private responsibility of patronage of the best that is made and written.[13]

Yet even against this, and for the reason given, Eliot offers nothing that can be called, in ordinary terms, a proposal. It is from this point, rather, that he begins his penetrating re-examination of the idea of culture in his next book. In *Notes towards the Definition of Culture*, Eliot's essential conservatism is very much more evident; but I think we can assume, and many who now look to him might remember, that his more recent enquiry was only undertaken from the standpoint of that far-reaching criticism of contemporary society and contemporary social philosophy which *The Idea of a Christian Society* so outspokenly embodies.

The *Notes towards the Definition of Culture* is a difficult work to assess. Although short, it differs very widely within itself both in method and in seriousness. At times, particularly in the Introduction and in the Notes on Education, the method is little more than an exposure of sentences which Eliot has found absurd or offensive, together with a brief running commentary which suddenly turns and assumes the status of argument. These parts of the book are the growling innuendoes of the correspondence columns rather than the prose of thought. The central chapters are very much more serious, and in parts of them there is that brilliance and nervous energy of definition which distinguishes Eliot's literary criticism. There is, however, an important difference from the literary criticism, of which a principal virtue was always the specificity, not only of definition, but of illustration. In these essays, on the other hand, the usefulness of the definitions is always in danger of breaking down because Eliot is unwilling or unable to illustrate. He makes, in the course of his argument, a number of important generalizations of a historical kind; but these are, at best, arbitrary, for there is hardly ever any attempt to demonstrate them. As a brief instance, this can be cited:

> You cannot expect to have all stages of development at once . . . a civilization cannot simultaneously produce great folk poetry at one cultural level and *Paradise Lost* at another.[14]

The general point is clearly very important, and it is built into much of the subsequent theory. Yet, historically, one wants very much more discussion, with actual examples, before one can reasonably decide whether it is true. The example he gives is indeed almost calculated to raise these doubts; because the fact, for instance, of the co-existence, within a generation, of *Paradise Lost* and *The Pilgrim's Progress* is an obvious, and obviously difficult, case for anyone who would think about levels of culture. It is not that one can be sure that Eliot is wrong, but that one can be even less sure that he is right. The substance of his general arguments is tentative and incidental, yet the manner in which they are communicated is often dogmatic to the point of insolence. For example, in his Introduction he writes:

> What I try to say is this: here are what I believe to be essential conditions for the growth and for the survival of culture.[15]

This is a fair claim, and the tone corresponds to what is in fact offered. But the sentence is at once followed by this:

> If they conflict with any passionate faith of the reader—if, for instance, he finds it shocking that culture and equalitarianism should conflict, if it seems monstrous to him that anyone should have 'advantages of birth'—I do not ask him to change his faith, I merely ask him to stop paying lip-service to culture.[16]

From *try to say* and *what I believe to be* there is an abrupt movement to something very different: the assertion, backed by the emotive devices of *passionate, shocking, monstrous* and *lip-service*, that if we do not agree with Eliot's conditions we stand self-convicted of indifference to culture. This, to say the least, is not proved; and in this jump from the academy to the correspondence column, which Eliot is far too able and experienced a writer not to know that he is making, there is evidence of other impulses behind this work than the patient effort towards definition; evidence, one might say, of the common determination to rationalize one's prejudices. Mr Laski, Mr Dent, Earl Attlee and the others in the pillory could hardly be blamed, at such moments, if they looked for Eliot not in the direction of the courtroom but alongside them, waiting to be pelted.

The most important disadvantage which has followed from these faults in the book is that they have allowed it to be plausibly dismissed by those of us whose prejudices are different, while its points of real importance are evaded. The major importance of the book, in my view, lies in two of its discussions: first, its adoption of the meaning of culture as 'a whole way of life', and the subsequent consideration of what we mean by 'levels' of culture within it; second, its effort to distinguish between 'élite' and 'class', and its penetrating criticism of the theories of an 'élite'. It is an almost physical relief to reach these discussions after the foregoing irritability; yet they seem to have been little considered.

The sense of 'culture' as 'a whole way of life' has been

most marked in twentieth-century anthropology and soci-
ology, and Eliot, like the rest of us, has been at least casu-
ally influenced by these disciplines. The sense depends, in
fact, on the literary tradition. The development of social
anthropology has tended to inherit and substantiate the
ways of looking at a society and a common life which had
earlier been wrought out from general experience of industrialism. The emphasis on 'a whole way of life' is continuous
from Coleridge and Carlyle, but what was a personal
assertion of value has become a general intellectual method.
There have been two main results in ordinary thinking.
First, we have learned something new about change: not
only that it need not terrify us, since alternative institutions
and emphases of energy have been shown to be practicable
and satisfying; but also that it cannot be piecemeal—one
element of a complex system can hardly be changed without
seriously affecting the whole. Second (and perhaps of more
doubtful value), we have been given new illustrations of an
alternative way of life. In common thinking, the mediaeval
town and the eighteenth-century village have been replaced,
as examples, by various kinds of recent simple societies.
These can reassure us that the version of life which industrialism has forced on us is neither universal nor permanent,
but can also become a kind of weakening luxury, if they lead
us to suppose that we have the 'whole arc' of human
possibilities to choose from, in life as in the documents. The
alternatives and variations which matter are those which can
become practical in our own culture; the discipline, rightly
emphasized, drives us back to look at these within our own
complex, rather than outwards to other places and other times.

Eliot's emphasis of culture as a whole way of life is useful
and significant. It is also significant that, having taken the
emphasis, he plays with it. For example:

Culture . . . includes all the characteristic activities and interests of
a people: Derby Day, Henley Regatta, Cowes, the twelfth of
August, a cup final, the dog races, the pin table, the dart board,
Wensleydale cheese, boiled cabbage cut into sections, beetroot in
vinegar, nineteenth-century Gothic churches, and the music of
Elgar.[17]

This pleasant miscellany is evidently narrower in kind than the general description which precedes it. The 'characteristic activities and interests' would also include steelmaking, touring in motor-cars, mixed farming, the Stock Exchange, coalmining and London Transport. Any list would be incomplete, but Eliot's categories are sport, food and a little art—a characteristic observation of English leisure. There is a suggestion that he does not fully accept the sense of 'a whole way of life', but in this illustration translates the older specialized sense of 'culture' (arts, philosophy) into 'popular culture' (sport, food and the Gothic churches). It is evident elsewhere in the book that at times he reverts to the specialized sense. He says that it is possible to conceive a future period which 'will have *no* culture',[18] by which he can surely only mean 'will have nothing recognizable as culture, in the sense of a religion, arts, learning'; for if one applies to the sentence the sense of 'a whole way of life', it amounts to saying that there could be a period in which there was no common life, at any level. There is often, in the book, this sense of a sliding of definitions.

Eliot distinguishes three senses of culture:

> according to whether we have in mind the development of an *individual*, of a *group* or *class*, or of a *whole society*.[19]

He observes that 'men of letters and moralists' have usually discussed the first two senses, and especially the first, without relation to the third. This is hardly true of, say, Coleridge, Carlyle, Ruskin and Morris, but it is probably true, or partly true, of Arnold, of whom he appears mainly to be thinking, and whom he quotes by name. The importance of the formulation, however, is not in this, but in the two deductions from it: first, that:

> a good deal of confusion could be avoided, if we refrained from setting before the group, what can be the aim only of the individual; and before society as a whole, what can be the aim only of a group;[20]

and, second, that:

> the culture of the individual cannot be isolated from that of the group, and . . . the culture of the group cannot be abstracted from

that of the whole society; . . . our notion of 'perfection' must take all three senses of 'culture' into account at once.[21]

These conclusions have, first, an important negative value. They rule out, if they are accepted, any attempt to make the individual's search for perfection into a plausible social ideal. They rule out also those extreme forms of the idea of a 'minority culture' in which it is supposed that the culture of a group can be maintained on its own terms, and within its own orbit, without reference to the progress of the culture of the whole society of which the group is a part. As ideas, these that are rejected seem evidently imperfect; yet, in terms of feeling, they are curiously persistent, and much contemporary effort seems in fact to be based upon them. It is essentially and ideally the function of a conservative thinker to show their inadequacy.

But the vital use of these conclusions, for Eliot, lies in the sentence: 'a good deal of confusion could be avoided, if we refrained from setting . . . before society as a whole, what can be the aim only of a group'. This observation at once initiates and supports his whole theory of class, in this way:

> Among the more primitive societies, the higher types exhibit more marked differentiations of function amongst their members than the lower types. At a higher stage still, we find that some functions are more honoured than others, and this division promotes the development of *classes*, in which higher honour and higher privilege are accorded, not merely to the person as functionary but as member of the class. And the class itself possesses a function, that of maintaining that part of the total culture of the society which pertains to that class. We have to try to keep in mind, that in a healthy society this maintenance of a particular level of culture is to the benefit, not merely of the class which maintains it, but of the society as a whole. Awareness of this fact will prevent us from supposing that the culture of a 'higher' class is something superfluous to society as a whole, or to the majority, and from supposing that it is something which ought to be shared equally by all other classes.[22]

This account, when it is set together with the insistence that culture is 'a whole way of life', forms the basis of the two important discussions to which I have referred: that of 'levels' of culture, and that of the nature of 'class' and its distinction from 'élite'. It is perhaps worth remarking, even at this stage, that Eliot's account of the development of classes is not, when historically viewed, such as will give us complete confidence in his subsequent reasoning. The slide from the differentiation of function in primitive society to what we call, and know as, *classes*, is adroitly managed, but it leaves out too much. In particular, the exclusion of the economic factor—of the tendency of function to turn into property—leaves the view of class narrow and misleading. Eliot seems always to have in mind, as the normal scheme of his thinking, a society which is at once more stable and more simple than any to which his discussion is likely to be relevant. The emergence of such 'functional' groups as the merchants, and then the industrial capitalists, and then the financiers has altered, in a very obvious way, the scheme which Eliot uses. For it is clear that it is possible, and has indeed widely occurred, that function can become divorced from the property which, at one stage, it created; and, further, that the maintenance of property, or, in the narrower sense, of money, can become a new 'function'. When this state of affairs has been complicated over many generations by inheritance and accumulation, and, further, has been radically penetrated and affected by the continual emergence of new economic functions, with their appropriate classes, it becomes misleading to equate class and function, or even to posit any consistent relation between them. It was the realization of this fact, in the confusion of the new industrial society, which led Eliot's predecessors in this tradition to demands for change. Coleridge, Southey, Carlyle, Ruskin and, in effect, Arnold, may be seen to have been working, above all, in the attempt to make 'class' into 'function'. It was the absence of any consistent relation between class and function which was the gravamen of their criticism of the new industrial society. One thinks indeed, at times, of Eliot as the contemporary of Burke, who was himself idealizing and simplifying his actual society. Certainly, in this later work—although not, as we have seen, in *The Idea of a Christian Society*—he seems guilty of the worst kind of abstraction and failure to observe.

The discussion of 'levels' of culture is, however, less vitiated by this failing than one would expect. In thinking of culture as 'a whole way of life' Eliot emphasizes that a large part of a way of life is necessarily unconscious. A large part of our common beliefs is our common behaviour, and this is the main point of difference between the two meanings of 'culture'. What we sometimes call 'culture'—a religion, a moral code, a system of law, a body of work in the arts—is to be seen as only a part—the conscious part—of that 'culture' which is the whole way of life. This, evidently, is an illuminating way of thinking about culture, although the difficulties which it at once exposes are severe. For, just as we could not assume a correspondence between function and class, so we can not assume a correspondence between conscious culture and the whole way of life. If we think of a simple, and stable, society, the correspondence is usually evident; but where there is complication, and tension, and change, the matter is no longer one of levels, a given percentage of a uniform whole. The consciousness can be a false consciousness, or partly false, as I think Eliot showed in *The Idea of a Christian Society*. Where this is so, the maintenance of that consciousness, which is often likely to be to the immediate interest of a particular class, is no longer, in any positive sense, a function. We should be wise, therefore, to distinguish between the general, theoretical relation between conscious culture and a whole way of life, and the actual relation or relations which may at any one time exist in society. In theory, the metaphor of 'levels' may be illuminating; in practice, because it derives from observation not only of a culture but of a system of social classes, and, further, because the degree of conscious culture is so easily confused with the degree of social privilege, it is misleading.

It is evident, however, that in any conceivable society, the degrees of consciousness of even a common culture will widely vary. Eliot's emphasis on this is important to the extent that it forces a revision of some of the simpler theses of the democratic diffusion of culture. There are three points here. First, it now seems evident that the idea of not a community but an equality of culture—a uniform culture evenly spread—is essentially a product of the primitivism (often expressed as mediaevalism) which was so important a response to the harsh complexities of the new industrial society. Such an idea ignores the *necessary* complexity of any community which employs developed industrial and scientific techniques; and the longing for identity of situation and feeling, which exerts so powerful an emotional appeal in such writers as Morris, is merely a form of the regressive longing for a simpler, non-industrial society. In any form of society towards which we are likely to move, it now seems clear that there must be, not a simple equality (in the sense of identity) of culture; but rather a very complex system of specialized developments—the whole of which will form the whole culture, but which will not be available, or conscious, as a whole, to any individual or group living within it. (This complex system has, of course, no necessary relation to a system of social classes based on economic discrimination.) Where this is realized, the idea of equal diffusion is commonly transferred to a few selected elements of the culture, usually the arts. It is certain, I think, that one can imagine a society in which the practice and enjoyment of the arts would be very much more widely diffused. But there are dangers, both to the arts and to the whole culture, if the diffusion of this abstracted part of the culture is planned and considered as a separate operation.

One aspect of these dangers may be seen in the second point: that ideas of the diffusion of culture have normally been dominative in character, on behalf of the particular and finished ideal of an existing class. This, which I would call the Fabian tone in culture, is seen most clearly in an ideal which has been largely built into our educational system, of leading the unenlightened to the particular kind of light which the leaders find satisfactory for themselves. A particular kind of work is to be extended to more persons, although, as a significant thing, it exists as a whole in the situation in which it was produced. The dominative element appears in the conviction that the product will not need to be changed, that criticism is merely the residue of misunderstanding, and, finally, that the whole operation can be carried out, and the product widely extended, without radically changing the general situation. This may be summarized as the belief that a culture (in the specialized sense) can be widely extended without changing the culture (in the sense of 'a whole way of life') within which it has existed.

Eliot's arguments help us to see the limitations of these ideas, although he hardly presses the discussion home. What he develops has more relevance to the third point, which follows from the second, that the specialized culture cannot be extended without being changed. His words for 'change' are, of course, 'adulteration' and 'cheapening'; and we must grant him, for his own purposes, his own valuations. Yet, while we may have other valuations, and see 'variation' and 'enrichment' as at least equal possibilities with those which Eliot foresees, his emphasis that any extension involves change is welcome. Nothing is to be gained by supposing that the values of one way of life can be transferred, unchanged, to another; nor is it very realistic to suppose that a conscious selection of the values can be made—the bad to be rejected and the good to be transferred. Eliot is right in insisting that the thought about culture which has led to these positions is confused and shallow.

Eliot, from his insistence on culture as 'a whole way of life', has valuably criticized the orthodox theories of the diffusion of culture, and there is, as he sees it, only one further obstacle to the acceptance of his general view. This obstacle is the theory, primarily associated with Mannheim, of the substitution of élites for classes. Mannheim's argument may be seen, fundamentally, as an epilogue to the long nineteenth-century attempt to reidentify class with function. This took the form, either of an attempt to revive obsolete classes (as in Coleridge's idea of the clerisy), or of an appeal to existing classes to resume their functions (Carlyle, Ruskin), or of an attempt to form a new class, the civilizing minority (Arnold). Mannheim, quite rightly, realizes that these attempts have largely failed. Further, he rejects the idea of classes based on birth or money, and, emphasizing the necessary specialization and complexity of modern society, proposes to substitute for the old classes the new élites, whose basis is neither birth nor money, but achievement. In practice, one can see our own society as a mixture of the old ideas of class and the new ideas of an élite: a mixed economy, if one may put it in that way. The movement towards acceptance of the idea of élites has, of course, been powerfully assisted by the doctrines of opportunity in education and of the competitive evaluation of merit. The degree of necessary specialization, and the imperative requirement for quality in it, have also exerted a strong and practical pressure.

Eliot's objections to Mannheim's theory can be summarized in one of his sentences: that 'it posits an *atomic* view of society'.[23] The phrase will be recognized as belonging to the tradition: the opposite to *atomic* is *organic*, a word on which (without more definition than is common) Eliot largely depends. His instinct, in this, is right: the theory of élites is, essentially, only a refinement of social *laissez-faire*. The doctrine of opportunity in education is a mere silhouette of the doctrine of economic individualism, with its emphasis on competition and 'getting-on'. The doctrine of *equal* opportunity, which appears to qualify this, was generous in its conception, but it is tied, in practice, to the same social end. The definition of culture as 'a whole way of life' is vital at this point, for Eliot is quite right to point out that to limit, or to attempt to limit, the transmission of culture to a system of formal education is to limit a whole way of life to certain specialisms. If this limited programme is vigorously pressed, it is indeed difficult to see how it can lead to anything but disintegration. What will happen in practice, of course, when the programme is combined with a doctrine of opportunity (as it now largely is) is the setting-up of a new kind of stratified society, and the creation of new kinds of separation. Orthodoxy, in this matter, is now so general and so confident that it is even difficult to communicate one's meaning when one says that a stratified society, based on merit, is as objectionable in every human term as a stratified society based on money or on birth. As it has developed, within an inherited economic system, the idea of such a society has been functionally authoritarian, and it has even (because of the illusion that its criteria are more absolute than those of birth or money, and cannot be appealed against in the same way) a kind of Utopian sanction, which makes criticism difficult or impossible.

Eliot's objections to an élite society are, first, that its common culture will be meagre, and, second, that the principle of élites requires a change of persons in each generation, and that this change is bound to be effected without the important guarantee of any continuity wider than the élite's own specialisms. The point rests again on the insistence that culture is 'a whole way of life', rather than certain special skills. Eliot argues that while an élite may have more of the necessary skills than a class, it will lack that wider social continuity which a class guaranteed. Mannheim himself has emphasized the importance of this continuity, but the idea of the selection and reselection of élites seems to deny it, unless some new principle is introduced. Eliot's emphasis is on the whole content of a culture—the special skills being contained, for their own health, within it. And certainly there is a good deal of evidence, from many parts of our educational and training systems, of the co-existence of fine particular skills with mediocre general skills: a state of affairs which has important effects, not only on the élites, but on the whole common way of life.

Eliot recognizes the need for élites, or rather for an élite, and argues that, to ensure general continuity, we must retain social classes, and in particular a governing social class, with which the élite will overlap and constantly interact. This is Eliot's fundamentally conservative conclusion, for it is clear, when the abstractions are translated, that what he recommends is substantially what now exists, socially. He is, of course, led necessarily to condemn the pressure for a class-less society, and for a national educational system. He believes, indeed, that these pressures have already distorted the national life and the values which this life supports. It is in respect of these recommendations (not always reached by the same paths) that he now commands considerable attention and support.

I have already indicated that I believe his criticism of certain orthodox ideas of 'culture' to be valuable, and I think that he has left the ordinary social-democratic case without many relevant answers. As a conservative thinker, he has succeeded in exposing the limitations of an orthodox 'liberalism' which has been all too generally and too complacently accepted. Where I find myself differing from him (and I differ radically) is not in the main in his critique of this 'liberalism'; it is rather in the present implications of considering culture as 'a whole way of life'. It seems to me that his theoretical persistence in this view is matched only by his practical refusal to observe (a refusal which was less evident, at certain points, in *The Idea of a Christian Society*). For what is quite clear in the new conservatism (and this makes it very different from, and much inferior to, the conservatism of a Coleridge or a Burke) is that a genuine theoretical objection to the principle and the effects of an 'atomized', individualist society is combined, and has to be combined, with adherence to the principles of an economic system which is based on just this 'atomized', individualist view. The 'free economy' which is the central tenet of contemporary conservatism not only contradicts the social principles which Eliot advances (if it were only this one could say merely that he is an unorthodox conservative), but also, and this is the real confusion, is the only available method of ordering society to the maintenance of those interests and institutions on which Eliot believes his values to depend. Against the actual and powerful programme for the maintenance of social classes, and against the industrial capitalism which actually maintains the human divisions that he endorses, the occasional observation, however deeply felt, on the immorality of exploitation or usury seems, indeed, a feeble velleity. If culture were only a specialized product, it might be afforded, in a kind of reserved area, away from the actual drives of contemporary society. But if it is, as Eliot insists it must be, 'a whole way of life', then the whole system must be considered and judged as a whole. The insistence, in principle, is on wholeness; the practice, in effect, is fragmentary. The triumphant liberalism of contemporary society, which the practice of conservatives now so notably sustains, will, as anyone who thinks about a 'whole way of life' must realize, colour every traditional value. The progress which Eliot deplores is in fact the product of all that is actively left of the traditional society from which his values were drawn. This is the root, surely, of that bleakness which Eliot's social writings so powerfully convey. His standards are too strict for him to turn, as other philosophical conservatives are turning, to the recovery of the bones of Burke, the nostalgia for 1788. The bleakness, which is a kind of discipline, is wholly salutary: the fashionable 'New Conservatism' has been much too easy. If Eliot, when read attentively, has the effect of checking the complacencies of liberalism, he has also, when read critically, the effect of making complacent conservatism impossible. The next step, in thinking of these matters, must be in a different direction, for Eliot has closed almost all the existing roads.

CHAPTER IV

TWO LITERARY CRITICS

1. I. A. Richards

IT is not too much to say that *Principles of Literary Criticism*, which I. A. Richards published in 1924, contained a programme of critical work for a generation. One is surprised, on re-reading the book, to see how certain paragraphs in it have been expanded into whole volumes, usually by other writers. Richards himself has followed up only a part of what is there indicated: his later work is almost wholly a study of language and communication, in which throughout he has been a pioneer. But the *Principles*, and the shorter *Science and Poetry*, published in 1926, offer and depend upon a particular idea of culture which is essentially a renewed definition of the importance of art to civilization.

The critical revolt of the 1920s has been described as a revolt against Romantic theory. Yet it is less this than a revolt against something nearer and more oppressive: not Romantic theory itself but one of its specialized consequences, Aesthetic theory. The isolation of aesthetic experience, which had been evident in England between Pater and Clive Bell, and which by the 'twenties had become a kind of orthodoxy, was attacked along several different lines. From Eliot came the re-emphasis of tradition and faith; from Leavis a rediscovery of the breadth of general emphasis which Arnold had given to culture; from the Marxists the application of a new total interpretation of society. From Richards, if we view his work as a whole, the theoretical attack came through the social facts of language and communication. But the judgement on which this attack was founded is (as in Leavis, and with a similar dependence on Arnold) a matter of the whole culture:

> Human conditions and possibilities have altered more in a hundred years than they had in the previous ten thousand, and the next fifty may overwhelm us, unless we can devise a more adaptable morality. . . . We pass as a rule from a chaotic to a better organized

state by ways which we know nothing about. Typically through the influence of other minds. Literature and the arts are the chief means by which these influences are diffused. It should be unnecessary to insist upon the degree to which high civilization, in other words, free, varied and unwasteful life, depends upon them in a numerous society.[1]

The word 'numerous' indicates Richards's diagnosis of one of the major changes of condition:

> With the increase of population the problem presented by the gulf between what is preferred by the majority and what is accepted as excellent by the most qualified opinion has become infinitely more serious and appears likely to become threatening in the near future. For many reasons standards are much more in need of defence than they used to be.[2]

The increase of population interacts with the other element of change which Richards identifies: what he calls the 'neutralization of nature':

> the transference from the Magical View of the world to the scientific. . . . Science can tell us about man's place in the universe and his chances. . . . But it cannot tell us what we are or what this world is; not because these are in any sense insoluble questions, but because they are not questions at all. And if science cannot answer these pseudo-questions no more can philosophy or religion. So that all the varied answers which have for ages been regarded as the keys of wisdom are dissolving together. The result is a biological crisis which is not likely to be decided without trouble.[3]

At one level the problem is the defence of standards: the finding of adequate reasons to support minority standards against the depredations of a commercialism that controls majority taste. At another level, the discovery of these reasons is the necessary advance in consciousness which man must make if he is to control his destiny now that the old orientations have gone: no longer 'a Rock to shelter under or to cling to', but 'an efficient aeroplane in which to ride . . . this tempestuous turmoil of change'. Richards's sketch of a solution to these problems is his 'Psychological Theory of Value'. Like Arnold, he is offering culture as an alternative to anarchy, but culture as an idea has to be founded on a conception of value dependent not on the old 'keys of wisdom' but on what can be discovered in the new consciousness.

Richards is careful in his subsequent arguments to emphasize the tentative nature of any such discovery, in our present state of knowledge. But he is prepared to offer an interpretation or formula on which most of his subsequent work will depend. The conduct of life, he argues,

> is throughout an attempt to organize impulses so that success is obtained for the greater number or mass of them, for the most important and the weightiest set.[4]

Impulses can be divided into 'appetencies' ('seekings after') and 'aversions', both of which may be unconscious. Then:

> anything is valuable which will satisfy an appetency without involving the frustration of some equal or *more important* appetency.[5]

Importance, here, is defined as

> the extent of the disturbance of other impulses in the individual's activities which the thwarting of the impulse involves.[6]

Such disturbance is disorganization. The adjustment of impulses is the process of organization. Right conduct then becomes a matter of such adjustment and such organization. Value is a question of the growth of order. When the question is transferred from the individual to the community, it can be answered in similar terms. The 'greatest happiness of the majority', in Bentham's term, becomes 'the highest degree of organization of the satisfaction of impulses'. A common standard will find some individuals above, some below it. The tensions thus set up should be resolved, not in terms of majorities, but

> of the actual range and degree of satisfaction which different possible systematizations of impulse yield.[7]

The danger of any public system is that it will waste and frustrate available energy. Social reform is a matter of liberation, through the kind of organization described, although the process will not be primarily conscious or planned. The importance of literature and the arts is that they offer supreme examples of such organization, and that in doing so they provide 'values' (not prescriptions or messages, but examples of a necessary common process). It is through experience of and attention to such values that the wider common reorganization can be initiated and maintained. It is in this sense that 'poetry can save us':

it is a perfectly possible means of overcoming chaos.[8]

Thus we return to Arnold's prescription of culture against anarchy, but both 'culture' and 'the process of perfection' have been newly defined.

Richards goes on from this theory of value to describe the psychology of the artist. Basically, the importance of the artist is that a wider area of experience is *available* to him than to the normal person. Or, to put it in another way, he is more capable of the kind of organization which has been described, and is therefore 'able to admit far more without confusion'. Yet his usefulness, in this, will depend upon his relative normality:

The ways . . . in which the artist will differ from the average will as a rule presuppose an immense degree of similarity. They will be further developments of organizations already well advanced in the majority. His variations will be confined to the newest, the most plastic, the least fixed part of the mind, the parts for which reorganization is most easy.[9]

Not all such variations can or ought to be generally followed. But often they will be significant advances which can serve as models for a general advance. Further, the existence of finely organized responses in the arts offers a continual standard by which what Richards calls the 'stock responses' can be seen and judged. At any time certain incomplete adjustments, certain immature and inapplicable attitudes, can be fixed into formulas and widely suggested and diffused:

The losses incurred by these artificial fixations of attitudes are evident. Through them the average adult is worse, not better adjusted to the possibilities of his existence than the child. He is even in the most important things functionally unable to face facts; do what he will he is only able to face fictions, fictions projected by his own stock responses. Against these stock responses the artist's internal and external conflicts are fought, and with them the popular writer's triumphs are made.[10]

The exploitation of these stock responses by commercialized art and literature, and by the cinema, is a notable fact of our own culture. While good art may serve the common process of finer organization, bad art will not only not serve it, but actively hinder it:

> The effects we are considering depend only upon the kind and degree of organization which is given to the experiences. If it is at the level of our own best attempts or above it (but not so far above as to be out of reach) we are refreshed. But if our own organization is broken down, forced to a cruder, a more wasteful level, we are depressed and temporarily incapacitated, not only locally but generally . . . unless the critical task of diagnosis is able to restore equanimity and composure.[11]

On this attitude to good and bad literature, a whole subsequent critical and educational programme has been based.

It remains to consider a final point made by Richards, about the social function of art. He takes the familiar theory of art as play and by redefining play returns art to a central position, instead of the marginal 'leisure-time' position which the description as play was meant to suggest. The redefinition rests again on the criterion of organization. Art is play in the sense that

> in a fully developed man a state of readiness for action will take the place of action when the full appropriate situation for action is not present.[12]

Play is the training of readiness for action, either in a special or in a general field. Art, in creating and offering us a situation, is in this sense experimental.

> In ordinary life a thousand considerations prohibit for most of us any complete working-out of our response; the range and complexity of the impulse-systems involved is less; the need for action, the comparative uncertainty and vagueness of the situation, the intrusion of accidental irrelevancies, inconvenient temporal spacing —the action being too slow or too fast—all these obscure the issue

and prevent the full development of the experience. We have to jump to some rough and ready solution. But in the 'imaginative experience' these obstacles are removed. Thus what happens here, what precise stresses, preponderances, conflicts, resolutions and interinanimations, what remote relationships between different systems of impulses arise, what before unapprehended and inexecutable connections are established, is a matter which, we see clearly, may modify all the rest of life.[13]

The experience of literature is thus a kind of training for general experience: a training, essentially, in that capacity for organization which is man's only profitable response to his altered and dangerous condition.

This summary of Richards's basic position serves to show, first, the degree to which he is an inheritor of the general tradition, and second, the extent to which, by offering a positive account, he has clarified certain of its contemporary issues. The clarification is real, as far as it goes, and its applications in criticism have been of major value. One of the most valuable points is Richards's return to that idea of the relative normality of the artist which Wordsworth had defined, but which later Romantic writing had rejected. Herbert Read also defines art as a 'mode of knowledge', and describes its social function in terms very similar to those of Richards. But Read, supported by Freud, reiterates that view of the artist's essential abnormality which as much as anything has denied art's social bearings. Read offers the model of three strata of the mind, with the artist as an example of a kind of 'fault' which exposes the strata to each other at unusual levels. In the matter of demonstrable psychology, our theories of art are still almost wholly speculative, but the crudeness of Freud's casual comment on the artist as 'neurotic' is sufficiently evident. Read's version of contact with deep levels of the mind through the 'fault', and of the actual making of art as an investment of this contact 'with superficial charms . . . lest the bare truth repel us',[14] is similarly unsatisfactory. The whole concept of 'levels of the mind', even if restricted to consideration as a model, is more static than experience appears to require. If we think, rather, of moving patterns and relations, the question of 'valuable derangement', and even of 'normality', seems a limiting term. To separate creation and execution is the mark of the Romantic disintegration of 'art' into the separable qualities of 'imaginative truth' and 'skill'. On the whole, Richards's version of art as 'organization' both restores the unity of conception and execution, and offers an emphasis which can be profitably investigated. We should add, however, that nearly all theoretical discussions of art since the Industrial Revolution have been crippled by the assumed opposition between art and the actual organization of society, which is important as the historical phenomenon that has been traced, but which can hardly be taken as an absolute. Individual psychology has been similarly limited by an assumption of opposition between individual and society which is in fact only a symptom of society's transitional disorganization. Until we have lived through this, we are not likely to achieve more than a limited theory of art, but we can be glad meanwhile that the starting point which has for so long misled us—the artist's necessary abnormality—is being gradually rejected in theory, and almost wholly rejected, in terms of practical feeling, among a majority of actual artists. The renewed emphasis on communication is a valuable sign of our gradual recovery of community.

Richards has had much that is useful to say about communication, but, in the general position within which this has been offered, there are, I think, two points of question. First, while what Richards says about the extension and refinement of organization is obviously useful, and corresponds in a general way to one's actual experience of literature, there is an element of passivity in his idea of the relationship between reader and work which might in the end be disabling. What one most wants to know about this process is the detail of its practical operation, at the highest and most difficult levels. The point can be illustrated, although this does not in itself affect the theory, from Richards's own criticism. He is always very good at the demonstration of a really crude organization, as in the Wilcox sonnet discussed in *Principles*. But he has not offered enough really convincing examples of the intense realization of a rich or complex organization, which in general terms he

TWO LITERARY CRITICS

has often described. He often notes the complexity, but the discussion that follows is usually a kind of return on itself, a return to the category 'complexity', rather than an indication of that ultimate refinement and adjustment which is his most positive general value. One has the sense of a manipulation of objects which are separate from the reader, which are *out there* in the environment. Further, and perhaps as a consequence of this, there is at times a kind of servility towards the literary establishment. This seems an astonishing thing to say about the writer who in *Practical Criticism* did more than anyone else to penetrate the complacency of literary academicism. So much, indeed, is willingly and gratefully granted. But the idea of literature as a training-ground for life *is* servile. Richards's account of the inadequacy of ordinary response when compared with the adequacy of literary response is a cultural symptom rather than a diagnosis. Great literature is indeed enriching, liberating and refining, but man is always and everywhere more than a reader, has indeed to be a great deal else before he can even become an adequate reader; unless indeed he can persuade himself that literature, as an ideal sphere of heightened living, will under certain cultural circumstances operate as a substitute. 'We shall then be thrown back . . . upon poetry. It is capable of saving us.' The very form of these sentences indicates the essential passivity which I find disquieting. Poetry, in this construction, is the new anthropomorph. Richards's general account may indeed be an adequate description of man's best *use* of literature, and such a use, if it comes to be articulated, will show itself in major criticism. But one has the feeling that Richards, overwhelmed, has picked out from a generally hostile environment certain redeeming features, and is concerned thereafter with finding a technique by means of which these features may be not so much used as enabled to *operate on* him and others.

This point is related to my second question, which formed itself, while I was reading, as the observation that Richards is remarkably innocent of company. By this I sought to mean, first, that his characteristic relationship is that of a sole man to a total environment, which is seen, again *out there*, as an object. His discussion, in the account of the theory of value, of the extension to 'communal affairs', is character-istically, as in Bentham, based on a minimal self-protective abstraction. His rational critique of custom is, as with the Utilitarians, often useful. But the basic attitude to custom is negative; the critic does not feel himself essentially involved. Few writers have referred more often than Richards to what may now be called global problems, and his own work towards 'the possibilities of World Communication which Basic English holds out' may be seen as a contribution to their solution. Yet this kind of concern is hardly social in the full sense. His advocacy of the rule of Reason (in the conclusion of *How to Read a Page*) is of course positive, as against the confusion which he and others have analysed. But where, in what bodies, do reason and confusion operate? Where, in what relationships, are they denied or confirmed? These questions, and surely both must be answered, are bound to lead into the whole complex of action and inter-action which is the practice of living, and which we cannot reduce to such an abstraction as 'the contemporary situation'. Richards's account of the genesis of our problems is a selection of certain products, not only science as a product but even, in the terms of the discussion, increased population as a product. His business, then, is to find another product that is redeeming. Yet this innocence of process, which follows naturally enough from an innocence of company, is disabling. We are faced not only with products but with the breath, the hand, that makes, maintains, changes or destroys. All that Richards has taught us about language and com-munication, and for which we acknowledge our debt, has to be reviewed, finally, when we have rid ourselves of those vestiges of Aesthetic Man—alone in a hostile environment, receiving and organizing his experience—which Richards, even as brilliant opponent, in fact inherited.

11. F. R. Leavis

F. R. Leavis, in the pamphlet *Mass Civilization and Minority Culture* published in 1930, outlined a particular view of culture which has become very widely influential. As in his literary criticism, there is a body of detailed judgements, and there is also an outline of history. In *Culture and Environment*, written jointly with Denys Thompson and published in 1933, the detailed judgements recur, and the outline of history is significantly enlarged. Thereafter, and mainly in *Scrutiny*, this essential case continued to be presented. It is natural to associate with it books like Q. D. Leavis's *Fiction and the Reading Public*, Denys Thompson's *Between the Lines* and *Voice of Civilization*, and L. C. Knights' work in *Drama and Society in the Age of Jonson* and *Explorations*. Leavis's own later writings in this field, which continually interact with his literary criticism, can be conveniently examined in *Education and the University* and *The Common Pursuit*. From this whole body of work, to which one must add a large number of minor contributions by other writers, the significant 'case' emerges clearly enough.

The basis of the case, and of the essential connexion with literary studies, appears in the opening pages of *Mass Civilization and Minority Culture*:

> In any period it is upon a very small minority that the discerning appreciation of art and literature depends: it is (apart from cases of the simple and familiar) only a few who are capable of unprompted, first-hand judgment. They are still a small minority, though a larger one, who are capable of endorsing such first-hand judgment by genuine personal response. The accepted valuations are a kind of paper currency based upon a very small proportion of gold. To the state of such a currency the possibilities of fine living at any time bear a close relation. . . . The minority capable not only of appreciating Dante, Shakespeare, Donne, Baudelaire, Hardy (to take major instances) but of recognizing their latest successors constitute the consciousness of the race (or of a branch of it) at a given time. For such capacity does not belong merely to an isolated aesthetic realm: it implies responsiveness to theory as well as to art, to science and philosophy in so far as these may affect the sense of the human situation and of the nature of life. Upon this minority depends our power of profiting by the finest human experience of the past; they keep alive the subtlest and most perishable parts of tradition. Upon them depend the implicit standards that order the finer living of an age, the sense that this is worth more than that,

this rather than that is the direction in which to go, that the centre is here rather than there. In their keeping . . . is the language, the changing idiom, upon which fine living depends, and without which distinction of spirit is thwarted and incoherent. By 'culture' I mean the use of such a language.[1]

In certain respects this is a new position in the development of the idea of Culture. Yet it mainly derives from Arnold, whom Leavis quite properly acknowledges as his starting point. What goes back to Arnold goes back also to Coleridge but there are significant changes on the way. For Coleridge the minority was to be a class, an endowed order of clerisy whose business was general cultivation, and whose allegiance was to the whole body of sciences. For Arnold, the minority was a remnant, composed of individuals to be found in all social classes, whose principal distinction was that they escaped the limitations of habitual class-feeling. For Leavis, the minority is, essentially, a literary minority, which keeps alive the literary tradition and the finest capacities of the language. This development is instructive, for the tenuity of the claim to be a 'centre' is, unfortunately, increasingly obvious. '"Civilization" and "culture" are coming to be antithetical terms,' Leavis writes a little later.[2] This is the famous distinction made by Coleridge, and the whole development of this idea of culture rests on it. Culture was made into an entity, a positive body of achievements and habits, precisely to express a mode of living superior to that being brought about by the 'progress of civilization'. For Coleridge the defence of this standard was to be in the hands of a National Church, including 'the learned of all denominations'. Since this could not in fact be instituted, the nature of the defending minority had continually, by the successors of Coleridge, to be redefined. The process which Arnold began, when he virtually equated 'culture' with 'criticism', is completed by Leavis, and had been similarly completed a little earlier, by I. A. Richards. Of course Leavis is right when he says that many of the 'subtlest and most perishable parts of tradition' are contained in our literature and language. But the decline from Coleridge's allegiance to all the sciences is unfortunately real. 'To science and philosophy in so far as these may affect the sense of the human situation and of the nature of life' is surely a little grudging. I agree with Leavis, as with Coleridge and Arnold and with Burke the common teacher of this point, that a society is poor indeed if it has nothing to live by but its own immediate and contemporary experience. But the ways in which we can draw on other experience are more various than literature alone. For experience that is formally recorded we go, not only to the rich source of literature, but also to history, building, painting, music, philosophy, theology, political and social theory, the physical and natural sciences, anthropology, and indeed the whole body of learning. We go also, if we are wise, to the experience that is otherwise recorded: in institutions, manners, customs, family memories. Literature has a vital importance because it is at once a formal record of experience, and also, in every work, a point of intersection with the common language that is, in its major bearings, differently perpetuated. The recognition of culture as the body of all these activities, and of the ways in which they are perpetuated and enter into our common living, was valuable and timely. But there was always the danger that this recognition would become not only an abstraction but in fact an isolation. To put upon literature, or more accurately upon criticism, the responsibility of controlling the quality of the whole range of personal and social experience, is to expose a vital case to damaging misunderstanding. English is properly a central matter of all education, but it is not, clearly, a whole education. Similarly, formal education, however humane, is not the whole of our gaining of the social experience of past and present. In his proposals on education (in *Education and the University*) Leavis makes, very clearly, the former point, and few men have done more to extend the depth and range of literary studies, and to relate them to other interests and other disciplines. But the damaging formulation of the nature of the minority remains. Leavis might have written:

> The minority capable not only of appreciating Shakespeare, the English common law, Lincoln Cathedral, committee procedure, Purcell, the nature of wage-labour, Hogarth, Hooker, genetic

theory, Hume (to take major instances) but of recognizing, either their successors, or their contemporary changes and implications, constitute the consciousness of the race (or of a branch of it) at a given time.

If he had done so (while apologizing for the arbitrariness of the selection), his claim that 'upon this minority depends our power of profiting by the finest human experience of the past' would have been, in some degree, more substantial. It is a matter not so much of theory as of emphasis. If, however, he had entered such dangerous lists, the whole question of the nature of the minority, of its position in society, and of its relations with other human beings, might have been forced more clearly into the open. The difficulty about the idea of culture is that we are continually forced to extend it, until it becomes almost identical with our whole common life. When this is realized, the problems to which, since Coleridge, we have addressed ourselves are in fact transformed. If we are to meet them honestly, we have to face very fine and very difficult adjustments. The assumption of a minority, followed by its definition in one's own terms, seems in practice to be a way of stopping short of this transformation of the problems, and of our own consequent adjustments. The particular view of what is valuable is taken, in experience, as a whole; the fixed point is determined; and, as in the literary criticism, a myth, a significant construction, is persuasively communicated. Leavis's myth seems to me rather more powerful than most of its competitors, but there is a point in its propagation when we begin to see its edges, and the danger, then, is that in fact we shall undervalue it.

For in fact, and against what has previously been said, the myth is to a considerable extent adequate, for the purposes to which Leavis actually passes. For he is faced, unlike Arnold, with the twentieth-century developments of the press, advertising, popular fiction, films, broadcasting, and that whole way of living for which Middletown (from the Lynds' study of an Illinois town) becomes his symbol. The critics who first formulated the idea of culture were faced with industrialism, and with its causes and consequences in thinking and feeling. Leavis, in 1930, faced not only these but certain ways of thinking and feeling embodied in immensely powerful institutions which threatened to overwhelm the ways that he and others valued. His pamphlet, given its reference to Richards, is the effective origin of that practical criticism of these institutions which has been of growing general importance in the last quarter-century. The kind of training indicated in *Culture and Environment*, which is an educational manual, has been widely imitated and followed, so that if Leavis and his colleagues had done only this it would be enough to entitle them to major recognition. It is not, of course, that the threat has been removed; indeed it may even be said to have grown in magnitude. 'That deliberate exploitation of the cheap response which characterises our civilization' is still very widely evident. But it is not negligible to have instituted a practical method of training in discrimination—a method which has been widely applied and can yet be greatly extended in our whole educational system. Because the exploitation is deliberate, and because its techniques are so powerful, the educational training has to be equally deliberate. And the magnificent contrasting vitality of literature is an essential control and corollary.

The Leavis who promoted this kind of work is the Leavis of detailed judgements. It is obvious, however, that the ways of feeling and thinking embodied in such institutions as the popular press, advertising and the cinema cannot finally be criticized without reference to a way of life. The questions, again, insistently extend. Is the deliberate exploitation a deliberate pursuit of profit, to the neglect or contempt of other considerations? Why, if this is so, should cheapness of expression and response be profitable? If our civilization is a 'mass-civilization', without discernible respect for quality and seriousness, by what means has it become so? What, in fact, do we mean by 'mass'? Do we mean a democracy dependent on universal suffrage, or a culture dependent on universal education, or a reading-public dependent on universal literacy? If we find the products of mass-civilization so repugnant, are we to identify the suffrage or the education or the literacy as the agents of decay? Or, alternatively, do we mean by mass-civilization an industrial civilization, dependent on machine-production and the factory system? Do we find institutions like the popular press and advertising to be the necessary consequences of such a system of production? Or, again, do we find both the machine-civilization and the institutions to be products of some great change and decline in human minds? Such questions, which are the commonplaces of our generation, inevitably underlie the detailed judgements. And Leavis, though he has never claimed to offer a theory of such matters, has in fact, in a number of ways, committed himself to certain general attitudes which amount to a recognizable attitude towards modern history and society.

The attitude will be quickly recognized by those who have followed the growth of the idea of culture. Its main immediate sources are D. H. Lawrence (whose relations to the earlier tradition have been noted) and the books of George Sturt ('George Bourne'), especially *Change in the Village* and *The Wheelwright's Shop*—works which, while original and valuable in their observation, go back, essentially, to Cobbett. A characteristic general statement by Leavis and Thompson is the following:

> Sturt speaks of 'the death of Old England and of the replacement of the more primitive nation by an "organized" modern state'. The Old England was the England of the organic community, and in what sense it was more primitive than the England that has replaced it needs pondering. But at the moment what we have to consider is the fact that the organic community has gone; it has so nearly disappeared from memory that to make anyone, however educated, realize what it was is commonly a difficult undertaking. Its destruction (in the West) is the most important fact of recent history—it is very recent indeed. How did this momentous change —this vast and terrifying disintegration—take place in so short a time? The process of the change is that which is commonly described as Progress.[3]

Several points in this are obscure: in particular, the exact weight of the adjective *organic* and its apparent contrast with *organized* (see note at the end of this chapter). But it seems clear, from the examples quoted in support, that the 'momentous change' is the Industrial Revolution. The 'organic community' is a rural community:

> The more 'primitive' England represented an animal naturalness, but distinctively human. Sturt's villagers expressed their human nature, they satisfied their human needs, in terms of the natural environment; and the things they made—cottages, barns, ricks, and waggons—together with their relations with one another constituted a human environment, and a subtlety of adjustment and adaptation, as right and inevitable (*sic*).[4]

In contrast with this way of life is set the urban, suburban, mechanized modernity, on which such comments as these are possible:

> The modern labourer, the modern clerk, the modern factory-hand live only for their leisure, and the result is that they are unable to live in their leisure when they get it. Their work is meaningless to them, merely something they have to do in order to earn a livelihood, and consequently when their leisure comes it is meaningless, and all the uses they can put it to come almost wholly under the head of what Stuart Chase calls 'decreation'. . . .[5]

> . . . The modern citizen no more knows how the necessaries of life come to him (he is quite out of touch, we say, with 'primary production') than he can see his own work as a significant part in a human scheme (he is merely earning wages or making profits).[6]

The points are familiar, but it is impossible to feel them to be adequate. The version of history is myth in the sense of conjecture, for while on such points as the adaptation to natural environment shown in building and tools, or on the related point about such traditional crafts as the carpenter's, it is possible, on the whole, to agree, it is a very different matter to assert, for instance, that the 'human environment . . . their relations with one another' was in fact 'right and inevitable'. This is, I think, a surrender to a characteristically industrialist, or urban, nostalgia—a late version of mediaevalism, with its attachments to an 'adjusted' feudal society. If there is one thing certain about 'the organic community', it is that it has always gone. Its period, in the contemporary myth, is the rural eighteenth century; but for Goldsmith, in *The Deserted Village* (1770), it had gone; for Crabbe, in

The Village (1783), it was hardly 'right and inevitable'; for Cobbett, in 1820, it had gone since his boyhood (that is to say, it existed when Goldsmith and Crabbe were writing); for Sturt it was there until late in the nineteenth century; for myself (if I may be permitted to add this, for I was born into a village, and into a family of many generations of farm-labourers) it was there—or the aspects quoted, the inherited skills of work, the slow traditional talk, the continuity of work and leisure—in the 1930s. What is being observed, and what, when rightly weighted, is important, is an important tradition of social and productive experience that has grown out of certain long-persistent conditions. It is useful to contrast this with the difficulties of comparable richness of adjustment to the urban and factory conditions of which experience is so much shorter. But it is misleading to make this contrast without making others, and it is foolish and dangerous to exclude from the so-called organic society the penury, the petty tyranny, the disease and mortality, the ignorance and frustrated intelligence which were also among its ingredients. These are not material disadvantages to be set against spiritual advantages; the one thing that such a community teaches is that life is whole and continuous—it is the whole complex that matters. 'That which is commonly described as Progress' saved spirit and blood.

The basic intellectual fault of such formulations as that in *Culture and Environment* is, curiously, the taking of aspects for wholes. A valid detailed judgement grows too quickly into a persuasive outline. The tendency to reduce experience to literary evidence alone is commonly tempting. *Middletown* is a frightening book; many advertisements and many newspapers are cheap and nasty. But do we not too easily construct from such evidence a contemptuous version of the lives of our contemporaries, which we should be hard put to it to prove from life, although we could prove it easily enough, or so it would seem, from print? Is it true, for instance, that to 'the modern labourer, the modern clerk, the modern factory-hand' all their work is 'meaningless', except as a means to money? Is it true that 'all the uses they can put' their leisure to are almost wholly 'decreation'? Is it true that 'the modern citizen' hardly knows 'how the necessaries of

life come to him'? What is true, I would argue, is that a
number of new kinds of unsatisfying work have come into
existence; a number of new kinds of cheap entertainment;
and a number of new kinds of social division. Against these
must be set a number of new kinds of satisfying work;
certain evident improvements, and new opportunities, in
education; certain important new kinds of social organization. Between all these and other factors, the balance has to
be more finely drawn than the myth allows.

My reason for making these points in relation to Leavis's
work, when they might equally have been made about other
work where the myth is more palpable, and, on occasion,
more sentimentally misleading, is that, in the case of Leavis,
these elements have become as it seems inextricably entangled with the advocacy of educational proposals that
are wholly valuable. *Culture and Environment* makes certain
reservations: 'we must beware of simple solutions . . . there
can be no mere going back . . . the memory of the old order
must be the chief incitement towards a new'.[7] These are
useful, and serve to introduce the primary stress on an education that will seek to control the disintegrating and cheapening forces, both by direct 'defensive' training, and by that
positive training in experience which literature is qualified
to offer. The making and extension of such an education are
so vital that one regrets the inclusion, in this advocacy, of
social conclusions and attitudes which are, to say the least,
doubtful. The point must be referred back to the earlier
point about the nature of the 'minority'. Leavis might
reasonably reply, to what I have there written, that to see
literature as a specialism among others is not to see literature
at all. I would agree with this. But the emphasis I am trying
to make is that, in the work of continuity and change, and
just because of the elements of disintegration, we cannot
make literary experience the sole test, or even the central
test. We cannot even, I would argue, put the important
stress on the 'minority', for the idea of the conscious
minority is itself no more than a defensive symptom, against
the general dangers. When Eliot combines the idea of a
minority culture with his rejection of the ideas of democracy,
he is on more consistent, if certainly sourer, ground. Leavis,

having made the vital connexion between a whole way of life and the capacity for valuable literary experience, is surely bound, for anything beyond the immediately necessary defensive measures, to a conception of the growth of a society, and its whole way of life, which should more adequately embody such kinds of experience. It is not so much a matter of announcing some political allegiance. It is a matter, rather, in our whole social experience, of declaring that 'this is worth more than that, this rather than that is the direction in which to go'. The difficulties are obvious, but I suspect that they are impossibly increased by continued allegiance to an outline of history which tends to suggest that 'what is commonly described as Progress' is almost wholly decline.

As I have understood Leavis's subsequent work, he has chosen to concentrate, on the one hand on persistent defensive actions, on the other hand, in criticism, on such re-creation as is possible. As a life's work (and one as yet unfinished) it has been a major achievement. Others have taken over the criticism of the popular press, advertising, the cinema and so on which is now almost a commonplace. Leavis, most valuably, has gone on with his criticism of some of the apparent alternatives to these: the 'better' press, the 'better' books. He has also, notably in his defence of Lawrence, come much nearer to acknowledging important elements in post-Industrial English society, which the outlines of *Culture and Environment* neglected. In his comments on Bunyan, on Dickens and on Mark Twain he has made a more positive theoretical commitment to actual and general social experience than the concept of a defensive minority (whose social experience is mainly from the past) seemed to allow. He has attacked what he calls the domination of the world of English letters by a small interlocking group, and has reduced to its proper impotence the ordinary conception of a superior minority which happens to coincide with a particular social class. He has, at the same time, continued to attack the Marxist version of a social alternative: intellectually, on the grounds of its abstraction; socially, on the nature of its realization in Russia. All this has brought him many enemies, but he has kept his course. And it is not so much, now, a matter of assessing his own life's work, as of assessing the value of the directions which he has initiated. I can only say, in conclusion, that the extremely valuable educational proposals, and the important and illuminating local judgements, which are real gains, have to be set against losses, some of which are serious. The concept of a culti- vated minority, set over against a 'decreated' mass, tends, in its assertion, to a damaging arrogance and scepticism. The concept of a wholly organic and satisfying past, to be set against a disintegrated and dissatisfying present, tends in its neglect of history to a denial of real social experience. The cultural training ought essentially to be a training in demo- cracy, which has to be a training in direct judgements. Yet the contingent elements in the myth have led, at worst to a pseudo-aristocratic authoritarianism, at best to a habitual scepticism which has shown itself very intolerant of any con- temporary social commitment. Leavis's distinction as a critic, and his equal distinction as a teacher, are unquestioned. But it is all the more necessary, if the distinction is to be insisted upon, to realize the inadequacies and the dangers of what is now the 'minority culture' dogma.

A Note on 'Organic'

Few English words are more difficult than 'organic', which has a vast and complicated semantic history. The Greek ὄργανον first meant 'tool' or 'instrument', and ὀργανικός was equivalent to our 'mechanical'. But there was a derived sense of 'physical organ' (the eye an 'instrument for seeing') and on this the whole association with living beings was subsequently made. In English, 'mechanical' and 'organical' are synonyms in the sixteenth century, but in the eighteenth century the physical and biological references begin to predominate. Then in Burke and Coleridge, 'organic' begins to be used to describe institutions and societies, and one of the senses of 'mechanical' (= 'artificial') is used to establish a now familiar contrast. The contrast is then extended into the 'organ' family itself: 'organ'='organ of sense', giving rise to praise-words such as 'organic' and 'organism', while 'organ'='instrument' produces 'organize' and 'organization'. Burke used 'organic' and 'organized' as synonyms, but by the middle nine- teenth century they are commonly opposed ('natural' vs. 'planned' society, etc.).

There are five apparent reasons why 'organic' became popular: to stress an idea of 'wholeness' in society; to stress the growth of a 'people', as in rising nationalisms; to stress 'natural growth', as in 'culture', with particular reference to slow change and adaptation; to reject 'mechanist' and 'materialist' versions of society; to criticize industrialism, in favour of a society 'in close touch with natural processes' (i.e. agriculture). The range is too wide and too tempting to be ordinarily scanned, and the word is now commonly used by writers of wholly opposed opinions: e.g. Marxists stressing 'a whole, formed State'; Conservatives 'a slowly adapting society and tradition'; critics of machine-production 'a predominantly agricultural society'; Bertrand Russell, on the other hand, 'a predominantly industrial society': 'when we are exhorted to make society "organize", it is from machinery that we shall necessarily derive our models, since we do not know how to make society a living animal' (*Prospects of Industrial Civilization*). At the very least, this complication indicates the need for caution in using the word without immediate definition. Perhaps all societies are organic (i.e. formed wholes), but some are more organic (agricultural/industrialized/conservative/planned) than others.

CHAPTER V

MARXISM AND CULTURE

I

MARX was the contemporary of Ruskin and George Eliot, but the Marxist interpretation of culture did not become widely effective in England until the 'thirties of our own century. William Morris had linked the cause of art with the cause of socialism, and his socialism was of the revolutionary Marxist kind. But the terms of Morris's position were older, an inheritance from the general tradition which came down to him through Ruskin. As he told the Northumberland miners, in 1887:

> Even supposing he did not understand that there was a definite reason in economics, and that the whole system could be changed ... he for one would be a rebel against it.[1]

The economic reasoning, and the political promise, came to him from Marxism; the general rebellion was in older terms.

Marx himself outlined, but never fully developed, a cultural theory. His casual comments on literature, for example, are those of a learned, intelligent man of his period, rather than what we now know as Marxist literary criticism. On occasion, his extraordinary social insight extends a comment, but one never feels that he is applying a theory. Not only is the tone of his discussion of these matters normally undogmatic, but also he is quick to restrain, whether in literary theory or practice, what he evidently regarded as an over-enthusiastic, mechanical extension of his political, economic and historical conclusions to other kinds of fact. Engels, though habitually less cautious, is very similar in tone. This is not to say, of course, that Marx lacked confidence in the eventual extension of such conclusions, or in the filling-in of his outline. It is only that his genius recognized difficulty and complexity, and that his personal discipline was a discipline to fact.

The outline which Marx drew, and which has proved to

be so fruitful and important, appears most clearly in the Preface to his *Critique of Political Economy* (1859):

> In the social production which men carry on they enter into definite relations that are indispensable and independent of their will; these relations of production correspond to a definite stage of development of their material powers of production. The sum total of these relations of production constitutes the economic structure of society—the real foundation, on which rise legal and political superstructures and to which correspond definite forms of social consciousness. The mode of production in material life determines the general character of the social, political and spiritual processes of life. It is not the consciousness of men that determines their existence, but, on the contrary, their social existence determines their consciousness. . . . With the change of the economic foundation the entire immense superstructure is more or less rapidly transformed. In considering such transformations the distinction should always be made between the material transformation of the economic conditions of production which can be determined with the precision of natural science, and the legal, political, religious, aesthetic, or philosophic—in short, ideological forms in which men become conscious of this conflict and fight it out.[2]

The distinction mentioned is obviously of great importance. Even if we accept the formula of structure and super-structure, we have Marx's word that changes in the latter are necessarily subject to a different and less precise mode of investigation. The point is reinforced by the verbal qualifications of his text: 'determines the *general* character'; '*more or less rapidly* transformed'. The superstructure is a matter of human consciousness, and this is necessarily very complex, not only because of its diversity, but also because it is always historical: at any time, it includes continuities from the past as well as reactions to the present. Marx indeed at times regards ideology as a false consciousness: a system of continuities which change has in fact undermined. He writes in *The Eighteenth Brumaire*:

> Upon the several forms of property, upon the social conditions of existence, a whole superstructure is reared of various and peculiarly shaped feelings, illusions, habits of thought, and conceptions of life.

The whole class produces and shapes these out of its material foundation and out of the corresponding social conditions. The individual unit to whom they flow through tradition and education may fancy that they constitute the true reasons for and premises of his conduct.[3]

If then a part of the superstructure is mere rationalization, the complexity of the whole is further increased.

This recognition of complexity is the first control in any valid attempt at a Marxist theory of culture. The second control, more controversial, is an understanding of the formula of structure and superstructure. In Marx this formula is definite, but perhaps as no more than an analogy. Certainly when we come to this comment by Engels there is need to reconsider:

> According to the materialist conception of history, the determining element in history is *ultimately* the production and reproduction in real life. More than this neither Marx nor I have ever asserted. If therefore somebody twists this into the statement that the economic element is the *only* determining one, he transforms it into a meaningless, abstract and absurd phrase. The economic situation is the basis, but the various elements of the superstructure—political forms of the class struggle and its consequences, constitutions established by the victorious class after a successful battle, etc.—forms of law—and then even the reflexes of all these actual struggles in the brains of the combatants: political, legal, and philosophical theories, religious ideas and their further development into systems of dogma —also exercise their influence upon the course of the historical struggles and in many cases preponderate in determining their *form*. There is an interaction of all these elements, in which, amid all the endless *host* of accidents (i.e. of things and events whose inner connection is so remote or so impossible to prove that we regard it as absent and can neglect it) the economic element finally asserts itself as necessary. Otherwise the application of the theory to any period of history one chose would be easier than the solution of a simple equation of the first degree.[4]

Here again the emphasis falls on complexity, but the result of the emphasis is a lessening of the usefulness of the formula which Marx used. Structure and superstructure, as terms of an analogy, express at once an absolute and a fixed relationship. But the reality which Marx and Engels recognize is both less absolute and less clear. Engels virtually introduces three levels of reality: the economic situation; the political situation; the state of theory. Yet any formula in terms of levels, as in terms of structure and superstructure, does less than justice to the factors of movement which it is the essence of Marxism to realize. We arrive at a different model, in which reality is seen as a very complex field of movement, within which the economic forces finally reveal themselves as the organizing element.

Engels uses the word 'interaction', but this does not imply any withdrawal of the claims for economic primacy. The point is clearly made by Plekhanov, in *The Development of the Monist Theory of History* (1895):

> Interaction exists . . . nevertheless, *by itself* it explains nothing. In order to understand interaction, one must ascertain the attributes of the interacting forces and these attributes cannot find their ultimate explanation in the fact of interaction, however much they may change thanks to that fact. . . . The qualities of the interacting forces, the attributes of the social organisms influencing one another, are explained in the long run by the cause we already know: the economic structure of these organisms, which is determined by the state of their productive forces.[5]

Plekhanov concedes that there are 'particular laws . . . in the development of human thought'; Marxists will not, for example, identify 'the laws of logic with the laws of the circulation of commodities'. All that a Marxist will deny is that the 'laws of thought' are the prime mover of intellectual development; the prime mover is economic change. He continues:

> Sensitive but weak-headed people are indignant with the theory of Marx because they take its first word to be its last. Marx says: in explaining the *subject*, let us see in what mutual relations people enter under the influence of *objective* necessity. Once these relations are known, it will be possible to ascertain how human self-consciousness develops under their influence. . . . Psychology adapts itself to economy. But this adaptation is a complex process . . . on

the one hand the 'iron laws' of movement of the 'string' . . . on the other, on the 'string' and precisely thanks to its movement, there grows up the 'garment of life' of ideology.[6]

Evidently Plekhanov is searching here (not altogether successfully) for a model more satisfactory than structure and superstructure. He is aware of Marx's reservation about the study of ideas, and admits:

> Much, very much, is still obscure for us in this sphere. But there is even more that is obscure for the idealists, and yet more for eclectics, who however never understand the significance of the difficulties they encounter, imagining that they will always be able to settle any question with the help of their notorious 'interaction'. In reality, they never settle anything, but only hide behind the back of the difficulties they encounter.[7]

There is then an interaction, but this cannot be positively understood unless the organizing force of the economic element is recognized. A Marxist theory of culture will recognize diversity and complexity, will take account of continuity within change, will allow for chance and certain limited autonomies, but, with these reservations, will take the facts of the economic structure and the consequent social relations as the guiding string on which a culture is woven, and by following which a culture is to be understood. This, still an emphasis rather than a substantiated theory, is what Marxists of our own century received from their tradition.

II

Marxist writing in England in the last thirty years has been very mixed in both quality and occasion. The political writing of the 'thirties was primarily a response to actual conditions in England and Europe, rather than a conscious development of Marxist studies. The conditions justified the response, even where it fell short of adequacy. But the result was that many English readers made their first acquaintance with Marxist theory in writings that were in fact local and temporary, both in affiliation and intention. It has of course been possible to compile from these the kind of fools' gallery which always appears in any general movement. I cannot see that this kind of smoking-out is fair dealing with Marxism as such, but equally it is as well for Marxists to remember that very many mistakes were made, and that these are less easy to forgive because of the tone of dogmatic infallibility which characterized some of the most popular writings. A collection of essays like *The Mind in Chains* was always mixed in quality, but it is now most clearly marked by its temporary character—the very thing which at the time must have seemed to guarantee its sense of reality. We are told in the Introduction that the 'belief which runs like a backbone through the whole of this book'[8] is R. E. Warner's conclusion:

> *Capitalism has no further use for culture.* On the one hand, the material stagnation of capitalism brings it about that fewer and fewer scholars, scientists, and technicians are required for the process of production. On the other hand, being no longer able to represent itself as a progressive force, capitalism can no longer invite the support of the general ideals of culture and progress.[9]

The general point is familiar, but capitalism, in its powers of recovery, even if indeed these are only temporary, was quite evidently underestimated, with the result that a whole set of attitudes, consequent on experience of depression, fell when the economic situation changed. Almost every kind of political prophecy has been wrong, but the Marxist claim to special insight into these matters of the life and death of an economic system makes concession of error less easy. Statements like that quoted above have, in general, not been reargued or revised, but merely dropped.

Yet Warner's general point about culture is reasonable:

> The progress of culture is dependent on the progress of the material conditions for culture; and, in particular, the social organization of any period of history limits the cultural possibilities of that period. Yet all through history there is a constant interaction between culture and social organization. Culture, it is true, cannot go beyond what is possible, but social organization can and does lag behind what, from the point of view of culture, is both possible and desirable. There is a continuity both between various forms of social organization and various forms of culture, but the cultural continuity is the more marked because, for one thing, it is easier

to envisage possibilities than to put them into practice, and also because change and progress in society have always been resisted for as long as possible by those interested persons who, being for the moment at the top, stand to lose by any readjustment within the whole. We find that, at those periods of history when a change of social organization is necessary, culture comes into opposition to the time-honoured standards of society, standards which, by the way, were elevated and properly honoured by the culture of the past, but which have proved inadequate and uninspiring for a further advance into the future.[10]

This is obviously relevant to the development of ideas and feelings, traced hitherto, which gave us the modern meanings of 'culture'. But I am not sure whether this is indeed a Marxist interpretation. While recognizing the material basis of culture, it seems to come very near to an Arnoldian definition, in which culture can be in advance of the economic and social organization, ideally embodying the future. In many Englishmen writing as Marxists I have noticed this. A tradition basically proceeding from the Romantics, and coming down through Arnold and Morris, has been supplemented by certain phrases from Marx, while continuing to operate in the older terms. Much of the 'Marxist' writing of the 'thirties was in fact the old Romantic protest that there was no place in contemporary society for the artist and the intellectual, with the new subsidiary clause that the workers were about to end the old system and establish Socialism, which would then provide such a place. The correlative protests against unemployment, poverty and Fascism were genuine; but the making-over of the workers' cause into the intellectuals' cause was always likely to collapse: either as the intellectuals found a place in different ways, or as the workers' cause asserted its primacy and moved in directions not so immediately acceptable or favourable. In seeing the literary Marxism of the 'thirties, in its general aspects, as a new case of the 'negative identification' described in relation to Gissing, I have of course the advantage of hindsight: it is a characteristic of the negative identification that it breaks up at points of real social crisis and reacts into an indifference to politics, recantation, or sometimes violent assault on the cause that has been abandoned. Because I believe this to be a law, its actions subject to the immense pressures of society, I have no desire to rehearse personalities. I note only the fact that 'culture' was not so far ahead, not so firmly affiliated to the future, as was then thought.

Alick West's *Crisis and Criticism* (1937) includes an account of the continuity between Romantic and Marxist ideas. He writes:

> Romantic criticism was a great achievement. Its conception of social relations as constituting beauty in art, of a conflict and antagonism in these relations and of the same conflict reconciled in art, of poetry as the voice of humanity against oppression and injustice and of the duty of the poets to cooperate in ending them— all these ideas are of the highest value. Instead of abusing them, or divorcing them from their social meaning, or preserving only their idealism, we have to use them. We cannot use them simply as they stand, because of that idealism. As indicated earlier, the romantic poets were unable in their particular circumstances to give a material meaning to their social conceptions. . . . Hence, in romantic criticism, the social relations which constitute beauty in art are not the actual social relations, but the conception of the relations.[11]

It is certainly true that the abstractions of Art and Culture were a substitute for satisfactory social relations, both in art itself and in general living. It is also true that the most evident weakness of the subsequent tradition was its failure to find any adequate social force by means of which the 'superior reality' of Art and Culture might be established and maintained. West, from his analysis, argues that Marx transformed Romantic idealism by giving it the content of material social relations. It is true at least that Morris, learning from Marx, found what he took to be a social force adequate to these ends in the working-class struggle for socialism. Yet this is not necessarily the Marxist way of putting the matter. E. P. Thompson, giving a recent Marxist account of Morris, writes:

> While this dialectical understanding of change, growth and decay was ever-present in his writing, he saw man's economic and social

development always as the master-process, and tended to suggest that the arts were passively dependent upon social change. . . . Morris has not emphasized sufficiently the *ideological* rôle of art, its active agency in *changing* human beings and society as a whole, its agency in man's class-divided history.[12]

The question is very difficult, but it is surely surprising to find a Marxist criticizing Morris for seeing 'man's economic and social development always as the master-process'. It has normally been assumed that this was precisely what Marx taught, and the position that Marxists wished to defend. One had understood that the arts *were* 'dependent upon social change'; but perhaps '*passively* dependent' makes the difference. Morris sometimes suggested that the cause of art must wait upon the success of socialism, and this (though it is purely an argument in the head: art of one kind or another in any case goes on being produced) may well be wrong. But wrong in what sense? That art is not subject to so simple an equation, as most non-Marxists would say? That good art can be produced in the struggle as well as in the success, which English Marxists, for obvious reasons, seem to wish to establish? The point is only of general interest in its bearings upon the basic Marxist position. Morris's 'master-process', which Thompson criticizes, is surely Marx's 'real foundation', which 'determines consciousness'. Engels spoke of 'the reflexes of all these actual struggles in the brains of the combatants'; surely, on a Marxist reading, art is one of these reflexes. Such reflexes, Engels said, 'exercise their influence upon the course of the historical struggles and in many cases preponderate in determing their *form*'. 'But only the form,'[13] insists Ralph Fox, in *The Novel and the People*, another Marxist view of literature. In what Marxist sense, then, has art this 'active agency in *changing* human beings and society as a whole'? Marx and Engels did not deny the effect of the 'reflexes' back upon the whole situation, but that one of them—art—might act to change 'human beings and society as a whole' is hardly consistent with their kind of emphasis. That art has this function is, however, a commonplace of the Romantic attitude: the poet as legislator. One had understood from West, however, that this was an idealist attitude based on an ignorance of social reality. It certainly seems relevant to ask English Marxists who have interested themselves in the arts whether this is not Romanticism absorbing Marx, rather than Marx transforming Romanticism. It is a matter of opinion which one would prefer to happen. Yet, in one way or another, the situation will have to be clarified. Either the arts are passively dependent on social reality, a proposition which I take to be that of mechanical materialism, or a vulgar misinterpretation of Marx. Or the arts, as the creators of consciousness, determine social reality, the proposition which the Romantic poets sometimes advanced. Or finally, the arts, while ultimately dependent, with everything else, on the real economic structure, operate in part to reflect this structure and its consequent reality, and in part, by affecting attitudes towards reality, to help *or hinder* the constant business of changing it. I find Marxist theories of culture confused because they seem to me, on different occasions and in different writers, to make use of all these propositions as the need serves.

It is clear that many English writers on culture who are also, politically, Marxists seem primarily concerned to make out a case for its existence, to argue that it is important, against a known reaction to Marxism which had established the idea that Marx, with his theory of structure and superstructure, had diminished the value hitherto accorded to intellectual and imaginative creation. Certainly there has been a quite shocking ignorance of what Marx wrote among those who have been prepared to criticize him, and the term 'superstructure' has been bandied about, as a kind of swearword, with wholly ridiculous implications. Political prejudice, obviously, has played its part in this. Yet I do not see how it can be denied that Marx did in one sense diminish the value of such work: not that he failed to respect it, and to consider it a great and important human achievement, but he denied, what had hitherto been commonly believed, that it was this kind of work that decided human development: 'it is not the consciousness of men that determines their existence, but, on the contrary, their existence determines their consciousness'. The shock of this, to thinkers and artists who had been accustomed to think of themselves as the pioneers of humanity, was real; it was a change of status comparable to that implied for men generally by Darwin. Much of the subsequent development of Marxism, it would seem, has been determined, in the matter of culture, by this reaction. It had to be shown that Marxists gave a high value to culture, although this proof that culture was important seemed, to other thinkers at least, unnecessary. It remains surprising, to others differently trained, that the normal Marxist book on, say, literature begins with a proof that literature is valuable: this had never seemed to be in any question, and one is reminded of Mill making the same point to the Utilitarians. But, while some of this writing can only be understood in such terms, a theory of culture was, of course, necessary, to the extent that Marxism became a major interpretative and active movement. Not only, it was thought, had past and present culture to be interpreted, in Marxist terms, but so also (and this has been very prevalent, although whether it is altogether Marxist is doubtful) future culture had to be predicted. In England, this work has been mainly done in relation to literature, and we must consider its nature.

The normal theoretical beginning is from the nature of language, as here in West:

> Language . . . grew as a form of social organization. Literature as art continues that growth. It lives language; it carries on the social activity of which language in its very existence is the creation and the creator.[14]

Here we are at once involved in the extremely complicated question of the origins of language. West relies on Noire, Paget and Marr; Caudwell, in *Illusion and Reality*, on assertion, which seems to derive from Darwin via Paget, but also from de Laguna. Linguistic theory is at once very specialized and very controversial, and the question of origins is necessarily to some extent speculative. A general stress on the social character of language can be readily accepted, and it would seem that, in practice, language does operate as a form of social organization, and that what it represents is an activity rather than a mere deposit. But the end of West's argument is already assumed in the special and extremely controversial senses in which he understands 'organization' and 'activity'. He continues:

> the source of value in the work of literature is the social energy and activity which makes the writer's vision a continuation of the development of the power to see, his use of language a continuation of . . . the power to speak; and not merely the consumer's use of what society has already produced. Our perception of that value is the stimulation in us of the same social energy and activity.[15]

This is saying much less than it seems to say. I cannot imagine anyone whom the middle phrases would surprise. And again, the end of the argument is assumed in the form of words. For West can now continue:

> The value of literature springs from the fact that it continues and changes the organization of social energy; we perceive value through the awakening of the same kind of energy in ourselves.[16]

And from this it is easy to identify valuable literature with that which proceeds from participation in 'the most active group and tendency of his time', and then, in contemporary terms, with the 'most creative movement . . . socialism'. 'Consequently',

> the criticism of our lives, by the test of whether we are helping forward the most creative movement in our society, is the only effective foundation of the criticism of literature.[17]

From this it is only a step (although West, to do him justice, does not take it, insisting on the reality of aesthetic judgement) to the kind of literary criticism which has made Marxism notorious: 'Is this work socialist or not in tendency? is it helping forward the most creative movement in society?' where literature is defined solely in terms of its political affiliations. Marxists, more than anyone else, need to repudiate this kind of end-product, in practice as firmly as in theory. But one can see how a potentially valuable argument is distorted, throughout, by an assumed need to arrive at this kind of conclusion, or at one resembling it. It is a conclusion, moreover, with which there seems no need for Marx to be saddled. Literature is quite obviously, in the general sense, a social activity, and value does seem to lie in the writer's access to certain kinds of energy which appear and can be discussed in directly literary terms (that is to say, as an intention that has become language), but which, by general agreement, have a more-than-literary origin, and lie in the whole complex of a writer's relations with reality. It is the identification of this energy with participation in a particular kind of social or political activity which is, to say the least, not proven. The positive evidence, where this kind of energy is manifest, suggests no such simple equation.

Christopher Caudwell remains the best-known of these English Marxist critics, but his influence is curious. His theories and outlines have been widely learned, although in fact he has little to say, of actual literature, that is even interesting. It is not only that it is difficult to have confidence in the literary qualifications of anyone who can give his account of the development of mediaeval into Elizabethan drama,[18] or who can make his paraphrase of the 'sleep' line from *Macbeth*,[19] but that for the most part his discussion is not even specific enough to be wrong. On the other hand, he is immensely prolific of ideas, over an unusually wide field of interest. It is now rather difficult to know which of these ideas may properly be described as Marxist. A recent controversy among English Marxists, on the value of Caudwell's work, revealed an extraordinary difference of opinion, ranging from George Thomson's view that *Illusion and Reality* is 'the first comprehensive attempt to work out a Marxist theory of art',[20] with the implication of major success, to J. D. Bernal's conclusion:

> It is largely on account of his use of the language of popular science that Caudwell's work has had, and still has, such an appeal to intellectuals, particularly to literary intellectuals.[21]

Bernal adds that the formulations in Caudwell's books

> are those of contemporary bourgeois scientific philosophy . . . and not those of Marxism.[22]

This is a quarrel which one who is not a Marxist will not attempt to resolve.

It is worth noting, however, that the hub of the Marxist controversy about Caudwell is very much the problem that has been discussed in the preceding pages. It is a matter of some importance that a number of writers, convinced of the economic and political usefulness of Marxism, have, in their attempts to account for the work of the 'superstructure', and in particular for the imaginative work of the arts, turned with some consistency to what other Marxists describe as an 'idealist muddle'. The difficulty comes down to one major point, which may be introduced by Caudwell's definition of the value of art:

> The value of art to society is that by it an emotional adaptation is possible. Man's instincts are pressed in art against the altered mould of reality, and by a specific organization of the emotions thus generated, there is a new attitude, an adaptation.[23]

The process of this, in the artist, is thus described:

> The artist is continually besieged by new feelings as yet unformulated, he continually attempts to grasp beauties and emotions not yet known; a tension between tradition and experience is constantly felt in his heart. Just as the scientist is the explorer of new realms of outer reality; the artist continually discovers new kingdoms of the heart. Both therefore are explorers, and necessarily therefore share a certain loneliness. But if they are individualists, it is not because they are non-social, but precisely because they are performing a social task. They are non-social only in this sense, that they are engaged in dragging into the social world realms at present non-social and must therefore have a foot in both worlds.[24]

What these two worlds are, in Caudwell's view, is the basic controversy. In *Illusion and Reality*, he wrote:

> The link between science and art, the reason they can live in the same language, is this: the subject of action is the same as the subject of cognition—the genotype. The object of action is the same as the object of cognition—external reality. Since the genotype is a part of reality, although it finds itself set up against another part of it, the two interact; there is development; man's thought and man's society have a history.[25]

It would certainly seem, at first sight, that this version of the 'genotype' interacting with 'external reality' is some way from Marx, and this is so not only in Caudwell's first writings, but, in the phrase about 'both worlds', in the late essay on Beauty. In effect, in writing of this kind, it would seem that Marx's basic conception of the relation between 'the real foundation' and 'consciousness', and hence between structure and superstructure, is being revalued. The point emerges, in practice, as a controversy about the rôle of art, and thence of culture (intellectual and imaginative work) generally. There is a clear controversy between the advocates of 'realism' (an analytical and synthetic embodiment of, in Engels' words, 'typical characters in typical circumstances', where the adequate 'reflex' of reality is seen as the purpose of art) and, on the other hand, those who add to this an additional clause, as here in Gorki:

> Myth is invention. To invent means to extract from the sum of a given reality its cardinal idea and embody it in imagery—that is how we get realism. But if to the idea extracted from the given reality we add—completing the idea by the logic of hypothesis—the desired, the possible, and thus supplement the image, we obtain that romanticism which is at the basis of myth, and is highly beneficial in that it tends to provoke a revolutionary attitude to reality, an attitude that changes the world in a practical way.[26]

This, I take it, is the advance of realism to 'socialist realism', for it is presumably only if 'the desired, the possible' is socialist that the 'revolutionary attitude to reality' will be provoked. The process is defined by identification with a political attachment. Otherwise, the method might be adequately described as 'socialist romanticism', the transformation of idealism by a material content, of which West wrote.

The difficulty remains that the source of 'the desired, the possible' has still to be defined. It is still Marxist to find this in emergent social forces, which are already active and conscious in the social process. But there has been a distinct tendency, in English writers, to find 'the desired, the possible' in terms of the 'inner energy' of the individual, of which Caudwell wrote. This, while it may be an improvement of Marx, would seem to deny his basic proposition about 'existence' and 'consciousness'. In fact, as we look at the English attempt at a Marxist theory of culture, what we see is an interaction between Romanticism and Marx, between the idea of culture which is the major English tradition and Marx's brilliant revaluation of it. We have to conclude that the interaction is as yet far from complete.

III

The one vital lesson which the nineteenth century had to learn—and learn urgently because of the very magnitude of its changes—was that the basic economic organization could not be separated and excluded from its moral and intellectual concerns. Society and individual experience were alike being transformed, and this driving agency, which there were no adequate traditional procedures to understand and interpret, had, in depth, to be taken into consciousness. Others besides Marx insisted on this, and worked towards it, but Marx, in giving a social and historical definition to the vaguer idea of 'industrialism', made the decisive contribution. The materials for restoring a whole and adequate consciousness of our common life were given into our hands. Meanwhile, underlying this, the practical means of community were being slowly learned, in experience.

Marx's emphasis has passed into the general mind, even if his particular teaching is still inevitably controversial. The questions we have now to ask—for the validity of his economic and political theory cannot here be discussed—relate to the Marxist impact on our thinking about culture. The basic question, as it has normally been put, is whether the economic element is in fact determining. I have followed the controversies on this, but it seems to me that it is, ultimately, an unanswerable question. The shaping influence of economic change can of course be distinguished, as most notably in the period with which this book is concerned. But the difficulty lies in estimating the final importance of a factor which never, in practice, appears in isolation. We can never observe economic change in neutral conditions, any more than we can, say, observe the exact influence of heredity, which is only available for study when it is already embodied in an environment. Capitalism, and industrial capitalism, which Marx by historical analysis was able to describe in general terms, appeared only within an existing culture. English society and French society are both, today, in certain stages of capitalism, but their cultures are observably different, for sound historical reasons. That they are both capitalist may be finally determining, and this may be a guide to social and political action, but clearly, if we are to understand the cultures, we are committed to what is manifest: the way of life as a whole. What many of us have felt about Marxist cultural interpretation is that it seems committed, by Marx's formula, to a rigid methodology, so that if one wishes to study, say, a national literature, one must begin with the economic history with which the literature co-exists, and then put the literature to it, to be interpreted in its light. It is true that on occasion one learns something from this, but, in general, the procedure seems to involve both forcing and superficiality. For, even if the economic element is determining, it determines a whole way of life, and it is to this, rather than to the economic system alone, that the literature has to be related. The interpretative method which is governed, not by the social whole, but rather by the arbitrary correlation of the economic situation and the subject of study, leads very quickly to abstraction and unreality, as for example in Caudwell's description of modern poetry (that is, since the fifteenth century) as '*capitalist* poetry',[27] where it remains to be shown that 'capitalist' is a relevant description of poetry at all. It leads also to the overriding of practical concrete judgements by generalizations, as for example in descriptions of Western European literature of this century as 'decadent' because its social system is judged 'decadent': a procedure which lumps together the bad art which reflects and exploits elements of disintegration, and the substantial art which, by the very seriousness of its procedure, shows the disintegration in process, and what it is like, in detail, to live through it. It leads also, I think, to very doubtful descriptions of a culture as a whole. To describe English life, thought and imagination in the last three hundred years simply as 'bourgeois', to describe English culture now as 'dying', is to surrender reality to a formula. I am glad to see that this point is still controversial among Marxists: some arguing that in a class society there is 'a polarization of mental activity' around the ruling class, so that if the ruling class is 'bourgeois' all the mental activity is 'bourgeois'; others denying this, and arguing that the consciousness of a whole society is always more diverse, and is not limited to the economically dominant class.[28] Whichever of these views may best accord with Marx, it would seem that the balance of evidence clearly lies with the latter. In all these points there would seem to be a general inadequacy, among Marxists, in the use of 'culture' as a term. It normally indicates, in their writings, the intellectual and imaginative products of a society; this corresponds with the weak use of 'superstructure'. But it would seem that from their emphasis on the interdependence of all elements of social reality, and from their analytic emphasis on movement and change, Marxists should logically use 'culture' in the sense of a whole way of life, a general social process. The point is not merely verbal, for the emphasis in this latter use would make impossible the mechanical procedures which I have criticized, and would offer a basis for more substantial understanding. The difficulty lies, however, in the terms of Marx's original formulation: if one accepts 'structure' and 'superstructure', not as the terms of a suggestive analogy, but as descriptions of reality, the errors naturally follow. Even if the terms are seen as those of an analogy, they need, as I have tried to suggest, amendment.

One practical result of this kind of Marxist interpretation of the past can be seen in the persistent attempts to define the culture of the socialist future. If you get into the habit of thinking that a bourgeois society produces, in a simple and direct way, a bourgeois culture, then you are likely to think that a socialist society will produce, also simply and directly, a socialist culture, and you may think it incumbent on you to say what it will be like. As a matter of fact, most of the speculation about the 'socialist culture' of the future has been no more than a Utopian habit; one cannot take it very seriously. But the point became practical in Russia, where, for example, the kind of literature appropriate to the new society has been commonly defined in advance, as an authoritative prescription. If there is a habit of thinking of the relation between literature and society as simple and direct, such a procedure seems plausible, a campaign for 'socialist realism' seems plausible, and of course literature of a kind, in response to the campaign, will always be got. But, if we are to agree with Marx that 'existence determines consciousness', we shall not find it easy to prescribe any particular consciousness in advance, unless, of course (this is how in theory it is usually done) the prescribers can somehow identify themselves with 'existence'. My own view is that if, in a socialist society, the basic cultural skills are made widely available, and the channels of communication widened and cleared, as much as possible has been done in the way of preparation, and what then emerges will be an actual response to the whole reality, and so valuable. The other way can be seen in these words of Lenin:

> Every artist . . . has a right to create freely according to his ideals, independent of anything. Only, of course, we communists cannot stand with our hands folded and let chaos develop in any direction it may. We must guide this process according to a plan and form its results.[29]

There is no 'of course' about it, and the growth of consciousness is cheapened (as in the mechanical descriptions of the past) by being foreseen as 'chaos'. Here, it is not ultimately a question of wise or unwise, free or totalitarian, policy; it is, rather, a question of inadequacy in the theory of culture.

The point can be put, finally, on a wider basis. Modern communist practice rests to a very large degree on Lenin, and it can be argued, in this matter of the development of consciousness, that Lenin is inconsistent with Marx. Lenin wrote, for instance:

> The history of all countries shows that the working class, exclusively by its own effort, is able to develop only trade-union consciousness.[30]

The working-class movement, unable to develop an ideology for itself, will be 'captured' either by 'bourgeois ideology' or by socialist ideology, which latter is itself created by bourgeois intellectuals. So much depends, here, on the ways in which 'ideology' and 'consciousness' are used, but

(i) if Lenin seriously and constantly maintained that the working class cannot create a socialist ideology, Marx's account of the relation between class and ideology, and between existence and consciousness, cannot easily be maintained;

(ii) if the 'bourgeois intelligentsia', working alone, can create 'socialist ideology', the relation between 'existence' and 'consciousness' has again to be redefined;

(iii) if the working people are really in this helpless condition, that they alone cannot go beyond 'trade-union consciousness' (that is, a negative reaction to capitalism rather than a positive reaction towards socialism), they can be regarded as 'masses' to be captured, the objects rather than the subjects of power. Almost anything can then be justified.

It is not easy to discover any single judgement on these questions which one can take as finally and authentically Marxist. The point is vital, for it would seem to lie at the root of a number of differences between the spirit of Marxist criticism and certain observable aspects of communist policy. We are interested in Marxist theory because socialism and communism are now important. We shall, to the degree that we value its stimulus, continue to look for its clarification in the field of culture as a whole.

CHAPTER VI

GEORGE ORWELL

'IT is not so much a series of books, it is more like a world.'[1] This is Orwell, on Dickens. 'It is not so much a series of books, it is more like a case.' This, today, is Orwell himself. We have been using him, since his death, as the ground for a general argument, but this is not mainly an argument about ideas, it is an argument about mood. It is not that he was a great artist, whose experience we have slowly to receive and value. It is not that he was an important thinker, whose ideas we have to interpret and examine. His interest lies almost wholly in his frankness. With us, he inherited a great and humane tradition; with us, he sought to apply it to the contemporary world. He went to books, and found in them the detail of virtue and truth. He went to experience, and found in it the practice of loyalty, tolerance and sympathy. But, in the end,

> it was a bright cold day in April, and the clocks were striking thirteen. Winston Smith, his chin nuzzled into his breast in an effort to escape the vile wind, slipped quickly through the glass doors of Victory Mansions, though not quickly enough to prevent a swirl of gritty dust from entering along with him.[2]

The dust is part of the case: the caustic dust carried by the vile wind. Democracy, truth, art, equality, culture: all these we carry in our heads, but, in the street, the wind is everywhere. The great and humane tradition is a kind of wry joke; in the books it served, but put them down and look around you. It is not so much a disillusion, it is more like our actual world.

The situation is paradox: this kind of tradition, this kind of dust. We have made Orwell the figure of this paradox: in reacting to him we are reacting to a common situation. England took the first shock of industrialism and its consequences, and from this it followed, on the one hand, that the humane response was early, fine and deep—the making of a real tradition; on the other hand that the material constitution of what was criticized was built widely into all our lives—a powerful and committed reality. The inter-action has been long, slow and at times desperate. A man who lives it on his own senses is subject to extraordinary pressures. Orwell lived it, and frankly recorded it: this is why we attend to him. At the same time, although the situation is common, Orwell's response was his own, and has to be dis-tinguished. Neither his affiliations, his difficulties nor his dis-illusion need be taken as prescriptive. In the end, for any proper understanding, it is not so much a case, it is a series of books.

The total effect of Orwell's work is an effect of paradox. He was a humane man who communicated an extreme of inhuman terror; a man committed to decency who actualized a distinctive squalor. These, perhaps, are elements of the general paradox. But there are other, more particular, para-doxes. He was a socialist, who popularized a severe and damaging criticism of the idea of socialism and of its adherents. He was a believer in equality, and a critic of class, who founded his later work on a deep assumption of inherent inequality, inescapable class difference. These points have been obscured, or are the subject of merely partisan debate. They can only be approached, adequately, through observa-tion of a further paradox. He was a notable critic of abuse of language, who himself practised certain of its major and typical abuses. He was a fine observer of detail, and appealed as an empiricist, while at the same time committing himself to an unusual amount of plausible yet specious generaliza-tion. It is on these points, inherent in the very material of his work, that we must first concentrate.

That he was a fine observer of detail I take for granted; it is the great merit of that group of essays of which *The Art of Donald McGill* is typical, and of parts of *The Road to Wigan Pier*. The contrary observation, on his general judgements, is an effect of the total reading of his work, but some examples may here stand as reminders:

> In each variant of socialism that appeared from about 1900 onwards the aim of establishing liberty and equality was more and more openly abandoned.[3]

The British Labour Party? Guild Socialism?

> By the fourth decade of the twentieth century all the main currents

of political thought were authoritarian. The earthly paradise had been discredited at exactly the moment when it became realisable.[4]

England in 1945?

The first thing that must strike any outside observer is that Socialism in its developed form is a theory confined entirely to the middle class.[5]

A Labour Party conference? Any local party in an industrial constituency? Trade-unions?

All left-wing parties in the highly industrialized countries are at bottom a sham, because they make it their business to fight against something which they do not really wish to destroy.[6]

On what total evidence?

The energy that actually shapes the world springs from emotions— racial pride, leader worship, religious belief, love of war—which liberal intellectuals mechanically write off as anachronisms, and which they have usually destroyed so completely in themselves as to have lost all power of action.[7]

But does the shaping energy spring from these emotions alone? Is there no other 'power of action'?

A humanitarian is always a hypocrite.[8]

An irritation masquerading as a judgement?

Take, for instance, the fact that all sensitive people are revolted by industrialism and its products. . . .[9]

All? By all its products?

I isolate these examples, not only to draw attention to this aspect of Orwell's method, but also to indicate (as all but one of them do) the quality of the disillusion which has, in bulk, been so persuasive. In many of the judgements there is an element of truth, or at least ground for argument, but Orwell's manner is normally to assert, and then to argue within the assertion. As a literary method, the influence of Shaw and Chesterton is clear.

The method has become that of journalism, and is some-times praised as clear forthright statement. Orwell, in his discussions of language, made many very useful points about the language of propaganda. But just as he used plausible assertion, very often, as a means of generalization, so, when he was expressing a prejudice, often of the same basic kind, he moved very easily into the propagandist's kind of emotive abuse:

> One sometimes gets the impression that the mere words 'Socialism and 'Communism' draw towards them with magnetic force every fruit-juice drinker, nudist, sandal-wearer, sex-maniac, Quaker, 'Nature Cure' quack, pacifist and feminist in England. . . .[10]

> . . . vegetarians with wilting beards . . . shock-headed Marxists chewing polysyllables . . . birth control fanatics and Labour Party backstairs-crawlers.[11]

Or consider his common emotive use of the adjective 'little':

> The typical socialist . . . a prim little man with a white-collar job, usually a secret teetotaller and often with vegetarian leanings. . . .[12]

> A rather mean little man, with a white face and a bald head, standing on a platform, shooting out slogans.[13]

> . . . The typical little bowler-hatted sneak—Strube's 'little man'—the little docile cit who slips home by the six-fifteen to a supper of cottage-pie and stewed tinned pears.[14]

> In the highbrow world you 'get on', if you 'get on' at all not so much by your literary ability as by being the life and soul of cocktail parties and kissing the bums of verminous little lions. . . .[15]

Of course, this can be laughed at, and one will only be annoyed if one is a socialist, nudist, feminist, commuter, or so on. But I agree with Orwell that good prose is closely connected with liberty, and with the social possibility of truth. I agree with him also (and so assemble this evidence) that

> modern writing at its worst . . . consists in gumming together long strips of words which have already been set in order by someone else, and making the results presentable by sheer humbug.[16]

To overlook this practice in Orwell himself would be ridiculous and harmful.

Now, in normal circumstances, any writer who at all

frequently wrote in the manner of the examples quoted might be simply disregarded. Yet I see this paradox, this permission of such writing by a man who accepted the standards which condemn it, as part of the whole paradox of Orwell, which I wish to describe. He is genuinely baffling until one finds the key to the paradox, which I will call the paradox of the exile. For Orwell was one of a significant number of men who, deprived of a settled way of living, or of a faith, or having rejected those which were inherited, find virtue in a kind of improvised living, and in an assertion of independence. The tradition, in England, is distinguished. It attracts to itself many of the liberal virtues: empiricism, a certain integrity, frankness. It has also, as the normally contingent virtue of exile, certain qualities of perception: in particular, the ability to distinguish inadequacies in the groups which have been rejected. It gives, also, an appearance of strength, although this is largely illusory. The qualities, though salutary, are largely negative; there is an appearance of hardness (the austere criticism of hypocrisy, complacency, self-deceit), but this is usually brittle, and at times hysterical: the substance of community is lacking, and the tension, in men of high quality, is very great. Alongside the tough rejection of compromise, which gives the tradition its virtue, is the felt social impotence, the inability to form extending relationships. D. H. Lawrence, still the most intelligent of these men in our time, knew this condition and described it. Orwell may also have known it; at least he lived the rejections with a thoroughness that holds the attention.

The virtues of Orwell's writing are those we expect, and value, from this tradition as a whole. Yet we need to make a distinction between exile and vagrancy: there is usually a principle in exile, there is always only relaxation in vagrancy. Orwell, in different parts of his career, is both exile and vagrant. The vagrant, in literary terms, is the 'reporter', and, where the reporter is good, his work has the merits of novelty and a certain specialized kind of immediacy. The reporter is an observer, an intermediary: it is unlikely that he will understand, in any depth, the life about which he is writing (the vagrant from his own society, or his own class, looking at another, and still inevitably from the outside). But a restless society very easily accepts this kind of achievement: at one level the report on the curious or the exotic; at another level, when the class or society is nearer the reporter's own, the perceptive critique. Most of Orwell's early work is of one of these two kinds (*Down and Out in Paris and London; The Road to Wigan Pier*). The early novels, similarly, are a kind of fictionalized report: even the best of them, *Coming up for Air*, has more of the qualities of the virtuoso reporter (putting himself in the place of the abstract, representative figure) than of the intensity of full imaginative realization. We listen to, and go about with, Orwell's Mr Bowling; Orwell, for the most part, is evidently present, offering his report.

Now, it would be absurd to blame Orwell for this 'vagrant' experience; he had good reasons for rejecting the ways of life normally open to him. But he saw that the rejection had in the end to be ratified by some principle: this was the condition of vagrancy becoming exile, which, because of his quality, he recognized as finer. The principle he chose was socialism, and *Homage to Catalonia* is still a moving book (quite apart from the political controversy it involves) because it is a record of the most deliberate attempt he ever made to become part of a believing community. Nor can such praise be modified because the attempt, in continuing terms, failed. While we are right to question the assertion of self-sufficiency, by vagrant and exile alike, we have also to recognize the complexity of what is being rejected and of what can be found. Orwell, in exploring this complexity, did work of real value.

But the principle, though affirmed, could not now (Orwell concluded) carry him directly through to actual community. It could, in fact, only be lived in controversy. Orwell's socialism became the exile's principle, which he would at any cost keep inviolate. The cost, in practice, was a partial abandonment of his own standards: he had often to curse, wildly, to keep others away, to avoid being confused with them. He did not so much attack socialism, which was safe in his mind, as socialists, who were there and might involve him. What he did attack, in socialism, was its disciplines, and, on this basis, he came to concentrate his attack on communism. His attacks on the denial of liberty are admirable: we have all, through every loyalty, to defend the basic liberties of association and expression, or we deny man. Yet, when the exile speaks of liberty, he is in a curiously ambiguous position, for while the rights in question may be called individual, the condition of their guarantee is inevitably social. The exile, because of his own personal position, cannot finally believe in any social guarantee: to him, because this is the pattern of his own living, almost all association is suspect. He fears it because he does not want to be compromised (this is often his virtue, because he is so quick to see the perfidy which certain compromises involve). Yet he fears it also because he can see no way of confirming, socially, his own individuality; this, after all, is the psychological condition of the self-exile. Thus in attacking the denial of liberty he is on sure ground; he is wholehearted in rejecting the attempts of society to involve him. When, however, in any positive way, he has to affirm liberty, he is forced to deny its inevitable social basis: all he can fall back on is the notion of an atomistic society, which will leave individuals alone. 'Totalitarian' describes a certain kind of repressive social control, but, also, any real society, any adequate community, is necessarily a totality. To belong to a community is to be a part of a whole, and, necessarily, to accept, while helping to define, its disciplines. To the exile, however, society as such is totalitarian; he cannot commit himself, he is bound to stay out.

Yet Orwell was at the same time deeply moved by what he saw of avoidable or remediable suffering and poverty, and he was convinced that the means of remedy are social, involving commitment, involving association, and, to the degree that he was serious, involving himself. In his essay *Writers and Leviathan*, which he wrote for a series in *Politics and Letters*, Orwell recognized this kind of deadlock, and his solution was that in such circumstances the writer must divide: one part of himself uncommitted, the other part involved. This indeed is the bankruptcy of exile, yet it was, perhaps, inevitable. He could not believe (it is not a matter of intellectual persuasion; it is a question of one's deepest experience and response) that *any* settled way of living exists in which a man's individuality can be socially confirmed. The writer's problem, we must now realize, is only one aspect of this general problem, which has certainly, in our own time, been acute. But because we have accepted the condition of exile, for a gifted individual, as normal, we have too easily accepted the Orwell kind of analysis as masterly. It is indeed a frank and honest report, and our kind of society has tied this knot again and again; yet what is being recorded, in Orwell, is the experience of a victim: of a man who, while rejecting the consequences of an atomistic society, yet retains deeply, in himself, its characteristic mode of consciousness. At the easy levels this tension is mediated in the depiction of society as a racket; a man may even join in the racket, but he tells himself that he has no illusions about what he is doing—he keeps a secret part of himself inviolate. At the more difficult levels, with men of Orwell's seriousness, this course is impossible, and the tension cannot be discharged. The consequent strain is indeed desperate; this, more than any objective threat, is the nightmare of *Nineteen Eighty-Four*.

A Marxist dismisses Orwell as 'petty bourgeois', but this, while one sees what it means, is too shallow. A man cannot be interpreted in terms of some original sin of class; he is where he is, and with the feelings he has; his life has to be lived with his own experience, not with someone else's. The only point about class, where Orwell is concerned, is that he wrote extensively about the English working class, and that this, because it has been influential, has to be revalued. On such matters, Orwell is the reporter again: he is often sharply observant, often again given to plausible generalization. In thinking, from his position, of the working class primarily as a class, he assumed too readily that observation of particular working-class people was an observation of all working-class behaviour. Because, however, he looked at people at all, he is often nearer the truth than more abstract left-wing writers. His principal failure was inevitable: he observed what was evident, the external factors, and only guessed at what was not evident, the inherent patterns of feeling. This failure is most obvious in its consequences: that he did come to think, half against his will, that the working people were really helpless, that they could never finally help themselves.

In *Animal Farm*, the geniality of mood, and the existence of a long tradition of human analogies in animal terms, allow us to overlook the point that the revolution that is described is one of animals against men. The men (the old owners) were bad, but the animals, left to themselves, divide into the pigs (the hypocritical, hating politicians whom Orwell had always attacked) and the others. These others have many virtues—strength, dumb loyalty, kindliness, but there they are: the simple horse, the cynical donkey, the cackling hens, the bleating sheep, the silly cows. It is fairly evident where Orwell's political estimate lies: his sympathies are with the exploited sheep and the other stupid animals, but the issue of government lies between drunkards and pigs, and that is as far as things can go. In *Nineteen Eighty-Four*, the same point is clear, and the terms are now direct. The hated politicians are in charge, while the dumb mass of 'proles' goes on in very much its own ways, protected by its very stupidity. The only dissent comes from a rebel intellectual: the exile against the whole system. Orwell puts the case in these terms because this is how he really saw present society, and *Nineteen Eighty-Four* is desperate because Orwell recognized that on such a construction the exile could not win, and then there was no hope at all. Or rather:

> If there was hope, it must lie in the proles. . . . Everywhere stood the same solid unconquerable figure, made monstrous by work and child-bearing, toiling from birth to death and still singing. Out of those mighty loins a race of conscious beings must one day come. You were the dead; theirs was the future. But you could share in that future if you kept alive the mind. . . .[17]

This is the conclusion of any Marxist intellectual, in specifically Marxist terms, but with this difference from at any rate some Marxists: that the proles now, like the animals, are 'monstrous' and not yet 'conscious'—one day they will be so, and meanwhile the exile keeps the truth alive. The only point I would make is that this way of seeing the working people is not from fact and observation, but from the pressures of feeling exiled: other people are seen as an undifferentiated mass beyond one, the 'monstrous' figure. Here, again, is the paradox: that the only class in which you can put any hope is written off, in present terms, as hopeless.

I maintain, against others who have criticized Orwell, that as a man he was brave, generous, frank and good, and that the paradox which is the total effect of his work is not to be understood in solely personal terms, but in terms of the pressures of a whole situation. I would certainly insist that his conclusions have no general validity, but the fact is, in contemporary society, that good men are driven again and again into his kind of paradox, and that denunciation of them—'he . . . runs shrieking into the arms of the capitalist publishers with a couple of horror comics which bring him fame and fortune'[18]—is arrogant and crass. We have, rather, to try to understand, in the detail of experience, how the instincts of humanity can break down under pressure into an inhuman paradox; how a great and humane tradition can seem at times, to all of us, to disintegrate into a caustic dust.

CONCLUSION

THE history of the idea of culture is a record of our reactions, in thought and feeling, to the changed conditions of our common life. Our meaning of culture is a response to the events which our meanings of industry and democracy most evidently define. But the conditions were created and have been modified by men. Record of the events lies elsewhere, in our general history. The history of the idea of culture is a record of our meanings and our definitions, but these, in turn, are only to be understood within the context of our actions.

The idea of culture is a general reaction to a general and major change in the conditions of our common life. Its basic element is its effort at total qualitative assessment. The change in the whole form of our common life produced, as a necessary reaction, an emphasis on attention to this whole form. Particular change will modify an habitual discipline, shift an habitual action. General change, when it has worked itself clear, drives us back on our general designs, which we have to learn to look at again, and as a whole. The working-out of the idea of culture is a slow reach again for control.

Yet the new conditions, which men have been striving to understand, were neither uniform nor static. On the contrary, they have, from the beginning, contained extreme diversity of situation, in a high and moving tension. The idea of culture describes our common inquiry, but our conclusions are diverse, as our starting points were diverse. The word, culture, cannot automatically be pressed into service as any kind of social or personal directive. Its emergence, in its modern meanings, marks the effort at total qualitative assessment, but what it indicates is a process, not a conclusion. The arguments which can be grouped under its heading do not point to any inevitable action or affiliation. They define, in a common field, approaches and conclusions. It is left to us to decide which, if any, we shall take up, that will not turn in our hands.

In each of the three major issues, those of Industry, of

Democracy and of Art, there have been three main phases of opinion. In industry, there was the first rejection, alike of machine-production and of the social relations embodied in the factory system. This was succeeded by a phase of growing sentiment against the machine as such, in isolation. Thirdly, in our own period, machine production came to be accepted, and major emphasis transferred to the problem of social relations within an industrial system of production.

In the question of democracy, the first phase was one of concern at the threat to minority values with the coming of popular supremacy: a concern which was emphasized by general suspicion of the power of the new masses. This, in turn, was succeeded by a quite different tendency, in which emphasis fell on the idea of community, of organic society, as against the dominant individualistic ethic and practice. Thirdly, in our own century, the fears of the first phase were strongly renewed, in the particular context of what came to be called mass democracy in the new world of mass communications.

In the question of art, the first emphasis fell, not only on the independent value of art, but on the importance to the common life of the qualities which it embodied. The contingent element of defiant exile passed into the second phase, in which the stress fell on art as a value in itself, with at times an open separation of this value from common life. Thirdly, emphasis came to be placed on a deliberate effort towards the reintegration of art with the common life of society: an effort which centred around the word 'communication'.

In these three questions I have listed the phases of opinion in the order in which they appeared, but of course opinion is persistent, and whether in relation to industry, to democracy or to art, each of the three phases could easily be represented from the opinions of our own day. Yet it is possible in retrospect to see three main periods, within each of which a distinct emphasis is paramount. In the first period, from about 1790 to 1870, we find the long effort to compose a general attitude towards the new forces of industrialism and democracy; it is in this period that the major analysis is undertaken and the major opinions and descriptions emerge. Then, from about 1870 to 1914, there is a breaking-down into narrower fronts, marked by a particular specialism in attitudes to art, and, in the general field, by a preoccupation with direct politics. After 1914 these definitions continue, but there is a growing pre-occupation, approaching a climax after 1945, with the issues raised not only by the inherited problems but by new problems arising from the development of mass media of communication and the general growth of large-scale organizations.

A great deal of what has been written in each of these three periods retains its relevance and importance. In particular, it is impossible to over-emphasize our debt to the first great critical period which gave us, in relation to these problems, the greater part of our language and manner of approach. From all the periods, indeed, certain decisive statements stand. Yet even as we learn, we realize that the world we see through such eyes is not, although it resembles, our world. What we receive from the tradition is a set of meanings, but not all of these will hold their significance if, as we must, we return them to immediate experience. I have tried to make this return, and I will set down the variations and new definitions that have followed from this, as a personal conclusion.

Mass and Masses

We now regularly use both the idea of 'the masses', and the consequent ideas of 'mass-civilization', 'mass-democracy', 'mass-communication' and others. Here, I think, lies a central and very difficult issue which more than any other needs revision.

Masses was a new word for mob, and it is a very significant word. It seems probable that three social tendencies joined to confirm its meaning. First, there was the concentration of population in the industrial towns, a physical massing of persons which the great increase in total population accentuated, and which has continued with continuing urbanization. Second, there was the concentration of workers into factories: again, a physical massing, made necessary by machine-production; also, a social massing, in the work-relations made necessary by the development of large-scale collective production. Third, there was the consequent development of an organized and self-organizing working class: a social and political massing. The masses, in practice, have been any of these particular aggregates, and because the tendencies have been interrelated, it has been possible to use the term with a certain unity. And then, on the basis of each tendency, the derived ideas have arisen: from urbanization, the mass meeting; from the factory, in part in relation to the workers, but mainly in relation to the things made, mass-production; from the working class, mass-action. Yet, masses was a new word for mob, and the traditional characteristics of the mob were retained in its significance: gullibility, fickleness, herd-prejudice, lowness of taste and habit. The masses, on this evidence, formed the perpetual threat to culture. Mass-thinking, mass-suggestion, mass-prejudice would threaten to swamp considered individual thinking and feeling. Even democracy, which had both a classical and a liberal reputation, would lose its savour in becoming mass-democracy.

Now mass-democracy, to take the latest example, can be either an observation or a prejudice; sometimes, indeed, it is both. As an observation, the term draws attention to certain problems of a modern democratic society which could not have been foreseen by its early partisans. The existence of immensely powerful media of mass-communication is at the heart of these problems, for through these public opinion has been observably moulded and directed, often by questionable means, often for questionable ends. I shall discuss this issue separately, in relation to the new means of communication.

But the term mass-democracy is also, evidently, a prejudice. Democracy, as in England we have interpreted it, is majority rule. The means to this, in representation and freedom of expression, are generally approved. But, with universal suffrage, majority rule will, if we believe in the existence of the masses, be mass-rule. Further, if the masses are, essentially, the mob, democracy will be mob-rule. This will hardly be good government, or a good society; it will, rather, be the rule of lowness or mediocrity. At this point, which it is evidently very satisfying to some thinkers to reach, it is necessary to ask again: who are the masses? In practice, in our society and in this context, they can hardly be other than the working people. But if this is so, it is clear that what is in question is not only gullibility, fickleness, herd-prejudice, or lowness of taste and habit. It is also, from the open record, the declared intention of the working people to alter society, in many of its aspects, in ways which those to whom the franchise was formerly restricted deeply disapprove. It seems to me, when this is considered, that what is being questioned is not mass-democracy, but democracy. If a majority can be achieved in favour of these changes, the democratic criterion is satisfied. But if you disapprove of the changes you can, it seems, avoid open opposition to democracy as such by inventing a new category, mass-democracy, which is not such a good thing at all. The submerged opposite is class-democracy, where democracy will merely describe the processes by which a ruling class conducts its business of ruling. Yet democracy, as interpreted in England in this century, does not mean this. So, if change reaches the point where it deeply hurts and cannot be accepted, either democracy must be denied or refuge taken in a new term of opprobrium. It is clear that this confusion of the issue cannot be tolerated. Masses = majority cannot be glibly equated with masses = mob.

A difficulty arises here with the whole concept of masses. Here, most urgently, we have to return the meanings to experience. Our normal public conception of an individual person, for example, is 'the man in the street'. But nobody feels himself to be only the man in the street; we all know much more about ourselves than that. The man in the street is a collective image, but we know, all the time, our own difference from him. It is the same with 'the public', which includes us, but yet is not us. 'Masses' is a little more complicated, yet similar. I do not think of my relatives, friends, neighbours, colleagues, acquaintances, as masses; we none of us can or do. The masses are always the others, whom we don't know, and can't know. Yet now, in our kind of society, we see these others regularly, in their myriad variations; stand, physically, beside them. They are here, and we are here with them. And that we are with them is of course the whole point. To other people, we also are masses. Masses are other people.

There are in fact no masses; there are only ways of seeing people as masses. In an urban industrial society there are many opportunities for such ways of seeing. The point is not to reiterate the objective conditions but to consider, personally and collectively, what these have done to our thinking. The fact is, surely, that a way of seeing other people which has become characteristic of our kind of society, has been capitalized for the purposes of political or cultural exploitation. What we see, neutrally, is other people, many others, people unknown to us. In practice, we mass them, and interpret them, according to some convenient formula. Within its terms, the formula will hold. Yet it is the formula, not the mass, which it is our real business to examine. It may help us to do this if we remember that we ourselves are all the time being massed by others. To the degree that we find the formula inadequate for ourselves, we can wish to extend to others the courtesy of acknowledging the unknown.

I have mentioned the political formula by means of which it seems possible to convert the majority of one's fellow human beings into masses, and thence into something to be hated or feared. I wish now to examine another formula, which underlies the idea of mass-communication.

Mass-communication

The new means of communication represent a major technical advance. The oldest, and still the most important, is printing, which has itself passed through major technical changes, in particular the coming of the steam-driven machine press in 1811, and the development of ever faster cylinder and rotary presses from 1815. The major advances in transport, by road, rail, sea and air, themselves greatly affected printing: at once in the collection of news and in the wide and quick distribution of the printed product. The development of the cable, telegraph and telephone services even more remarkably facilitated the collection of news. Then, as new media, came sound broadcasting, the cinema and television.

We need to look again at these familiar factual elements if we are to be able adequately to review the idea of 'mass-communication' which is their product. In sum, these changes have given us more and normally cheaper books, magazines and newspapers; more bills and posters; broadcasting and television programmes; various kinds of film. It would be difficult, I think, to express a simple and definite judgement of value about all these very varied products, yet they are all things that need to be valued. My question is whether the idea of 'mass-communication' is a useful formula for this.

Two preliminary points are evident: first, that there is a general tendency to confuse the techniques themselves with the uses to which, in a given society, they have been put; second, that, in considering these uses, our argument is commonly selective, at times to an extreme degree.

The techniques, in my view, are at worst neutral. The only substantial objection that is made to them is that they are relatively impersonal, by comparison with older techniques serving the same ends. Where the theatre presented actors, the cinema presents the photographs of actors. Where the meeting presented a man speaking, the wireless presents a voice, or television a voice and a photograph. Points of this kind are relevant, but need to be carefully made. It is not relevant to contrast an evening spent watching television with an evening spent in conversation, although this is often done. There is, I believe, no form of social activity which the use of these techniques has replaced. At most, by adding alternatives, they have allowed altered emphases in the time given to particular activities. But these alterations are obviously conditioned, not only by the techniques, but mainly by the whole circumstances of the common life. The point about impersonality often carries a ludicrous rider. It is supposed, for instance, that it is an objection to listening to wireless talks or discussions that the listener cannot answer the speakers back. But the situation is that of almost any reader; printing, after all, was the first great impersonal medium. It is as easy to send an answer to a broadcast speaker or a newspaper editor as to send one to a contemporary author; both are very much easier than to try to answer Aristotle, Burke or Marx. We fail to realize, in this matter, that much of what we call communication is, necessarily, no more in itself than transmission: that is to say, a one-way sending. Reception and response, which complete communication, depend on other factors than the techniques.

What can be observed as a fact about the development of these techniques is a steady growth of what I propose to call *multiple transmission*. The printed book is the first great model of this, and the other techniques have followed. The new factor, in our own society, is an expansion of the potential audience for such transmissions, so great as to present new kinds of problem. Yet it is clear that it is not to this expansion that we can properly object, at least without committing ourselves to some rather extraordinary politics. The expansion of the audience is due to two factors: first, the growth of general education, which has accompanied the growth of democracy; second, the technical improvements themselves. It is interesting, in the light of the earlier discussion of 'masses', that this expansion should have been interpreted by the phrase 'mass-communication'.

A speaker or writer, addressing a limited audience, is often able to get to know this audience well enough to feel a directly personal relationship with them which can affect his mode of address. Once this audience has been expanded, as with everything from books to televised parlour-games it has been expanded, this is clearly impossible. It would be rash, however, to assume that this is necessarily to his and the audience's disadvantage. Certain types of address, notably serious art, argument and exposition, seem indeed to be distinguished by a quality of impersonality which enables them frequently to survive their immediate occasion. How far this ultimate impersonality may be dependent on a close immediate relationship is in fact very difficult to assess. But it is always unlikely that any such speaker or writer will use, as a model for communication, any concept so crude as 'masses'. The idea of mass-communication, it would seem, depends very much more on the intention of the speaker or writer, than on the particular technique employed.

A speaker or writer who knows, at the time of his address, that it will reach almost immediately several million persons, is faced with an obviously difficult problem of interpretation. Yet, whatever the difficulty, a good speaker or writer will be conscious of his immediate responsibility to the matter being communicated. He cannot, indeed, feel otherwise, if he is conscious of himself as the source of a particular transmission. His task is the adequate expression of this source, whether it be of feeling, opinion or information. He will use for this expression the common language, to the limit of his particular skill. That this expression is then given multiple transmission is a next stage, of which he may well be conscious, but which cannot, of its nature, affect the source. The difficulties of expressing this source—difficulties of common experience, convention and language—are certainly always his concern. But the source cannot in any event be denied, or he denies himself.

Now if, on this perennial problem of communication, we impose the idea of masses, we radically alter the position. The conception of persons as masses springs, not from an inability to know them, but from an interpretation of them according to a formula. Here the question of the intention of the transmission makes its decisive return. Our formula can be that of the rational being speaking our language. It can be that of the interested being sharing our common experience. Or—and it is here that 'masses' will operate—it can be that of the mob: gullible, fickle, herdlike, low in taste and habit. The formula, in fact, will proceed from our intention. If our purpose is art, education, the giving of information or opinion, our interpretation will be in terms of the rational and interested being. If, on the other hand, our purpose is manipulation—the persuasion of a large number of people to act, feel, think, know, in certain ways—the convenient formula will be that of the masses.

There is an important distinction to be drawn here between source and agent. A man offering an opinion, a proposal, a feeling, of course normally desires that other persons will accept this, and act or feel in the ways that he defines. Yet such a man may be properly described as a source, in distinction from an agent, whose characteristic is that his expression is subordinated to an undeclared intention. He is an agent, and not a source, because the intention lies elsewhere. In social terms, the agent will normally in fact be a subordinate—of a government, a commercial firm, a newspaper proprietor. Agency, in the simple sense, is necessary in any complex administration. But it is always dangerous unless its function and intention are not only openly declared but commonly approved and controlled. If this is so, the agent becomes a collective source, and he will observe the standards of such expression if what he is required to transmit is such that he can wholly acknowledge and accept it—re-create it in his own person. Where he cannot thus accept it for himself, but allows himself to be persuaded that it is in a fit form for others—presumably inferiors—and that it is his business merely to see that it reaches them effectively, then he is in the bad sense an agent, and what he is doing is inferior to that done by the poorest kind of source. Any practical denial of the relation between conviction and communication, between experience and expression, is morally damaging alike to the individual and to the common language.

Yet it is certainly true, in our society, that many men, many of them intelligent, accept, whether in good or bad faith, so dubious a rôle and activity. The acceptance in bad faith is a matter for the law, although we have not yet gone very far in working out this necessary common control. The acceptance in good faith, on the other hand, is a matter of culture. It would clearly not be possible unless it appeared to be ratified by a conception of society which relegates the majority of its members to mob-status. The idea of the masses is an expression of this conception, and the idea of mass-communication a comment on its functioning. This is the real danger to democracy, not the existence of effective and powerful means of multiple transmission. It is less a product of democracy than its denial, springing from that half-world of feeling in which we are invited to have our being. Where the principle of democracy is accepted, and yet its full and active practice feared, the mind is lulled into an acquiescence, which is yet not so complete that a fitful conscience, a defensive irony, cannot visit it. 'Democracy would be all right,' we can come to say, 'it is indeed what we personally would prefer, if it were not for the actual people. So, in a good cause if we can find it, in some other if we can not, we will try to get by at a level of communication which our experience and training tell us is inferior. Since the people are as they are, the thing will do.' But it is as well to face the fact that what we are really doing, in such a case, is to cheapen our own experience and to adulterate the common language.

Mass-observation

Yet the people are as they are, the objection is returned. Of course the masses are only other people, yet most other people are, on the evidence, a mob. In principle, we would wish it not to be so; in practice, the evidence is clear.

This is the negative side of the idea of mass-communication. Its evidence is collected under the title of mass-culture, or popular culture. It is important evidence, and much of it is incontrovertible. There remains, however, the question of its interpretation. I have said that our arguments on this matter are normally selective, often to an extreme degree. I will try now to illustrate this.

We are faced with the fact that there is now a great deal of bad art, bad entertainment, bad journalism, bad advertisement, bad argument. We are not likely to be diverted from this conclusion by the usual diversionary arguments. Much that we judge to be bad is known to be bad by its producers. Ask any journalist, or any copywriter, if he will now accept that famous definition: 'written by morons for morons'. Will he not reply that in fact it is written by skilled and intelligent people for a public that hasn't the time, or hasn't the education, or hasn't, let's face it, the intelligence, to read anything more complete, anything more careful, anything nearer the known canons of exposition or argument? Had we not better say, for simplicity, anything good? Good and bad are hard words, and we can, of course, find easier ones. The strip newspaper, the beer advertisement, the detective novel—it is not exactly that they are good, but they are good of their (possibly bad) kind; they have the merits at least of being bright, attractive, popular. Yet, clearly, the strip newspaper has to be compared with other kinds of newspaper; the beer advertisement with other kinds of description of a product; the detective novel with other novels. By these standards—not by reference to some ideal quality, but by reference to the best things that men exercising this faculty have done or are doing—we are not likely to doubt that a great deal of what is now produced, and widely sold, is mediocre or bad.

But this is said to be popular culture. The description has a ready-made historical thesis. After the Education Act of 1870, a new mass-public came into being, literate but untrained in reading, low in taste and habit. The mass-culture followed as a matter of course. I think always, when I hear this thesis, of an earlier one, from the second half of the eighteenth century. Then, the decisive date was between 1730 and 1740, and what had emerged, with the advance of the middle classes to prosperity, was a new middle-class reading public. The immediate result was that vulgar phenomenon, the novel. As a matter of fact there is in both theses a considerable element of truth. If the former is not now so commonly mentioned, it is only because it would be indiscreet, in a situation where 'good' and 'middle class' are equivalent terms. And of course we can properly see the earlier situation in its true perspective. We can see that what the rise of the middle classes produced was not only the novel but many other things good and bad. Further, now that the bad novels are all out of print, and the good ones are among our classics, we see that the novel itself, while certainly a phenomenon, cannot be lightly dismissed as vulgar. Of the situation after 1870 we are not able to speak so clearly. For one thing, since the emergence as a whole still divides us, we can resent the cultural situation for political reasons and not realize this. For another, since the period has not fallen into settled history, we can be much more subjective in our selection of evidence.

1870 is in fact very questionable as a decisive date. There had been widespread literacy much earlier than this, the bad popular press is in fact also earlier. The result of the new educational provision was in part an actual increase in literacy, in part an evening-up between the fortunate places and the unfortunate. The increase is certainly large enough to be important, but it was no kind of sudden opening of the flood-gates. In itself, it is far from enough to account for the institution of the now characteristic features of popular culture.

Further, we need to remember that the new institutions were not produced by the working people themselves. They were, rather, produced for them by others, often (as most notably with the cheap newspaper and commercial advertisement on a large scale) for conscious political or commercial advantage. Such things in this sphere as the working people produced for themselves (radical newspapers, political pamphlets and publicity, trade-union banners and designs) were, if by no means always good, at least quite different in important respects. Again, it is wrong to see the new institutions as catering only for the new class. The new types of newspaper and advertisement were and are much more widely received. If the masses are to be defined as those for whom these institutions now cater, and by whom they are now received with apparent satisfaction, then the masses extend far beyond the categories of, say, the manual workers, or those whose education has been restricted to an elementary stage. I make this point because 'masses= working and lower-middle class' is so commonly confused with 'masses= mob'. The mob, if there is one, is at almost everyone's elbow; it may, indeed, be even nearer than that.

And if this is so of the new newspapers and advertisements, it is even more true of the other bad work which has been noted, in the novel, in the theatre, in the cinema, in the wireless and television programmes. If, in this kind of entertainment, there has been a continual decline of standards, then it is not from 1870 that we shall date this, but at least from 1740. As a matter of fact, I see little evidence why the backward dating should stop there, but then I am not so sure about the continual decline in standards. The multiplication of transmission, and the discovery of powerful media, seem to me mainly to have emphasized and made more evident certain long-standing tastes and means of satisfying them. I shall return to this point when I have made a further observation about our practices of selection.

In the matter of selection, there are two main points. First, it is clear that in an anxiety to prove their case, which is indeed an important one if the badness is not to go unchallenged, the contemporary historians of popular culture have tended to concentrate on what is bad and to neglect what is good. If there are many bad books, there are also an important number of good books, and these, like the bad books, circulate much more widely than in any previous period. If the readers of bad newspapers have increased in number, so have the readers of better newspapers and periodicals, so have the users of public libraries, so have students in all kinds of formal and informal adult education. The audiencies for serious music, opera and ballet have increased, in some cases to a remarkable degree. Attendances at museums and exhibitions have, in general, steadily risen. A significant proportion of what is seen in the cinemas, and of what is heard on the wireless, is work of merit. In every case, certainly, the proportions are less than we could desire, but they are not negligible.

Secondly, it is important to remember that, in judging a culture, it is not enough to concentrate on habits which coincide with those of the observer. To the highly literate observer there is always a temptation to assume that reading plays as large a part in the lives of most people as it does in his own. But if he compares his own kind of reading with the reading-matter that is most widely distributed, he is not really comparing levels of culture. He is, in fact, comparing what is produced for people to whom reading is a major activity with that produced for people to whom it is, at best, minor. To the degree that he acquires a substantial proportion of his ideas and feelings from what he reads he will assume, again wrongly, that the ideas and feelings of the majority will be similarly conditioned. But, for good or ill, the majority of people do not yet give reading this importance in their lives; their ideas and feelings are, to a large extent, still moulded by a wider and more complex pattern of social and family life. There is an evident danger of delusion, to the highly literate person, if he supposes that he can judge the quality of general living by primary reference to the reading artifacts. He will, in particular, be driven to this delusion if he retains, even in its most benevolent form, the concept of the majority of other people as 'masses', whom he observes as a kind of block. The error resembles that of the narrow reformer who supposes that farm labourers and village craftsmen were once uneducated, merely because they could not read. Many highly educated people have, in fact, been so driven in on their reading, as a stabilizing habit, that they fail to notice that there are other forms of skilled, intelligent, creative activity: not only the cognate forms of theatre, concert and picture-gallery; but a whole range of general skills, from gardening, metalwork and carpentry to active politics. The contempt for many of these activities, which is always latent in the highly literate, is a mark of the observers' limits, not those of the activities themselves. Neglect of the extraordinary popularity of many of these activities, as evidence of the quality of living in contemporary society, is the result of partisan selection for the reasons given.

This point comes to be of particular importance when we remember that the general tendency of modern development has been to bring many more levels of culture within the general context of literacy than was ever previously the case. A number of tastes which would formerly have been grati-fied in pre-literate and therefore largely unrecorded ways are now catered for and even fostered in print. Or, to put it in another way, the historical counterpart of a modern popular newspaper, in its informing function, is not an earlier minority newspaper, but that complex of rumour and travellers' tales which then served the majority with news of a kind. This is not to surrender the finest literacy we have, which at all times offers a standard for the newly literate functions. But, equally, to look at the matter in this way helps us to keep a just sense of proportion.

Our problem is one of adapting our social training to a widely literate culture. It is clear that the highest standards of literacy in contemporary society depend on a level of instruction and training far above that which is commonly available. For this reason it is still much too early to conclude that a majority culture is necessarily low in taste. The danger of such a judgement is that it offers a substitute righteousness—the duty of defending a standard against the mob. Right action is not of this kind, but is a matter of ensuring that the technical changes which have made our culture more dependent on literate forms are matched by a proportionate increase in training for literacy in its full sense. It is obvious that we have allowed the technical changes to keep far ahead of the educational changes, and the reasons for this neglect, which in its own terms is so plainly foolish, lie in a combination of interest and inertia, deeply rooted in the organization of society. An interpretation of the majority as a mob has served, paradoxically, to still or weaken the most active consciences in this matter. Loutishness is always easy, and there can be few things more loutish than to turn, at the end of a long training, and sneer at those who are just entering on it, and who, harassed and insecure, are making the inevitable mistakes.

Such a view might settle the matter if we could be sure that our only problem was to ensure that educational provision matched the extension of literacy. A generation of work would lie ahead of us, but the path at least would be clear. Yet evidently such questions are not settled within a specialized field. The content of education, as a rule, is the content of our actual social relations, and will only change as part of a wider change. Further, the actual operation of the new techniques is extremely complicated, in social terms, because of their economic bearings. The technical changes made necessary a great increase in the amount and concentration of capital, and we are still on the upward curve of this increase, as is most evident in the management of newspapers and television. These facts have led, in our society, to an extreme concentration of production of work of this kind, and to extraordinary needs and opportunities for controlling its distribution. Our new services tend to require so much capital that only a very large audience can sustain them. This in itself is not a difficulty; the potential audience is there. But everything depends on the attitude of those who control these services to such an audience. Our broadcasting corporation, for example, holds, in general, a reasonable interpretation of its particular responsibilities in this situation, even if this is no more surely founded than in a vestigial paternalism. Yet we are constantly being made aware how precarious this interpretation must be, under the pressures which come from a different attitude. The scale of capital involved has given an entry to a kind of person who, a hundred years ago, would never have thought of running a newspaper or a theatre. The opportunity to exploit the difficulties of a transitional culture was open, and we have been foolish enough to allow it to be widely taken. The temptation to make a profit out of ignorance or inexperience is present in most societies. The existence, in our own, of powerful media of persuasion and suggestion made it virtually irresistible. The cheapjack, whether he is the kind of vagrant who attached himself to Huckleberry Finn, or the more settled individual of our own society, always interprets his victims as an ignorant mob; this, to him, is his justification. It is a question for society, however, whether it will allow such an interpretation and its consequent activities, not merely to lead the fugitive existence of a vagrant, but, as now, to establish itself in some of the seats of power, with a large and settled material organization.

The ways of controlling such activities are well known; we lack only the will. All I am concerned to point out is that the cheapjack has had allies of a surprising kind. He has an ally in whoever concedes his interpretation of his fellow-beings. He has an ally, also, in that old kind of democrat who rested on the innate nobility of man. The delusions which led to this unholy alliance are of a complementary kind. The old democrat is often too sure of man's natural nobility to concern himself with the means of its common assurance. The new sceptic observes what happens when such means are not assured, and seeks an explanation in man's natural baseness. The failure, in each case, is a failure of consciousness of change. The old rural culture, which is so widely (and sometimes sentimentally) admired, rested on generations of experience within a general continuity of common condition. The speed and magnitude of the changes which broke up this settlement were never fully realized, and, even if they had been, the search for a new common control was bound to be slow. It is now becoming clear, from all kinds of evidence, that a society can, if it chooses, train its members in almost any direction, with only an occasional failure. The failures will be interpreted in terms of virtue or of recidivism, according to circumstances. But what is important is not that we are all malleable—any culture and any civilization depend on this—but the nature and origin of the shaping process. The contributions of old democrat and new sceptic are alike irrelevant to this decisive question; and the cheapjack has jumped in on the irrelevance and the general confusion.

The local newspaper, of all things, stands as a most important piece of controlling evidence. For it is read by people at least as simple, at least as poorly educated, as the readers of the worst strip paper. Yet in method and content it is still remarkably like the older journalism of minority reading, even to its faults. The devices which are said to be necessary to reach the ordinary mind are not employed, yet the paper is commonly read and understood. This is a case which, because of special circumstances, illumines the general problem. Produced for a known community on a basis of common interest and common knowledge, the local newspaper is not governed by a 'mass' interpretation. Its communication, in fact, rests on a community, in sharp contrast with most national newspapers, which are produced for a market, interpreted by 'mass' criteria. The methods of the popular newspaper do not rest on the fact that simple people read it, for then the local paper would hardly be read or understood at all. They rest on the fact that it and its readers are organized in certain kinds of economic and social relation. If we realize this we will concentrate our attention, not on man's natural goodness or badness, but on the nature of the controlling social relations. The idea of the masses, and the technique of observing certain aspects of mass-behaviour—selected aspects of a 'public' rather than the balance of an actual community—formed the natural ideology of those who sought to control the new system and to profit by it. To the degree that we reject this kind of exploitation, we shall reject its ideology, and seek a new definition of communication.

CONCLUSION

Communication and Community

Any governing body will seek to implant the 'right' ideas in the minds of those whom it governs, but there is no government in exile. The minds of men are shaped by their whole experience, and the most skilful transmission of material which this experience does not confirm will fail to communicate. Communication is not only transmission; it is also reception and response. In a transitional culture it will be possible for skilful transmission to affect aspects of activity and belief, sometimes decisively. But, confusedly, the whole sum of experience will reassert itself, and inhabit its own world. Mass-communication has had its evident successes, in a social and economic system to which its methods correspond. But it has failed, and will continue to fail, when its transmissions encounter, not a confused uncertainty, but a considered and formulated experience.

Observing this, the practitioners of mass-communication turn to the improvement of what they call their science: that is to say, to scraps of applied psychology and linguistic. It is of the greatest importance to attend to what they are doing, but at the same time any real theory of communication is a theory of community. The techniques of mass-communication will be irrelevant to a genuine theory of communication, to the degree that we judge them to be conditioned, not by a community, but by the lack or incompleteness of a community. It is very difficult to think clearly about communication, because the pattern of our thinking about community is, normally, dominative. We tend, in consequence, if not to be attracted, at least to be preoccupied by dominative techniques. Communication becomes a science of penetrating the mass mind and of registering an impact there. It is not easy to think along different lines.

It is easy to recognize a dominative theory if, for other reasons, we think it to be bad. A theory that a minority should profit by employing a majority in wars of gain is easily rejected. A theory that a minority should profit by employing a mass of wage-slaves is commonly rejected. A theory that a minority should reserve the inheritance of human knowledge to itself, and deny it to the majority, is occasionally rejected. But (we say) nobody, or only a few bad people, can be found to support such theories. We are all democrats now, and such things are unthinkable. As a matter of fact, mass-communication has served and is in some places still serving all the theories I have mentioned. The whole theory of mass-communication depends, essentially, on a minority in some way exploiting a majority. We are not all democrats now.

Yet 'exploiting', of course, is a tendentious word. What of the case where a minority is seeking to educate a majority, for that majority's ultimate good? Such minorities abound, seeking to educate majorities in the virtues of capitalism, communism, culture, contraception. Surely here mass-communication is necessary and urgent, to bring news of the good life, and of the ways to get it, and the dangers to avoid in getting it, to the prejudiced, servile, ignorant and multiplying masses? If workmen are impoverishing themselves and others by restrictive practices; if peasants are starving themselves and others by adhering to outdated ways; if men and women are growing up in ignorance, when so much is known; if families are breeding more children than can be fed: surely, urgently, they must be told this, for their own good?

The objection, as a matter of fact, is not to telling anyone anything. It is a question of how one tells them, and how one would expect to be told oneself. Nor is this merely a matter of politeness, of politeness being the best policy. It is really a matter of how one would be told oneself: telling as an aspect of living; learning as an element of experience. The very failure of so many of the items of transmission which I have listed is not an accident, but the result of a failure to understand communication. The failure is due to an arrogant preoccupation with transmission, which rests on the assumption that the common answers have been found and need only to be applied. But people will (damn them, do you say?) learn only by experience, and this, normally, is uneven and slow. A governing body, in its impatience, will often be able to enforce, by any of a number of kinds of pressure, an apparent conformity. This can on occasion be made substantial by subsequent experience; such a fact is the sharpest temptation to any dominative policy—that events will substantiate what at first people would not accept. As a matter of politics, this is perhaps the most difficult contemporary issue. As a matter of communication, however, such a point only substantiates what has already been said; it will be the experience that teaches. In a society which lacks the experience of democratic practice, a zealous reforming minority will often be forced to take this kind of chance. Yet, even here, it has great dangers; the process of learning depends so much on the conscious need to learn, and such a need is not easily imposed on anyone.

It is clear, on the other hand, that even in contemporary democratic communities the dominative attitude to communication is still paramount. Almost every kind of leader seems to be genuinely afraid of trusting the processes of majority discussion and decision. As a matter of practice this is usually whittled away to the merest formula. For this, the rooted distrust of the majority, who are seen as masses or more politely as the public, is evidently responsible. Democratic theory remains theory, and this practical scepticism breeds the theoretical scepticism which is again becoming, even in our own society, dangerously marked. The consequences are unsatisfactory from most points of view. If people cannot have official democracy, they will have unofficial democracy, in any of its possible forms, from the armed revolt or riot, through the 'unofficial' strike or restriction of labour, to the quietest but most alarming form—a general sullenness and withdrawal of interest. Faced with this set of facts, it is always possible to fall back on the other part of the 'mass' interpretation; to see these symptoms as 'proving' the unfitness of the masses—they *will* riot, they *will* strike, they *will not* take an interest—such is the nature of that brute, the mob. I am arguing, on the contrary, that these characteristic marks of our civilization are not interpretable in this mode; that they are, rather, symptoms of a basic failure in communication. It is possible to say this, and to conclude that the answer lies in educational projects, the feeding of information, or a new publicity drive. But this is to go on thinking of communication as transmission alone, a renewal, perhaps by new means, of the long dominative effort. The point is very difficult to see, in practice, when a group is certain that its case is right and urgent, and that for their own good, and urgently, people must be brought to recognize this.

Yet the uneasy symptoms are, precisely, a response to a dominative organization. In a revolt, in most riots, in many strikes, it is a positive response: the assertion of a different kind of answer. The answer that is then finally adopted will depend on the balance of power. But often it is less formulated than this: a confused, vague reaction against the dominative habit. What I have called sullenness is the obvious example of this. I think it is now a very prevalent reaction to the dominative kinds of mass-communication. People don't, of course, believe all they read in the newspapers, and this, often, is just as well. But for one small area of discriminating reading, almost always the product of training, there is a huge area of general suspicious disbelief, which, while on particular occasions it may be prophylactic, is as a general habit enfeebling. Inertia and apathy have always been employed by the governed as a comparatively safe weapon against their governors. Some governing bodies will accept this, as at least being quiet. But in our own society, because of the way we produce, there is so large a degree of necessary common interest and mutual effort that any widespread withdrawal of interest, any general mood of disbelief, can quite certainly be disastrous. The answer to it, however, does not lie in exhortation. It lies, rather, in conceding the practice of democracy, which alone can substantiate the theory. It lies, in terms of communication, in adopting a different attitude to transmission, one which will ensure that its origins are genuinely multiple, that all the sources have access to the common channels. This is not possible until it is realized that a transmission is always an offering, and that this fact must determine its mood: it is not an attempt to dominate, but to communicate, to achieve reception and response. Active reception, and living response, depend in their turn on an effective community of experience, and their quality, as certainly, depends on a recognition of practical equality. The inequalities of many kinds which still divide our community make effective communication difficult or impossible. We lack a genuinely common experience, save in certain rare and dangerous moments of crisis. What we are paying for this lack, in every kind of currency, is now sufficiently evident. We need a common culture, not for the sake of an abstraction, but because we shall not survive without it.

I have referred to equality, but with some hesitation, for the word is now commonly confusing. The theoretical emphasis on equality, in modern society, is in general an opponent response; it is less a positive goal than an attack on inequality, which has been practically emphasized in exact proportion to equalitarian ideas. The only equality that is important, or indeed conceivable, is equality of being. Inequality in the various aspects of man is inevitable and even welcome; it is the basis of any rich and complex life. The inequality that is evil is inequality which denies the essential equality of being. Such inequality, in any of its forms, in practice rejects, depersonalizes, degrades in grading, other human beings. On such practice a structure of cruelty, exploitation and the crippling of human energy is easily raised. The masses, the dominative mood, the rejection of culture, are its local testaments in human theory.

A common culture is not, at any level, an equal culture. Yet equality of being is always necessary to it, or common experience will not be valued. A common culture can place no absolute restrictions on entry to any of its activities: this is the reality of the claim to equality of opportunity. The claim to such opportunity is of course based on the desire to become unequal, but this can mean any of a number of things. A desired inequality which will in practice deny the essential equality of being, is not compatible with a culture in common. Such inequalities, which cannot be afforded, have continually to be defined, out of the common experience. But there are many inequalities which do not harm this essential equality, and certain of these are necessary, and need to be encouraged. The point becomes practical in examples, and I would suggest these. An inequality in other than personal property—that is to say an inequality in ownership of the means of life and production—may be found intolerable because in practice it may deny the basic processes of equality of being. Inequality in a particular faculty, however, or unequal developments of knowledge, skill and effort, may not deny essential equality: a physicist will be glad to learn from a better physicist, and will not, because he is a good physicist, think himself a better man than a good composer, a good chess-player, a good carpenter, a good runner. Nor, in a common culture, will he think himself a better human being than a child, an old woman, or a cripple, who may lack the criterion (in itself inadequate) of useful service. The kind of respect for oneself and one's work, which is necessary to continue at all, is a different matter from a claim to inequality of being, such as would entitle one to deny or dominate the being of another. The inequalities which are intolerable are those which lead to such denial or domination.

But some activities *are* better than others, the objection is returned. An insistence on equality may be, in practice, a denial of value. I have followed the course of this objection with some care, for it is important indeed. Is not a teacher to dominate a child, so that he may learn? Some facts will be right, and others wrong: the teacher must insist on their distinction, whether or not it is right to dominate. I agree, but most good teaching, in fact, is a transmission of the skills of discrimination alongside statements of the conclusions and judgements which have been received, and which have, provisionally, to be used. This offering, alike of a statement to be confirmed, and of the means of decision, is the proper working of general communication. A child will only learn the skills if he practises them; a teacher will only be skilled if he is aware of the process while offering the product. The utmost emphasis on distinctions of value, in all the things that man makes and does, is not an emphasis on inequality of being. It is, rather, a common process of learning, which, indeed, will only ever be undertaken if the primary concession of equality of being, which alone can remove such a process from the dominative sphere, is made. Nobody can raise anybody else's cultural standard. The most that can be done is to transmit the skills, which are not personal but general human property, and at the same time to give open access to all that has been made and done. You cannot stop a child reading a horror comic, or a man reading a strip newspaper, by order (unless you attempt the indignity of physical power over him), or even by argument, by telling him that it is bad. You can only give him the opportunity of learning what has been generally and commonly learned about reading, and see that he has access to all that is available to be read. In the end, and rightly, his choice will in any case be his own. A man's concern for value—for standards, as we say—properly expresses itself in the effort towards a community of experience on which these standards can rest. Further, if his concern for value is something more than dogma, he will hold himself open to learn other values, in the shaping of a new common experience. The refusal of either course is a petulant timidity. If one cannot believe in men, and in their common efforts, it is perhaps only in caricature that one can believe in oneself.

Culture and Which Way of Life?

We live in a transitional society, and the idea of culture, too often, has been identified with one or other of the forces which the transition contains. Culture is the product of the old leisured classes who seek now to defend it against new and destructive forces. Culture is the inheritance of the new rising class, which contains the humanity of the future; this class seeks, now, to free it from its restrictions. We say things like this to each other, and glower. The one good thing, it seems, is that all the contending parties are keen enough on culture to want to be identified with it. But then, we are none of us referees in this; we are all in the game, and playing in one or other direction.

I want to say something about the idea of 'working-class culture', because this seems to me to be a key issue in our own time, and one in which there is a considerable element of misunderstanding. I have indicated already that we cannot fairly or usefully describe the bulk of the material produced by the new means of communication as 'working-class culture'. For neither is it by any means produced exclusively for this class, nor, in any important degree, is it produced by them. To this negative definition we must add another: that 'working-class culture', in our society, is not to be understood as the small amount of 'proletarian' writing and art which exists. The appearance of such work has been useful, not only in its more self-conscious forms, but also in such material as the post-Industrial ballads, which were worth collecting. We need to be aware of this work, but it is to be seen as a valuable dissident element rather than as a culture. The traditional popular culture of England was, if not annihilated, at least fragmented and weakened by the dislocations of the Industrial Revolution. What is left, with what in the new conditions has been newly made, is small in quantity and narrow in range. It exacts respect, but it is in no sense an alternative culture.

This very point of an alternative is extremely difficult, in terms of theory. If the major part of our culture, in the sense of intellectual and imaginative work, is to be called, as the Marxists call it, bourgeois, it is natural to look for an alternative culture, and to call it proletarian. Yet it is very doubtful whether 'bourgeois culture' is a useful term. The body of intellectual and imaginative work which each generation receives as its traditional culture is always, and necessarily, something more than the product of a single class. It is not only that a considerable part of it will have survived from much earlier periods than the immediately pre-existing form of society; so that, for instance, literature, philosophy and other work surviving from before, say, 1600, cannot be taken as 'bourgeois'. It is also that, even within a society in which a particular class is dominant, it is evidently possible both for members of other classes to contribute to the common stock, and for such contributions to be unaffected by or in opposition to the ideas and values of the dominant class. The area of a culture, it would seem, is usually proportionate to the area of a language rather than to the area of a class. It is true that a dominant class can to a large extent control the transmission and distribution of the whole common inheritance; such control, where it exists, needs to be noted as a fact about that class. It is true also that a tradition is always selective, and that there will always be a tendency for this process of selection to be related to and even governed by the interests of the class that is dominant. These factors make it likely that there will be qualitative changes in the traditional culture when there is a shift of class power, even before a newly ascendant class makes its own contributions. Points of this kind need to be stressed, but the particular stress given by describing our existent culture as bourgeois culture is in several ways misleading. It can, for example, seriously mislead those who would now consider themselves as belonging to the dominant class. If they are encouraged, even by their opponents, to think of the existing culture (in the narrow sense) as their particular product and legacy, they will deceive themselves and others. For they will be encouraged to argue that, if their class position goes, the culture goes too; that standards depend on the restriction of a culture to the class which, since it has produced it, alone understands it. On the other hand, those who believe themselves to be representatives of a new rising class will, if they accept the proposition of 'bourgeois culture', either be tempted to neglect a common human inheritance, or, more intelligently, be perplexed as to how, and how much of, this bourgeois culture is to be taken over. The categories are crude and mechanical in either position. Men who share a common language share the inheritance of an intellectual and literary tradition which is necessarily and constantly revalued with every shift in experience. The manufacture of an artificial 'working-class culture', in opposition to this common tradition, is merely foolish. A society in which the working class had become dominant would, of course, produce new valuations and new contributions. But the process would be extremely complex, because of the complexity of the inheritance, and nothing is now to be gained by diminishing this complexity to a crude diagram.

The contrast between a minority and a popular culture cannot be absolute. It is not even a matter of levels, for such a term implies distinct and discontinuous stages, and this is by no means always the case. In Russian society in the nineteenth century one finds perhaps the clearest example of a discontinuous culture within recent history; this is marked, it should be noted, by a substantial degree of rejection of even the common language by the ruling minority. But in English society there has never been this degree of separation, since English emerged as the common language. There has been marked unevenness of distribution, amounting at times to virtual exclusion of the majority, and there has been some unevenness of contribution, although in no period has this approached the restriction of contribution to members of any one class. Further, since the beginning of the nineteenth century it has been difficult for any observer to feel that the care of intellectual and imaginative work could be safely entrusted to, or identified with, any existing social or economic class. It was in relation to this situation that the very idea of culture was, as we have seen, developed.

The most difficult task confronting us, in any period where there is a marked shift of social power, is the complicated process of revaluation of the inherited tradition. The common language, because in itself it is so crucial to this matter, provides an excellent instance. It is clearly of vital importance to a culture that its common language should not decline in strength, richness and flexibility; that it should, further, be adequate to express new experience, and to clarify change. But a language like English is still evolving, and great harm can be done to it by the imposition of crude categories of class. It is obvious that since the development, in the nineteenth century, of the new definition of 'standard English', particular uses of the common language have been taken and abused for the purposes of class distinction. Yet the dialect which is normally equated with standard English has no necessary superiority over other dialects. Certain of the grammatical clarifications have a common importance, but not all even of these. On the other hand, certain selected sounds have been given a cardinal authority which derives from no known law of language, but simply from the fact that they are habitually made by persons who, for other reasons, possess social and economic influence. The conversion of this kind of arbitrary selection into a criterion of 'good' or 'correct' or 'pure' English is merely a subterfuge. Modern communications make for the growth of uniformity, but the necessary selection and clarification have been conducted, on the whole, on grounds quite irrelevant to language. It is still thought, for instance, that a double negative ('I don't want none') is *incorrect* English, although millions of English-speaking persons use it regularly: not, indeed, as a misunderstanding of the rule, which they might be thought too ignorant to apprehend; but as the continuation of a habit which has been in the language continuously since Chaucer. The broad 'a', in such words as 'class', is now taken as the mark of an 'educated person', although till the eighteenth century it was mainly a rustic habit, and as such despised. Or 'ain't', which in the eighteenth century was often a mark of breeding, is now supposed to be a mark of vulgarity: in both cases, the valuation is the merest chance. The extraordinary smugness about aspirates, vowel-sounds, the choice of this or that synonym ('couch' 'sofa'), which has for so long been a normal element of middle-class humour, is, after all, not a concern for good English ,but parochialism. (The current controversy about what are called 'U' and 'non-U' speech habits clearly illustrates this; it is an aspect, not of major social differences, but of the long difficulty of drawing the lines between the upper and lower sections of the *middle* class.) Yet, while this is true, the matter is complicated by the fact that in a society where a particular class and hence a particular use of the common language is dominant a large part of the literature, carrying as it does a body of vital common experience, will be attracted to the dominant language mode. At the same time, a national literature, as English has never ceased to be, will, while containing this relation, contain also elements of the whole culture and language. If we are to understand the process of a selective tradition, we shall not think of exclusive areas of culture but of degrees of shifting attachment and interaction, which a crude theory either of class or of standards is incompetent to interpret.

A culture can never be reduced to its artifacts while it is being lived. Yet the temptation to attend only to external evidence is always strong. It is argued, for instance, that the working class is becoming 'bourgeois', because it is dressing like the middle class, living in semi-detached houses, acquiring cars and washing-machines and television sets. But it is not 'bourgeois' to possess objects of utility, nor to enjoy a high material standard of living. The working class does not become bourgeois by owning the new products, any more than the bourgeois ceases to be bourgeois as the objects he owns change in kind. Those who regret such a development among members of the working class are the victims of a prejudice. An admiration of the 'simple poor' is no new thing, but it has rarely been found, except as a desperate rationalization, among the poor themselves. It is the product either of satiety or of a judgement that the material advantages are purchased at too high a human cost. The first ground must be left to those who are sated; the second, which is more important, is capable of a false transference. If the advantages were 'bourgeois' because they rested on economic exploitation, they do not continue to be 'bourgeois' if they can be assured without such exploitation or by its diminution. The worker's envy of the middle-class man is not a desire to be that man, but to have the same kind of possessions. We all like to think of ourselves as a standard, and I can see that it is genuinely difficult for the English middle class to suppose that the working class is not desperately anxious to become just like itself. I am afraid this must be unlearned. The great majority of English working people want only the middle-class material standard and for the rest want to go on being themselves. One should not be too quick to call this vulgar materialism. It is wholly reasonable to want the means of life in such abundance as is possible. This is the materialism of material provision, to which we are all, quite rightly, attentive. The working people, who have felt themselves long deprived of such means in any adequacy, intend to get them and to keep them if they can. It would need more evidence than this to show that they are becoming vulgar materialists, or that they are becoming 'bourgeois'.

The question then, perhaps, is whether there is any meaning left in 'bourgeois'? Is there any point, indeed, in continuing to think in class terms at all? Is not industrialism, by its own momentum, producing a culture that is best described as classless? Such questions, today, command a significant measure of assent, but again, while drawing support from the crudities of certain kinds of class interpretation, they rest, essentially, on an external attitude alike to culture and to class. If we think of culture, as it is important to do, in terms of a body of intellectual and imaginative work, we can see that with the extension of education the distribution of this culture is becoming more even, and, at the same time, new work is being addressed to a public wider than a single class. Yet a culture is not only a body of intellectual and imaginative work; it is also and essentially a whole way of life. The basis of a distinction between bourgeois and working-class culture is only secondarily in the field of intellectual and imaginative work, and even here it is complicated, as we have seen, by the common elements resting on a common language. The primary distinction is to be sought in the whole way of life, and here, again, we must not confine ourselves to such evidence as housing, dress and modes of leisure. Industrial production tends to produce uniformity in such matters, but the vital distinction lies at a different level. The crucial distinguishing element in English life since the Industrial Revolution is not language, not dress, not leisure—for these indeed will tend to uniformity. The crucial distinction is between alternative ideas of the nature of social relationship.

'Bourgeois' is a significant term because it marks that version of social relationship which we usually call individualism: that is to say, an idea of society as a neutral area within which each individual is free to pursue his own development and his own advantage as a natural right. The course of recent history is marked by a long fighting retreat from this idea in its purest form, and the latest defenders would seem to the earliest to have lost almost the entire field. Yet the interpretation is still dominant: the exertion of social power is thought necessary only in so far as it will protect individuals in this basic right to set their own course. The classical formula of the retreat is that, in certain defined ways, no individual has a right to harm others. But, characteristically, this harm has been primarily interpreted in relation to the individual pursuit—no individual has a right to prevent others from doing *this kind of thing*.

The reforming bourgeois modification of this version of society is the idea of service, to which I shall return. But

325

both this idea and the individualist idea can be sharply contrasted with the idea that we properly associate with the working class: an idea which, whether it is called communism, socialism or cooperation, regards society neither as neutral nor as protective, but as the positive means for all kinds of development, including individual development. Development and advantage are not individually but commonly interpreted. The provision of the means of life will, alike in production and distribution, be collective and mutual. Improvement is sought, not in the opportunity to escape from one's class, or to make a career, but in the general and controlled advance of all. The human fund is regarded as in all respects common, and freedom of access to it as a right constituted by one's humanity; yet such access, in whatever kind, is common or it is nothing. Not the individual, but the whole society, will move.

The distinction between these versions of society has been blurred by two factors: the idea of service, which is the great achievement of the Victorian middle class, and is deeply inherited by its successors; and the complication of the working-class idea by the fact that England's position as an imperial power has tended to limit the sense of community to national (and, in the context, imperialist) lines. Further, the versions are blurred by a misunderstanding of the nature of class. The contending ideas, and the actions which follow from them, are the property of that part of a group of people, similarly circumstanced, which has become conscious of its position and of its own attitude to this position. Class feeling is a mode, rather than a uniform possession of all the individuals who might, objectively, be assigned to that class. When we speak, for instance, of a working-class idea, we do not mean that all working people possess it, or even approve of it. We mean, rather, that this is the essential idea embodied in the organizations and institutions which that class creates: the working-class movement as a tendency, rather than all working-class people as individuals. It is foolish to interpret individuals in rigid class terms, because class is a collective mode and not a person. At the same time, in the interpretation of ideas and institutions, we can speak properly in class terms. It depends, at any time, on which kind of fact we are considering. To dismiss an individual because of his class, or to judge a relationship with him solely in class terms, is to reduce humanity to an abstraction. But, also, to pretend that there are no collective modes is to deny the plain facts.

We may now see what is properly meant by 'working-class culture'. It is not proletarian art, or council houses, or a particular use of languages; it is, rather, the basic collective idea, and the institutions, manners, habits of thought and intentions which proceed from this. Bourgeois culture, similarly, is the basic individualist idea and the institutions, manners, habits of thought and intentions which proceed from that. In our culture as a whole, there is both a constant interaction between these ways of life and an area which can properly be described as common to or underlying both. The working class, because of its position, has not, since the Industrial Revolution, produced a culture in the narrower sense. The culture which it has produced, and which it is important to recognize, is the collective democratic institution, whether in the trade unions, the cooperative movement or a political party. Working-class culture, in the stage through which it has been passing, is primarily social (in that it has created institutions) rather than individual (in particular intellectual or imaginative work). When it is considered in context, it can be seen as a very remarkable creative achievement.

To those whose meaning of culture is intellectual or imaginative work, such an achievement may be meaningless. The values which are properly attached to such work can, at times, seem overriding. On this, I would only point out that while it may have seemed reasonable to Burke to anticipate the trampling down of learning by the irruption of the 'swinish multitude', this has not in fact happened, and the swinish multitude itself has done much to prevent it happening. The record of the working-class movement in its attitudes to education, to learning and to art is on the whole a good record. It has sometimes wrongly interpreted, often neglected where it did not know. But it has never sought to destroy the institutions of this kind of culture; it has, on the contrary, pressed for their extension, for their wider social recognition, and, in our own time, for the application of a larger part of our material resources to their maintenance and development. Such a record will do more than stand comparison with that of the class by which the working class has been most actively and explicitly opposed. This, indeed, is the curious incident of the swine in the night. As the light came, and we could look around, it appeared that the trampling, which we had all heard, did not after all come from them.

The Idea of Community

The development of the idea of culture has, throughout, been a criticism of what has been called the bourgeois idea of society. The contributors to its meaning have started from widely different positions, and have reached widely various attachments and loyalties. But they have been alike in this, that they have been unable to think of society as a merely neutral area, or as an abstract regulating mechanism. The stress has fallen on the positive function of society, on the fact that the values of individual men are rooted in society, and on the need to think and feel in these common terms. This was, indeed, a profound and necessary response to the disintegrating pressures which were faced.

Yet, according to their different positions, the idea of community, on which all in general agree, has been differently felt and defined. In our own day we have two major interpretations, alike opposed to bourgeois liberalism, but equally, in practice, opposed to each other. These are the idea of service, and the idea of solidarity. These have in the main been developed by the middle class and the working class respectively. From Coleridge to Tawney the idea of function, and thence of service to the community, has been most valuably stressed, in opposition to the individualist claim. The stress has been confirmed by the generations of training which substantiate the ethical practice of our professions, and of our public and civil service. As against the practice of *laissez-faire*, and of self-service, this has been a major achievement which has done much for the peace and welfare of our society. Yet the working-class ethic, of solidarity, has also been a major achievement, and it is the difference of this from the idea of service which must now be stressed.

A very large part of English middle-class education is devoted to the training of servants. This is much more its characteristic than a training for leadership, as the stress on conformity and on respect for authority shows. In so far as it is, by definition, the training of upper servants, it includes, of course, the instilling of that kind of confidence which will enable the upper servants to supervise and direct the lower servants. Order must be maintained there, by good management, and in this respect the function is not service but government. Yet the upper servant is not to think of his own interests. He must subordinate these to a larger good, which is called the Queen's peace, or national security, or law and order, or the public weal. This has been the charter of many thousands of devoted lives, and it is necessary to respect it even where we cannot agree with it.

I was not trained to this ethic, and when I encountered it, in late adolescence, I had to spend a lot of time trying to understand it, through men whom I respected and who had been formed by it. The criticism I now make of it is in this kind of good faith. It seems to me inadequate because in practice it serves, at every level, to maintain and confirm the *status quo*. This was wrong, for me, because the *status quo*, in practice, was a denial of equity to the men and women among whom I had grown up, the lower servants, whose lives were governed by the existing distributions of property, remuneration, education and respect. The real personal unselfishness, which ratified the description as service, seemed to me to exist within a larger selfishness, which was only not seen because it was idealized as the necessary form of a civilization, or rationalized as a natural distribution corresponding to worth, effort and intelligence. I could not share in these versions, because I thought, and still think, that the sense of injustice which the 'lower servants' felt was real and justified. One cannot in conscience then become, when invited, an upper servant in an establishment that one thus radically disapproves.

Now it is true that much of this service has gone to improving the conditions of the 'lower servants', but, because of its nature, this has been improvement within a framework which is thought, in its main lines, inviolate. I have seen this psychology of service extend to the working-class movement itself, until the phraseology of 'making a man a useful citizen', 'equipping him to serve the community', has become common form. A particular climax of this, for me, was a book called *How we are Governed*, written by a left-wing democrat. It is at this point, on the basis of a different social ethic, that one becomes awkward.

How we are Governed, as an explanation of democracy, is an expression of the idea of service at its psychological limit. The break through to 'How we govern ourselves' is impossible, on the basis of such a training: the command to conformity, and to respect for authority as such, is too strong. Of course, having worked for improvement in the conditions of working people, in the spirit of service, those who are ruled by the idea of service are genuinely dismayed when the workers do not fully respond: when, as it is put, they don't play the game, are lacking in team-spirit, neglect the national interest. This has been a crisis of conscience for many middle-class democrats and socialists. Yet the fact is that working-class people cannot feel that this *is* their community in anything like the sense in which it is felt above them. Nor will education in their responsibilities to a community thus conceived convince them. The idea of service breaks down because while the upper servants have been able to identify themselves with the establishment, the lower servants have not. What 'they' decide is still the practical experience of life and work.

The idea of service, ultimately, is no substitute for the idea of active mutual responsibility, which is the other version of community. Few men can give the best of themselves as servants; it is the reduction of man to a function. Further, the servant, if he is to be a good servant, can never really question the order of things; his sense of authority is too strong. Yet the existing order is in fact subject to almost overwhelming pressures. The break through, into what together we want to make of our lives, will need qualities which the idea of service not only fails to provide, but, in its limitation of our minds, actively harms.

CONCLUSION

The idea of service to the community has been offered to the working class as an interpretation of solidarity, but it has not, in the circumstances, been fully accepted, for it is, to them, inferior in feeling. Another alternative to solidarity which has had some effect is the idea of individual opportunity—of the ladder. It has been one of the forms of service to provide such a ladder, in industry, in education and elsewhere. And many working-class leaders, men in fact who have used the ladder, have been dazzled by this alternative to solidarity. Yet the ladder is a perfect symbol of the bourgeois idea of society, because, while undoubtedly it offers the opportunity to climb, it is a device which can only be used individually: you go up the ladder alone. This kind of individual climbing is of course the bourgeois model: a man should be allowed to better himself. The social conscience, which produced the idea of service, argued that no greater benefit could be conferred on the working people than that this ladder should be extended to them. The actual process of reform, in so far as it has not been governed by working-class pressure, has been, in large part, the giving of increasing opportunity to climb. Many indeed have scrambled up, and gone off to play on the other side; many have tried to climb and failed. Judged in each particular case, it seems obviously right that a working man, or the child of a working-class family, should be enabled to fit himself for a different kind of work, corresponding to his ability. Because of this, the ladder idea has produced a real conflict of values within the working class itself. My own view is that the ladder version of society is objectionable in two related respects: first, that it weakens the principle of common betterment, which ought to be an absolute value; second, that it sweetens the poison of hierarchy, in particular by offering the hierarchy of merit as a thing different in kind from the hierarchy of money or of birth. On the educational ladder, the boy who has gone from a council school to Oxford or Cambridge is of course glad that he has gone, and he sees no need to apologize for it, in either direction. But he cannot then be expected to agree that such an opportunity constitutes a sufficient educational reform. A few voices, softened by the climb, may be found to say this, which they are clearly expected to say. Yet, if he has come from any conscious part of the working class, such a boy will take leave to doubt the proffered version. The education was worth the effort, but he sees no reason why it should be interpreted as a ladder. For the ladder, with all its extra-educational implications, is merely an image of a particular version of society; if he rejects the version, he will reject the image. Take the ladder image away, and interest is returned to what is, for him, its proper object: to the making of a common educational provision; to the work for equity in material distribution; to the process of shaping a tradition, a community of experience, which is always a selective organization of past and present, and which he has been given particular opportunities to understand. The ladder, which is a substitute for all these things, must be understood in all its implications; and it is important that the growing number who have had the ladder stamped on their brows should interpret it to themselves and to their own people, whom, as a class, it could greatly harm. For in the end, on any reckoning, the ladder will never do; it is the product of a divided society, and will fall with it.

The Development of a Common Culture

In its definition of the common interest as true self-interest, in its finding of individual verification primarily in the community, the idea of solidarity is potentially the real basis of a society. Yet it is subject, in our time, to two important difficulties. For it has been, basically, a defensive attitude, the natural mentality of the long siege. It has in part depended, that is to say, on an enemy; the negative elements thus produced will have to be converted into positives in a fully democratic society. This will at best be profoundly difficult, for the feelings involved are fundamental.

The issue can be defined as one in which diversity has to be substantiated within an effective community which disposes of majority power. The feeling of solidarity is, although necessary, a primitive feeling. It has depended, hitherto, on substantial identity of conditions and experience. Yet any predictable civilization will depend on a wide variety of highly specialized skills, which will involve, over definite parts of the culture, a fragmentation of experience. The attachment of privilege to certain kinds of skill has been traditionally clear, and this will be very difficult to unlearn, to the degree that is necessary if substantial community of condition is to be assured. A culture in common, in our own day, will not be the simple all-in-all society of old dream. It will be a very complex organization, requiring continual adjustment and redrawing. At root, the feeling of solidarity is the only conceivable element of stabilization in so difficult an organization. But in its issue it will have to be continually redefined, and there will be many attempts to enlist old feelings in the service of an emerging sectional interest. The emphasis that I wish to place here is that this first difficulty —the compatibility of increasing specialization with a genuinely common culture—is only soluble in a context of material community and by the full democratic process. A skill is only an aspect of a man, and yet, at times, it can seem to comprehend his whole being. This is one kind of crisis, and it can only be overcome as a man becomes conscious that the value he places on his skill, the differentiation he finds in it, can only ultimately be confirmed by his constant effort not only to confirm and respect the skills of others, but also to confirm and deepen the community which is even larger than the skills. The mediation of this lies deep in personal feeling, but enough is known to indicate that it is possible. Further, there can be no effective participation in the whole culture merely on the basis of the skill which any particular man may acquire. The participation depends on common resources, and leads a man towards others. To any individual, however gifted, full participation will be impossible, for the culture will be too complex. Yet effective participation is certainly possible. It will, at any time, be selective from the whole culture, and there will be difference and unevenness in selection, as there will be in contribution. Such selection, such unevenness, can be made compatible with an effective community of culture, but only by genuine mutual responsibility and adjustment. This is the conversion of the defensive element of solidarity into the wider and more positive practice of neighbourhood. It is, in practice, for any man, a long conversion of the habitual elements of denial; a slow and deep personal acceptance of extending community. The institutions of cynicism, of denial and of division will perhaps only be thrown down when they are recognized for what they are: the deposits of practical failures to live. Failure—the jaunty hardness of the 'outsider'—will lose its present glamour, as the common experience moves in a different direction. Nobody will be proud any longer to be separate, to deny, or to ratify a personal failure in unconcern.

The second difficulty, in the development of the idea of solidarity, is related to the first: in that it is again a question of achieving diversity without creating separation. Solidarity, as a feeling, is obviously subject to rigidities, which can be dangerous in a period of change. The command to common action is right, but there is always the danger that the common understanding will be inadequate, and that its enforcement will prevent or delay right action. No community, no culture, can ever be fully conscious of itself, ever fully know itself. The growth of consciousness is usually uneven, individual and tentative in nature. An emphasis of solidarity which, by intention or by accident, stifles or weakens such growth may, evidently, bring a deep common harm. It is necessary to make room for, not only variation, but even dissidence, within the common loyalty. Yet it is difficult to feel that, even in the English working-class movement, with its long democratic tradition, this need has been clearly and practically recognized.

A culture, while it is being lived, is always in part unknown, in part unrealized. The making of a community is always an exploration, for consciousness cannot precede creation, and there is no formula for unknown experience. A good community, a living culture, will, because of this, not only make room for but actively encourage all and any who can contribute to the advance in consciousness which is the common need. Wherever we have started from, we need to listen to others who started from a different position. We need to consider every attachment, every value, with our whole attention; for we do not know the future, we can never be certain of what may enrich it; we can only, now, listen to and consider whatever may be offered and take up what we can.

The practical liberty of thought and expression is less a natural right than a common necessity. The growth of understanding is so difficult that none of us can arrogate to himself, or to an institution or a class, the right to determine its channels of advance. Any educational system will reflect the content of a society; any emphasis in exploration will follow from an emphasis of common need. Yet no system, and no emphasis, can be adequate, if they fail to allow for real flexibility, real alternative courses. To deny these practical liberties is to burn the common seed. To tolerate only this or only that, according to some given formula, is to submit to the phantasy of having occupied the future and fenced it into fruitful or unfruitful ground. Thus, in the working-class movement, while the clenched fist is a necessary symbol, the clenching ought never to be such that the hand cannot open, and the fingers extend, to discover and give a shape to the newly forming reality.

We have to plan what can be planned, according to our common decision. But the emphasis of the idea of culture is right when it reminds us that a culture, essentially, is unplannable. We have to ensure the means of life, and the means of community. But what will then, by these means, be lived, we cannot know or say. The idea of culture rests on a metaphor: the tending of natural growth. And indeed it is on growth, as metaphor and as fact, that the ultimate emphasis must be placed. Here, finally, is the area where we have most need to reinterpret.

To rid oneself of the illusion of the objective existence of 'the masses', and to move towards a more actual and more active conception of human beings and relationships, is in fact to realize a new freedom. Where this can be experienced, the whole substance of one's thinking is transformed. There is a further shift in experience, cognate with this, when we think again about human growth, and its human tending, in a spirit other than that of the long dominative mode. The forces which have changed and are still changing our world are indeed industry and democracy. Understanding of this change, this long revolution, lies at a level of meaning which

335

it is not easy to reach. We can in retrospect see the dominative mood as one of the mainsprings of industry: the theory
and practice of man's mastering and controlling his natural
environment. We are still rephrasing this, from experience,
as we learn the folly of exploiting any part of this environment in isolation. We are learning, slowly, to attend to our
environment as a whole, and to draw our values from that
whole, and not from its fragmented parts, where a quick
success can bring long waste. In relation to this kind of
learning, we come to realize, again slowly, that where the
dominative mood extends to man himself, where human
beings also are isolated and exploited, with whatever temporary success, the issue in the long run is a cancelling in
spirit of the full opportunities offered by the material gains.
A knot is tied, that has come near to strangling our whole
common life, in this century. We live in almost overwhelming danger, at a peak of our apparent control. We
react to the danger by attempting to take control, yet still
we have to unlearn, as the price of survival, the inherent
dominative mode. The struggle for democracy is the
pattern of this revaluation, yet much that passes as democratic is allied, in spirit, with the practice of its open
enemies. It is as if, in fear or vision, we are now all determined to lay our hands on life and force it into our own
image, and it is then no good to dispute on the merits of
rival images. This is a real barrier in the mind, which at
times it seems almost impossible to break down: a refusal
to accept the creative capacities of life; a determination to
limit and restrict the channels of growth; a habit of thinking,
indeed, that the future has now to be determined by some ordinance in our own minds. We project our old images into the
future, and take hold of ourselves and others to force energy
towards that substantiation. We do this as conservatives,
trying to prolong old forms; we do this as socialists, trying
to prescribe the new man. A large part of contemporary
resistance to certain kinds of change, which are obviously
useful in themselves, amounts to an inarticulate distrust of
this effort at domination. There is the hostility to change of
those who wish to cling to privilege. There is also the
hostility to one's life being determined, in a dominative

mood masked by whatever idealism or benevolence. This latter hostility is valuable, and needs to be distinguished from the former with which it is often crudely compounded. It is the chafing of any felt life against the hands which seek to determine its course, and this, which was always the democratic impulse, remains essential within the new definitions of society. There are still major material barriers to democracy, but there is also this barrier in our minds, behind which, with an assumption of virtue, we seek to lay hands on others, and, from our own constructions, determine their course. Against this the idea of culture is necessary, as an idea of the tending of *natural* growth. To know, even in part, any group of living processes, is to see and wonder at their extraordinary variety and complexity. To know, even in part, the life of man, is to see and wonder at its extraordinary multiplicity, its great fertility of value. We have to live by our own attachments, but we can only live fully, in common, if we grant the attachments of others, and make it our common business to keep the channels of growth clear. Never yet, in the great pattern of inheritance and response, have two wholly identical individuals been formed. This, rather than any particular image of virtue, is our actual human scale. The idea of a common culture brings together, in a particular form of social relationship, at once the idea of natural growth and that of its tending. The former alone is a type of romantic individualism; the latter alone a type of authoritarian training. Yet each, within a whole view, marks a necessary emphasis. The struggle for democracy is a struggle for the recognition of equality of being, or it is nothing. Yet only in the acknowledgement of human individuality and variation can the reality of common government be comprised. We stress natural growth to indicate the whole potential energy, rather than the selected energies which the dominative mode finds it convenient to enlist. At the same time, however, we stress the social reality, the tending. Any culture, in its whole process, is a selection, an emphasis, a particular tending. The distinction of a culture in common is that the selection is freely and commonly made and re-made. The tending is a common process, based on common decision, which then, within itself, comprehends the actual variations of life and growth. The natural growth and the tending are parts of a mutual process, guaranteed by the fundamental principle of equality of being.

The evident problems of our civilization are too close and too serious for anyone to suppose that an emphasis is a solution. In every problem we need hard, detailed inquiry and negotiation. Yet we are coming increasingly to realize that our vocabulary, the language we use to inquire into and negotiate our actions, is no secondary factor, but a practical and radical element in itself. To take a meaning from experience, and to try to make it active, is in fact our process of growth. Some of these meanings we receive and re-create. Others we must make for ourselves, and try to communicate. The human crisis is always a crisis of understanding: what we genuinely understand we can do. I have written this book because I believe the tradition it records is a major contribution to our common understanding, and a major incentive to its necessary extensions. There are ideas, and ways of thinking, with the seeds of life in them, and there are others, perhaps deep in our minds, with the seeds of a general death. Our measure of success in recognizing these kinds, and in naming them making possible their common recognition, may be literally the measure of our future.

REFERENCES

INTRODUCTION

xiv   1. *Words Ancient and Modern*; E. Weekley; 1926; p. 34.

PART I

CHAPTER I

(i)

Page Note No.

4   1. Letter, 21 November 1791, to Fitzwilliam; cit. *Edmund Burke, A Life*; Philip Magnus; London, 1939; Appendix 5; p. 348.

4   2. *Essays in Criticism*; M. Arnold (1918 edn.); p. 18.

5   3. Lord Charlemont, 19 August 1797; cit. Magnus, op. cit., p. 296.

6   4. *Reflections on the Revolution in France*; Edmund Burke (World's Classics edn.), 1950; pp. 184-185.

7   5. Ibid., pp. 186-187.

7   6. *Letter to a Noble Lord*; *Works*, Vol. V, p. 186.

7   7. *Reflections*, p. 12.

8   8. Ibid., p. 138.

9   9. Ibid., p. 65.

9   10. Ibid., p. 95.

9   11. *Appeal from the New to the Old Whigs*; *Works*, Vol. III, p. 82.

10   12. *Reflections*; pp. 105-106.

10   13. Ibid., p. 107.

10   14. *Thoughts on French Affairs*; ibid., p. 375.

11   15. *Reform of Representation in the House of Commons*; *Works*, Vol. VI, p. 147.

12   16. *Reflections*; p. 168.

12   17. Ibid., p. 156.

13   18. *The Bloody Buoy*; 1796; Vol. III, *Porcupine's Works* (1801).

13   19. *Porcupine's Works*, Vol. XII, p. 1.

13   20. *Political Register*, 28 February 1807.

14   21. Ibid., 15 March 1806.

14   22. Ibid., 6 December 1806.

14   23. Ibid., 12 July 1817.

14   24. Ibid., 21 November 1807.

Page *Note No.*
15   25. Ibid., 14 April 1821.
15   26. Ibid., 10 July 1824.
15   27. Ibid., 8 March 1834.
16   28. Ibid., 16 July 1808.
16   29. Ibid., 13 November 1830.
16   30. Ibid., 2 May 1812.
16   31. Ibid., 25 July 1812.
17   32. Ibid., 19 December 1818.
17   33. Ibid., 19 December 1818.
17   34. Ibid., 27 August 1825.
17   35. *Lectures on the French and Belgian Revolutions*, I, p. 1.
18   36. *Political Register*, 7 December 1833.
19   37. Letter to T. J. Street, 22 March 1817; Nonesuch Coleridge; pp. 668-669.
20   38. *Political Register*, 8 June 1816.

(ii)

21   1. *Sir Thomas More: or, Colloquies on the Progress and Prospects of Society*; Robert Southey; 2 vols., 1829; VI, p. 132.
21   2. Ibid., p. 132.
21   3. Ibid., pp. 132-133.
22   4. *The Vision of Judgment*, Stanza XCVI; *Poetical Works of Lord Byron* (1945), p. 168.
22   5. Cit. *William Morris, Mediaevalist and Revolutionary*; M. Grennan; King's Crown Press, New York, 1945; p. 12.
22   6. *Letters of Robert Southey*; ed. Fitzgerald; p. 273.
23   7. *Colloquies*, VII, pp. 193-194.
23   8. Ibid., p. 197.
23   9. Ibid., VII, p. 170.
24   10. Ibid., p. 174.
24   11. Ibid., Vol. 2, Coll. XIII, p. 246.
24   12. Ibid., Vol. 2, p. 262.
24   13. Ibid., Vol. 2, Coll. XV, pp. 424-425, et supra.
25   14. Ibid., Coll. IV, p. 79.
25   15. Ibid., Vol. 2, Coll. XV, p. 418.
25   16. Ibid., p. 420.
25   17. Ibid., VIII, p. 206.
26   18. *Observations on the Effect of the Manufacturing System, with hints for the improvement of those parts of it which are most injurious to health and morals, dedicated most respectfully to the British Legislature*; London, 1815; p. 5.

REFERENCES

27   19. Ibid., pp. 10-11.

27   20. *A New View of Society*; London, 1813; *Essay First on the Formation of Character*; repr. *A New View of Society and Other Writings*, by Robert Owen; ed. Cole; Everyman, 1927; p. 16.

28   21. Address prefixed to Third Essay, *A New View of Society*; ed. Cole; pp. 8-9.

28   22. *The Life of Robert Owen, by Himself*; repr. London, 1920; pp. 186-189 *passim*.

28   23. Ibid., pp. 122-123.

29   24. Ibid., p. 105.

29   25. *A New View of Society*; pp. 178-179.

CHAPTER II

33   1. *Wordsworth's Poetical Works*; ed. Hutchinson; Oxford, 1908; p. 953.

34   2. Ibid., p. 952.

34   3. Draft of *The Wealth of Nations*, in *Adam Smith as Student and Professor*; W. R. Scott; p. 344.

35   4. Ibid., p. 345.

35   5. *The Autobiography of Sir Egerton Brydges*; 1834; Vol. II, pp. 202-203.

35   6. *Memoirs, Journal and Correspondence of Thomas Moore*; Vol. VII, p. 46.

37   7. *Conjectures on Original Composition*; Edward Young; 1759; p. 12.

37   8. Ibid., p. 19.

38   9. *William Blake*; Nonesuch edn. (Keynes); p. 664.

38   10. Ibid., p. 624.

38   11. Ibid., p. 637.

40   12. *Poetical Works*, p. 260.

40   13. Ibid., p. 938.

41   14. Ibid., pp. 951-952.

41   15. Ibid., pp. 938-939.

42   16. Ibid., p. 938.

43   17. *A Defence of Poetry*; P. B. Shelley; repr. *English Prose of the Romantic Period* (Macintyre and Ewing); p. 270.

43   18. Ibid., p. 271.

44   19. *Letters of John Keats*; ed. Forman; Letter 90, p. 223.

45   20. *Coleridge's Essays and Lectures on Shakespeare*; Everyman, p. 46.

45   21. Op. cit., p. 130.

Page Note No.
45 22. Ibid., pp. 67-68.
45 23. Ibid., p. 72.
45 24. Ibid., p. 67.
46 25. *Poetical Works*, p. 941.
46 26. Ibid., p. 939.
47 27. Ibid., p. 939.
47 28. Op. cit., p. 273.
48 29. Ibid., p. 274.
48 30. Ibid., p. 275.

CHAPTER III

50   1. *Coleridge*; repr. *Mill on Bentham and Coleridge*; introd.
        F. R. Leavis; London, 1950; p. 105.
51   2. Ibid., p. 105.
51   3. Ibid., p. 105.
51   4. Ibid., p. 106.
53   5. Ibid., pp. 106-107.
53   6. Ibid., p. 107.
53   7. Ibid., p. 108.
54   8. Ibid., p. 99.
54   9. Ibid., p. 84.
54 10. Ibid., p. 63.
55 11. Cit. *John Stuart Mill*; K. Britton; London, 1953; p. 13.
55 12. *Letters of John Stuart Mill*; ed. Elliot (1910); Vol. I,
        p. 88.
56 13. *Bentham*; repr. *Mill on Bentham and Coleridge*; p. 84.
57 14. Ibid., p. 148.
57 15. Ibid., p. 70.
57 16. Ibid., p. 73.
57 17. *On the Constitution of Church and State* (1837 edn.), p. 67.
58 18. Table Talk, recorded by T. Allsop; repr. Nonesuch
        Coleridge; pp. 476-477.
59 19. *Coleridge*; repr. *Mill on Bentham and Coleridge*; pp. 129-
        130.
60 20. Ibid., pp. 131-133.
61 21. Ibid., p. 140.
61 22. *On the Constitution of Church and State*, V.
62 23. Ibid., V.
62 24. *Bentham*; repr. *Mill on Bentham and Coleridge*; p. 66.
63 25. *Church and State*, V.
64 26. Ibid., V.
64 27. Ibid., V.

REFERENCES

Page Note No.

64 28. Ibid., VI.
65 29. Ibid., VI.
65 30. *Coleridge*; repr. *Mill on Bentham and Coleridge*; p. 147.
66 31. *Autobiography*; J. S. Mill; repr. World's Classics; p. 125.
66 32. Ibid., p. 113.
68 33. Letter to Wordsworth, 30 May 1815; repr. Nonesuch
       Coleridge; p. 661.
69 34. *The Friend*, Section 2, Essay 11.
69 35. Letter to Poole, 23 March 1801.
69 36. Notebooks (1801); repr. Nonesuch Coleridge; p. 158.
69 37. *The Friend* (1818), Section 2, Essay 11.
70 38. Notebooks (1801); repr. Nonesuch Coleridge; p. 159.

CHAPTER IV

72   1. *Works of Thomas Carlyle*; Vol. II, p. 233.
72   2. Ibid., p. 233.
72   3. Ibid., pp. 233-234.
73   4. Ibid., pp. 234, 235, 236.
73   5. Ibid., p. 238.
73   6. Ibid., pp. 239-240.
73   7. Ibid., p. 245.
74   8. Ibid., p. 247.
74   9. Ibid., pp. 248-249.
74 10. Ibid., p. 249.
74 11. Ibid., p. 249.
74 12. Ibid., pp. 244-245.
75 13. Ibid., pp. 250-252.
76 14. *Works*, Vol. VI (1869); p.154.
76 15. *Reflections on the French Revolution*, p. 12.
78 16. *Works*, Vol. VI, pp. 109-110.
78 17. Ibid., p. 111.
79 18. Ibid., p. 152.
79 19. Ibid., p. 153.
79 20. Ibid., p. 137.
79 21. Ibid., p. 145.
80 22. Ibid., p. 144.
81 23. Ibid., pp. 174-175.
81 24. Ibid., p. 183.
82 25. Ibid., p. 178.
82 26. Ibid., p. 175.
83 27. *Past and Present*; *Works*, Vol. VII, p. 231.

REFERENCES

Page Note No.

CHAPTER VI

110   1. *On the Scope and Nature of University Education*; J. H. Newman; 1852; pp. 201-202.
111   2. Ibid., p. 255.
111   3. Ibid., pp.197-198.
111   4. *On the Constitution of Church and State*; S. T. Coleridge; V.
112   5. *Chartism*; T. Carlyle.
112   6. *Alton Locke*; C. Kingsley (1892 edn.); pp. xxx-xxxi.
113   7. Cit. *Continuation Schools in England and Elsewhere*; Sadler; London, 1908; pp. 38-39.
113   8. Ibid.
114   9. *Englishman's Register*. See *Life and Correspondence*, Ch. vi.
114 10. *13 Letters on our Social Condition*; *Sheffield Courant*; 1832; Letter II, pp. 4-5.
114 11. Letter XII, *Hertford Reformer*; *Misc. Works*, p. 481.
114 12. Letter VI, *Hertford Reformer*; *Misc. Works*, pp. 453 seq.
114 13. Letter XVI, *Hertford Reformer*; *Misc. Works*, p. 500.
115 14. *Culture and Anarchy*; M. Arnold (Murray); p. viii.
115 15. Ibid., p. xi.
115 16. Ibid., p. 10.
116 17. Ibid., pp. 12-13.
116 18. Ibid., p. 13.
117 19. *Friendship's Garland*; M. Arnold (1903 edn.); p. 141.
118 20. Ibid., p. 141.
118 21. *Culture and Anarchy*, p. viii, and p. 8.
118 22. Ibid., p. 9.
119 23. Ibid., p. 150.
119 24. Ibid., p. 27.
120 25. *Reflections on the French Revolution*, p. 107.
121 26. *Culture and Anarchy*, p. 43.
121 27. Ibid., p. 70.
122 28. Ibid., p. 164.
123 29. Ibid., p. 87.
123 30. Ibid., p. 88.
123 31. Ibid., p. 37.
124 32. Ibid., p. 42.
124 33. Ibid., p. 160.
124 34. Ibid., pp. 157-158. My italics.
126 35. Ibid., p. 30.
126 36. *The Scope and Nature of University Education*, p. 313.
126 37. *Culture and Religion, in some of their relations*; J. C. Shairp; 1870; p.5.

Page Note No.

126   38. *The Choice of Books*; Harrison, p. 103.
128   39. *Democracy*, in *Mixed Essays* (1903 edn.); p. 47.
129   40. *Culture and Anarchy*, p. 28.

CHAPTER VII

130   1. *The Gothic Revival*; Kenneth Clark; London (2nd (revised) edn.); p. 188.
132   2. *Contrasts*; A.W. Pugin; London, 1841 (2nd edn.); pp. 49-50.
133   3. *Life of George Eliot*; J. W. Cross; London, n.d.; p. 239.
134   4. *Ruskin*; D. Larg; London, 1932; p. 95.
135   5. *Modern Painters*, II, Part III, Sec. I, Ch. 3, para. 16.
136   6. *Lectures on Art*; Library edn., Vol. XX, p. 39.
136   7. In the manuscript printed as an appendix to *Modern Painters* (Library edn.), Vol. 2, pp. 388-389.
137   8. *Stones of Venice*, Vol. I, Appendix 15.
138   9. *Praeterita*, ii, p. 205.
139   10. *Modern Painters*, II, Part III, Sec. I, Ch. 3, para. 16.
140   11. *John Ruskin, Social Reformer*; J. A. Hobson; London, 1889; p. 82.
141   12. *Stones of Venice*, Vol. 2, Ch. VI, *The Nature of Gothic* (1899 edn.); p. 165.
142   13. Ibid., pp. 163 and 165.
142   14. *Unto this Last*; Essay IV, *Ad Valorem* (1900 edn.); pp. 118-119.
143   15. *Munera Pulveris* (1899 edn.), p. 1.
143   16. *Unto this Last*; Essay III, *Qui Judicatis Terram* (1900 edn.); p. 102.
143   17. *Unto this Last*, p. 123.
144   18. *The Two Paths* (1887 edn.), pp. 129-131.
145   19. *The Crown of Wild Olive* (1886 edn.), p. 73.
145   20. Ibid., p. 101.
146   21. *Time and Tide*, paras. 138, 139.
147   22. *Sesame and Lilies*, para. 52.
148   23. *The Two Paths* (1887 edn.), p. 125.
148   24 a, b, c, d. *How I Became a Socialist*; repr. Nonesuch Morris; pp. 657-658.
150   25. Ibid., p. 659. My italics.
151   26. Letter to *Pall Mall Gazette*; in *Letters of William Morris*; ed. Henderson; p. 262.
151   27. Letter to *Daily News*; in *Letters*; pp. 242-243.
152   28. *Art and Socialism*; repr. Nonesuch Morris; p. 630.
152   29. *The Aims of Art*; repr. Nonesuch Morris; pp. 598-599.

REFERENCES

Page Note No.

152 30. *Communism*; repr. Nonesuch Morris; p. 669.
153 31. *The Beauty of Life*; repr. Nonesuch Morris; pp. 542-543.
153 32. *The Aims of Art*; repr. Nonesuch Morris; pp. 592-593.
154 33. *The Art of the People*; repr. Nonesuch Morris; p. 527.
154 34. *Art and Socialism*; repr. Nonesuch Morris; p. 635.
154 35. Ibid., p. 636.
154 36. *How we Live and How we might Live*; repr. Nonesuch Morris; p. 581 and pp. 584-585.
156 37. *Communism*; repr. Nonesuch Morris; p. 660.
156 38. Ibid., p. 661.
157 39. Ibid., p. 660.
157 40. Ibid., pp. 662-663.
157 41. *The Art of the People*; repr. Nonesuch Morris; p. 520.
157 42. *Communism*; repr. Nonesuch Morris; p. 663.
158 43. Ibid., p. 665.

PART II

INTERREGNUM

(i)

163 1. *The New Republic; or, Culture, Faith, and Philosophy in an English Country House*; W. H. Mallock; repr. London, 1945; p. 147.
163 2. Ibid., p. 155.
163 3. Ibid., p. 157.
163 4. Ibid., pp. 281-282.
164 5. *The Limits of Pure Democracy*; London, 1918; p. 351.
164 6. Ibid., p. 348.
164 7. Ibid., p. 352.
164 8. Ibid., p. 392.
165 9. Ibid., p. 280.
165 10. Ibid., p. 288.

(ii)

167 1. *Appreciations, with an Essay on Style*; Walter Pater; London, 1907 (3rd edn.); pp. 62-63.
167 2. *The Renaissance*; Walter Pater; 1904 edn.; p. 239.
168 3. Ibid., p. 229.
168 4. *Mr Whistler's 'Ten O'Clock'*; London, Chatto & Windus, 1888; passim.
169 5. *Whistler v. Ruskin; Art and Art Critics*; (4th edn.: n.d.); pp. 14-15.

Page Note No.

169   6. 'Ten O'Clock', p. 7.
169   7. Ibid., p. 9.
170   8. Ibid., p. 29.
170   9. Wilde v. Whistler, being an acrimonious correspondence between Oscar Wilde and James A. McNeill Whistler; London, 1906, privately printed; p. 8.
170   10. The Soul of Man under Socialism; Oscar Wilde; repr. Essays by Oscar Wilde (ed. Pearson); London, 1950; p. 232.
170   11. The Critic as Artist; ibid., p. 157.
170   12. Ibid., pp. 156-157.
170   13. The Decay of Lying; ibid., passim.
171   14. The Critic as Artist; ibid., pp. 152-153.
171   15. The Soul of Man under Socialism; ibid., p. 245.
171   16. Ibid., p. 227.
171   17. Ibid., p. 266.
171   18. Ibid., pp. 230-231.
172   19. Ibid., p. 228.
172   20. The Critic as Artist; ibid., p. 125.

(iii)

173   1. New Grub Street; G. Gissing; repr. London, 1927; Ch. i; A Man of his Day; pp. 4-5.
174   2. Ibid., Ch. xxxiii; The Sunny Way; p. 419.
174   3. Ibid., Ch. xxxiv; A Check; p. 436.
175   4. The Nether World; G. Gissing (1890 new edn.); Ch. xl; p. 392.
175   5. Ibid., pp. 391-392.
176   6. The Unclassed; G. Gissing (new edn., repr. 1901); Ch. xxv; Art and Misery; p. 211.
177   7. Demos, a story of English Socialism; G. Gissing (1897 new edn.); Ch. xxxi; p. 407.
177   8. The Conservative Mind; R. Kirk; London, 1954; p. 337.
178   9. Demos, Ch. xv, p. 202.
179   10. Ibid., Ch. xxix, p. 381.
179   11. Ibid., Ch. xxxvi, p. 470.

(iv)

179   1. Death of an Old Revolutionary Hero; Bernard Shaw.
180   2. The Intelligent Woman's Guide to Socialism and Capitalism; Bernard Shaw; London, 1928; p. 219.
180   3. Ibid., p. 456.

REFERENCES

Page Note No.

182   4. *Fabian Essays in Socialism* (1931 edn.); pp. 186-187.
182   5. Ibid., pp. 31-35 *passim*.
183   6. *Signs of Change*; W. Morris; London, 1888; p. 46.
183   7. *Fabian Essays*, p. 37.
183   8. Review in *Commonweal*, 25 January 1890.
183   9. Ibid.
183 10. *Fabian Essays*; Introd. to 1920 edn. (1931 edn.); pp. xxi-xxix *passim*.
184 11. Ibid.; Preface to 1931 edn.; p. ix.
184 12. *Intelligent Woman's Guide*, pp. 452-453.
184 13. Ibid., p. 164.
185 14. Ibid., p. 454.
185 15. Ibid., p. 459.

(v)

186   1. *The Servile State*; H. Belloc (3rd edn., 1927); p. 53 and p. 72.
186   2. Ibid., p. 53.
186   3. Ibid., p. 51.
187   4. Ibid., p. 116.
187   5. Ibid., p. 127.
187   6. Ibid., p. viii.
187   7. *Guilds and the Social Crisis*; A. J. Penty; London, 1919; p. 46.
188   8. Ibid., pp. 46-47.
188   9. Ibid., p. 47.
188 10. Ibid., p. 57.
188 11. *Old Worlds for New: a study of the post-industrial State*; A. J. Penty; pp. 28-29.
188 12. Ibid., p. 33.
188 13. Ibid., p. 33.
188 14. Ibid., p. 35.
188 15. Ibid., p. 176.
189 16. *Essays in Social Theory*; G. D. H. Cole; London, 1950; p. 90.
190 17. Ibid., p. 93.

(vi)

191   1. *Speculations: essays on humanism and the philosophy of art*; T. E. Hulme; ed. H. Read; London (2nd edn.), repr. 1954; p. 116.
191   2. Ibid., pp. 255-256.

Page Note No.

192   3. Ibid., pp. 32-34.

192   4. Ibid., p. 117.

192   5. Ibid., p. 118.

193   6. Ibid., p. 37.

194   7. Ibid., p. 254.

194   8. Ibid., p. 259, note.

194   9. Ibid., p. 259, note.

194 10. Ibid., p. 133.

194 11. Ibid., p. 127.

194 12. Ibid., p. 120.

194 13. Ibid., p. 77 *et al.*

194 14. Ibid., p. 97.

195 15. Ibid., p. 104.

PART III

CHAPTER I

200   1. *Climbing down Pisgah; Selected Essays* (Penguin), p. 50.

200   2. Ibid., p. 53.

201   3. *Nottingham and the Mining Country; Selected Essays*, p. 120.

201   4. *Democracy; Selected Essays*, p. 94.

201   5. *Nottingham and the Mining Country*, p. 119.

201   6. *Lady Chatterley's Lover; Works*, repr. 1950; pp. 173-174.

203   7. *Nottingham and the Mining Country*, p. 119.

205   8. Ibid., pp. 121-122.

208   9. *Democracy; Selected Essays*, p. 88.

208 10. Ibid., p. 89.

208 11. Ibid., pp. 91-92.

208 12. Ibid., p. 89.

209 13. Ibid., p. 93.

210 14. Ibid., p. 94.

210 15. Ibid., p. 95.

210 16. Ibid., p. 76.

211 17. Ibid., pp. 92-93.

212 18. *Studies in Classic American Literature*; p. 12.

212 19. Ibid.

212 20. *Democracy; Selected Essays*, p. 95.

214 21. *Letters*; p. 286.

214 22. Ibid., p. 196.

214 23. *John Galsworthy; Selected Essays*, p. 227.

215 24. *Sex versus Loveliness; Selected Essays*, p. 18.

215 25. *The State of Funk; Selected Essays*, pp. 100-101.

REFERENCES

CHAPTER II

Page   Note No.

217   1. *The Acquisitive Society*; R. H. Tawney; London, 1921; p. 7.
217   2. Ibid., pp. 12-14.
218   3. Ibid., pp. 19-20.
218   4. Ibid., p. 21.
218   5. Ibid., p. 19.
219   6. Ibid., pp. 47-48.
219   7. Ibid., pp. 48-49.
220   8. Ibid., p. 42.
220   9. *Equality*; R. H. Tawney; London (revised edn.), 1931; pp. 30-31.
221   10. Ibid., pp. 46-50, *passim*.
221   11. Ibid., p. 50.
222   12. Ibid., p. 53.
223   13. Ibid., p. 103.
223   14. Ibid., p. 103.
224   15. Ibid., p. 103.
224   16. Ibid., p. 112.
224   17. Ibid., p. 113.
225   18. Ibid., p. 116.
225   19. Ibid., pp. 116-117, and p. 106.

CHAPTER III

227   1. *Mill on Bentham and Coleridge*; introd. F. R. Leavis; London, 1950; p. 140.
227   2. Ibid., p. 167.
227   3. *The Idea of a Christian Society*; T. S. Eliot; London, 1939; p. 8.
228   4. Ibid., p. 9.
228   5. Ibid., p. 64.
228   6. Ibid., p. 34.
228   7. Ibid., p. 34.
228   8. Ibid., p. 33.
229   9. Ibid., p. 33 and pp. 61-62.
229   10. Ibid., pp. 30-31.
229   11. Ibid., p. 21.
230   12. Ibid., p. 39.
230   13. Ibid., pp. 39-40.
231   14. *Notes towards the Definition of Culture*; T. S. Eliot; London, 1948; p. 25.

Page Note No.

232   15. Ibid., p. 16.
232   16. Ibid., p. 16.
233   17. Ibid., p. 31.
234   18. Ibid., p. 19.
234   19. Ibid., p. 21.
234   20. Ibid., p. 22.
235   21. Ibid., p. 24.
235   22. Ibid., p. 35.
240   23. Ibid., p. 37.

CHAPTER IV

(i)

245   1. *Principles of Literary Criticism*; I. A. Richards; London, 1924; pp. 56-57.
245   2. *Principles*, p. 36.
245   3. *Science and Poetry*; I. A. Richards; London, 1926; pp. 47 and 53-54.
246   4. *Principles*, p. 46.
246   5. Ibid., p. 48.
246   6. Ibid., p. 51.
246   7. Ibid., p. 55.
247   8. *Science and Poetry*, pp. 82-83.
247   9. *Principles*, p. 196.
248   10. Ibid., p. 203.
248   11. Ibid., p. 236.
248   12. *Science and Poetry*, p. 20.
249   13. *Principles*, pp. 237-238.
249   14. *Art and Society*; Herbert Read; pp. 94-95.

(ii)

254   1. *Mass Civilization and Minority Culture*; Cambridge, 1930; pp. 3-5.
254   2. Ibid., p. 26.
258   3. *Culture and Environment: the Training of Critical Awareness*; F. R. Leavis and Denys Thompson; London, 1933; p. 87.
259   4. Ibid., p. 91.
259   5. Ibid., pp. 68-69.
259   6. Ibid., pp. 91-92.
261   7. Ibid., pp. 96-97.

REFERENCES

CHAPTER V

Page Note No.

265   1. *Newcastle Chronicle*, 12 April 1887; cit. *William Morris, Romantic to Revolutionary*; E. P. Thompson; London, 1955; p. 522.

266   2. *Critique of Political Economy*; Karl Marx; *Preface*; Eng. trans., Stone; pp. 11 ff.

267   3. *The Eighteenth Brumaire of Louis Bonaparte*; Karl Marx; Eng. trans., de Leon; 1898; p. 24.

267   4. Engels, letter to J. Bloch, 21 September 1890; *Selected Correspondence*, p. 475.

268   5. English translation as *In Defence of Materialism*; G. V. Plekhanov; trans., A. Rothstein; London, 1947; V, p. 207.

269   6. Ibid., pp. 223 and 237.

269   7. Ibid., p. 237.

270   8. *The Mind in Chains;* ed. C. Day Lewis; London, 1937; p. 15.

270   9. Ibid., p. 24.

271 10. Ibid., pp. 21-22.

272 11. *Crisis and Criticism*; Alick West; London, 1937; pp. 88-89.

273 12. Op. cit., pp. 770 and 763.

273 13. *The Novel and the People*; Ralph Fox; London, 1937; p. 22.

275 14. Op. cit., p. 114.

276 15. Ibid., p. 133.

276 16. Ibid., p. 138.

276 17. Ibid., pp. 138-139.

277 18. *Illusion and Reality*; C. Caudwell (new edn.); 1946; p. 257.

277 19. Ibid., p. 214.

277 20. Ibid., *Biographical Note*, by G. T.; p. 5.

277 21. *Modern Quarterly*, New Series, Vol. 6, No. 4; Autumn 1951; p. 346.

277 22. Ibid., p. 346.

278 23. *Studies in a Dying Culture*; C. Caudwell; London; 1938; repr. 1948; pp. 53-54.

278 24. *Further Studies in a Dying Culture*; C. Caudwell; London, 1949; p. 109.

278 25. *Illusion and Reality*, p. 265.

279 26. Cit. M. Slater; *Modern Quarterly*, New Series, Vol. 6, No. 3; Summer 1951; p. 265.

281 27. *Illusion and Reality*, p. 55.

Page Note No.

282   28. See e.g. Cornforth; *Modern Quarterly,* New Series, Vol. 6, No. 4; Autumn 1951; p. 357.

283   29. Cit. Blunt; *Art under Capitalism and Socialism,* in *Mind in Chains;* p. 122 ('Remarks to Clara Zetkin').

283   30. *Collected Works;* Lenin; Vol. IV, Book 2, p. 114.

CHAPTER VI

285   1. *Critical Essays;* George Orwell; London, 1946; p. 45.

285   2. *Nineteen Eighty-Four.* George Orwell; London, 1951; p. 5.

286   3. Ibid., p. 208.

287   4. Ibid., p. 210.

287   5. *The Road to Wigan Pier;* Orwell; London, 1937; p. 205.

287   6. *Rudyard Kipling,* in *Critical Essays;* London, 1946; p. 103.

287   7. *Wells, Hitler and the World State,* in *Critical Essays;* p. 84.

287   8. *Rudyard Kipling, Critical Essays,* p. 103.

287   9. *Politics and Letters;* Summer 1948; p. 39.

288   10. *The Road to Wigan Pier,* p. 206.

288   11. Ibid., p. 248.

288   12. Ibid., p. 205.

288   13. *Coming up for Air;* London; 2nd edn., 1948; p. 148.

288   14. *Keep the Aspidistra Flying;* London, 1936; p. 64.

288   15. *The Road to Wigan Pier,* p. 196.

288   16. *Politics and the English Language,* in *Shooting an Elephant,* p. 93.

293   17. *Nineteen Eighty-Four.* pp. 73 and 227.

294   18. *George Orwell,* by J. Walsh; *Marxist Quarterly,* Vol. 3, No. 1, January 1956; pp. 35-36.

INDEX

(Main sections in bold type)

A. WORKS AND AUTHORS

355

B. WORDS, THEMES AND PERSONS

INDEX

Bertrand Russell
Philosophical Writings

Illustration © Hans Erni

Logic and Knowledge

Logic and Knowledge brings together Russell's most important writings in logic and the theory of knowledge.

Firmly established as a classic, it comprises ten essays which have profoundly influenced the course of philosophy. They include his landmark paper *On Denoting*.

£15.00 - ISBN: 978 085124 734 2

Mysticism and Logic
£12.00 - ISBN: 978 085124 735 9

Political Ideals
£10.00 - ISBN: 978 085124 731 1

The Analysis of Mind
£15.00 - ISBN: 978 085124 741 0

The Analysis of Matter
£15.00 - ISBN: 978 085124 740 3

My Philosophical Development
£15.00 - ISBN: 978 085124 736 6

An Inquiry into Meaning and Truth
£18.00 - ISBN: 978 085124 737 3

Introduction to Mathematical Philosophy
£15.00 - ISBN: 978 085124 738 0

Foundations of Geometry
£12.00 - ISBN: 978 085124 739 7

The Philosophy of Leibniz
£15.00 - ISBN: 978 085124 742 7

Available from
www.spokesmanbooks.com

KEY WORDS JOURNAL
A journal of cultural materialism
distributed by Spokesman

Key Words is committed to developing the tradition of cultural materialism derived from the founding analysis of culture and society in the work of Raymond Williams.

The journal provides a forum for radical thought on history and politics, and explores the role of literary, media and cultural forms in the contemporary global era.

After *The Long Revolution* - *Key Words* 10
Price: £12.50 | ISBN: 978 0 95315 03-8-0

Raymond Williams in Japan - *Key Words* 9
Price: £15.00 | ISBN: 978 0 95315 03-6-6

Labouring-Class Writing - *Key Words* 8
Price: £15.00 | ISBN: 978 0 95315 03-5-9

The Century's Wide Margin - *Key Words* 7
Price: £15.00 | ISBN: 978 0 95315 03-1-1

Seeing Ourselves in History - *Key Words* 6
Price: £12.50 | ISBN: 978 0 95315 03-0-4

Modernism - *Key Words* 4
Price: £12.50 | ISBN: 978 0 95315 03-4-2

Futures - *Key Words* 3
Price: £12.50 | ISBN: 978 0 95315 03-3-5

Ecocriticism - *Key Words* 2
Price: £12.50 | ISBN: 978 0 95315 03-2-8

RAYMOND WILLIAMS

The Country & the City

The Country and the City
by Raymond Williams

A brilliant survey of English literature in terms of changing attitudes toward country and city, Raymond Williams's perceptive study reveals the shifting images and associations between these two tradtional poles of life throughout the major developmental period of English culture. The author, who was a foremost social and cultural critic, finds the English experience especially significant because of the early occurrence of the Industrial Revolution, which so decisively transformed relations between the country and the city. This new edition makes available, once again, a seminal work.

'A long, painstaking and beautiful examination of English literature in the search for shifting images of "country" and "city" through history and the often class-freighted and ahistorical meanings we give them. I challenge anyone to read his first chapter and not be eager to go on. As with Joyce and Irishness, so Williams with Welshness: two national cultural elements in my own background that have resonated within my own thought and work.'

Trevor Griffiths

'... Raymond Williams still speaks to us, at the start of the 21st century, as a roadman cutting and clearing the choked thoroughfares of our culture, a signalman indicating passable routes through the social, economic and political histories that shaped him – and us.'

Stan Smith, from his new Foreword

Price: £19.95 | ISBN: 978 0 85124 7991